IBM

International Technical S

# WebSphere MQ Integrator for z/OS V2.1 Implementation Guide

February 2002

SG24-6528-00

**Take Note!** Before using this information and the product it supports, be sure to read the general information in "Special notices" on page 361.

**First Edition (February 2002)**

This edition applies to Version 2, Release 1 of WebSphere MQ Integrator for z/OS, Program Number 5655-G97 for use with the z/OS and OS/390 Operating Systems.

Comments may be addressed to:
IBM Corporation, International Technical Support Organization
Dept. HZ8 Building 662
P.O. Box 12195
Research Triangle Park, NC 27709-2195

When you send information to IBM, you grant IBM a non-exclusive right to use or distribute the information in any way it believes appropriate without incurring any obligation to you.

**© Copyright International Business Machines Corporation 2002. All rights reserved.**
Note to U.S Government Users – Documentation related to restricted rights – Use, duplication or disclosure is subject to restrictions set forth in GSA ADP Schedule Contract with IBM Corp.

# Contents

Preface . . . . . . . . . . . . . . . . . . . . . . . . . . . . . . . . . . . . . . . . . . . . . . . . . . . . . ix
The team that wrote this redbook. . . . . . . . . . . . . . . . . . . . . . . . . . . . . . . . . . ix
Special notice. . . . . . . . . . . . . . . . . . . . . . . . . . . . . . . . . . . . . . . . . . . . . . . . xi
IBM trademarks . . . . . . . . . . . . . . . . . . . . . . . . . . . . . . . . . . . . . . . . . . . . . xii
Comments welcome. . . . . . . . . . . . . . . . . . . . . . . . . . . . . . . . . . . . . . . . . . xii

**Part 1. Introduction** . . . . . . . . . . . . . . . . . . . . . . . . . . . . . . . . . . . . . . . . . . . . . . . . . . . . 1

**Chapter 1. Product overview** . . . . . . . . . . . . . . . . . . . . . . . . . . . . . . . . . . . 3
1.1 WebSphere MQ Integrator basics. . . . . . . . . . . . . . . . . . . . . . . . . . . . . . . 4
  1.1.1 Architecture of WebSphere MQ Integrator . . . . . . . . . . . . . . . . . . . . 8
  1.1.2 The role of the Configuration Manager . . . . . . . . . . . . . . . . . . . . . . 9
  1.1.3 The functionality of the broker. . . . . . . . . . . . . . . . . . . . . . . . . . . . 11
  1.1.4 Publish/subscribe and the User Name Server . . . . . . . . . . . . . . . 13
  1.1.5 The user interface: the Control Center . . . . . . . . . . . . . . . . . . . . . 15
1.2 Anatomy of a message flow . . . . . . . . . . . . . . . . . . . . . . . . . . . . . . . . . 17
1.3 Enhanced Message Repository Manager . . . . . . . . . . . . . . . . . . . . . . . 22
1.4 XML support . . . . . . . . . . . . . . . . . . . . . . . . . . . . . . . . . . . . . . . . . . . . . 26
1.5 Database support . . . . . . . . . . . . . . . . . . . . . . . . . . . . . . . . . . . . . . . . . 26
1.6 New ESQL features. . . . . . . . . . . . . . . . . . . . . . . . . . . . . . . . . . . . . . . . 27
1.7 Summary of new features . . . . . . . . . . . . . . . . . . . . . . . . . . . . . . . . . . . 29
1.8 Software prerequisites for z/OS and OS/390 platform . . . . . . . . . . . . . . 30
  1.8.1 Mandatory requirements . . . . . . . . . . . . . . . . . . . . . . . . . . . . . . . . 30
  1.8.2 Functional requirements . . . . . . . . . . . . . . . . . . . . . . . . . . . . . . . . 30

**Chapter 2. z/OS UNIX System Services** . . . . . . . . . . . . . . . . . . . . . . . . . 31
2.1 In brief . . . . . . . . . . . . . . . . . . . . . . . . . . . . . . . . . . . . . . . . . . . . . . . . . . 32
2.2 UNIX System Services concepts and tools. . . . . . . . . . . . . . . . . . . . . . 32
2.3 Working with UNIX System Services . . . . . . . . . . . . . . . . . . . . . . . . . . 35
  2.3.1 Permissions. . . . . . . . . . . . . . . . . . . . . . . . . . . . . . . . . . . . . . . . . . 36
  2.3.2 Useful TSO/E commands . . . . . . . . . . . . . . . . . . . . . . . . . . . . . . . 36
  2.3.3 Useful MVS console commands . . . . . . . . . . . . . . . . . . . . . . . . . . 37
2.4 Basic shell commands. . . . . . . . . . . . . . . . . . . . . . . . . . . . . . . . . . . . . . 38
2.5 Shared HFS in a Parallel Sysplex . . . . . . . . . . . . . . . . . . . . . . . . . . . . . 41
  2.5.1 Using HFS on OS/390 V2.8 . . . . . . . . . . . . . . . . . . . . . . . . . . . . . 41
  2.5.2 Using HFS on OS/390 V2.9 and higher . . . . . . . . . . . . . . . . . . . . 42

**Chapter 3. z/OS Resource Recovery Services and transactional message flows** . . . . . . . . . . . . . . . . . . . . . . . . . . . . . . . . . . . . . . . . . . 43

3.1  Resource Recovery Services introduction . . . . . . . . . . . . . . . . . . . . . . . . . 44
3.2  RRS prerequisites and setup . . . . . . . . . . . . . . . . . . . . . . . . . . . . . . . . . . 45
3.3  RRS support with MQSeries 5.2. . . . . . . . . . . . . . . . . . . . . . . . . . . . . . . . 46
3.4  Transactional support . . . . . . . . . . . . . . . . . . . . . . . . . . . . . . . . . . . . . . . . 48
    3.4.1  Message flow coordination . . . . . . . . . . . . . . . . . . . . . . . . . . . . . . 51
    3.4.2  Transactional support on MQInput . . . . . . . . . . . . . . . . . . . . . . . . 52
    3.4.3  Transactional support on MQOutput. . . . . . . . . . . . . . . . . . . . . . . 54
    3.4.4  Transactional support on Database node . . . . . . . . . . . . . . . . . . 55

**Part 2. Configuration and migration** . . . . . . . . . . . . . . . . . . . . . . . . . . . . . . . . . . . . . . . . 59

**Chapter 4.  Configuration of WMQI on z/OS and Windows platforms**. . . . 61
4.1  Configuration of components on z/OS . . . . . . . . . . . . . . . . . . . . . . . . . . 62
    4.1.1  Before you start. . . . . . . . . . . . . . . . . . . . . . . . . . . . . . . . . . . . . . 62
    4.1.2  Configuration overview . . . . . . . . . . . . . . . . . . . . . . . . . . . . . . . . 62
4.2  Customizing brokers . . . . . . . . . . . . . . . . . . . . . . . . . . . . . . . . . . . . . . . 65
4.3  Customizing the User Name Server (UNS) . . . . . . . . . . . . . . . . . . . . . 75
4.4  Setup of the Configuration Manager . . . . . . . . . . . . . . . . . . . . . . . . . . 81
    4.4.1  Installing the Configuration Manager . . . . . . . . . . . . . . . . . . . . . 82
    4.4.2  Creating the Configuration Manager. . . . . . . . . . . . . . . . . . . . . . 82
4.5  Setup of the Control Center. . . . . . . . . . . . . . . . . . . . . . . . . . . . . . . . . . 85
    4.5.1  Install the Control Center . . . . . . . . . . . . . . . . . . . . . . . . . . . . . . 85
    4.5.2  Connect to the Configuration Manager. . . . . . . . . . . . . . . . . . . . 85
    4.5.3  Add your broker to topology . . . . . . . . . . . . . . . . . . . . . . . . . . . . 88

**Chapter 5.  WMQI operations on the z/OS platform** . . . . . . . . . . . . . . . . . . 89
5.1  Review typical message flows. . . . . . . . . . . . . . . . . . . . . . . . . . . . . . . . 90
    5.1.1  A simple message flow . . . . . . . . . . . . . . . . . . . . . . . . . . . . . . . 90
    5.1.2  Filter nodes and Compute nodes in a message flow . . . . . . . . . 93
    5.1.3  A simple database access example . . . . . . . . . . . . . . . . . . . . . 95
5.2  Common administrative tasks . . . . . . . . . . . . . . . . . . . . . . . . . . . . . . . 100
5.3  Problem determination techniques . . . . . . . . . . . . . . . . . . . . . . . . . . . 106
    5.3.1  Sources for proper problem determination . . . . . . . . . . . . . . . . 106
    5.3.2  Most commons problems or errors . . . . . . . . . . . . . . . . . . . . . 109
    5.3.3  Checklist for deployment problems. . . . . . . . . . . . . . . . . . . . . . 113
    5.3.4  Using tracing to assist with problem determination. . . . . . . . . . 113

**Chapter 6.  Overview of New Era of Networks support in WebSphere MQ
            Integrator**. . . . . . . . . . . . . . . . . . . . . . . . . . . . . . . . . . . . . . . . . . . . 115
6.1  History of New Era of Networks support . . . . . . . . . . . . . . . . . . . . . . 116
6.2  WebSphere MQ Integrator with New Era of Networks . . . . . . . . . . . . 117
6.3  New Era of Networks new features. . . . . . . . . . . . . . . . . . . . . . . . . . . 118
    6.3.1  UNIX Systems Services . . . . . . . . . . . . . . . . . . . . . . . . . . . . . 119
    6.3.2  New parameter file . . . . . . . . . . . . . . . . . . . . . . . . . . . . . . . . . . 119

  6.3.3 The new Rules GUI. . . . . . . . . . . . . . . . . . . . . . . . . . . . . . . . . . . . . . 119
  6.3.4 Format permissions. . . . . . . . . . . . . . . . . . . . . . . . . . . . . . . . . . . . . 119
  6.3.5 The new map function. . . . . . . . . . . . . . . . . . . . . . . . . . . . . . . . . . 119
  6.3.6 Binary literals. . . . . . . . . . . . . . . . . . . . . . . . . . . . . . . . . . . . . . . . . 120
  6.3.7 NNFie -p option. . . . . . . . . . . . . . . . . . . . . . . . . . . . . . . . . . . . . . . 120
  6.3.8 Reload Rules and Formats . . . . . . . . . . . . . . . . . . . . . . . . . . . . . . 120
 6.4 Migration planning. . . . . . . . . . . . . . . . . . . . . . . . . . . . . . . . . . . . . . . . 120

**Chapter 7. Configuring New Era of Networks Support** . . . . . . . . . . . . . . 123
 7.1 Broker configuration . . . . . . . . . . . . . . . . . . . . . . . . . . . . . . . . . . . . . . 124
  7.1.1 Customizing the broker for New Era of Networks support . . . . . . . 124
  7.1.2 Building the Rules and Formats database . . . . . . . . . . . . . . . . . . 125
  7.1.3 Configuring the broker UNIX System Services environment . . . . . 126
 7.2 Setup of the Configuration Manager . . . . . . . . . . . . . . . . . . . . . . . . . . . 128
  7.2.1 Defining the connection to the Rules and Formats database . . . . . 129
  7.2.2 Create the nnsyreg.dat . . . . . . . . . . . . . . . . . . . . . . . . . . . . . . . . . 129
  7.2.3 Amending the system environment variables . . . . . . . . . . . . . . . . 130
  7.2.4 Restart the Configuration Manager. . . . . . . . . . . . . . . . . . . . . . . . 131
 7.3 Workstation configuration . . . . . . . . . . . . . . . . . . . . . . . . . . . . . . . . . . 133
  7.3.1 Defining the connection to the Rules and Formats database . . . . . 133
  7.3.2 Creating the nnsyreg.dat file . . . . . . . . . . . . . . . . . . . . . . . . . . . . . 133
  7.3.3 Configuring the System Environment variables . . . . . . . . . . . . . . . 133
  7.3.4 Starting the Control Center and New Era of Networks GUI . . . . . . 134
 7.4 Verification. . . . . . . . . . . . . . . . . . . . . . . . . . . . . . . . . . . . . . . . . . . . . . 137
  7.4.1 Build a simple NEONTransform flow. . . . . . . . . . . . . . . . . . . . . . . 138
  7.4.2 Configure the node properties. . . . . . . . . . . . . . . . . . . . . . . . . . . . 139
  7.4.3 Define queues . . . . . . . . . . . . . . . . . . . . . . . . . . . . . . . . . . . . . . . 143
  7.4.4 Deploy and test the message flow . . . . . . . . . . . . . . . . . . . . . . . . 143
  7.4.5 Verification of the Configuration Manager. . . . . . . . . . . . . . . . . . . 144
  7.4.6 Configuration problem determination . . . . . . . . . . . . . . . . . . . . . . 149

**Chapter 8. Migrating New Era of Networks Rules and Formats from**
      **MQSeries Integrator Version 1.11** . . . . . . . . . . . . . . . . . . . . . . 151
 8.1 Migration overview . . . . . . . . . . . . . . . . . . . . . . . . . . . . . . . . . . . . . . . 152
 8.2 Copying your export files to UNIX System Services . . . . . . . . . . . . . . . 153
 8.3 Importing your rules and formats. . . . . . . . . . . . . . . . . . . . . . . . . . . . . 153
  8.3.1 Configuring NNFie and NNRie . . . . . . . . . . . . . . . . . . . . . . . . . . . 153
  8.3.2 Importing formats . . . . . . . . . . . . . . . . . . . . . . . . . . . . . . . . . . . . 155
  8.3.3 Importing rules . . . . . . . . . . . . . . . . . . . . . . . . . . . . . . . . . . . . . . 156
 8.4 Running the consistency checker . . . . . . . . . . . . . . . . . . . . . . . . . . . . 157
 8.5 Creating your migration message flow . . . . . . . . . . . . . . . . . . . . . . . . 157
  8.5.1 NNSY.IN . . . . . . . . . . . . . . . . . . . . . . . . . . . . . . . . . . . . . . . . . . . 158
  8.5.2 NEONRulesEvaluation1 node. . . . . . . . . . . . . . . . . . . . . . . . . . . . 160

        8.5.3   NNSY.RULES.FAILED and NNSY.NOHITS . . . . . . . . . . . . . . . . . . 161
        8.5.4   NNSY.PUTQUEUE.ACTION. . . . . . . . . . . . . . . . . . . . . . . . . . . . . . 161
    8.6  Other migration considerations . . . . . . . . . . . . . . . . . . . . . . . . . . . . . . . . . 162
        8.6.1   Configuring WMQI to match your Rules Engine . . . . . . . . . . . . . . 162
        8.6.2   User exits . . . . . . . . . . . . . . . . . . . . . . . . . . . . . . . . . . . . . . . . . . . . 164
        8.6.3   Multiple databases and Rules Engines . . . . . . . . . . . . . . . . . . . . . 164
    8.7  Other New Era of Networks features. . . . . . . . . . . . . . . . . . . . . . . . . . . . . 165
        8.7.1   NEONRulesEvaluation node terminals . . . . . . . . . . . . . . . . . . . . . 165
        8.7.2   NEONMap node . . . . . . . . . . . . . . . . . . . . . . . . . . . . . . . . . . . . . . 170
        8.7.3   NEONTransform node . . . . . . . . . . . . . . . . . . . . . . . . . . . . . . . . . 170
        8.7.4   NeonRules and NeonFormatter nodes . . . . . . . . . . . . . . . . . . . . . 171
        8.7.5   Exploiting ESQL with New Era of Networks messages . . . . . . . . . 171

    **Chapter 9. Migration from distributed platforms to WMQI for z/OS** . . . . 181
    9.1  Considerations for migration . . . . . . . . . . . . . . . . . . . . . . . . . . . . . . . . . . . 182
    9.2  Migrating from MQSeries Integrator V2.02 . . . . . . . . . . . . . . . . . . . . . . . . 183
        9.2.1   Upgrading your MQSeries Integrator V2.02 Configuration Manager183
        9.2.2   Upgrading your MQSeries Integrator V2.02 Control Center . . . . . . 186
        9.2.3   Upgrading your MQSeries Integrator V2.02 brokers. . . . . . . . . . . . 186
        9.2.4   Migrating New Era of Networks Rules and Formats from V2.02. . . 187
    9.3  Migrating from MQSeries Integrator V2.0.1. . . . . . . . . . . . . . . . . . . . . . . . 187
    9.4  Migrating from MQSeries Integrator V2.0 . . . . . . . . . . . . . . . . . . . . . . . . . 188

    **Chapter 10. WMQI in a Parallel Sysplex environment** . . . . . . . . . . . . . . . 191
    10.1  The Parallel Sysplex concept . . . . . . . . . . . . . . . . . . . . . . . . . . . . . . . . . 192
    10.2  MQSeries message sharing . . . . . . . . . . . . . . . . . . . . . . . . . . . . . . . . . . 193
        10.2.1   Queue-sharing groups . . . . . . . . . . . . . . . . . . . . . . . . . . . . . . . . 193
        10.2.2   Shared objects . . . . . . . . . . . . . . . . . . . . . . . . . . . . . . . . . . . . . . 194
        10.2.3   Remarks . . . . . . . . . . . . . . . . . . . . . . . . . . . . . . . . . . . . . . . . . . . 195
    10.3  WMQI configuration in a Parallel Sysplex . . . . . . . . . . . . . . . . . . . . . . . . 197
        10.3.1   Introduction . . . . . . . . . . . . . . . . . . . . . . . . . . . . . . . . . . . . . . . . 197
        10.3.2   Overview . . . . . . . . . . . . . . . . . . . . . . . . . . . . . . . . . . . . . . . . . . 197
        10.3.3   WMQI sample architecture . . . . . . . . . . . . . . . . . . . . . . . . . . . . . 198
        10.3.4   Execution of message flows in the sysplex. . . . . . . . . . . . . . . . . . 202
        10.3.5   Transactional behavior . . . . . . . . . . . . . . . . . . . . . . . . . . . . . . . . 210
        10.3.6   Automatic Restart Management (ARM) planning . . . . . . . . . . . . 217
        10.3.7   Configuration for publishing and subscribing in a sysplex . . . . . . 220
        10.3.8   Topic-based security in a Parallel Sysplex environment. . . . . . . . 228

**Part 3. Advanced features** . . . . . . . . . . . . . . . . . . . . . . . . . . . . . . . . . . . . . . . . . . . 233

    **Chapter 11. New MRM and XML features** . . . . . . . . . . . . . . . . . . . . . . . . . 235
    11.1  Put, get, and view MQSeries messages . . . . . . . . . . . . . . . . . . . . . . . . . 236
    11.2  Testing the MRM in a message flow . . . . . . . . . . . . . . . . . . . . . . . . . . . . 237

11.3 Defining delimited messages .................................. 238
   11.3.1 Building the message set ................................. 239
   11.3.2 Creating a message flow to convert CSV to XML ............. 254
   11.3.3 Testing the message flow ................................. 260
11.4 Building tagged messages ..................................... 261
   11.4.1 Build the message set .................................... 261
   11.4.2 Creating a message flow to convert tagged messages to XML .. 265
   11.4.3 Test the message flow .................................... 267
11.5 Importing an XML DTD ......................................... 270
   11.5.1 DTDs explained ........................................... 270
   11.5.2 Importing the DTD ........................................ 271
   11.5.3 Creating a message flow to test the DTD import ............ 277
   11.5.4 Testing the message flow ................................. 282
   11.5.5 Modifying the location attribute in a Compute node ........ 283
11.6 Additional XML MRM features .................................. 284
   11.6.1 Multiple XML entities .................................... 284
   11.6.2 Mixing MRM and generic XML ............................... 287
   11.6.3 Using ESQL reference variables ........................... 289

**Chapter 12. Developing and deploying custom nodes in Java ....... 293**
12.1 What can you do with a Java plug-in? ......................... 294
   12.1.1 Plug-in nodes ............................................ 294
   12.1.2 MbInputNodeInterface ..................................... 295
   12.1.3 MbNodeInterface .......................................... 295
12.2 Getting started .............................................. 296
   12.2.1 System requirements ...................................... 296
   12.2.2 Programming requirements ................................. 296
   12.2.3 Debugging and logging .................................... 296
12.3 Implementing an input node ................................... 297
   12.3.1 Working with the example provided with the product ....... 297
   12.3.2 Taking a look at the Java source ......................... 298
   12.3.3 Packaging and loading the input node ..................... 300
   12.3.4 A simple message flow to test the input node ............. 302
   12.3.5 How to test the input node ............................... 309
   12.3.6 How to use the input node to read a telnet stream ........ 311
12.4 Implementing a plug-in node .................................. 313
   12.4.1 Let us start ............................................. 313
   12.4.2 A look at another Java source ............................ 314
   12.4.3 Packaging and loading the plug-in node ................... 316
   12.4.4 A simple message flow to test the plug-in node ........... 316
12.5 Summary ...................................................... 320

**Appendix A. Running a message flow trace ........................ 321**

**Appendix B. Source code for the Java extensions to WebSphere MQ Integrator** . . . . . . . . . . . . . . . . . . . . . . . . . . . . . . . . . . . . . . . . 333

**Appendix C. Using the Control Center Debugger** . . . . . . . . . . . . . . . . . . 347

**Appendix D. Additional material** . . . . . . . . . . . . . . . . . . . . . . . . . . . . . . . 355
Locating the Web material . . . . . . . . . . . . . . . . . . . . . . . . . . . . . . . . . . . . . 355
Using the Web material . . . . . . . . . . . . . . . . . . . . . . . . . . . . . . . . . . . . . . . 355
    System requirements for downloading the Web material . . . . . . . . . . . . 356
    How to use the Web material . . . . . . . . . . . . . . . . . . . . . . . . . . . . . . . . 356

**Related publications** . . . . . . . . . . . . . . . . . . . . . . . . . . . . . . . . . . . . . . . . 357
IBM Redbooks . . . . . . . . . . . . . . . . . . . . . . . . . . . . . . . . . . . . . . . . . . . . . . 357
    Other resources . . . . . . . . . . . . . . . . . . . . . . . . . . . . . . . . . . . . . . . . . . 357
Referenced Web sites . . . . . . . . . . . . . . . . . . . . . . . . . . . . . . . . . . . . . . . . 358
How to get IBM Redbooks . . . . . . . . . . . . . . . . . . . . . . . . . . . . . . . . . . . . . 358
    IBM Redbooks collections . . . . . . . . . . . . . . . . . . . . . . . . . . . . . . . . . . . 359

**Special notices** . . . . . . . . . . . . . . . . . . . . . . . . . . . . . . . . . . . . . . . . . . . . 361

**Glossary** . . . . . . . . . . . . . . . . . . . . . . . . . . . . . . . . . . . . . . . . . . . . . . . . . 363

**Abbreviations and acronyms** . . . . . . . . . . . . . . . . . . . . . . . . . . . . . . . . . 367

**Index** . . . . . . . . . . . . . . . . . . . . . . . . . . . . . . . . . . . . . . . . . . . . . . . . . . . . 369

# Preface

This redbook looks at the new WebSphere MQ Integrator V2.1 product on the z/OS and OS/390 platforms. Its focus is entirely on the deployment of WMQI applications to the z/OS and OS/390 environments. It takes you through the usage of the IBM development, deployment, and debugging tools, and explains how to set up the broker environment in the most appropriate way.

In the first part of the redbook, we introduce the new product and provide some background information about the use of UNIX System Services on the z/OS and OS/390 platforms. The topics covered are:

- WebSphere MQ Integrator 2.1 overview
- z/OS UNIX System Services overview
- z/OS Resource Recovery Services

In the second part of the redbook, we discuss WMQI customization, migration from earlier releases and Parallel Sysplex considerations. The topics include:

- Configuration setup
- Operational considerations
- Migrating New Era of Networks Rules and Formats
- Migrating existing message flows from distributed platforms to z/OS platform
- WMQI in a Parallel Sysplex environment

In the third part of the redbook we introduce advanced features of this release. The features we look at are:

- Support for delimited and tagged messages (MRM2)
- XML support enhancements
- Java plug-in and custom node support

## The team that wrote this redbook

This redbook was produced by a team of specialists from around the world working at the International Technical Support Organization, Raleigh Center

**Geert Van de Putte** is an IT Specialist at the International Technical Support Organization, Raleigh Center. He has six years of experience in the design and implementation of MQSeries-based solutions. Before joining the ITSO, Geert worked in IBM Global Services, Belgium. Geert designed and prepared this project.

**Eugene Deborin** is a Consulting Information Technology Specialist at the International Technical Support Organization, Raleigh Center. He writes extensively and teaches IBM classes worldwide on all areas of transaction and message processing. Eugene has been working for IBM Israel since 1984, first as a Systems Engineer and, more recently, as Software Technical Sales Specialist. He joined the ITSO San Jose Center five years ago as CICS Transaction Server Specialist and is now a member of WebSphere MQ/ WebSphere MQ Integrator ITSO team located in Raleigh and Hursley, UK.

**Corinthian Carpenter** is an IT Architect in the IBM Business Innovation Services group based in Charlotte, NC. He has over 10 years' industry experience in software life cycle development and over four years with IBM working as a practitioner with the WebSphere MQSeries product line. He holds an undergraduate degree in Chemical Engineering and graduate degree in Computer Science and is completing his MBA. His areas of expertise include enterprise application development using WebSphere technologies on multiple operating system platforms.

**Graham French** is a senior consultant in MQSolutions in the United Kingdom. MQSolutions is an IBM Business Partner and offers a wide range of consultancy and services across the WebSphere MQ product range. Graham has over 18 years in Information Technology and has spent the last six years working with MQSeries, NeoNet and what are now the WebSphere MQ products. He has worked with many large corporations in Europe, planning, implementing and managing these products and has written SupportPacs and provided presentations from his based on his experience.

**David Long** is a Senior e-Business Software Sales Specialist for zServers with IBM based in Dallas, TX. He has 28 years' experience in the software and IT services industries. He holds a BS degree in Aerospace Engineering, an MBA and an MS in Accounting. He was an adjunct professor in MIS for over 10 years at the University of Texas at Dallas with an expertise in database concepts. He has experience in software development, technical support, project management, marketing and sales.

**Angel L Montero Sanchez** is an Application Designer working in the IBM Center for e-business Innovation in Madrid, Spain. His main area of expertise is application development for MQSeries, CICS and DB2 on the mainframe as well as on distributed platforms. Angel was actively involved in Sydney 2000 Olympic Games information technology project where the infrastructure was MQSeries based. One of systems he developed within the framework of this project is currently being patented by IBM.

Thanks to the following people for their contributions to this project:

**Julian Barker**, IBM United Kingdom, Hursley Laboratories

**Chris Griego**, IBM Global Services, IBM US

**Robert Haimowitz**, International Technical Support Organization

**Miriam Kastner**, IBM Learning Services, IBM Germany

**Brian McCarty**, Independent MQSeries Technical Support Specialist

**Roy Saxton**, IBM United Kingdom, Hursley Laboratories

**Peter Toogood**, Royal and Sun Alliance Insurance, United Kingdom

**Ralf Ziegler**, Integration Technology Services, IBM Germany

# Special notice

This publication is intended to help WebSphere MQ System Administrators and WebSphere MQ Integrator Application Developers to customize and use the WebSphere MQ Integrator product on z/OS and OS/390 platforms. The information in this publication is not intended as the specification of any programming interfaces that are provided by WebSphere MQ or WebSphere MQ Integrator. See the PUBLICATIONS section of the IBM Programming Announcement for WebSphere MQ Integrator for z/OS product for more information about what publications are considered to be product documentation.

# IBM trademarks

The following terms are trademarks of the International Business Machines Corporation in the United States and/or other countries:

e (logo)® @
AIX®
CICS®
Database 2™
DB2®
DB2 Universal Database™
DRDA®
Everyplace™
IBM®
IMS™
Language Environment®
MQIntegrator®
MQSeries®
MVS™
NetView®
OS/390®
Parallel Sysplex®
RACF®
Redbooks Logo
Redbooks™
S/390®
SP™
SP1®
SupportPac™
System/390®
Tivoli®
VisualAge®
VTAM®
WebSphere®
z/OS™
Lotus®
Domino™

# Comments welcome

Your comments are important to us!

We want our Redbooks to be as helpful as possible. Send us your comments about this or other Redbooks in one of the following ways:

- Use the online **Contact us** review redbook form found at:

    ibm.com/redbooks

- Send your comments in an Internet note to:

    redbook@us.ibm.com

- Mail your comments to the address on page ii.

# Part 1

# Introduction

# Product overview

WebSphere MQ Integrator for z/OS V2.1 extends MQ message broker availability to the z/OS platform and adds significant capabilities to those previously provided by the MQSeries Integrator for OS/390 and DB2 V1.1.

This program offering, previously known on other platforms as the MQSeries Integrator, is central to the WebSphere MQ software platform.

WebSphere MQ Integrator (WMQI) helps you to:
- Create, deploy, and control message-based solutions
- Integrate existing applications with new e-business requirements
- Integrate applications within enterprises
- Connect applications between enterprises and their suppliers

## 1.1 WebSphere MQ Integrator basics

WebSphere MQ Integrator (formerly called MQSeries Integrator) is IBM's *message broker* product. It extends the messaging capabilities of MQSeries by adding message routing and transformation features. It is used for Enterprise Application Integration (EAI) and is a part of the WebSphere MQ family of products.

WMQI V2.1 is available for Windows NT, Windows 2000, the IBM pServers (AIX), IBM iServers (AS400 under NT Emulation), SUN Solaris, HP-UX and the IBM zServers (OS/390 and z/OS). This document specifically deals with the zServers that require OS/390 V2.8 or above or z/OS V1R1 or above. When z/OS is referenced herein, it refers to both OS/390 on S/390 and z/OS on z900 at the operating system levels just listed.

Business rules can be defined by graphically developing *message flows,* which consist of a sequence of *nodes*. Message flows are processes that can encapsulate logic ranging from simple to extremely complex. They can be designed to perform a wide variety of functions including (but not limited to):

- Routing of messages to zero or more destinations based on the contents of the message or message header (both one-to-many and many-to-one messaging topologies are supported).
- Transformation of messages into different formats so that diverse applications can exchange messages that each of them can understand.
- Enrichment of the message content en-route (for example, by using a database lookup performed by the message broker).
- Storing information extracted from messages en-route to a database (using the message broker to perform this).
- Publishing messages (and using topic/content based criteria for subscribers to select which messages to receive).
- Interfacing with other transport mechanisms such as MQSeries Everyplace.
- Extending the base function of WebSphere MQ Integrator with *plug-in* nodes (which can be developed by installations as well as by IBM and ISVs).

Message content can be handled in a number of message domains, including:

- XML domain, which handles self-defining (or generic) XML messages.
- Message Repository Manager (MRM) domain, which handles messages predefined in *message sets* in the message repository database, as:
  - XML (defined)
  - Tagged data

- Custom Wire Format (similar to a COBOL copybook layout)
- Delimited data
- PDF (not Adobe, but a specialized financial data format).

▶ NEONMSG domain, which handles messages defined using the New Era of Networks (NEON) formatter.

▶ BLOB domain, which handles messages with no predefined structure.

## WebSphere MQ Integrator background

WebSphere MQ Integrator builds on the assured messaging capability of MQSeries, and a typical message flow uses MQSeries messages for input and output. There are MQSeries adapters and connectors available for various systems and applications, and Release 2.1 of WebSphere MQ Integrator also allows other interfaces to be linked directly to broker message flows.

WebSphere MQ (formerly known as MQSeries) provides support for applications with a number of application programming interfaces (Message Queuing Interface (MQI), Application Messaging Interface (AMI), Java Messaging Services (JMS)) in several programming languages and for a number of communication models (including point-to-point and publish/subscribe). WebSphere MQ also provides a number of connectors and gateways to other products such as Lotus Domino, Microsoft Exchange, SAP/R3, CICS, and IMS.

WebSphere MQ Integrator extends the messaging capabilities of MQSeries by adding message broker functionality driven by business rules. It provides the intelligence to route and transform messages, the possibility to filter messages (topic-based or content-based), and database capabilities for enrichment of the messages or for warehousing the messages. Also, it provides a framework for extending the functionality with plug-ins to user-written or third-party solutions.

MQSeries Workflow(MQWF) is the third component of IBM's family of products for business integration. MQSeries Workflow is the process engine for IBM Business Process Management (BPM) software. MQWF executes process definitions captured during modeling and ensures that business functions are performed accurately and reliably using the transactional integrity of MQSeries. MQWF facilitates the integration of services provided by IT and organizational infrastructures, integrating bought and built applications - even with customers, business partners, suppliers and employees. MQWF can transform traditional business models into e-business models.

## WebSphere MQ Integrator for z/OS

Most businesses today have a heterogeneous IT processing environment, that is, they have small, midsize and large processors. In the past, this made application development, integration and maintenance costly. WebSphere MQ Integrator is the industry-leading tool for Enterprise Application Integration. WMQI plays a significant role in simplifying the integration of heterogeneous applications and thus reducing the cost for an organization to tie together the entire enterprise and also to interface with vendor partners and clients. WMQI for z/OS V2.1 extends the MQ message broker to the z/OS platform. WMQI on z/OS is designed to allow customers to leverage existing hardware and existing OS/390 and z/OS administrative skills to provide a highly available, robust messaging environment while taking advantage of the strengths of the mainframe. Customers will choose a mainframe environment:

- When applications require highest availability
- When high levels of I/O are required
- When they desire to consolidate numerous smaller servers
- When the application benefits from proximity to mainframe-based data or application components.

Advantages of WebSphere MQ Integrator on z/OS are:

- Quality of Service
  - Scalability:
    - Parallel Sysplex exploitation
  - Availability:
    - WorkLoad Manager exploitation
    - Automatic Restart Manager
    - Geographically distributed failover
    - Highest reliability server hardware with industry's most advanced self-healing and recovery capabilities
  - Data Integrity
    - Integrated transaction support with other z/OS Work Managers
    - Transactional services based on RRS
    - Two-phase distributed transactions spanning CICS, IMS and DB2
    - Sysplex wide data sharing
  - Data Protection and Security
    - Integrated security via System Authorization Facility
    - Security integration with RACF
    - Strongest inter process isolation and system security

- Performance
  - Optimization of communication protocols
  - Asynchronous socket I/O parallelism
  - IIOP optimizations to exploit local communications within a sysplex cluster
- Proximity to enterprise data and applications
  - Short path length to enterprise data and applications
  - Gigabit I/O access to enterprise data and applications
  - Enablement of single unit of work (UOW) management of assets
- Administration and Management
  - Processing administration and operations matured and refined over decades
  - Geared to production-level, high transaction volume, mission-critical processing
  - Practical 24 x 7 operation
  - Tools refined to require fewer people to manage large, complex environments
  - Tools refined to quickly determine, isolate, circumvent, and repair problems
  - Well-established problem and change management procedures
  - Ability to tailor many processing environments on one box for specific application needs

## WebSphere MQ Integrator applications

These applications can be existing MQSeries-enabled applications that do not need to be aware of WebSphere MQ Integrator. In this case, the message flows will set the correct configuration defined to handle the messages. Alternatively the application can prefix the user data of the message with a WebSphere MQ Integrator header (MQRFH or MQRFH2) to control the way the broker handles the message.

WebSphere MQ Integrator supports two models for application communication:

- Point to Point - which can include one to many and many to one (that is, where the number of message producers and consumers are different).
- Publish/Subscribe - which includes and extends the existing MQSeries publish/subscribe model.

Figure 1-1 on page 8 shows the members of the WebSphere MQ family.

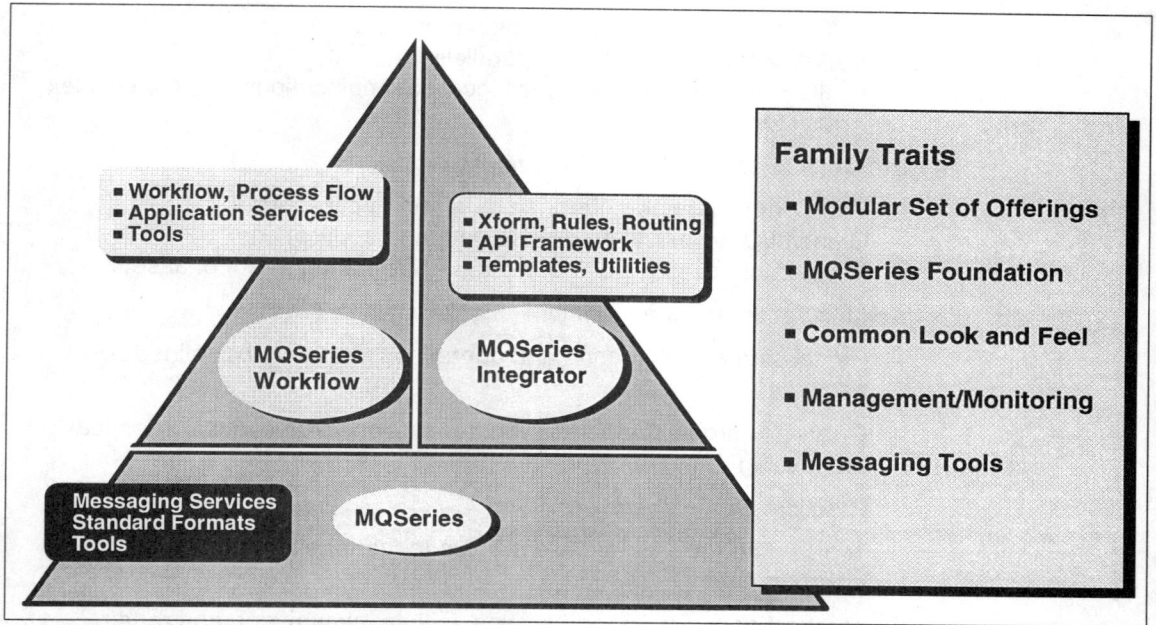

Figure 1-1   WebSphere MQ family

### 1.1.1  Architecture of WebSphere MQ Integrator

The components of a WebSphere MQ Integrator environment include:

- Control Center. This is a Windows NT graphical user interface (GUI) for the message broker administration and it is also used to develop message flows and message sets.
- Configuration Manager, with its configuration and message repository.
- One or more brokers (which can be on different platforms or systems).
- User Name Server (used to control publish/subscribe topic security).
- MQSeries Queue Manager(s) - at least one is needed per broker.
- Database software to support the Configuration Manager and broker(s).
- Client applications (source and target) which produce and consume messages (or use the other supported types of interfaces).
- Optionally, system management software such as Tivoli products that monitor the broker and Queue Manager's operational status.

Figure 1-2 shows the product architecture.

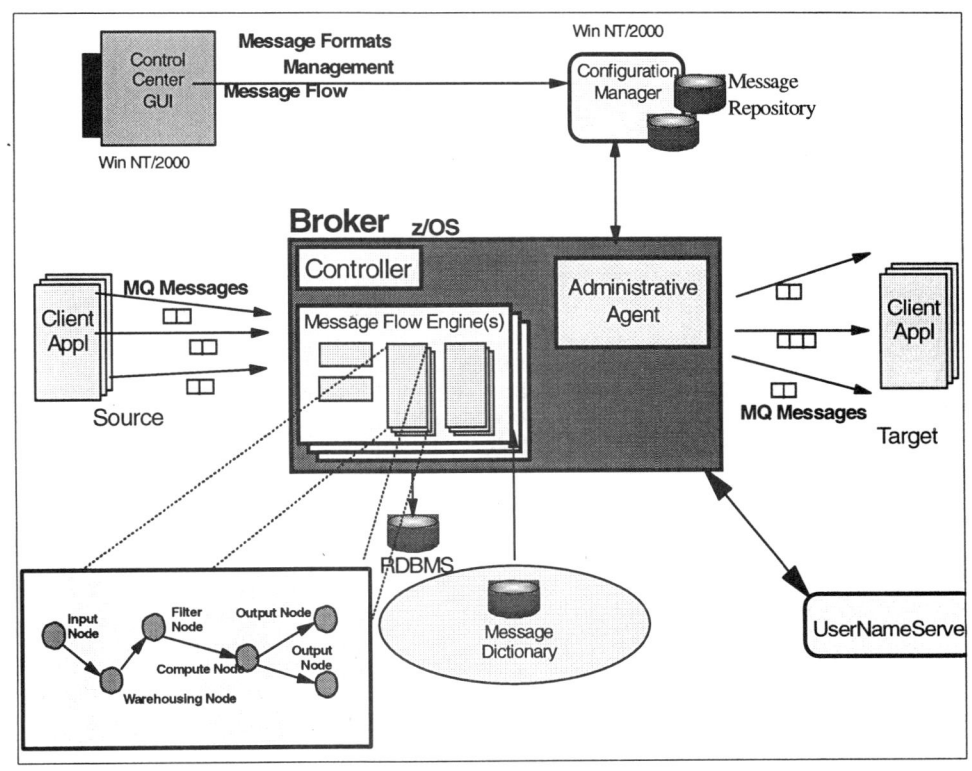

*Figure 1-2   WebSphere MQ Integrator architecture*

## 1.1.2  The role of the Configuration Manager

A WebSphere MQ Integrator system is controlled by the *Configuration Manager,* which manages the components and resources within the *broker domain.* The domain configuration information is maintained in the configuration repository and administered by using the Control Center.

The Configuration Manager has these main functions:

- Maintains the configuration repository - this set of database tables records the configuration of the components in the broker domain including the flows.
- Manages the initialization and deployment of message brokers and flows.
- Maintains message set information in the message repository database (these are the definitions of message contents and layout).
- Checks the authority of defined user IDs to initiate control actions.

Chapter 1. Product overview   **9**

Figure 1-3 shows the relationships of the Configuration Manager with other product components.

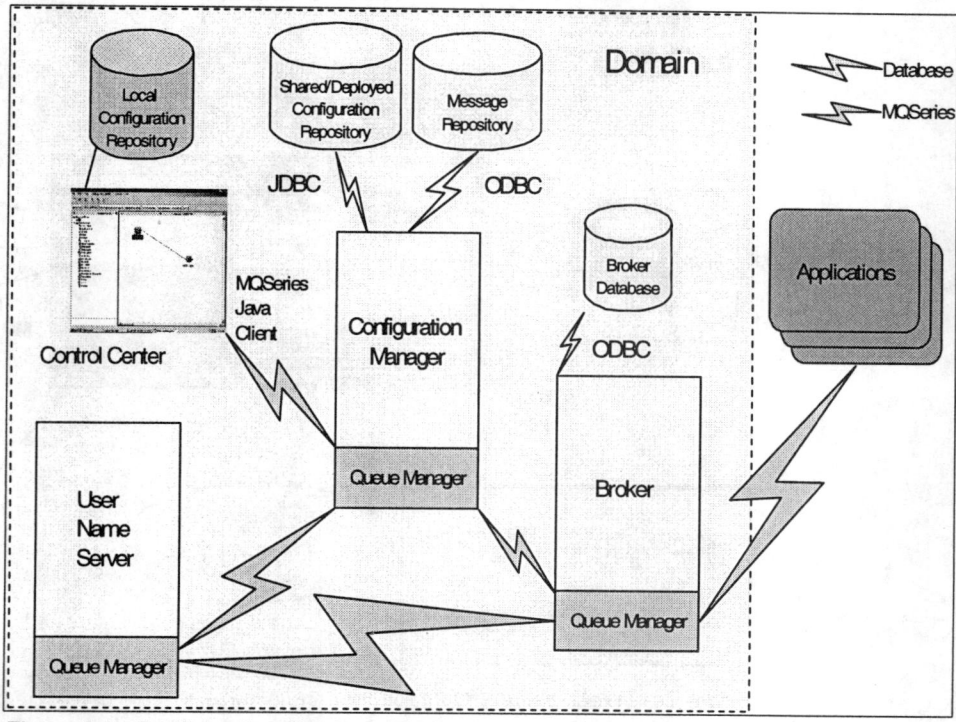

*Figure 1-3   Configuration Manager relationships*

The Configuration Manager provides services to the other broker domain components, performing the configuration updates in response to the Control Center actions.

The Configuration Manager uses MQSeries messages to communicate with the other components in the broker domain. Windows NT (or Windows 2000) with DB2 must be used to host the Configuration Manager and its databases. Only one Configuration Manager is used for a given broker domain.

A set of tables in a database, known as the configuration repository, is defined. This database must be created using DB2 Universal Database for Windows NT. The Configuration Manager uses a Java Database Connectivity (JDBC) connection to this database.

A set of tables in a database, known as the message repository, is also defined. This database must also be created using DB2 Universal Database for Windows NT. The Configuration Manager uses an Open Database Connectivity (ODBC) connection to this database

A set of fixed name queues is defined on the MQSeries Queue Manager that hosts the Configuration Manager. This MQSeries Queue Manager must exist on the same physical system as the Configuration Manager, and is identified at the time the Configuration Manager is created.

These queues are created when the `mqsicreateconfigmgr` (including associated variables) command is executed through either the GUI or the command prompt. No actions are required by the administrator to add the required definitions.

A server connection channel is defined to the MQSeries Queue Manager that hosts the Configuration Manager. This connection is used by all instances of the Control Center that communicate with the Configuration Manager.

Sender and receiver channels are defined to each broker in the broker domain except for a broker that shares its Queue Manager with the Configuration Manager.

### 1.1.3 The functionality of the broker

A broker is the named resource that executes the business logic defined in the message flows. Applications send and receive messages to and from a broker (which is the deployed runtime, or execution, part of the product) using MQSeries queues (or the other supported methods of communication). The broker component is defined and executes on UNIX Systems Services in z/OS.

More than one broker can be defined per WebSphere MQ Integrator domain, either on the same or on a different physical system. If you plan to use the publish/subscribe service, you can connect a number of brokers together into a *collective,* which allows optimization of the subscriber connections.

Message flows run within *execution groups* on the broker. An execution group is an operating system process, and flows within it are mapped to threads. Individual flows and execution groups can be stopped and started using the Control Center. By default, only one execution group is defined, but more can be added easily.

It's a good practice to run message flows belonging to different applications in different execution groups to give some isolation between them in the event of problems. To give even more isolation between applications you can use different brokers, but remember that each will need a different Queue Manager.

Figure 1-4 is an overview of the broker component.

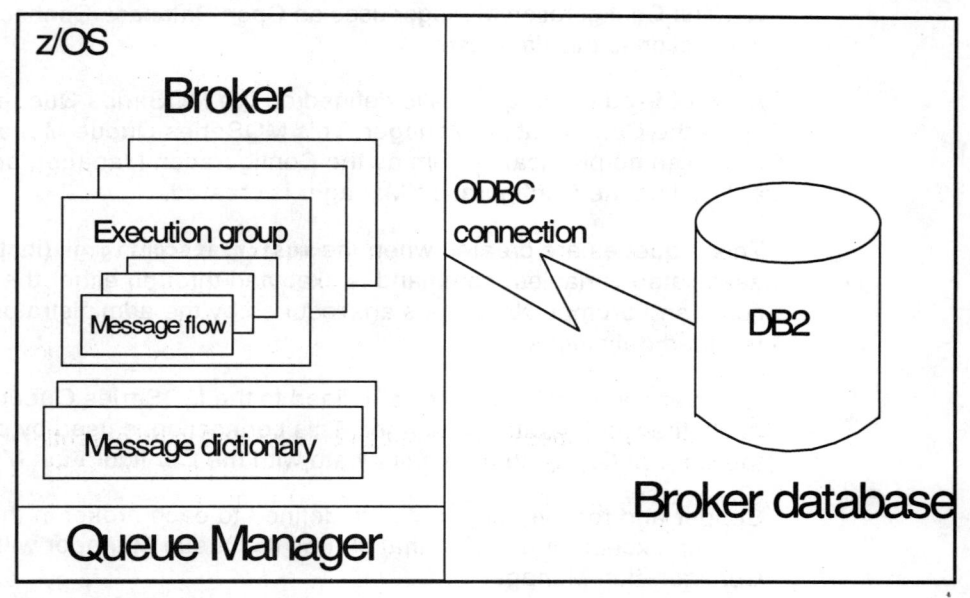

*Figure 1-4   Broker overview*

WebSphere MQ Integrator for z/OS brokers run on z/OS.

Each broker has a related *local* MQSeries Queue Manager (which cannot be shared with another broker) and a set of database tables to hold the broker definitions which are accessed via an ODBC connection.

For the z/OS version of the product, these tables are created in DB2. (WebSphere MQ Integrator for z/OS only supports DB2.)

Each broker requires:

- A set of tables in DB2 to hold the broker's local data. This data is accessed using the ODBC connection.
- A set of named queues on the Queue Manager associated with the broker domain (these are created automatically when the `mqsicreatebroker` command is issued).
- Each broker needs its own Queue Manager. It can share the Queue Manager hosting either or both the Configuration Manager (not on z/OS) and the optional User Name Server.

Because the broker uses a set of predetermined queue names there is a dependency of an MQSeries Queue Manager per broker.

- For operation, a broker requires both configuration and initialization data. *Configuration* and *initialization data* are logically separate and are stored in different physical repositories.

Each broker instance needs an assigned, everlasting and fixed name. This is the *Broker Instance* name. This name, which is similar to the static identifier assigned to databases before they are created, is used to distinguish tables pertaining to one broker from another, where multiple brokers have been set up using the same database.

Creating a broker on the target execution platform does not itself update the Configuration Manager. You need to create a reference to it using the Control Center. Once this is done, and the broker deployed (to initialize it), then message flows and sets can be assigned to the broker. Deploying the flows starts their execution.

Several different message flows can be assigned to an execution group, although using different execution groups gives better application isolation. A particular message flow can also be configured to run more than one instance of itself inside the execution group.

The execution group environment is also known as a data flow (or message flow) engine. The engine is responsible for loading any *plug-in nodes* that can be developed or provided to extend the function beyond the supplied IBM nodes. These are known as *loadable implementation libraries* (or .lil files).

Brokers provide information in the form of published event messages in response to changes. These can be used by system management tools to update their management agents on the status of the broker components.

## 1.1.4 Publish/subscribe and the User Name Server

Message flows that include a *publication node* provide a publish/subscribe service. Publishing applications generate input to such flows and subscribing applications register a subscription with the broker based on the topic and/or content of interest to them. Within a broker collective, subscribers can register with their local broker and messages are automatically routed to them.

With publish/subscribe, the broker is providing interaction between publishers and subscribers. Subscribers can use a mixture of topic and content criteria to select which messages to receive.

Topic-based security can be implemented to provide administrative control over who can publish and who can subscribe - the WebSphere MQ Integrator User Name Server (which is optional and only needed for publish/subscribe security) is used to interface with the Windows NT security system and the z/OS External Security Manager (ESM). It provides information about users and groups to the Configuration Manager and brokers. The User Name Server can run on UNIX System Services on z/OS.

When a User Name Server is created, a set of fixed named queues are defined to its hosting Queue Manager (which may be a Queue Manager shared with the Configuration Manager or a broker if they are installed on the same system).

Figure 1-5 illustrates the publish/subscribe mechanism.

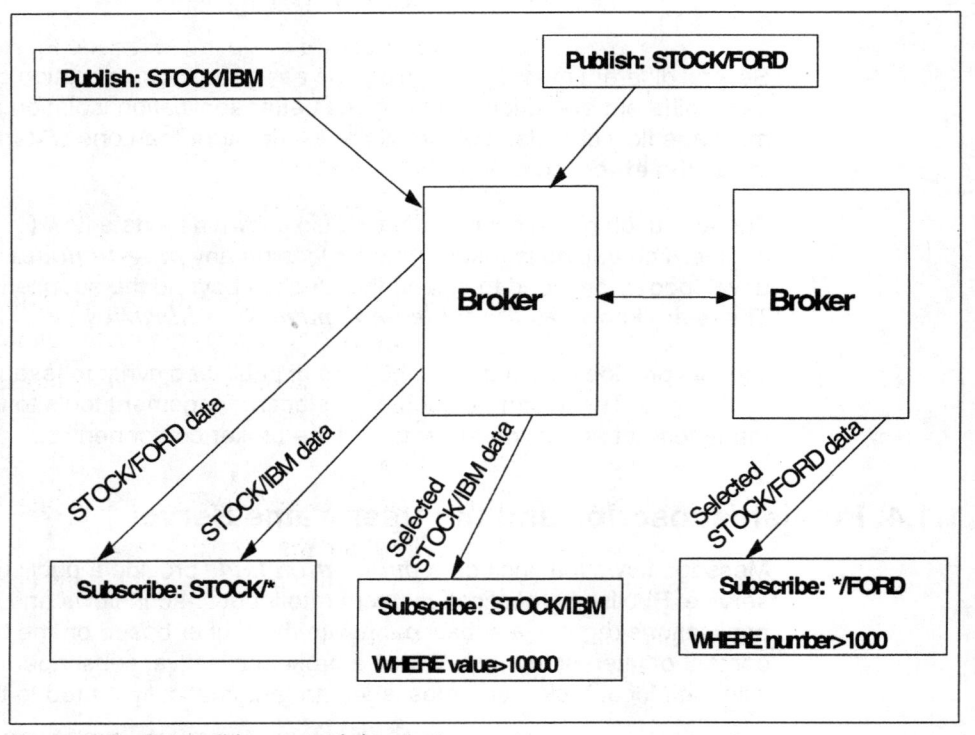

*Figure 1-5  Subscribing on topic/content*

## 1.1.5 The user interface: the Control Center

The Control Center is a graphical user interface (GUI) running on Windows NT (or Windows 2000) that allows you to configure and control your brokers. The Control Center connects, using the MQSeries client for Java, to the Configuration Manager over TCP/IP. It can be installed on the same physical system as the Configuration Manager but is typically used on another PC connected over a LAN.

Any number of Control Center instances can be connected to the Configuration Manager. The Control Center is used by the message flow developers as well as by broker administrators. Several user roles are predefined:

- Message flow and message set developer.
    - Can create message flows and message sets.
    - Can access the Message Sets view and the Message Flows view.
- Message flow and message set assigner.
    - Can create execution groups within brokers, then assign and deploy message flows and sets to brokers.
    - Can access the Assignments view only.
- Operational domain controller.
    - Can create brokers and collectives, and define the topology.
    - Can deploy all types of data and monitor the operational domain.
    - Can access the Topology view, the Assignments view, the Topics view, the Operations view and the Subscriptions view.
- Topic Security Administrator
    - Can create topics and their access control lists and deploy these.
    - Can access the Topics view and the Topology view.
- All Roles
    - Perform all Control Center tasks.
    - Access all views.

There are four Windows NT security groups (mqbrdevt, mqbrasgn, mqbrops, mqbrtpic) which are to used to grant the privileges. Standard Windows user administration is used to assign membership of one or more of these groups to users, and then the role is selected in the Control Center Preference window.

Figure 1-6 shows a sample Control Center window layout.

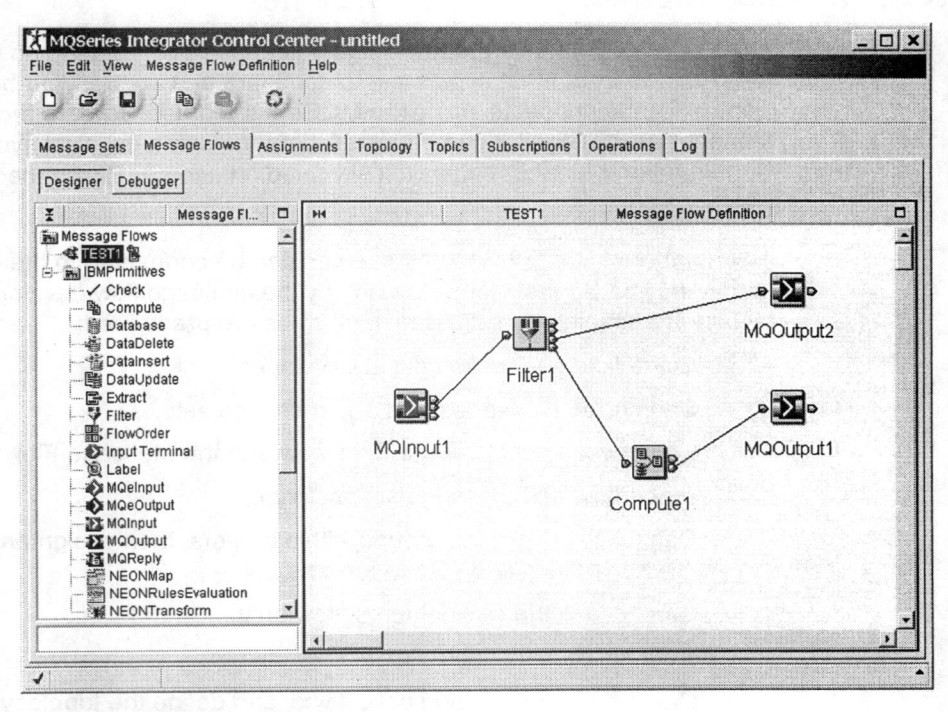

Figure 1-6   A Control Center view

When you decide to make changes to a resource managed by the Control Center, you must *check out* the resource. This gives you exclusive control over a locked copy until you *check in* or unlock the resource. You can save a local copy of the changed resource without checking it back in, if you wish to.

Control Center resources can exist in three states:

- Local. A copy of the configuration data being worked on - usually obtained by checking out the resource from the shared copy. Changes made to the local copy are not visible to other users until it is checked in.
- Shared. The version of the resource stored by the Configuration Manager and visible to all users. Note that only one level exists and no previous version is saved. SupportPac IC04, available from http://www.software.ibm.com/ts/mqseries/txppacs, offers procedures for version management.
- Deployed. The active copy of the configuration data that is in the broker (and also stored in the deployment database of the Configuration Manager).

The Control Center allows the export and import of message flows to and from a flat file in XML format. Message sets can be imported and exported with the `mrmimpexpmsgset` command.

## 1.2 Anatomy of a message flow

Message flows consist of a number of nodes (or primitives) that are *wired* together to form a broker application. Each node has t*erminals* for input or output or both (most nodes have several output terminals, in fact). The Control Center message flow view is used to construct the flows using nodes like these:

- MQInput node - encapsulates an `MQGET` operation.
- MQOutput node - encapsulates an `MQPUT` operation.
- Extract node - extracts specified fields from a message.
- Filter node - routes a message according to an ESQL expression.
- Compute node - modifies message or database contents with ESQL.
- Database node - performs a database operation.
- Reset Content Descriptor - re-parses the message format.

There are many other IBM primitive nodes available and these are described in *Using the Control Center,* SC34-5602. Each node has properties that can be set to define parameters (for example the Queue Manager name is an optional property of the MQInput node).

Some nodes have their function controlled by ESQL statements. This is a free-format high-level programming language derived from Structured Query Language (SQL) Version 3. By coding ESQL statements, it is possible to develop complex logic for manipulating either message and database contents (or both), without using excessive nodes in a flow.

ESQL, like most programming languages, can be used to develop business logic but is generally coded to select and analyze message and/or database contents, and perform the more complicated conversions of data values. For more information about ESQL, refer to the *WebSphere MQ Integrator ESQL Reference*, SC34-5923.

Although ESQL does not provide subroutines to reuse common code, it is possible to include smaller message flows as *subflows*. Such flows can be used for generic parts of message flows such as error handling routines. In addition, the use of subflows improves readability of the logic, regardless of reuse.

## Extending the nodes available

WebSphere MQ Integrator allows you to develop and implement custom nodes and custom parsers. These can be written in C or Java and might also be provided by an ISV. A number of useful plug-ins are available as SupportPacs and freely downloadable from the IBM WebSphere MQ Integrator Web site. It is important to check that any such custom node is compatible with all the target broker platforms that you may wish to deploy the message flows onto.

Figure 1-7 shows a sample view of a message flow.

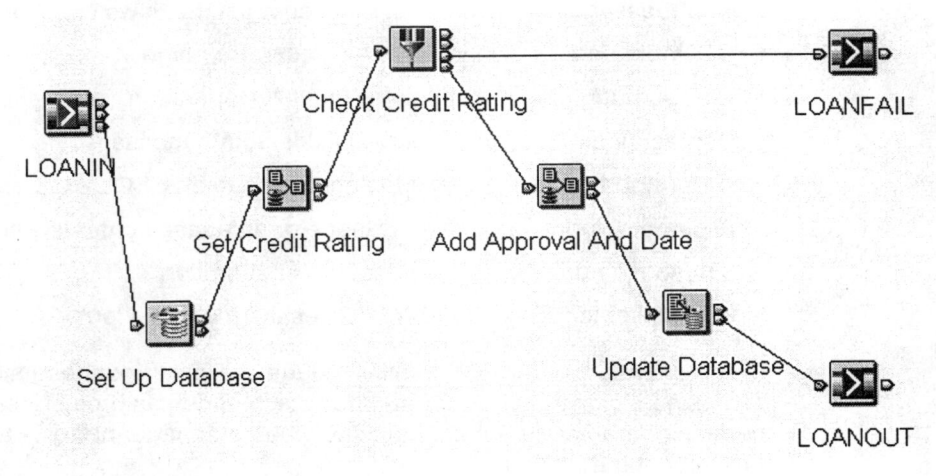

*Figure 1-7  Example of a message flow*

Each node has properties that must be set; for example, with the MQInput node you would specify the input queue name (the Queue Manager is always the same as the broker's), conversion and other `MQGET` options, transaction mode, message domain and so forth. Generally, it is necessary to specify more of these values when handling messages that do not have an MQRFH2 header.

Figure 1-8 shows one of the property windows on the MQInput node.

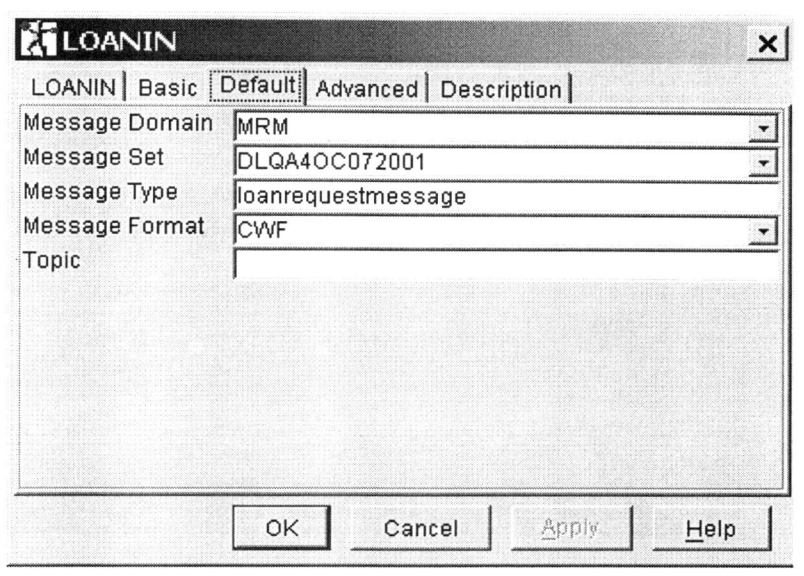

*Figure 1-8   Properties of MQInput node*

In most cases the (parsed) message is passed unchanged from one node to another, except in the case of the *Compute* node, which can modify it, and then the output message of the Compute node becomes the input to the next node in the flow. Some nodes provide a drag-and-drop graphical interface to assist with element selection, for example the Data Update node (Figure 1-9 on page 20) for its output database table.

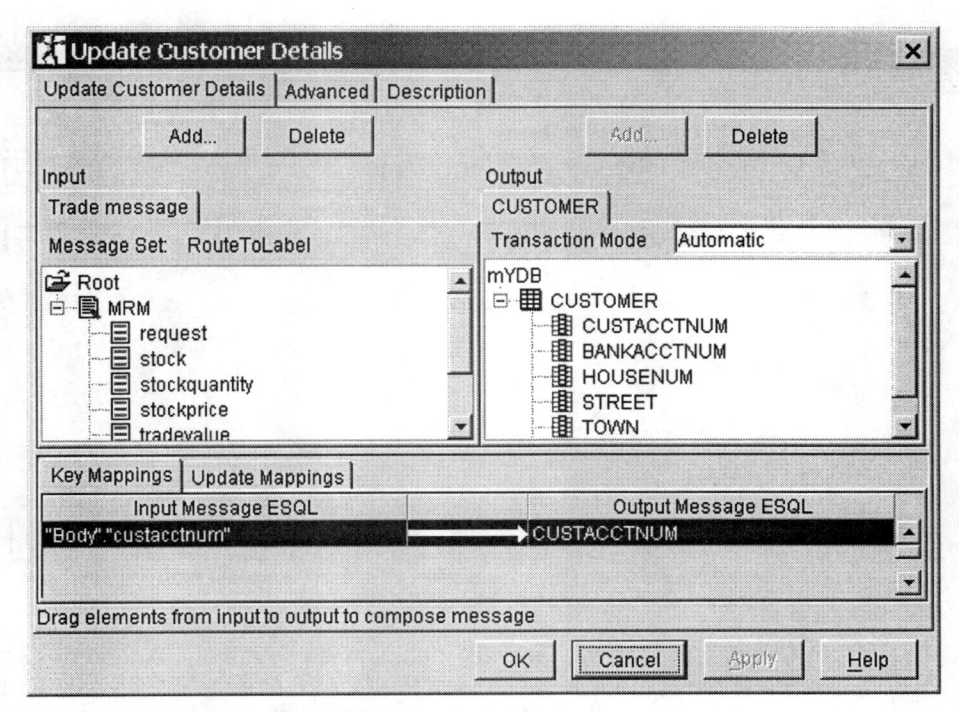

*Figure 1-9 Example of Data Update node field selection*

ESQL statements are added using the ESQL tab window on the properties page of WebSphere MQ Integrator nodes such as compute and filter. As well as simple assignments, ESQL includes branching and looping capability. Example 1-1 shows an example of a sequence of ESQL statements.

*Example 1-1 ESQL statements*

```
SET OutputRoot = InputRoot;
DECLARE TotalItemQuantity INTEGER;
SET TotalItemQuantity = (SELECT SUM(CAST(T.itemquantity AS INT))
FROM InputBody.Message.receiptmsg.transactionlog.purchaseselement[] AS T
WHERE CAST(T.itemname AS CHAR) = 'Shampoo');
SET
OutputRoot.XML.Message.receiptmsg.transactionlog.totalselement.totalitemquantit
y = TotalItemQuantity;
```

The visual message flow builder in the Control Center can be used to assemble sequences of nodes (or primitives) that provide similar logic to a programming language. Loops and branches can be performed using nodes.

The message flow shown on Figure 1-10 shows a *Filter* node that tests a counter stored in the message tree; if the comparison is false, the flow passes to a Data Insert node. This node is followed by a Compute node, which increments the counter. When the filter comparison test is eventually true, control passes to the MQOutput node.

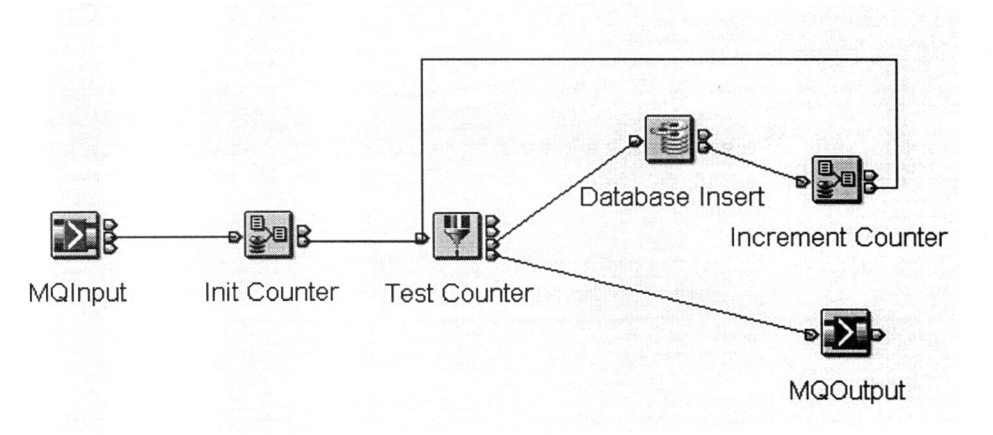

*Figure 1-10   Example of loop control in a flow*

In traditional programming languages, subroutines are used to group commonly used statements. With WebSphere MQ Integrator message flows, this is achieved using subflows. These flows are comprised of the same nodes as main-line flows, except that they have Input and Output *Terminal* nodes.

Main message flows (or higher level subflows) simply include the desired subflow as if it were another node, and wire up its terminals accordingly. This technique is valuable for very complex message flows as it structures the flow into a series of smaller, more readable subflows.

Compute nodes are similar to groups of executable statements in other languages and can be inserted into flows when there is a need to perform calculations or make assignments, especially when converting data formats. ESQL has branching and looping features that work inside the Compute node.

Compute nodes can modify the message tree contents and update databases. They are therefore the most powerful nodes available. ESQL is also used extensively in Filter and Database nodes. WebSphere MQ Integrator V2.1 offers an ESQL code palette to allow drag-and-drop development.

## 1.3 Enhanced Message Repository Manager

WebSphere MQ Integrator supports self-defining XML and JMS messages. Their message formats do not have to be defined to the Message Repository Manager (although you can do this to exploit the MRM features). Defining your message formats to the MRM gives you greater control over the formats and enables increased functionality within the Control Center to manipulate messages in the flows.

Predefined message formats are stored in *message sets*. These message formats are created in the Control Center, or imported from exported copies. Message sets allow message flows to understand the structure of incoming message data and therefore need to be deployed to the runtime (or broker) environment.

You can transform any message in the MRM domain into any other format defined to the MRM, with most of the transformation being provided automatically by the broker. Drag-and-drop element selection is available in the node properties because the message structure is known at build time.

The MRM components are:

- At build time
  - GUI - the Control Center Message Sets tab
  - Repository - Configuration Manager
  - Importers
  - Extractors
  - Deployment
- At runtime
  - Message parsers
  - Run Time dictionaries
  - Physical format descriptors

The MRM message model consists of meta-data representing logical message definitions that are platform and language independent. It has layers of additional data used for mapping to physical formats. Definitions are made up of reusable components or objects and organized into message sets.

Logical structures consist of one or more *compound types* that are made up of simple types, elements or other compound types. Often it is easier to import the definitions than it is to create them in the Control Center; for example, a COBOL or C structure can be imported to create a new compound type.

Figure 1-11 shows the composition of a message set.

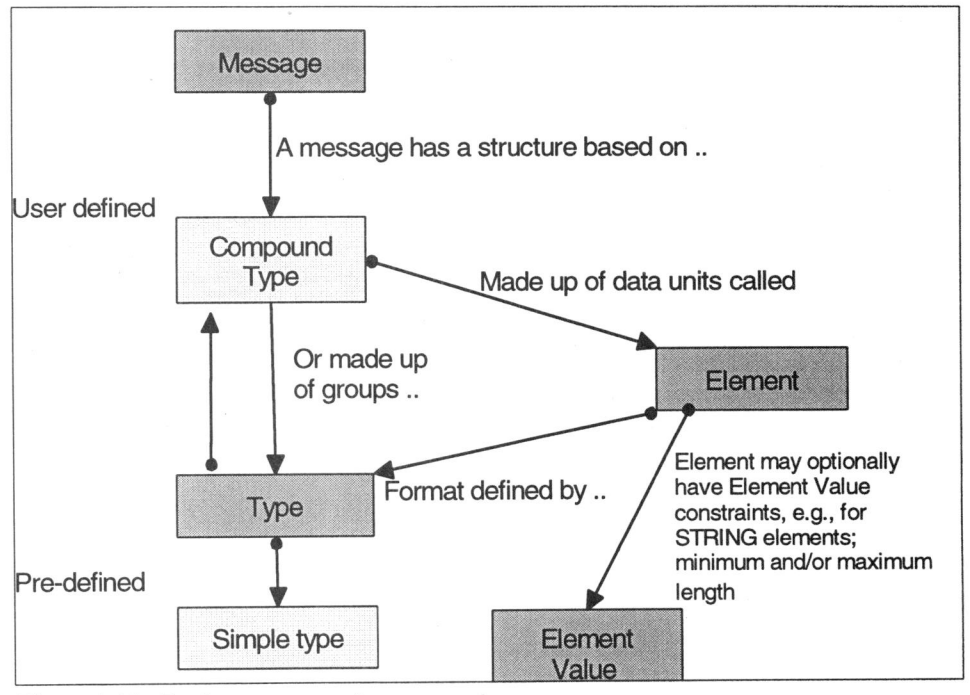

*Figure 1-11   Basic message set components*

A *message set* is a group of messages that are related in some way. A *message* defines the format of a single unit of information to be exchanged between applications. A message can contain (embed) other messages (multi-part). An *element* defines the format of a single unit of information within a message. A *type* defines the format of an element and can be a simple or compound type. A *category* groups messages and transactions within a message set. A *transaction* (in this sense) is a logical grouping of messages within a message set.

MRM Type composition options:

- Empty
- Choice
- Unordered set
- Ordered set (default)
- Sequence
- Simple unordered set
- Message

Figure 1-12 shows the simple types recognized by the MRM.

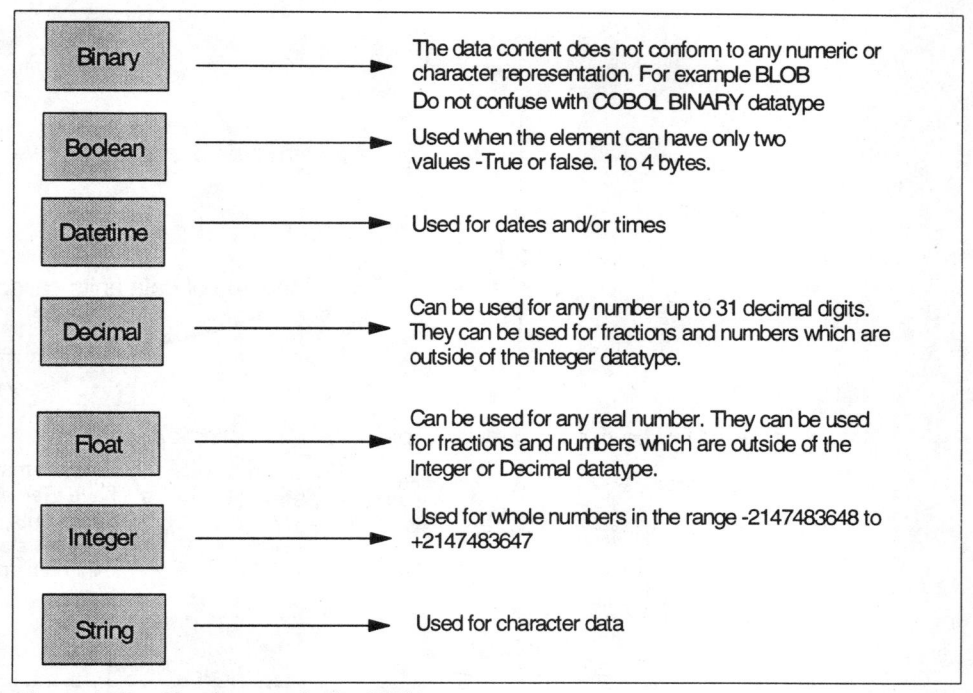

| Type | Description |
|---|---|
| Binary | The data content does not conform to any numeric or character representation. For example BLOB. Do not confuse with COBOL BINARY datatype |
| Boolean | Used when the element can have only two values -True or false. 1 to 4 bytes. |
| Datetime | Used for dates and/or times |
| Decimal | Can be used for any number up to 31 decimal digits. They can be used for fractions and numbers which are outside of the Integer datatype. |
| Float | Can be used for any real number. They can be used for fractions and numbers which are outside of the Integer or Decimal datatype. |
| Integer | Used for whole numbers in the range -2147483648 to +2147483647 |
| String | Used for character data |

*Figure 1-12   Simple types in the MRM*

*Value constraints* can be defined for elements for such things as minimum length, scale, default value and so forth. This is primarily for documentation purposes, as currently the broker does not perform runtime validation.

A message in the MRM domain can have one of these wire formats:

- CWF (Custom Wire Format or Legacy messages)
- TDWF (Tagged / Delimited Wire Format, such as SWIFT).
- XML (defined as opposed to self-defining or generic)
- PDF (not Adobe but a specialized financial format)

CWF messages are often defined by importing a C or COBOL structure. XML messages can be defined by importing a DTD. Some tagged formats are predefined to the MRM and others can be configured in the Control Center.

Message sets can be imported and exported (to XML format flat files) using the supplied `mqsiimpexpmsgset` command. This can be used both for version control and to copy message sets between Configuration Managers.

## Tagged data formats

The following messaging standards can be selected in the Control Center:

- Unknown (this is the default)
- ACORD AL3
- SWIFT
- EDIFACT
- X12

Tagged/Delimited messages consist of:

- Text strings
- Optionally preceded by *fixed text*
- followed by child elements
    - May be fixed length or separated by a delimiter
    - Each of which may be preceded by a *tag* that uniquely identifies it
    - Tag may be fixed length or separated from the data by a delimiter
    - Data for child elements may represent simple values or sub-structures
- Followed optionally by fixed text

Example 1-2 shows a sample message in a SWIFT format.

*Example 1-2   A SWIFT message*

```
{1:F01BANKBEBBAXXX2222123456}{2:I100IBMADEF0AXXXN}{4:
:20:X
:32A:940930USD1000000,
:50:LINE1
:59:LINE1
-}
```

The sample SWIFT message comprises two headers and a message body.

Each header is wrapped within curly braces ({...})

| | |
|---|---|
| { | Is the group indicator |
| : | Is the tag data separator |
| }{ | Is the delimiter |
| } | Is the group terminator |
| 1, 2, 4 | Are tags |

## 1.4 XML support

XML messages are supported by WebSphere MQ Integrator as either generic (or undefined) XML or as MRM XML. This determines whether the generic parser or the MRM parser is used to interpret them. Defining XML messages in the MRM enables more comprehensive facilities for processing them, such as the broker performing message transformation to Custom Wire Format.

When you define XML messages to the MRM, you can specify an XML format layer. This specification allows the output XML format to be customized, for example, the data elements can be given attributes.

Output XML format can be created with:

- Tags and/or attributes
- Attribute identifiers or without them
- DOCTYPE, Root Tag Name, XML Name, Render, Format, Encoding

You can now import a Document Text Definition (DTD) into the Control Center. This can be a DTD generated from a WebSphere MQ Integrator message repository, or a DTD from another source. You can then use the MRM to model these XML messages. Example 1-3 shows a simple XML message.

*Example 1-3   A simple XML message*

```
<PurchaseOrder>
<CustomerName>IBM</CustomerName>
<OrderDetail><PartNum>1234-L</PartNum>
<PartDesc>Large Widget</PartDesc>
</OrderDetail>
<OrderDetail>
<PartNum>1234-M</PartNum>
<PartDesc>Medium Widget</PartDesc>
</OrderDetail>
<OrderDetail>
<PartNum>1234-S</PartNum>
<PartDesc>Small Widget</PartDesc>
</OrderDetail>
</PurchaseOrder>
```

## 1.5 Database support

WebSphere MQ Integrator uses DB2 databases for the Configuration Manager, which must run on Windows NT (or 2000). On z/OS brokers can use DB2 only.

User databases are where the message flows can (optionally) access or store database records. Several nodes are provided to assist with developing message flows that use database information. It is not mandatory to use a database in a flow, although the broker uses its own for configuration data.

When a message flow updates one or more user databases, an important consideration is the *transactionality* of the flow. Many business transactions require that all updates are committed or rolled back, in a single unit of work. This normally includes updates to message queues as well as databases.

MQSeries is able to coordinate transactions between Queue Managers and databases through RRS transaction manager.

Message flows can be made transactional for message queue and database interaction by selecting the appropriate option in the node properties.

Supported releases are DB2 V6.1 and higher.

For the correct configuration of the databases including the ODBC connections for each broker platform, please refer to the *WebSphere MQ Integrator Administration Guide,* SC34-5792 and *WebSphere MQ Integrator for z/OS Customization and Administration Guide,* SC34-5919.

## 1.6 New ESQL features

SQL is the industry-standard language for accessing and updating database data. ESQL is a language derived from SQL Version 3 and is particularly suited to manipulating both database and message data. An ESQL program consists of a number of statements that are executed in the order they are written.

ESQL programs form an essential part of WebSphere MQ Integrator nodes such as the Compute, Filter and Database nodes. In common with other high-level programming or scripting languages, ESQL has statements, operators, expressions, functions, data types, variables, reserved words and so forth.

Example 1-4 shows an example of ESQL code used in a Compute node.

*Example 1-4   Some ESQL from a Compute node*

```
DECLARE C INTEGER;
SET C = CARDINALITY(InputRoot.*[]);
DECLARE I INTEGER;
SET I = 1;
WHILE I < C DO
   SET OutputRoot.*[I] = InputRoot.*[I];
   SET I=I+1;
```

```
END WHILE;
DECLARE elementnum INTEGER;
SET elementnum="InputBody"."totalselement"."f_reserve";
SET
"OutputRoot"."MRM"."purchaseselement"."q_reserve"="InputBody"."purchaseselement"
"[elementnum]"."itemquantity";
```

WebSphere MQ Integrator V2.1 provides some new ESQL features compared to earlier releases:

- Environment (pass user-defined variable information between nodes)
- ESQL UUID function (creates a universally unique identifier)
- Field references variables (these act as variable pointers)
- Binary and Date/Time casting
- SQLCODE and SQLSTATE database indicators introduced
- ESQL node rationalization for Compute, Filter and Database nodes
    - They each can modify both DBMS data and environment variables. Performance is improved by avoiding the need to create new message tree elements for passing data between nodes in a flow.
    - Have drag-and-drop facility for ESQL code, selectable from a palette.
- Improved support of NULLs

Figure 1-13 shows the ESQL palette.

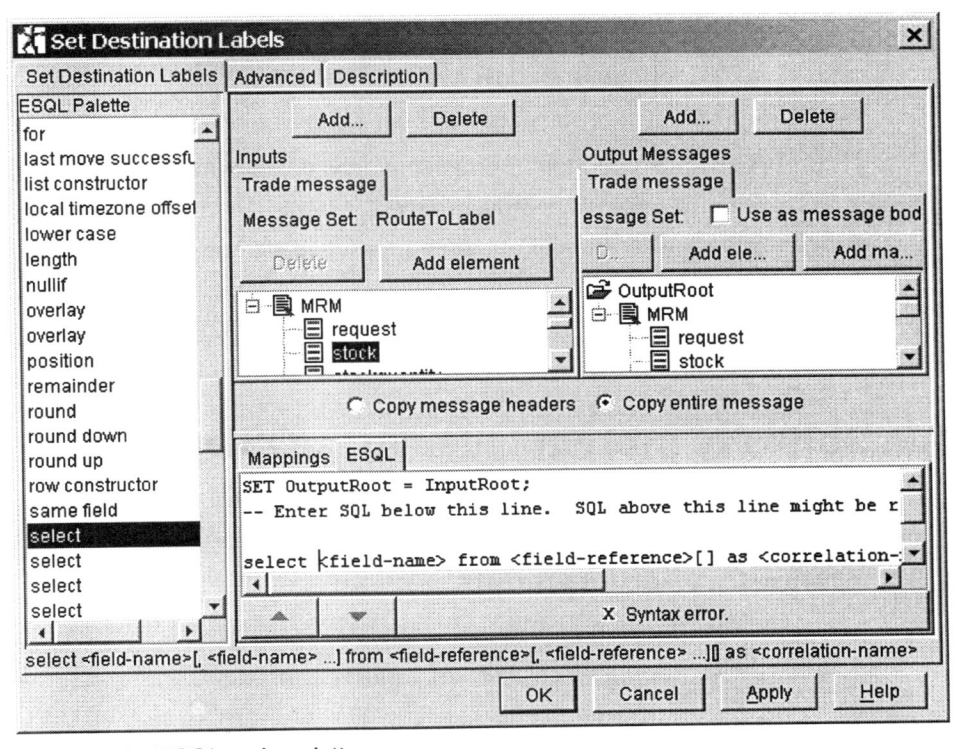

*Figure 1-13   ESQL code palette*

## 1.7 Summary of new features

WebSphere MQ Integrator V2.1 adds the following new features compared to earlier releases:

- ▶ z/OS (OS/390) platform support (using UNIX System Services)
- ▶ XML improvements (mixed content, attribute support, DTD import)
- ▶ Tagged Message Support (user-specified delimiters)
- ▶ Industry-standard messages (SWIFT, EDIFACT, X12, AL3)
- ▶ Plug-in API extensions (input nodes can now be developed)
- ▶ Java environment available for plug-in nodes (but not parsers)
- ▶ ESQL enhancements include environment variable storage
- ▶ New SupportPacs including command-line deployment
- ▶ Control Center security exit available

- Message aggregation capability (refer to SupportPac IA72)
- Improvements to the MRM (logical message model extensions)
- Performance improvements for the MRM
- New Era of Networks Version 5.2 libraries and improved integration
- Visual debugger for message flow development
- Performance improvements
- Support for MQSeries 5.2 and Windows 2000
- Usability improvements and plug-in node development wizard
- A new manual - *WebSphere MQ Integrator ESQL Reference*, SC34-5923

## 1.8 Software prerequisites for z/OS and OS/390 platform

In this section we provide the software requirements for WMQI for z/OS.

### 1.8.1 Mandatory requirements

- OS/390 2.8 or higher
- MQSeries for OS/390 V5.2 must be installed
- SYSLOGD must be installed
- DB2 UDB Server for OS/390 V6.1 or higher (for broker tables and shared queue access) including Call Level Interface (all PTFs valid up to 01/07/01)
- RRS must be operational

### 1.8.2 Functional requirements

- High-level assembler V1.2 or higher (For assembler applications)
- IBM OS/390 C/C++ (For C and C++ applications)
- HFS PTFs (UW69626, UW70296, UW70297, OW44631, UW74186, UW74187)
- RRS PTFs (OW49327, UW72071, UW72074, UW72077, UW72080)
- Java Runtime Environment V1.3 plus PTF

# 2

# z/OS UNIX System Services

In this chapter, we introduce the UNIX System Services (previously known as OpenEdition) component of z/OS operating system as the processing environment for WebSphere MQ Integrator V2.1 for z/OS. The WMQI brokers are installed on Hierarchical File System (HFS) used by UNIX System Services and execute as UNIX System Services processes.

In this chapter we do not attempt to cover UNIX System Services in depth as manuals are devoted to that. We provide an overview of UNIX System Services concepts by listing common terms, definitions, and providing command examples. These commands are used later in the book in the process of installing and customizing the WMQI environment.

## 2.1 In brief

For WebSphere MQSeries Integrator for z/OS, the broker, the component directory and, optionally, the User Name Server and NEON components reside and execute on UNIX System Services.

UNIX System Services provides a set of system and application services to support UNIX applications. These services are:

- ISPF shell
- OMVS shell
- TSO/E commands to enter the shell environment and to manage files
- A shell environment for developing and running applications
- Utilities to administer and develop in a UNIX environment
- The dbx debugger
- Support for socket applications
- rlogin (remote login) and inetd functions
- Direct telnet based on TCP/IP protocol
- Support for full-screen applications
- Communications Server login monitor support.

The UNIX System Services file system is known as Hierarchical File System (HFS).

## 2.2 UNIX System Services concepts and tools

In this section we introduce some important concepts and useful tools that have to do with UNIX System Services.

### BPXPRMxx

BPXPRMxx is a SYS1.PARMLIB member that contains parameters that control the z/OS UNIX System Services environment including the HFS. This information is used at z/OS IPL time. The ROOT entry defines the HFS to be mounted on the '/' mountpoint at IPL.

```
ROOT FILESYSTEM('OMVS.MVS66.OS39028.ROOT.D1999351')
     TYPE(HFS)
     MODE(RDWR)
```

Additional parameters are:

/u contains directories for users, for example, MQRES1

/usr is more of a base for products, containing directories

Installed products can usually be located under /usr/lpp directory, for example, /usr/lpp/wmqi.

### Daemon
A daemon is a long-lived process that runs unattended to perform continuous or periodic system functions, such as network control. It is similar in function to a started task in OS/390. Examples of daemons are cron, inetd, and rlogin.

### Dubbing
Dubbing is a process of connecting an MVS address space to UNIX.

### rlogin (telnet)
rlogin is a process that establishes a workstation connection to UNIX System Services. It is handled by the inetd daemon rlogin as a TCP/IP connection.

### Mount
The mount process makes the HFS data set available for use and connects a file system to an existing directory structure.

The **MOUNT** command may be issued by a superuser or you can add an entry to BPXPRMxx member in SYS1.PARMLIB. A site can use a Direct Mount or the Automount Facility (preferred method). Your WMQI HFS data sets must be mounted for use.

### Mountpoint
The mountpoint is the directory (pathname) where the file system is mounted. The root mountpoint is "/".

### Environment variable (ENV)
An ENV is the name associated with a string of characters that is available to programs. It is similar to symbolic parms used in JCL or information stored in a parmlib. Environment variables can define things such as the command search path, Dynamic Link Libraries (DLL) files, and the current time zone, to name a few.

### Fork
Creates a copy of a parent process in a child process. It is usually followed by an exec that starts a new program running in the child process. It is similar to creating an address space. The forked address space is provided by the z/OS WorkLoad Manager (WLM) mechanism.

### Spawn
Creates a copy of a parent process in a child process and the execution of the new program using a single UNIX system call.

### Archive
An archive is a single file that contains the complete contents of a set of other files. It preserves the directory hierarchy that contained the original files.

### Tar (Tape ARchiver)
`tar` is a command that manipulates archives. It is used frequently on UNIX systems to bundle files together before copying or moving them, such as in an FTP process.

### Shell interface
- The shell interface is an execution environment analogous to TSO/E, with a programming language of shell commands analogous to Restructured eXtended eXecutor (REXX) language.
- A shell program interprets sequences of text input as commands. It may operate on an input stream, or it may interactively prompt and read commands from a terminal. Shell programs can be run interactively by shell users.
- Shell commands and scripts can be run interactively by shell users or as batch jobs.
- The shell has a command interpreter that provides a user interface to the operating system and its commands.
- The shell is a layer, above the kernel, that provides a flexible interface between users and the rest of the system.
- The shell allows a kernel program to run under different operating system environments.

### Standard in (stdin)
stdin is a standard input file similar to the one specified on SYSIN DDcard.

### Standard out (stdout)
stdout is a standard output file destination similar to the one specified on SYSOUT DDcard.

### Standard error (stderr)
stderr is a standard destination for output error messages.

### Users, user groups and superusers

On UNIX systems, each user needs an account that is made up of a user name and a password. Internally, the UNIX operating system uses a numeric ID to refer to a user. This ID is referred to as the user identifier, or UID. Each user has a unique UID. UNIX operating systems differ, but generally these UIDs are unsigned 16-bit numbers, ranging from 0 to 65535. z/OS UNIX System Services supports UID numbers up to 2,147,483,647.

UNIX systems also have the concept of groups, where you group together many users who need to access a set of common files, directories, or devices. Like user names and UIDs, groups have both group names and group identification numbers (GIDs). Each user belongs to a primary group, the name of which is stored in /etc/passwd file on UNIX systems. There is no convention for assigning GID numbers, and unlike UIDs, number 0 has no special significance.

A superuser is a system user who has special rights and privileges to be able to manage processes and files. The UID of a superuser is set to 0.

### Path statements

There are two environment variables that are of particular interest. The PATH variable specifies the location of platform-dependent executables that can be directly invoked. The CLASSPATH variable specifies the location of platform-independent Java classes. LIBPATH is used to locate dynamic link libraries.

### HFS - Hierarchical File System

HFS is a stream (byte) oriented file system used by UNIX, unlike MVS data sets, which are record oriented. A UNIX System Services user can allocate an HFS data set and mount it at a certain location on the HFS tree. Similarly to data sets created by TSO users, HFS data sets can have high-level qualifiers that identify the creator.

## 2.3 Working with UNIX System Services

You can access the UNIX System Services shell either with telnet or rlogin TCP/IP services or from a TSO session. As a TSO user you can either use an **OMVS** command that provides you with access to a UNIX command-line (prompt) or an **ISHELL** command that allows you to manipulate HFS files through ISPF panels.

Whenever you log on to the UNIX System Services shell, a profile script is executed. The environment variables and commands used by most shell and utilities users are placed in the /etc/profile file. An optional $HOME/.profile file can contain commands that set or change the values of environment variables for an individual user. $HOME specifies the location of the user's home directory. The values set in $HOME/.profile override those set in /etc/profile.

Once you have accessed the UNIX System Services shell, you can allocate directories or files. In UNIX systems, general information about each file is stored with the files in the file system. Included with this general information is security information about the file, such as the owner (UID), the group (GID), and UNIX access controls (permission bits).

### 2.3.1 Permissions

All UNIX files have three types of permissions:

- Read (displayed as r)
- Write (displayed as w)
- Execute (displayed as x)

For every UNIX file, read, write and execute (rwx) permissions are maintained for three different types of file users:

- The file owner
- The group that owns the file
- All other users

The permission bits are stored as three octal numbers (3 bits for each type of file user) totalling 9 bits. When displayed by commands, such as `ls -l`, a 10-character field is shown, consisting of 9 for permission, preceded by 1 for file type.

### 2.3.2 Useful TSO/E commands

In this section we discuss the TSO/E commands that can be used to invoke the UNIX System Services shell and to work with the HFS file system. The commands to work with the HFS file system are:

- Start a shell
  - `ISHELL` - Invokes the UNIX System Services ISPF shell
  - `OSHELL` - Invokes BPXBATCH from TSO/E
  - `OMVS` - Invokes the UNIX System Services shell

- **BPXBATCH** - Runs shell commands, shell scripts or executable files
► Edit or browse an HFS file
- **OBROWSE** - Browses an HFS file
- **OEDIT** - Edits an HFS file
► Copy a file
- **OCOPY** - Copies an MVS data set member or an HFS file to another member or file
- **OGET** and **OGETX** - Copy an HFS file from a directory to an MVS file or a PDS or a PDSE
- **OPUT** and **OPUTX** - Copy members from an MVS PDS or PDSE to an HFS directory

You can enter the TSO/E commands mentioned above from:
► TSO/E command line
► The ISPF command processor panel (option 6 on the ISPF menu)
► The ISPF command shell

ISPF option 6 is usually preferable, because it does not convert into uppercase the commands that you enter (UNIX System Services, as any other UNIX environment, is case-sensitive).

Note that:
► The path name you use is relative to the working directory (usually the home directory) of the TSO/E session, not the shell session.
► Use absolute path names when you enter a TSO/E command.
► Avoid using spaces or single quotes within path names.

### 2.3.3 Useful MVS console commands

You can obtain valuable information using the following MVS console commands:

`D OMVS, O`
- Displays the current OMVS settings
- Values specified in SYS1.PARMLIB(BPXPRMxx)

`D OMVS,A=ALL`
- Lists all UNIX System Services processes

`D GRS,C`
- Provides a contention report

**D A,OMVS**
- Produces a list of dataspaces

**D OMVS,F**
- Produces a file system report

### Spawned region sizes

You should be aware of region sizes allocated to UNIX System Services sessions. If the session is started through BPXBATCH process and this process forks another, the new region size will be the same as the original BPXBATCH. If the OMVS command was used, the new region size will be the value from the TSO logon panel. If you use telnet or rlogin, the region size of the new process will be the value specified by the MAXASSIZE parameter.

## 2.4 Basic shell commands

Table 2-1 provides a summary of useful UNIX shell commands and examples of their use.

*Table 2-1  A summary of shell commands*

| Description | Command | Example |
|---|---|---|
| List the contents of a file | `cat file` | `cat fileA fileB fileC` |
| Change Directory | `cd directory` | `cd       -goes to login directory`<br>`cd   /usr/merlin/mydir`<br>`cd   mydir`<br>`cd /  -goes to the root dir` |
| Change file nodes<br>  user, group, other<br>  +add, -sub, = exact<br>  read, write, execute | `chmod` | `chmod u+rw fileA`<br>`chmod +x fileA fileB`<br>`chmod o=rx fileC`<br>`chmod u=rwx,g=r,o=fileD` |
| Copy file | `cp oldfile, newfile` | `cp fileA fileB`<br>`cp file* ../mydir/tm` |
| List value of a variable | `echo $variable` | `echo $DFHJVPIPE` |
| Show all environment variables | `env` | `env` |
| Set a global variable | `export variable` | `export JAVA_HOME=/usr/`<br>`/lpp/java118/J1.1` |

| Description | Command | Example |
|---|---|---|
| Sets, resets, and displays extended file attributes (file owner or superuser) | `extattr` | `extattr +p bin/mvs/native/*`<br>　　`-view the attributes with ls -alE` |
| List files in the current dir | `ls [-ltax] directory`<br>　　`-l long    -t time`<br>　　`-a all     -x across`<br>　　`-E extended attributes` | `ls`<br>`ls -l /tmp`<br>`ls -x /usr/merlin`<br>`ls -alE/u/cheby` |
| Make directory | `mkdir` | `mkdir jims` |
| Edit using OMVS | `oedit file` | `oedit .profile - edit my profile`<br>`like using ISPF` |
| Print the current working directory | `pwd` | `pwd` |
| Remove (delete) files | `rm file` | `rm oldfile` |
| Create an empty file | `touch` | `touch newfile` |
| Edit a file using telnet/rlogin connection | `vi file` | `vi myfile`<br>　`the data is saved in EBCDIC` |
| Change file owner | `chown user file` | `chown merlin fileA` |
| Check spelling | `spell [-b] file`<br>`-b British spelling` | `spell fileA`<br>`spell -b fileA>oops` |
| Determine file type | `file file1 file2` | `file fileA fileB` |
| Find a file<br>　-user username<br>　-size blocks<br>　-atime days<br>　-exec {command} | `find path . .condition` | `find .;name myfile -print`<br>`find /mp -user merlin -print`<br>`find /-size +100 -print`<br>`find /usr -atime +10 -print`<br>`find .-name core -exec rm {}\` |
| Link file | `ln original newname` | `ln fileA ../mydir/other` |
| List end of file | `tail file` | `tail fileA` |

Chapter 2. z/OS UNIX System Services   **39**

| Description | Command | Example |
|---|---|---|
| Move a file | `mv oldfile newfile`<br>`mv file . .directory`<br>`mv olddir newdir` | `mv myfile ../mydir/xyz`<br>`mv * ../mydir`<br>`mv mydir junk` |
| Paging to the terminal, view a file a page at a time | `pg file`<br>`more file` | `pg fileA`<br>`more fileB` |
| Save and pipe | `tee file` | `grep abc fileA \|tee fileB\|wc` |
| Sort a file | `sort [+n] [-n] file`<br>    `+n start of field n`<br>    `-n stop of field n` | `sort fileA`<br>`sort +1 fileA`<br>`sort +2 -4 fileA>fileB` |
| Search a file<br>  -v non-matching<br>  -i ignore case<br>  -n line numbers | `grep [-vin] pattern file` | `grep UNIX myfile`<br>`grep -vi unix myfile` |
| Translate file, change a string in a file | `tr oldstring newstring` | `tr unix UNIX <fileA>fileB` |
| Word count | `wc file` | `wc fileA` |
| List print queue | `lpstat [-t]`<br>`lpstat printer` | `lpstat -t`<br>`lpstat laser` |
| Paginate for printing | `pr [-h title] file`<br>`pr [-l lines] file` | `pr -h "merlin's spells"fileA>tmp`<br><br>`pr -18C fileB fileC \| lp` |
| Print file | `lp [-dprinter] file` | `lp dlaser fileA fileB` |
| Tape archive | `cpio [-iocvB]>device`<br>    `input, output`<br>    `verbose,`<br>`Bigblocks`<br><br>`tar` | `find -print\|cpio -ocvB>/dev/mt0`<br><br>`cpio -itcvB</dev/mt0`<br>`cpio -icvB</dev/mt0`<br>`tar -cv *`<br>`tar -xv` |
| Execute commands at specific time | `at time[day]<file` | `at 4 pm tomorrow<commands`<br><br>`at 0400 04/012/02 <shellfile` |

| Description | Command | Example |
|---|---|---|
| Calculator | bc<br>to finish CTRL D | bc<br>scale=4<br>((345*32.1)+56.78) |
| Calendar | cal year<br>cal month year | cal 2000<br>cal 12 2000 |
| Stop a process | kill pid<br>kill -signal pid | kill 4321<br>kill -9 12345 |
| List current user | id | id |
| List date/time | date | date |
| List disk space free | df | df |
| List disk space usage | du | du |
| List logged on users | who | who |
| Process status | ps [-al]{-u user]<br>    -a all   -l long | ps -a<br>ps -lu merlin |
| Terminal name | tty | tty |
| Where am I? | pwd | pwd |

## 2.5 Shared HFS in a Parallel Sysplex

If you have more than one MVS image, consider how you will use the HFS file system. On OS/390 V2.9 and above, you can share files in an HFS across different members of a sysplex. The file system is mounted on one MVS image and requests to the file are routed to the owning system using XCF from systems that do not have it mounted. On OS/390 V2.8, an HFS is not easily sharable between different images in a sysplex. You need to consider this when planning your system. Specific space requirements for WebSphere MQ Integrator are covered in the *WebSphere MQ Integrator for z/OS Customization and Administration Guide*, SC34-5919. Your use of shared HFS entales a decision on your part between storage utilization and performance.

### 2.5.1 Using HFS on OS/390 V2.8

OS/390 V2.8 does not support shared HFS. Therefore, you need to install WebSphere MQ Integrator on each image and you should allow enough space for multiple sets of libraries. You will need to allocate the same amount of space on each z/OS image where you will be running WebSphere MQ Integrator for z/OS. Each broker or User Name Server requires its own space for its own files. These files include customization files, output files, and trace files. If you allocate a file system for each broker, it is possible to unmount and remount the file system on a different MVS image. In contrast, if you have brokers sharing a file system, all the brokers and User Name Servers have to run on the same image to be able to use the file system.

You cannot create your component directory in a file system that is mounted using the Network File System (NFS) because this is not supported by WebSphere MQ Integrator.

If you have multiple z/OS images and the HFS is not shared, a file can have the same name on different images, but reside in separate file systems. You need to log on to the z/OS image to access files on that system. If your files are not where you expect them to be or contain unexpected data, ensure you are using the correct z/OS system.

Before you copy product libraries from one system to another, make sure that both systems are at the same level of maintenance for the operating system, MQSeries and Language Environment. To be on the safe side, you should prefer to do an SMP/E installation of WMQI on the new system rather than copy libraries.

To copy the product libraries from one system to another you need to:

1. Tar the files. For example:

   ```
   tar -cvz -f wmqi.tar.z /usr/lpp/wmqi
   ```

2. Copy the tarred files to a sequential file and access the sequential file from a different system. Alternatively you can use FTP to copy the tar files around.

3. Untar the files. For example:

   ```
   tar -xvozf wmqi.tar.z
   ```

## 2.5.2 Using HFS on OS/390 V2.9 and higher

Your files can be shared between different members of the sysplex. Moving a broker or User Name Server from one image to another is straightforward.

The files for each broker or User Name Server can be shared. However, there is a performance impact when using files shared between images in an HFS because data flows through the Coupling Facility (this is true for trace and other diagnostic data).

Note that sharing HFS file can have a significant performance impact.

# z/OS Resource Recovery Services and transactional message flows

WebSphere MQ Integrator for z/OS uses Resource Recovery Service (RRS) to coordinate changes to MQSeries and DB2 Resources. In this chapter we discuss some basics of RRS and transactional support within message flows.

MQSeries offers assured and once-only delivery. WebSphere MQ Integrator adds significant additional functionality to basic MQ but does require an understanding of transactional support to ensure the integrity of transactional delivery as required by the application.

Also be aware that there are minor but subtle differences caused by the use of RRS on the z/OS and XA Transaction Manager on distributed platforms.

## 3.1 Resource Recovery Services introduction

WebSphere MQ Integrator for z/OS uses Resource Recovery Services (RRS) to coordinate changes to MQSeries and DB2 resources. It must be configured and active on your system for your broker to connect to DB2. This is different from the WMQI distributed environment, which is optionally coordinated by MQSeries as an XA-conformant Transaction Manager.

Refer to the following manuals for detailed information about RRS: *OS/390 MVS Setting up a Sysplex,* GC28-1779 and *OS/390 MVS Programming: Resource Recovery,* GC28-1739.

RRS was first made available with OS/390 Version 1 Release 3. Each follow-on release of OS/390 saw improvements and enhancements to enable RRS to become the mature component it now is and to fulfill its role in mission-critical applications. RRS is:

- A system-wide syncpoint coordinator. It is *not* a resource manager but it coordinates "commit changes" made by resource managers. This coordination happens by driving "enabled exits" of the enrolled/interested resource managers.
- A S/390 component, running as a subsystem in one address space, and started by a procedure. When you want to use distributed syncpointing, this component becomes mandatory.

As a syncpoint coordinator RRS must keep track of all work that is executed by resource managers and WorkLoad Managers that want to participate in a global Unit of Work. To be able to coordinate the changes made by all these different managers, they must be registered with RRS.

WebSphere Application Server for z/OS and OS/390 V4, CICS Transaction Server V1.3 and higher, IMS, DB2, and MQSeries are resource managers that must or can register with RRS. A CICS region, for example, registers with RRS by specifying RRMS=YES in its System Initialization Table (SIT).

Notice that you can include CICS or IMS functionality in a plug-in node. You invoke CICS programs through External CICS Interface (EXCI) or Enterprise Java Beans (EJBs) deployed in CICS through the Internet Inter-ORB Protocol (IIOP). The RRS context can be passed by the EXCI or J2EE client (your plug-in node) and two-phase commit is supported. An EJB deployed in WebSphere Application Server can be accessed in a similar way.

For more information on how to develop an EXCI client that uses RRS facilities, refer to *CICS Transaction Server Version 1 Release 3 Implementation Guide*, SG24-5274. For more information on how to access EJBs deployed in WebSphere Application Server for z/OS and CICS, refer to *Enterprise Java Beans for z/OS and OS/390 WebSphere Application Server V4.0*, SG24-6283 and *Enterprise Java Beans for z/OS and OS/390 CICS Transaction Server Version 2 Release 1*, SG24-6284.

Similarly, RRS coordination can be achieved with IMS using an APPC protected conversation or through a customer-developed Open Transaction Manager Access (OTMA) client.

Keep in mind that WMQI plug-ins on z/OS are not allowed to issue syncpoint or rollback requests. The RRS unit of recovery (UR) is set up by the broker for the message flow and the broker commits (or rolls back, in case of a failure) the whole transaction.

## 3.2 RRS prerequisites and setup

For MQSeries to be able to use RRS, you need at least OS/390 V2.4. RRS requires a Parallel Sysplex environment with a Coupling Facility. Other software products besides MQSeries that support RRS are:

- CICS Transaction Server V1.3 or higher
- DB2 V5.1 or higher
- IMS V6 or higher
- WebSphere Application Server for z/OS V4 or higher

The minimum OS/390 requirement for MQSeries V5.2 in a queue sharing environment is OS/390 V2.9 or higher.

RRS uses five logstreams that are shared by all the systems in the Parallel Sysplex. Every MVS image with RRS needs access to the Coupling facility and to DASD on which the system logger logstreams reside. To define the RRS logstreams, use the IXCMIAPU utility provided in the SYS1.MIGLIB library. For more information on defining logstreams, refer to *OS/390 MVS Setting Up a Sysplex*, GC28-1779.

You should also define RRS as an MVS subsystem. You need to update the IEFSSNxx member of your SYS1.Parmlib with the following statement, ensuring it comes after the statement defining the primary subsystem:

```
SUBSYS SUBNAME(RRS)
```

You can then start RRS specifying the name of its procedure. In our case, we used the **S RRS** command for this purpose.

RRS provides ISPF panels that allow you to:

- View the RRS logs
- View unit of recovery (UR) information
- View resource manager information
- Determine where a resource manager can restart after a system failure
- Remove a resource manager's interest in a UR

## 3.3 RRS support with MQSeries 5.2

One of the functions of the RRS adapter is to keep data synchronized between MQSeries and other RRS-participating resource managers. If a failure occurs when MQSeries has completed phase one of the commit and is waiting for a decision from RRS (the commit coordinator), the unit of recovery enters the in-doubt state.

When communication is reestablished between RRS and MQSeries, RRS automatically commits or backs out each unit of recovery, depending on whether there was a log record marking the beginning of the commit. MQSeries cannot resolve these in-doubt units of recovery (that is, commit or back out the changes made to MQSeries resources) until the connection to RRS is reestablished.

Under some circumstances, RRS cannot resolve in-doubt units of recovery. When this happens, MQSeries sends one of the following messages to the z/OS console:

- CSQ3011I
- CSQ3013I
- CSQ3014I
- CSQ3016I

For details of what these messages mean, see the *MQSeries for OS/390 Messages and Codes* manual.

For all resolved units of recovery, MQSeries updates the queues as necessary and releases the corresponding locks. Unresolved units of recovery can remain after restart.

Both MQSeries and RRS provide tools to display information about in-doubt units of recovery, and techniques for manually resolving them.

In MQSeries, use the `DISPLAY THREAD` command to display information about in-doubt MQSeries threads. The output from the command includes RRS unit of recovery IDs for those MQSeries threads that have RRS as a coordinator. This can be used to determine the outcome of the unit of recovery.

Use the MQSeries `RESOLVE INDOUBT` command to resolve the MQSeries in-doubt thread manually. This command can be used to either commit or back out the unit of recovery after you have determined what the correct decision is. You can use the QMNAME keyword to specify the name of the inactive Queue Manager. For example, if you issue the following command:

`+CSQ1 DISPLAY THREAD(*) TYPE(INDOUBT) QMNAME(QM01)`

You receive the following messages:

```
CSQV436I +CSQ1 INDOUBT THREADS FOR QM01
NAME         THREAD-XREF          URID    NID
USER1        B145A34D7EB970000000750      CSQ:0001.0
USER2        B035D65C6FA780000005501      CSQ:0001.0
  DISPLAY THREAD REPORT COMPLETE
```

If the Queue Manager specified is not inactive, MQSeries does not return information about in-doubt threads, but issues the following message:

`CSQV435I CANNOT USE QMNAME KEYWORD, QM01 IS ACTIVE`

If a Queue Manager that is a member of a queue-sharing group fails and cannot be restarted, other Queue Managers in the group can perform peer recovery, and take over from it. However, the Queue Manager might have in-doubt units of recovery that cannot be resolved by peer recovery because the final disposition of that unit of recovery is known only to the failed Queue Manager. These units of recovery will be resolved when the Queue Manager is eventually restarted, but until then, they remain in doubt. You can display these units of work with the `DISPLAY THREAD` command and resolve them if necessary with the `RESOLVE INDOUBT` command.

This means that certain resources (for example, messages) might be locked, making them unavailable to other Queue Managers in the group.

The RRS adapter enables MQSeries to become a full participant in RRS coordination. Applications can participate in the two-phase commit processing with other products that support RRS (for example DB2).

The RRS adapter provides two stubs; application programs that want to use RRS must be link-edited with one of these stubs.

- CSQBRSTB

    This stub allows you to use two-phase commit and backout for applications by using the RRS callable resource recovery services instead of the MQI calls MQCMIT and MQBACK (both for single phase commit).

    You must also link-edit module ATRSCSS from library SYS1.CSSLIB with your application. If you use the MQI calls MQCMIT and MQBACK, you will receive the message MQRC_ENVIRONMENT_ERROR.

- CSQBRSSI

    This stub allows you to use MQI calls MQCMIT and MQBACK; MQSeries actually implements these calls as the SRRCMIT and SRRBACK RRS calls.

    For information about building application programs that use the RRS adapter, see the *MQSeries Application Programming Guide,* SC33-0807.

## 3.4 Transactional support

Message flows hosted by brokers might handle vital processing and data manipulation that must have full transactional integrity. That is, the message flow must complete all processing successfully, or must complete none. Any part of the processing that completed successfully (for example, the reading of the input queue) must be rolled back if there are problems that prevent later processing from completing successfully.

Only transactions coordinated by MQSeries are supported by WebSphere MQ Integrator. An externally coordinated unit of work (for example, one coordinated by CICS) is not supported. A transaction can, optionally, begin upon receiving a message at an input node, and can be committed or rolled back when all processing has completed.

If the message flow processing includes interaction with an external database, the transaction can be coordinated to ensure all participants can maintain or return to a consistent state. The external coordination is provided by MQSeries on distributed and on RRS on z/OS.

> **Note:** On z/OS, message flows are always coordinated by RRS. Message flows are always coordinated on z/OS, regardless of whether the Coordinated Transaction box is checked in the Control Center or not.

WebSphere MQ Integrator on z/OS differs from WMQI on distributed platforms in this regard. In a distributed environment (UNIX or Windows NT) a message flow can be fully globally coordinated, fully broker-coordinated by default, or partially broker-coordinated.

A fully globally coordinated message flow means that MQSeries is used as an XA Transaction Manager to coordinate the transaction associated with the message flow. In a distributed environment, a Queue Manager must be defined with the proper XA resource manager settings. This is done within the MQSeries Services function. Click the **Queue Manager** to be put under XA control. Doing so displays the Queue Manager services in the right-hand results pane. Right-click the **Queue Manager** in the results pane and select **Properties**. Within the Queue Manager Properties, select **Resources** and complete the XA resource manager settings.

Figure 3-1 shows the window where you define a Queue Manager as an XA Transaction Manager on a Windows NT platform.

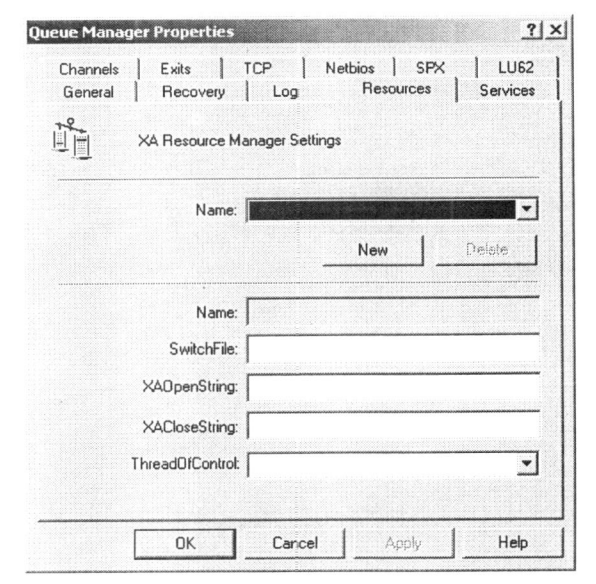

*Figure 3-1   MQSeries Services, Queue Manager Properties, Resources*

The reading and writing of MQSeries messages and all interactions with capable external databases (DB2 only on z/OS) are coordinated in a single unit of work (UOW). On z/OS, RRS coordinates the message syncpointing in coordination with MQSeries and DB2 as the resource managers.

You must coordinate external databases and MQSeries appropriately to enable this support. All actions in the message flow therefore either complete successfully or are rolled back to the point where the original input message is restored on the input queue. Note that on z/OS with RRS control, the Coordinated Transaction property does not need to be checked. If you are processing in a multi-platform environment and you want the distributed message flows to behave similarly to the z/OS message flows, then what follows applies. This feature is controlled using the Coordinated Transaction property of the message flow:

The default is for the transaction not to be globally coordinated. To change this property, right-click the message flow and select **Properties** (Figure 3-2 and Figure 3-3 on page 51).

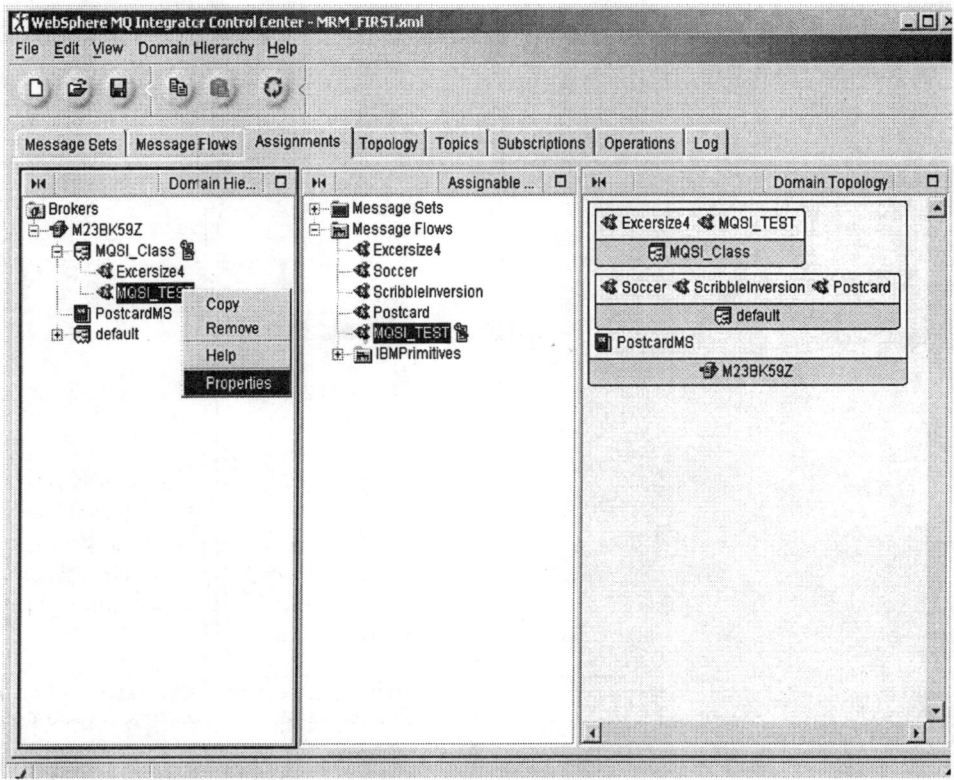

*Figure 3-2   WMQI Control Center, message flow properties*

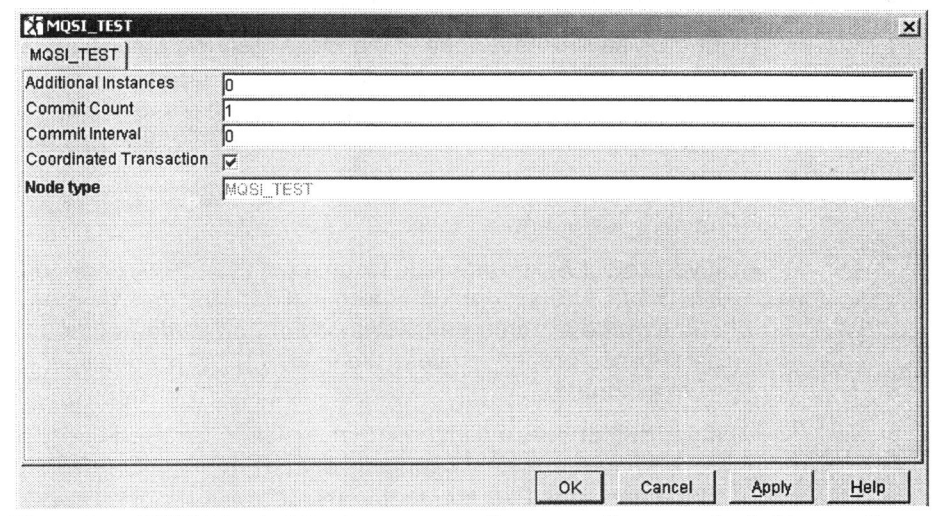

*Figure 3-3 WMQI Control Center, message flow properties, coordinated transaction*

## 3.4.1 Message flow coordination

Message flows that run on distributed platforms can be fully or partially broker-coordinated.

A message flow that is not fully globally coordinated is said to be fully broker-coordinated by default. The reading and writing of MQSeries messages and interactions with external databases are not coordinated within a single unit of work (UOW). However, the message flow ensures that all database transactions are committed automatically at the completion of processing a message through that flow.

A message flow can also be partially broker-coordinated. This means that some message processing nodes will commit their operation immediately, instead of waiting until message flow completion as in a fully broker-coordinated message flow. You can specify property values on the message flow nodes that interact with the databases to allow their processing to be committed immediately.

In a fully globally coordinated message flow, all messages subsequently sent by any MQOutput node in the same instance of the message flow are put under syncpoint, unless you set the output node properties to explicitly override this. If you do this, then the message flow is also said to be partially broker-coordinated.

## 3.4.2 Transactional support on MQInput

Right-click an MQInput node in the Message Flow Definition pane in the Control Center and select **Properties**. Click the **Advanced** tab to set properties that define how the message is processed, for example its transactional characteristics. Many of these properties map to options on the MQGet call.

Select the Transaction Mode from the drop-down list to define the transactional characteristics of how a message is handled:

- If you select **Automatic**, the incoming message is received under syncpoint if it is marked persistent; otherwise it is not. Any derived messages sent by an output node are sent transactionally or not, as determined by the incoming persistence property, unless the output node has explicitly overridden transactionality.

- If you select **Yes**, the incoming message is received under syncpoint. Any derived messages subsequently sent by an output node in the same instance of the message flow are sent transactionally, unless the output node has explicitly overridden transactionally.

- If you select **No**, the incoming message is not received under syncpoint. Any derived messages subsequently sent by an output node in the flow is sent non-transactionally, unless the output node has specified that the message should be put under syncpoint.

By setting the property on the MQInput node, you ensure it is set for every instance of the flow, on any broker or execution group.

Figure 3-4 shows how to select a Property feature of an MQInput node.

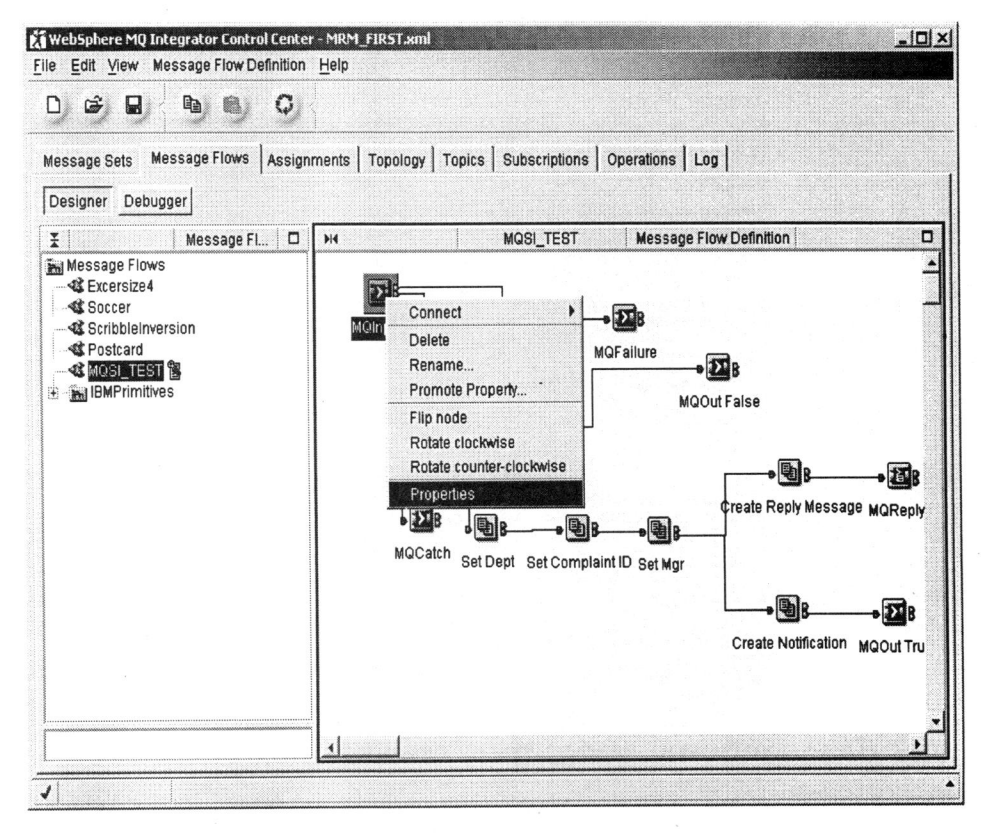

*Figure 3-4 Selecting properties on an MQInput node*

Figure 3-5 shows the window where you specify the desired properties.

Chapter 3. z/OS Resource Recovery Services and transactional message flows **53**

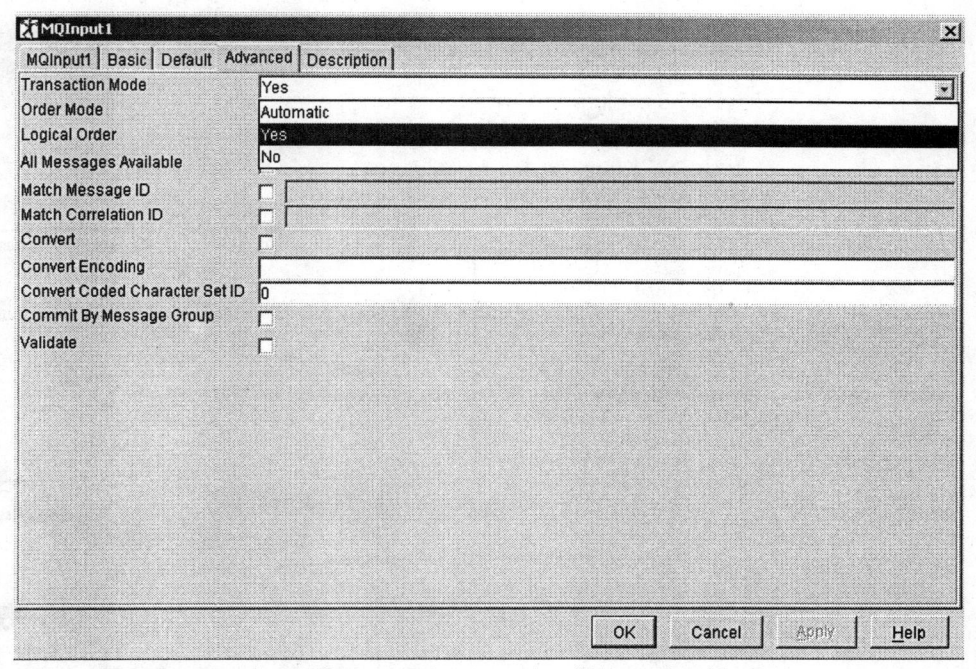

*Figure 3-5   Message flow MQInput node properties, Transaction Mode*

## 3.4.3 Transactional support on MQOutput

When you define an MQOutput node, the option you select for the Transaction Mode property defines whether the message is written under syncpoint:

- If you select **Yes**, the message is written under syncpoint (that is, within an MQSeries unit of work).
- If **Automatic** (the default), the message is written under syncpoint if the incoming input message is marked persistent.
- If **No**, the message is not written under syncpoint.

Another property of the MQOutput node, Persistence Mode, defines whether the output message is marked as persistent when it is put to the output queue:

- If you select **Yes**, the message is marked as persistent.
- If **Automatic** (the default), the desired message persistence is determined by the properties of the incoming message, as set in the MQMD (the MQSeries message descriptor).
- If **No**, the message is not marked as persistent.

► If you select **As Defined for Queue**, the message persistence is set as defined in the MQSeries queue by the MQOutput node specifying the MQPER_PERSISTENCE_AS_Q_DEF option in the MQMD.

Figure 3-6 shows the window where you specify the Transaction Mode on the MQOutput node.

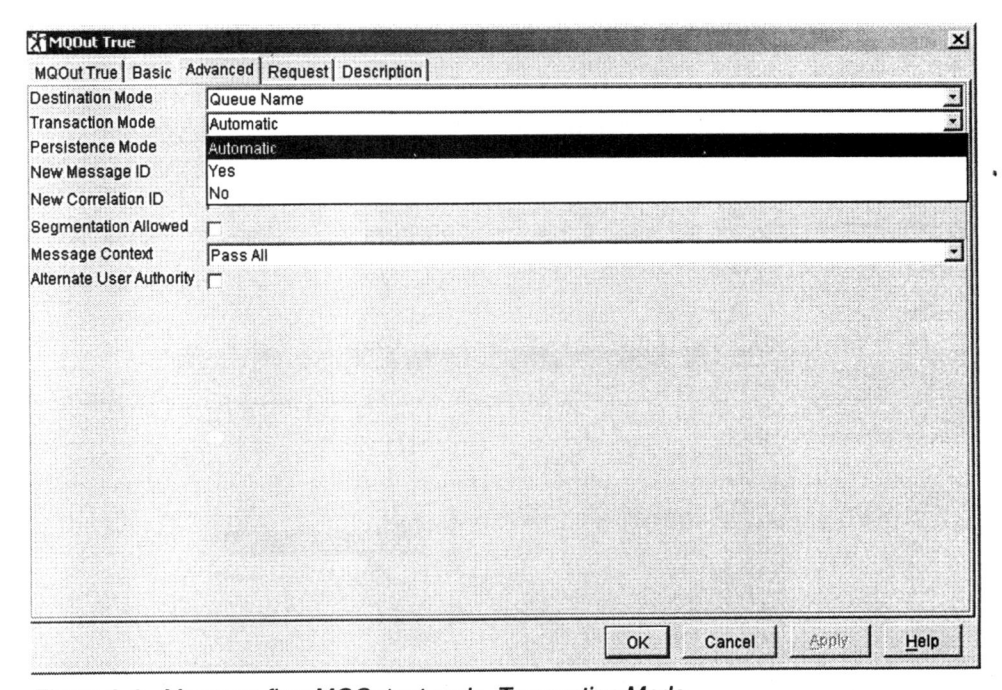

*Figure 3-6  Message flow MQOutput node, Transaction Mode*

## 3.4.4 Transactional support on Database node

When you define an Database node, the option you select for the Transaction Mode property defines whether the update to the database is committed immediately, or deferred until the completion of processing of the message flow, at which time the update is committed or rolled back according to the overall completion status of the message flow. The values are:

**No** (the default)  The actions on the database are not committed.

**Automatic**   The message flow, of which the Database node is a part, is committed if it is successful. That is, the actions that you define in the customizer are performed and the message continues through the message flow. If the message flow fails, it is rolled back. Therefore choosing **Automatic** means that the ability to commit or roll back the action of the Database node on the database depends on the success or failure of the entire message flow.

**Commit**  If you want to commit any uncommitted actions performed in this message flow on the database connected to this node, irrespective of the success or failure of the message flow as a whole, select **Commit**. The changes to the database will be committed even if the message flow itself fails.

**Tip:** If you select **Commit** on one Database node and **Automatic** on another, you must use a different session. To achieve this, you can change the case of the data source name.

Figure 3-7 shows the window where you define the Transaction Mode for a Database node.

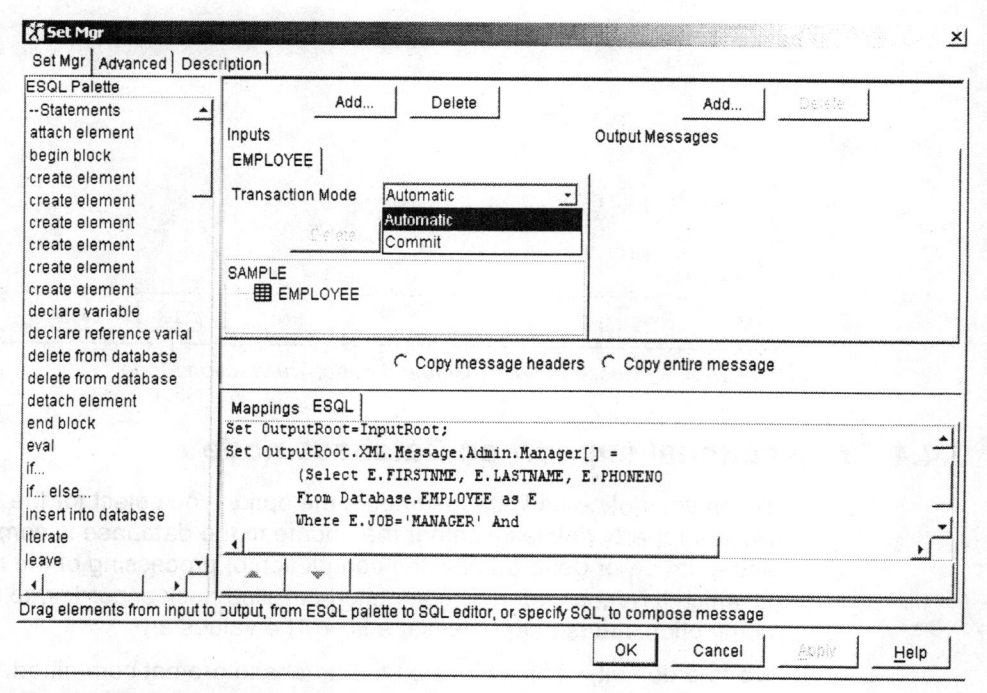

*Figure 3-7   Message flow Database node, Transaction Mode*

Figure 3-8 shows the message flow that we used to test transactional behavior and a table that documents this behavior upon failure in this flow on z/OS. The message flow includes two database nodes that perform database updates. This flow has no failure or backout nodes. Therefore, the failed message either goes to the Dead Letter Queue (DLQ) or is disposed (Disp) of. The backout threshold for the input node was set to zero.

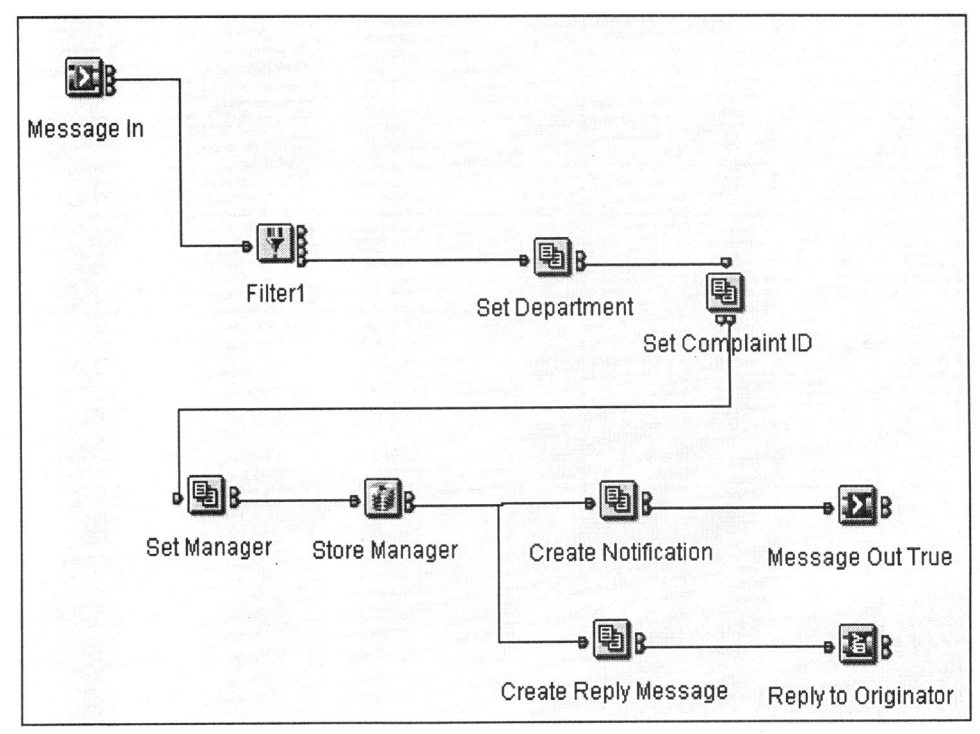

*Figure 3-8   Message flow with two Database nodes*

Table 3-1 shows the results of our tests. The first column defines message persistence. The second column is the Transaction Mode property for an Input node. The third column is the Transaction Mode property for a Database node. The fourth column is the result to the database record itself; that is, the change is either committed or rolled back. The last column is what happens to the message, that is, it is either sent to the DLQ or disposed.

Chapter 3. z/OS Resource Recovery Services and transactional message flows    57

Table 3-1  Flow transactional behavior upon failure

| Message Persistence | Flow Tx Mode | DB Node Tx Mode | Results on Flow Failure Database Rec | MQ Msg |
|---|---|---|---|---|
| Yes | Yes | Automatic | Roll Back | DLQ |
| Yes | Yes | Commit | Commit | DLQ |
| Yes | Automatic | Automatic | Roll Back | DLQ |
| Yes | Automatic | Commit | Commit | DLQ |
| Yes | No | Automatic | Roll Back | Disp |
| Yes | No | Commit | Commit | Disp |
| No | Yes | Automatic | Roll Back | DLQ |
| No | Yes | Commit | Commit | DLQ |
| No | Automatic | Automatic | Roll Back | Disp |
| No | Automatic | Commit | Commit | Disp |
| No | No | Automatic | Roll Back | Disp |
| No | No | Commit | Commit | Disp |

# Part 2

# Configuration and migration

# Configuration of WMQI on z/OS and Windows platforms

In this chapter, we provide information about setting up a simple architecture for running WebSphere MQ Integrator on multiple platforms. We explain the tasks and techniques used to install and configure the Control Center, Configuration Manager, and brokers on appropriate platforms. In Chapter 5, "WMQI operations on the z/OS platform" on page 89, we discuss operations performed to verify proper functioning of this simple architecture and in Chapter 10, "WMQI in a Parallel Sysplex environment" on page 191 we discuss a more complex architecture.

The information presented in this chapter is based on implementation of tasks introduced in *WebSphere MQ Integrator Administration Guide*, SC34-5792, *WebSphere MQ Integrator Using the Control Center*, SC34-5602, *WebSphere MQ Integrator Introduction and Planning*, GC34-5599, *WebSphere MQ Integrator for Windows NT and Windows 2000 Installation Guide*, GC34-5600, and *WebSphere MQ Integrator for z/OS Customization and Administration Guide*, SC34-5919.

## 4.1 Configuration of components on z/OS

The information in this section is based on implementation of the tasks introduced in *WebSphere MQ Integrator for z/OS Customization and Administration Guide*, SC34-5919. Prior to working through this section, make sure that the prerequisites are installed (MQSeries, DB2, and WMQI).

All the tasks to be done in the UNIX System Services that are described in this chapter may be done in the OMVS command prompt, in a telnet session to the UNIX System Services or using `rlogin`. We mostly used the OMVS prompt to perform configuration tasks and we assume that system administrators to be involved in the WMQI customization in z/OS are probably more used to OMVS operation and utilities.

### 4.1.1 Before you start

You should make yourself familiar with information in Chapter 1, "Preparing for Customization" in the *Customization and Administration Guide* for details to be taken into account before you start configuration of MQ Integrator components that refer to environment, security, DB2, MQSeries, Hierarchical File System and UNIX System Services.

### 4.1.2 Configuration overview

Figure 4-1 shows the configuration setup described in this section.

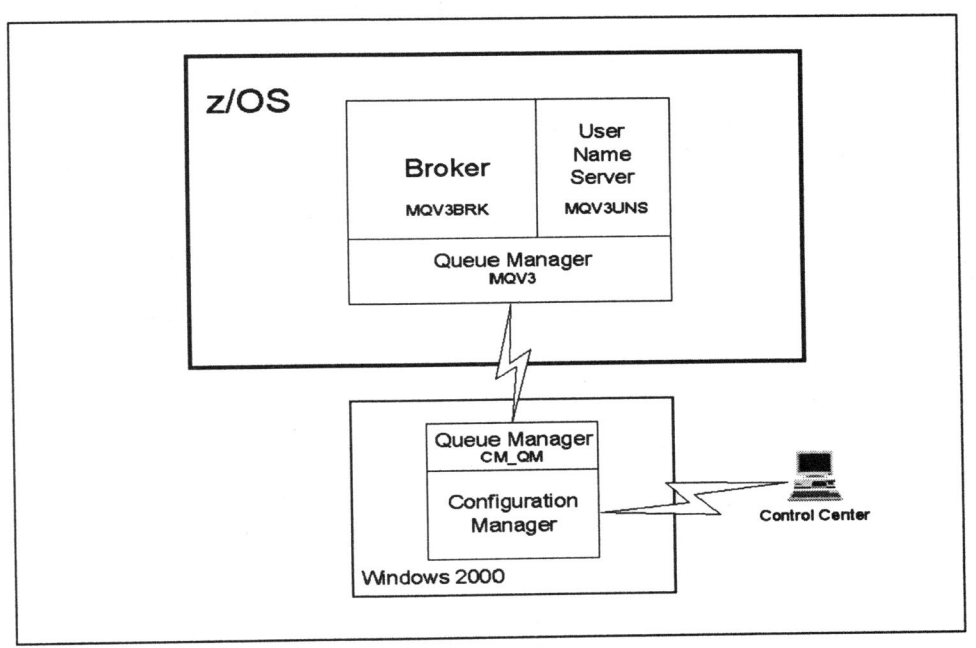

*Figure 4-1   Overview of the described configuration*

This section describes a configuration which involves:

- A Configuration Manager, running in a Windows 2000 server, with a local Queue Manager in the same server. The name of the Queue Manager is CM_QM.
- A broker running in a z/OS system, with a local MQ Manager. The MQ Manager name is MQV3. The broker name is MQV3BRK.
- A User Name Server, running in the same z/OS and sharing the Queue Manager with the broker. The name of the User Name Server is MQV3UNS.

The naming convention used in this configuration is based on the following:

- The first four characters of the component name correspond to the Queue Manager name.
- The remaining three characters describe the component: BRK for broker and UNS for User Name Server.

**Tip:** It is a good idea to follow this naming convention in your installation, so all the elements will be consistent. The component started task has a maximum of 7 characters, and this way it will correspond to the component name.

Chapter 4. Configuration of WMQI on z/OS and Windows platforms

To perform this configuration, there are some MQ definitions to be made. Those definitions are needed to achieve the proper communication between the different components that is performed using MQ queues. These definitions are:

- MQ Manager CM_QM:
  - Transmit queue MQV3, associated to the channel CM_QM.TO.MQV3 (the name of the channel specified in the queue trigger data). The maximum message length in this queue is set to 100 Mb.
  - Sender channel to the Queue Manager on z/OS, CM_QM.TO.MQV3, associated to the queue MQV3 (name provided as the channel transmission queue).
  - Receiver channel from Queue Manager in the z/OS, MQV3.TO.CM_QM.

- MQ Manager MQV3:
  - Transmit queue CM_QM, associated to the channel MQV3.TO.CM_QM (the name of the channel specified in the queue trigger data), and starting process MQV3.TO.CM_QM.PROCESS. The maximum message length in this queue is set to 100 Mb.
  - Process MQV3.TO.CM_QM.PROCESS, application type MVS, application ID CSQX START. This process is intended to start the channel when it is inactive and the first message comes into the transmit queue.
  - Sender channel to the Queue Manager in the Windows 2000 system, MQV3.TO.CM_QM, associated to the queue CM_QM (name provided as the channel transmission queue).
  - Receiver channel from Queue Manager in the Windows 2000 system, CM_QM.TO.MQV3.

**Note:** The maximum message length to be set in the transmit queues definition should be set to 100 Mb because some messages between a Configuration Manager and a broker may require large storage space, depending on the size of the flows to be deployed.

For any other installation, you should set the proper naming convention for these elements. For details about creation of these elements in both MQ managers, refer to MQSeries documentation.

**Tip:** Check that your channels are defined correctly and that the triggering mechanism works. You can save a lot of time and effort later if you make this verification at this stage.

## 4.2 Customizing brokers

The configuration process combines UNIX System Services tasks, such as running scripts and configuring environments, running batch JCL in native MVS, and configuring the Windows environment. The steps to follow can be found in Chapter 2, "Customization" of the *Customization and Administration Guide*. We follow the steps to customize a broker called MQV3BRK, using an MQSeries Queue Manager called MQV3, in a z/OS system.

### Setting up an OMVS user ID for the customizing user

You have to set up the .profile of the user performing the customization on UNIX System Services, so that WMQI commands can be found and executed. The .profile file should contain the following lines that you can change with the **oedit** command:

In OMVS, issue: **oedit .profile**

Add the following:

```
export NLSPATH=/usr/lpp/wmqi/messages/En_US/%N:$NLSPATH
export PATH= .:/usr/lpp/wmqi/bin:$PATH
```

where /usr/lpp/wmqi/ is the installation path of the WebSphere MQ Integrator libraries. Additional variables should be set if you intend to provide New Era of Networks support. Refer to Chapter 7, "Configuring New Era of Networks Support" on page 123 for details.

To activate the .profile for the user ID, you can both:

► Place the .profile file in the home directory of the user ID, and then exit and reconnect to OMVS.

► Execute the command **. .profile** in the directory where .profile is placed.

### Check APF attributes of bipimain

Use the **extattr** command to display the attributes of the object bipimain. For example:

**extattr /usr/lpp/wmqi/bin/bipimain**

The bipimain program should be set to APF authorized= YES; otherwise use **extattr +a bipimain** to set the attribute (this has to be done by a user with authority to execute this command).

## Create the broker PDSE

Each broker requires a separate data set for its JCL customization streams. The data set can be a PDS or PDSE.

A PDS can be defined using option 3.2 of ISPF (see Example 4-1).

*Example 4-1   PDS definition for the broker*

```
Data Set Name  . . . : WMQI210.MQV3BRK.CNTL

General Data                        Current Allocation
  Volume serial . . . : TOTTSU        Allocated tracks  . : 15
  Device type . . . . : 3390          Allocated extents . : 1
  Organization  . . . : PO            Maximum dir. blocks : 8
  Record format . . . : FB
  Record length . . . : 80
  Block size  . . . . : 27920       Current Utilization
  1st extent tracks . : 15            Used tracks . . . . : 1
  Secondary tracks  . : 15            Used extents  . . . : 1
                                      Used dir. blocks  . : 1
  Creation date . . . : 2001/11/29    Number of members . : 0
  Referenced date . . : ***None***
  Expiration date . . : ***None***
```

## Create a broker directory

Use the TSO `OMVS` command or telnet to the UNIX System Services. Create the broker root directory using:

`mkdir /var/wmqi/MQV3BRK`

Ensure that the broker user ID is assigned to the broker root directory or the directory belongs to a group of which that user is a member. The broker user ID is used later to run the broker started task procedure (refer to "Define the broker started task user ID" on page 73). The directory must have rwx permissions for both the user and group. Use the following commands:

- `id userID` to obtain the group set of the user ID of the broker.
- `chgrp group /var/wmqi/MQV3BRK` to assign the path name to the group the user ID is a member.
- `chmod g=RWX /var/wmqi/MQV3BRK` to grant proper permissions to the group.

## Create the broker runtime environment

Ensure that the user ID executing the customization has permissions to read and execute programs from the product installation libraries, /usr/lpp/wmqi. The commands referenced in "Create a broker directory" on page 66 can be used to set up the permissions for the user.

Enter in the broker root directory:

`cd /var/wmqi/MQV3BRK`

Create the broker called MQV3BRK in its runtime environment:

`mqsicreateBroker MQV3BRK -c /var/wmqi/MQV3BRK -q MQV3 [-s MQV3] [-g ConfigurationTimout] [-k ConfigurationDelayTimeout`

The optional parameters are:

- **-s MQV3**     Is the name of the Queue Manager of the User Name Server. If this parameter is omitted here then the broker has to be modified later to add the User Name Server.
- **-g ConfigurationTimeOut**   The length of time in seconds that an execution group in the broker is allowed to take to apply a change in configuration.
- **-k ConfigurationTimeout**   The length of time in second and broker is allowed to take to process a minimal change in configuration.

For details on the **-g** and **-k** options, refer to the *Customization and Administration Guide*.

Example 4-2 shows output after execution of the **mqsicreatebroker** command.

*Example 4-2 Output for the mqsicreatebroker command.*

```
MQRES1 @ SC66:/SYSTEM/var/wmqi>mqsicreateBroker MQV3BRK -c /var/wmqi/MQV3BRK -q
MQV3 -s MQV3UNS
BIP9171I: Installation Path is    : /usr/lpp/wmqi
Component Name is                 : MQV3BRK
Component Path is                 : /var/wmqi/MQV3BRK
Queue Manager Name is             : MQV3
UNS Queue Manager Name is         : MQV3
Configuration Timeout is          : 300
Configuration Timeout Delay is    : 60
BIP9182I: All parameters correct? (Y|y) or (N|n)?

y
BIP9177I: Component MQV3BRK will be created.
BIP9169I: Copy template/data/mqsicompcif...
```

```
BIP9169I: Copy template/shell/mqsicustomize...
BIP9173I: Component MQV3BRK created successfully.
```

> **Note:** The `mqsicreatebroker` command is different in z/OS from other platforms. It only creates the runtime environment for the broker. There are more tasks to be done for the broker before it can be started.

## Edit the customization input file (CIF)

Use the check list found in the *Customization and Administration Guide* to enter your machine's specific information for the CIF file.

When the broker was created, the customization input file, mqsicompcif, was copied to the broker's root directory. You need to edit this file. The file on your machine has to be provided with values similar to those shown in Table 4-1, which shows the values we used to customize our broker.

*Table 4-1   Sample values for the CIF file*

| Attribute | Value | Example |
|---|---|---|
| DB2_SAMPLE_PGMNAME | Name of the DB2 sample program for executing SQL in batch mode | DSNTEP2 |
| DB2_SAMPLE_PGMPLAN | Name of the DB2 Plan for the sample program execution | DSNTEP71 |
| DB2_DSNACLI_PLANNAME | Name of the DB2 Plan for execution of DSNACLI program | DSNACLI |
| DB2_SUBSYSTEM | Name of the DB2 subsystem | D7V3 |
| DB2_LOCATION | Name of the location of the DB2 subsystem, used by ODBC connections (see note below) | DB7V |
| DB2_TABLE_OWNER | Name of the DB2 Tables qualifier | MQV3BRK |
| DB2_STORAGE_GROUP | Name of the DB2 storage group | MQV3BRK |
| DB2_STOR_GROUP_VCAT | Name of the VCAT for the DB2 storage group | DB7VU |

| Attribute | Value | Example |
|---|---|---|
| DB2_STOR_GROUP_VOL | Name of the DB2 storage group volume (or "*" for SMS managed volumes) | TOTDCR |
| DB2_DATABASE | Name of DB2 database for the Broker | MQV3BRK |
| COMPONENT_PDS | Name of the Broker PDSE (or PDS) | WMQI210.MQV3BRK.CNTL |
| COMPONENT_KEY | Unique Component Key for Broker or User Name Server | MQV3BRK |
| USER_PROCLIB_PDS | Name of the User Procedures Library (see note below) | SYS1.PROCLIB |
| STEPLIB_NAME | Name of the STEPLIB Names Member (see note below) | WMQISTEP |
| JAVAHOME | Root directory of the JAVA installation | /usr/lpp/java/IBM/J1.3 |
| CLASSPATH | CLASSPATH environment variable | /usr/lpp/wmqi/classes:/usr/lpp/java/IBM/J1.3/lib |
| PATH | Path to the WMQI and JAVA executables | /usr/lpp/wmqi/bin:/usr/lpp/java/IBM/J1.3/bin |
| LIBPATH | Path to the DLLs (Dynamic Link Libraries) | /usr/lpp/wmqi/lib:/usr/lpp/java/IBM/J1.3/lib:/usr/lpp/java/IBM/J1.3/bin |
| LILPATH | Path to WMQI .lil and/or customer .lil files | /usr/lpp/wmqi/lil |
| LANG | Local Language | C |
| LC_ALL | Local Language, overriding other LC_* environment variables | C |
| TZ | Time zone (see note below) | EST5 |
| NLSPATH | Contains the location of the message catalog(s) | /usr/lpp/wmqi/messages/En_US/%N |

| Attribute | Value | Example |
|---|---|---|
| CONSOLE_NLSPATH | Used to locate the messages for the console. | /usr/lpp/wmqi/messages/En_US |
| MC_MESSAGES | Needed by WMQI setting if messages should appear in mixed case or uppercase | YES |
| USE_ARM | Automatic Restart Management switch (see note below) | NO |
| ARM_ELEMENTNAME | Element Name used by ARM | MQV3BRK |
| ARM_ELEMENTTYPE | ElementType used by ARM | SYSWMQI |

Additional attributes have to be specified if you need support for New Era of Networks. Refer to Chapter 7, "Configuring New Era of Networks Support" on page 123 for details.

The DB2 administrator should provide the name of the DB2 LOCATION. The DB2 LOCATION name is found in the system log at startup, after a message DSNL004I DDF START COMPLETE.

The DB2_LOCATION is also the name to be provided, in message flows, as data source when accessing DB2 tables, instead of using the subsystem name, because it is the name used as the ODBC connection.

The User Procedures Library is used to contain the STEPLIB Names Member, and also the procedure for starting the broker. It is recommended that you not use the SYS1.PROCLIB library, but any other library concatenated as the Procedures Library.

The STEPLIB Names Member is a member created in the broker's PDSE, which has to be copied into the User Procedures Library. See "Create the STEPLIB member" on page 71 for details.

The value EST5 is the default value provided with the customization input file. This value corresponds to US Eastern Time Zone. For more details, refer to the z/OS *UNIX System Services User's Guide,* SA22-7801.

WebSphere MQ Integrator allows you to register a component in the Automatic Restart Manager. See "Automatic Restart Management (ARM) planning" on page 217 for details.

Refer to "Broker configuration" on page 124 for the values to be set for NEON support if you are planning to add this support in your installation.

You can edit the file by using the following command:

```
cd /var/wmqi/MQV3BRK
oedit mqsicompcif
```

### Customize the broker

At the broker root directory, /var/wmqi/MQV3BRK, run the command to customize the broker:

```
mqsicustomize
```

It is always a good idea to browse the customization log, which is in the output directory under the broker root directory. This can be done by using the following command:

```
obrowse output/Customizelog
```

If you get any messages beginning with `Could not find message...` refer to "Setting up an OMVS user ID for the customizing user" on page 65.

It is very important that you specify the correct parameters when you modify the mqsicompcif file. If you find that you have specified parameters in mqsicompcif incorrectly, change the mqsicompcif file and repeat the step of customizing the broker. Also, remember to rerun `mqsicustomize` every time you modify the mqsicompcif file.

### Create the STEPLIB member

When you execute the `mqsicustomize` command, it creates a member called BIPSLIB containing some libraries needed in the broker's runtime, such as WebSphere MQ, DB2 and Language Environment libraries; also some ISPF libraries for the DUMP formatter. Update the member properly if some of the libraries are already in the LINKLIST and don't need to be in the task STEPLIB. Also, give these libraries proper names that correspond to your installation.

The `mqsicustomize` command creates this member in the broker's PDSE. Copy this member into the User Procedures Library, and be careful that its name matches the value set in the customization input file, because that is the name used by the started task procedure.

### Create the broker database

Submit the following jobs created in your broker PDSE. You need SYSADM or SYSCTRL authority to submit the DB2 jobs. You should get step return code 0 from all the steps and should see that the step named BAD was flushed. Wait for the successful completion of the job before submitting the next request.

| Submission Order | DB2 job | Description |
|---|---|---|
| 1 | BIP$DB01 | Create a storage group |
| 2 | BIP$DB02 | Create a database |
| 3 | BIP$DB03 | Create the table spaces |
| 4 | BIP$DB04 | Create the tables |
| 5 | BIP$DB05 | Grant authority to the tables |

**Note:** The SQL statements in the broker PDSE member BIPDBGR grant unlimited access to the tables by default. You should review and change this statement before submitting BIP$DB05.

If you encounter problems, use the job BIP#DB01 to delete the definitions, review the CIF settings, recustomize, and begin submitting the create jobs again starting with BIP$DB01.

You may have to change DSNTIAD to DSNTEP2 in the mqsicompcif file and run **mqsicustomize** again if you get none/zero return codes from BIP#DB01.

In a Parallel Sysplex installation, you should add a System Affinity clause to the job card, in order to ensure the jobs are executed in the same system they have been submitted in. The complete job card would look like this:

```
//BIP$DB01 JOB 5655-G97,MSGLEVEL=(1,1),MSGCLASS=A,NOTIFY=&SYSUID
/*JOBPARM SYSAFF=*
```

## Create the broker queues

Ensure that the user customizing the broker has the proper authorizations to access the MQSeries Queue Manager and associated queues. Start the Queue Manager if necessary before continuing.

Submit the following job from the broker PDSE to define the MQSeries objects needed by the broker. Take into account the recommendation in "Create the broker database" on page 71 about the System Affinity clause in the job card, if your installation is a Parallel Sysplex.

| MQSeries job | Description |
|---|---|
| BIP$MQ01 | Create the Broker queues |

**Note:** If you encounter problems, use the job BIP#MQ01 to delete MQSeries objects, review the CIF settings, recustomize, and begin submitting the create jobs again starting with BIP$MQ01.

### Define the broker started task user ID

Define the user ID the broker started task will be assigned to, and assign the broker procedure with this user ID.

See "Setting up z/OS security" and "Authorizations required for the WebSphere MQ Integrator started task user ID" in the *Customization and Administration Guide* for details about setting the proper permissions for the broker started task user ID.

> **Restriction:** The user ID of the broker started task should not have OMVS UID=0. This would prevent some commands sent to the broker started task, such as STOP, from being executed properly. Take this into account when determining the OMVS settings for the broker started task user ID.

### Copy the broker started task procedure

The started task procedure has to be copied to the User Procedures Library. This is performed by submitting the job BIP$UT1. Ensure the User Procedures Library is properly set as destination of the started task procedure in the BIP$UT1 job, and also that the User Procedures Library is already set in the SYS1.PROCLIB concatenation.

### Run the Customization Verification Program

Submit the BIP$JCVP job from the broker PDSE. If the return code of the job execution is different from 00, refer to Run the Customization Verification Program in *Customization and Administration Guide* for details about the operations this jobs performs, and check your customization. Take into account the recommendation in "Create the broker database" on page 71 about the System Affinity clause in the job card, if your installation is a Parallel Sysplex.

### Start the broker

You can start the broker using the z/OS console START command.

```
S MQV3BRK
```

where MQV3BRK is the name of the broker started task procedure.

If an SDSF window is used, you can use this command preceded by a slash:

`/S MQV3BRK`

The expected output in the system log when the broker starts successfully is:

`BIP914W MQV3BRK 0 The component was started`

If the broker fails to start, refer to "Broker failed to start" in the *Customization and Administration Guide*.

> **Important:** If it is not planned in your installation to add NEON support, and no appropriate NEON customizations are taken, possibly the broker started task dumps a 4039 abend, although this does not prevent the broker from working. To prevent this dump from being produced, rename or remove after backing up the file imbdfneo.lil. It is in the .lil file of the WebSphere MQ Integrator product (/usr/lpp/wmqi/lil). If you rename this file, make sure that the new name does not have the extension .lil.

## Connect the broker to the WebSphere MQ Integrator network

For the broker to be connected to the WebSphere MQ Integrator Network, the MQ settings have to be done as described at the beginning of this chapter. If the broker does not run in a configuration like that described here, ensure the needed queues and channels are created among the different WMQI components.

After you define the broker in the Configuration Manager, you can deploy message flows and execute them.

## Verify availability of threads

A remarkable factor to pay attention to is the *number of threads* to be used by the WMQI components in runtime, given that it involves configuration in both UNIX System Services and MQSeries.

The number of threads to run by the WMQI components depend on the application, that means number of Execution Groups and number of message flows. The way to calculate the threads to be used by a message flow is:

*Threads for a Flow = Number of Input Nodes * (Additional instances + 1)*

Where *Additional instances* is the configuration parameter on the properties of the message flow, when parallel flow execution is desired.

Each execution group starts a thread within the Queue Manager.

As a rule of thumb, to calculate the maximum number of threads open by WMQI in a configuration of one broker and one User Name Server sharing the Queue Manager, use the following formula:

*Max Threads = Total Threads for all Flows + Number of Execution Groups + 10*

Consider this value when setting:

- The MAXTHREADS and MAXTHREADTASKS value in UNIX System Services (see "Preparing for Customization" in the *Customization and Administration Guide*).
- The number of threads to be reserved for *background tasks,* when assembling the MQSeries system parameters module (the IDBACK parameter). Increase this value if needed, depending on the number of threads to be open by WMQI. If there are not enough threads available for opening, an MQ RC=2025 is reached by the task attempting to open an MQ connection. The current IDBACK value may be determined by browsing the output of the Queue Manager started task.

### Deleting a broker

Refer to "Common administrative tasks" on page 100 for the procedure of deleting a broker from your system.

> **Important:** Before you delete a broker from a z/OS system, you have to delete it from your Topology using the Control Center, if the broker is in your Topology, and deploy the changes. If you do not do so, rebuilding the broker in the same or other system will cause conflicts of component identifiers.

## 4.3 Customizing the User Name Server (UNS)

A User Name Server has the following roles:

- Supplying the Configuration Manager with the users and groups list, so that ACLs can be built in the Control Center for a specific topic.
- Providing the broker, at runtime, for information about users and groups, so that the broker may determine whether a publish or subscribe operation may be performed by a given user.

A User Name Server has to be configured if you plan to use the WebSphere MQ Integrator publish/subscribe facilities, providing user/group-based security.

In z/OS, the UNS obtains the users/groups list from the Security Subsystem (RACF in most cases).

## Setting up a User Name Server

The configuration steps for a UNS are very similar to those taken for the broker customization. The configuration process combines UNIX System Services tasks, such as running scripts and configuring environments, running batch JCL in native MVS, and configuring the Windows environment. The steps to follow can be found in Chapter 2 "Customization" of the *Customization and Administration Guide*. We follow the steps to customize a User Name Server called MQV3UNS, using an MQSeries Queue Manager called MQV3, in a z/OS system.

> **Note:** If you have defined your brokers before you start to define the UNS, you must change the brokers' configuration to add the UNS. See "Common administrative tasks" on page 100 for details.

## Previous steps

You have to customize your OMVS user ID and check the APF attributes of the bipimain object as explained in the broker customization (see "Customize the broker" on page 71), if you are customizing the UNS in a system where these operations have not been already done.

## Create the User Name Server PDSE

Each UNS requires a separate data set for its JCL customization streams. The data set can be a PDS or PDSE.

A PDS can be defined using option 3.2 of ISPF (Example 4-3).

*Example 4-3   PDS Definition for the User Name Server*

```
Data Set Name . . . : WMQI210.MQV3UNS.CNTL

General Data                         Current Allocation
  Volume serial . . . : TOTTS3         Allocated tracks  . : 15
  Device type . . . . : 3390           Allocated extents . : 1
  Organization  . . . : PO             Maximum dir. blocks : 8
  Record format . . . : FB
  Record length . . . : 80
  Block size  . . . . : 27920        Current Utilization
  1st extent tracks . : 15             Used tracks . . . . : 3
  Secondary tracks  . : 15             Used extents  . . . : 1
                                       Used dir. blocks  . : 2
  Creation date . . . : 2001/11/21     Number of members . : 16
  Referenced date . . : 2001/11/30
  Expiration date . . : ***None***
```

## Create the User Name Server directory

Use the TSO OMVS command or telnet to the UNIX System Services. Create the UNS root directory using the following command:

**mkdir /var/wmqi/MQV3UNS**

Ensure that the User Name Server user ID is assigned to the UNS root directory or the directory belongs to a group of which that user is a member. The directory must have rwx permissions for both the user and group. Use the commands:

- **id userID** to obtain the group set of the user ID of the broker.
- **chgrp group /var/wmqi/MQV3UNS** to assign the path name to the group the user ID is a member.
- **chmod g=RWX /var/wmqi/MQV3UNS** to grant proper permissions to the group.

## Create the User Name Server runtime environment

Ensure that the user ID executing the customization has permissions to read and execute programs from the product installation libraries, /usr/lpp/wmqi. The commands referenced in the above topic can be used to set up the permissions for the user. Execute this command:

**cd /var/wmqi/MQV3UNS**

Create the User Name Server called MQV3UNS in its runtime environment:

**mqsicreateusernameserver -c /var/wmqi/MQV3UNS -q MQV3 [-r RefreshInterval]**

The optional parameter is -r RefreshInterval. This is the interval in seconds used by the UNS to refresh the users/group list, from the information provided by the security subsystem. The default value is 60 seconds.

*Example 4-4 Sample output for the mqsicreateusernameserver command*

```
MQRES1 @ SC66:/SYSTEM/var/wmqi/MQV3UNS>mqsicreateusernameserver -c
/var/wmqi/MQV3UNS -q MQV3
BIP9172E: Installation Path is : /usr/lpp/wmqi
Component Path is            : /var/wmqi/MQV3UNS
Queue Manager Name is        : MQV3
Refresh Interval is          : 60
BIP9182I: All parameters correct? (Y|y) or (N|n)?
Y
BIP9177I: Component UserNameServer will be created.
BIP9169I: Copy template/data/mqsicompcif...
BIP9169I: Copy template/shell/mqsicustomize...
BIP9173I: Component UserNameServer created successfully.
```

For details refer to the *Customization and Administration Guide*.

### Edit the customization input file (CIF)

Use the check list found in the *Customization and Administration Guide* to enter your machine's specific information for the CIF file.

When the UNS was created the customization input file, mqsicompcif, was copied to the UNS root directory. You need to edit this file. In the customization described, the CIF file is the same as that used for the broker. So, the CIF for the broker may be copied into the UNS root directory. Refer to Table 4-1 on page 68 for a list of values to be provided to the CIF. The values to be changed with respect to those provided for the broker definitions are:

- Component key
- ARM-element name
- COMPONENT_PDSE
- STPN

### Customize the User Name Server

At the UNS root directory, /var/wmqi/MQV3UNS, run the command to customize the UNS:

**mqsicustomize**

It is always a good idea to browse the customization log. This can be done by using the command:

**obrowse output/Customizelog**

If you get any messages beginning with `Could not find message...` refer to "Setting up an OMVS user ID for the customizing user" on page 65.

> **Note:** It is very important that you specify the correct parameters when you modify the mqsicompcif file. If you find that you have specified parameters in mqsicompcif incorrectly, change the mqsicompcif file and repeat the step of customizing the broker. Also remember to rerun **mqsicustomize** every time you modify the mqsicompcif file.

## Create the STEPLIB member

When executing the `mqsicustomize` command, a PDS member called BIPSLIB is automatically created (see Table 4-1 on page 68). This member contains a list of libraries needed in the broker's runtime STEPLIB, such as WebSphere MQ, DB2 and Language Environment libraries, as well as some ISPF libraries for the DUMP formatter. Update the member properly if some of the libraries are already in the LINKLIST and do not need to be in the task STEPLIB. Also give these libraries the proper name that corresponds to your installation.

The `mqsicustomize` command creates this member in the broker's PDSE. Copy this member into the User Procedures Library, and be careful that its name matches the value set in the customization input file, because that is the name used by the started task procedure to refer to this member.

The `mqsicustomize` command creates this member in the User Name Server PDSE. Copy this member into the User Procedures Library, and be careful that its name matches the value set in the customization input file.

If these steps have already been taken for a broker creation in the same z/OS system, maybe they are not needed, and the same STEPLIB member is used for both components.

## Create the User Name Server queues

Ensure that the user customizing the UNS has the proper authorizations to access the MQSeries Queue Manager and associated queues. Start the Queue Manager if necessary before continuing.

Submit the following job from the broker PDSE to define the MQSeries objects needed by the UNS.

| MQSeries job | Description |
| --- | --- |
| BIP$MQ01 | Create the User Name Server queues |

**Note:** If you encounter problems, use the job BIP#MQ01 to delete MQSeries objects, review the CIF settings, recustomize, and submit BIP$MQ01 again.

If you run the job in a Parallel Sysplex, take into account the recommendation for System Affinity jobs submission given in "Create the broker database" on page 71.

## Define the User Name Server started task user ID

Define the user ID the UNS started task will be assigned to, and assign the UNS procedure with this user ID.

See "Setting up z/OS security" and "Authorizations required for the WebSphere MQ Integrator started task user ID" in the *Customization and Administration Guide* for details about setting the proper permissions for the UNS started task user ID.

### Copy the UNS started task procedure

The started task procedure has to be copied to the User Procedures Library. This is performed by submitting the job BIP$UT1. Ensure that the User Procedures Library is properly set as the destination of the started task procedure in the BIP$UT1 job, and also that the User Procedures Library is already set in the SYS1.PROCLIB concatenation.

### Run the Customization Verification Program

Submit the BIP$JCVP job from the broker PDSE. If the return code of the job execution is different from 00, refer to "Run the Customization Verification Program" in the *Customization and Administration Guide* for details about the operations this jobs performs, and check your customization.

If you run the job in a Parallel Sysplex, take into account the recommendation for System Affinity jobs submission given in "Create the broker database" on page 71.

### Start the User Name Server

You can start the UNS using the z/OS console command:

```
S MQV3UNS
```

where `MQV3UNS` is the name of the UNS started task procedure.

If an SDSF panel is used, you can use this command preceded by a slash:

```
/S MQV3UNS
```

The expected output in the system log when the broker starts successfully is:

```
BIP9141W UserNameServer 0 The component was started
```

### Connect the UNS to the WebSphere MQ Integrator network

For the UNS to be connected to the WebSphere MQ Integrator Network, the MQ Settings have to be configured as described at the beginning of this chapter. If the UNS does not run in a configuration like that described here, ensure the needed queues and channels are created among the different WMQI components.

### Making the User Name Server available to other components

The User Name Server may be made known to the broker and to the Configuration Manager when these are created, by supplying the UNS Queue Manager name in the appropriate parameter in the `mqsicreateBroker` and `mqsicreateconfigmgr` commands (see "Create the broker runtime environment" on page 67 for parameters to be supplied when creating a broker).

If the UNS Queue Manager is not made known to the broker and Configuration Manager at creation time, both may be modified later for this purpose. In z/OS, the command changing the broker to provide it with the name of the User Name Server's Queue Manager is:

```
F MQV3BRK,cb s='MQV3'
```

A command may be sent to the started task from the system console or SDSF, and from the OMVS command line. Refer to "WMQI operations on the z/OS platform" on page 89 for details about sending commands to WMQI started tasks.

### Deleting a User Name Server

Refer to "Common administrative tasks" on page 100 for the procedure of deleting a UNS from your system.

> **Important:** If you delete a UNS from your system, you have to remove the UNS references from the rest of the components. That means modifying the Configuration Manager not to continue registering with the UNS and modifying all the brokers with the same purpose.

## 4.4 Setup of the Configuration Manager

The information presented in this section is based on implementation of the tasks introduced in *WebSphere MQ Integrator for Windows NT and Windows 2000 Installation Guide*, SC34-5600. When you set up the Configuration Manager, remember these points:

- The Configuration Manager exists on the Windows NT or Windows 2000 platforms only.
- DB2 is the only RDBMS database that can be used to build the configuration repository and the message repository.
- Create only one instance of the Configuration Manager in your broker domain.
- The Configuration Manager requires an MQSeries Queue Manager.

- The Configuration Manager requires access to a database to create and maintain internal data in two sets of tables:
    - A table, known as the Configuration Repository, to hold configuration and definition information for the whole broker domain.
    - A table, known as the Message Repository, to hold definition information for messages defined or imported thorough the Control Center.

    You must create these repositories using DB2.
- The Configuration Manager requires MQSeries, DB2, and Microsoft Data Access Component (MDAC) be installed before its installation.

### 4.4.1 Installing the Configuration Manager

The installation program checks that prerequisites are installed, and display a window if anything is missing. It is recommended that you cancel your installation of the Configuration Manager and install any missing prerequisites.

WebSphere MQ Integrator contains a number of components that work together to provide the full function of a broker domain. You can choose which components to install at the start of the install procedure, by selecting a setup type. You should choose either the **Full** or **Custom** setup type to install the Configuration Manager.

**Note:** If you encounter problems during the installation you should check the readme.txt file, WebSphere MQ Integrator installation log, MQSI2.log, or WebSphere MQ Integrator Messages guide, as appropriate, for problem determination and resolution.

### 4.4.2 Creating the Configuration Manager

The tasks described in this section use specific resource names and user IDs. You should use your own naming convention for MQSeries.

Perform the following tasks to create and configure the Configuration Manager:
- Create a new user ID called the 'service userid'(mqsiuid).
- Assign an existing user ID to all the WebSphere MQ Integrator groups.
- Create the databases
- Connect to the databases
- Set up database authorizations
- Customize the database
- Create the Configuration Manager

## Create a new user ID and assign it to appropriate groups

Use Windows NT User Manager to create a user ID and password for WebSphere MQ Integrator, for example mqsiuid with a password of mqsipw. See "Setting up user IDs and groups" in Chapter 4 of the *WebSphere MQ Integrator Installation Guide for Windows NT and Windows 2000*, GC34-5600, for details.

> **Note:** Do not create a new user ID with the same name as your machine. If you do, an Unable to start the component error will be generated.

Use the Windows NT User Manager utility to add the user ID created above to the Windows NT Administrator and WebSphere MQ Integrator groups (mqbrkrs, mqbrasgn, mqbrdevt, mqbrops, and mqbrtpic).

## Create databases and connect to them

Use the DB2 Control Center to create the two databases used by the Configuration Manager. See "Creating and connecting to the databases" in Chapter 4 of the *WebSphere MQ Integrator Installation Guide for Windows NT and Windows 2000*, GC34-5600, for details on creating a database using the Create Database Wizard.

An ODBC connection is needed for the message repository. The configuration repository dose not need an ODBC connection.

## Set up database authorizations

To authorize users to access the databases you have created in previous sections follow the steps below:

- Start the DB2 Control Center.
- For each database you created:
  - Expand the Object tree until you find the database
  - Click **User and Group Objects**
  - Right-click **DB Users**
  - Select **Add** from the pop-up menu
  - Select the user ID used for WebSphere MQ Integrator
  - Select the appropriate options

See "Setting up database authorizations" in Chapter 4 of the *WebSphere MQ Integrator Installation Guide for Windows NT and Windows 2000*, GC34-5600 for more details.

> **Note:** You can omit this task if you specify your DB2 administrator ID and password as parameters for the Create Configuration Manager command. See the *WebSphere MQ Integrator Administration Guide* for further information.

## Customize the database

DB2 Version 7.1 requires a database heap size of at least 900 pages (4 KB). To change the heap size:

- Start the DB2 Control Center
- For each database you have created:
    - Expand the Object tree until you find the database
    - Right-click and select **Configure...**
    - Select the **Performance** tab and **Database Heap Size** parameter
    - Set this value to 900
    - Click **OK**

## Create the Configuration Manager

To create the Configuration Manager complete the following steps:

- Access the Create Configuration Manager via the Command Assistant (**Start -> Programs ->IBM WebSphere MQ Integrator -> Command Assistant**).
- Complete the high lighted fields
- Click **Next** to check the full command
- Click **Finish** to run the command

Alternatively, enter the following command on the command line:

```
mqsicreateconfigmgr -i <user ID> -a <password> -q <queue manager> -n
<configuration repository> -m <message repository>
```

## Start the Configuration Manager

To start the Configuration Manager, enter the following command on the Windows command line:

```
mqsistart configmgr
```

`mqsistart configmgr` starts the Windows NT services for the Configuration Manager and reports whether the services have started successfully. You must also check the application log of the Windows NT Event Viewer for any warnings or errors.

Configure Windows NT services for automatic starting of the Configuration Manager by selecting **Start ->Settings ->Control Panel -> Services,** right-click **IBM MQSeries Broker Configmgr,** select **Properties,** and select **Automatic** from the drop-down menu of the Startup Type parameter.

## 4.5 Setup of the Control Center

The information presented in this section is based on implementation of the tasks introduced in *WebSphere MQ Integrator for Windows NT and Windows 2000 Installation Guide*, GC34-5600. When setting up the Control Center remember these points:

- ► The Control Center can only be installed on the Windows NT or Windows 2000 platform. You can install and use the Control Center on any number of systems in your broker domain.
- ► The Control Center is where you will develop and modify message flows and message sets in the broker domain.
- ► Other uses of the Control Center are to assign resources to the broker, define the broker topology, control the publish/subscribe network, and manage the broker domain.
- ► The modifications you make to the broker domain are deployed to the Configuration Manager for long term storage and use.
- ► You must use MQSeries Client for Java to connect to the Configuration Manager.
- ► The Control Center does not require any prerequisite software except MQSeries Client for Java.

### 4.5.1 Install the Control Center

Install the Control Center by selecting either the **Full** or **Custom** setup types from the product installation CD.

### 4.5.2 Connect to the Configuration Manager

To connect to the Configuration Manager follow the tasks below:

- ► Start the MQSeries Listener for the Configuration Manager's Queue Manager

- Start the Configuration Manager
- Start the Control Center and connect to the Configuration Manager

> **Important:** Check that your broker on z/OS is started before making any changes to the broker domain.

### Start the Configuration Manager MQSeries Listener

You need to start the Listener on the Queue Manager to enable the control Center to communication with the Configuration Manager. To perform this step use the MQSeries Services:

- Access the **MQSeries Services** from the Program Files menu.
- Locate and click the **Queue Manager** to display its services.
- Right-click the **Listener** and select **ALL Tasks -> Start**.

If the Listener is not listed, right-click the **Queue Manager** and select **New -> Listener**. Select the transport protocol **TCP**, and specify the port number 1414. Click **OK** to start the Listener. When it has been created, right-click the **Listener** and select **Start** to start the Listener as a background task.

Alternatively, run the following command on the command line:

```
runmqlsr -t tcp -p 1414 -m <queue manager>
```

The Listener is started as a foreground task, and is not displayed in the MQSeries Services window.

> **Note:** If the default MQSeries port 1414 is not available, assign an alternative port value. Set the new port value in the Listener properties window. If the port is already in use, the Control Center cannot contact the Configuration Manager.

### Start the Configuration Manager

To start the Configuration Manager, enter the following command on the Windows command line:

```
mqsistart configmgr
```

Check the Application Log of the Windows NT Event Viewer for any warnings.

## Start the broker

The command to start the broker on z/OS is issued as a using native MVS command. To start the broker, enter the following command on the command line:

S <broker name>

For example:

S MQV3BRK

Check that the broker starts up properly without error.

## Connect to the Configuration Manager

To connect to the Configuration Manager follow the tasks below:

- Access the WebSphere MQ Integrator Control Center by selecting **Start -> Programs -> Program File -> IBM WebSphere MQ Integrator -> Control Center**.
- Complete the field shown in Figure 4-2 to provide the information required to connect your Control Center session to the Configuration Manager.

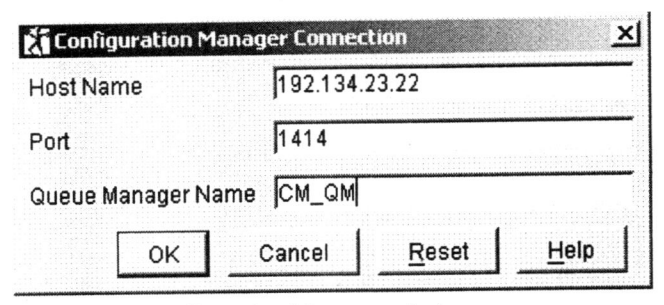

*Figure 4-2  Configuration Manager window*

- Click **OK**.

The Control Center contacts the Configuration Manager. If you want to check or change these settings later, select **File -> Connection...** to display the Configuration Manager Connection window.

If the Control Center fails to contact the Configuration Manager, check the following:

- The Configuration Manager is started
- The Queue Manager Listener is started

- ▶ The Queue Manager is started
- ▶ The user ID logged on to the computer is in the right groups

### 4.5.3 Add your broker to topology

To add a broker to the topology view perform the following steps:

- ▶ In the Control Center, select the **Topology** tab.
- ▶ Check out the Topology from the configuration repository by right-clicking the root of the Topology tree and selecting **Checkout**..
- ▶ Create the broker reference by right-clicking the root of the topology pane and select **Create -> Broker**. Fill in the Name and Queue Manager fields and click **Finish** in the Create new Broker window.

You are now ready to develop message flows and verify your broker domain.

# 5

# WMQI operations on the z/OS platform

Operating a broker domain in a multiple platform architecture that includes the z/OS platform introduces a bit more complexity than without the z/OS. In this chapter we describe some common operations for the z/OS platform and discuss how to manage WMQI components successfully. We cover the following areas:

- Typical operational message flows
- Common administrative functions
- Basic problem determination and resolution techniques

The information presented in this chapter is based on the implementation of tasks introduced in *WebSphere MQ Integrator of z/OS Customization and Administration Guide*, SC34-5919, *WebSphere MQ Integrator ESQL Reference*, SC34-5923, *WebSphere MQ Integrator Using the Control Center*, SC34-5602, *WebSphere MQ Integrator Administration Guide, MQ Integrator Working with Messages*, SC34-6039, *and WebSphere MQ Integrator Problem Determination Guide*, GC34-5920.

## 5.1 Review typical message flows

When the broker domain, Configuration Manager, and Control Center are configured and function properly on their individual platforms (see Chapter 4, "Configuration of WMQI on z/OS and Windows platforms" on page 61 for details on configuration issues), it is time to test and operate the system as a whole. This is done by developing message flows and message sets in the Control Center that exercise the capability of your integrator architecture. Below are some simple tests and exercises.

The information discussed in this section is based on implementation of tasks presented in *WebSphere MQ Integrator Using the Control Center, WebSphere MQ Integrator Working with Messages,* and *WebSphere MQ Integrator ESQL Reference.*

### 5.1.1 A simple message flow

The following sample message flow simulates a generic complaints input process where a user on the Web fills in a complaint form that results in an XML message arriving at the WebSphere MQ Integrator V2.1 broker via MQSeries. The message will be read from an input queue and written to an output queue.

In this example we do the following:

- Create a message flow
- Deploy the message flow to the broker
- Test the message flow

**Create a message flow**

Create MQInput and MQOutput nodes configured as shown in Figure 5-1 using the Control Center. Define an input queue, an output queue, and a failure queue using MQSeries on the z/OS platform. Make sure the MQSeries Queue Manager and listener is started, and that the MQSeries channels for the Configuration Manager and broker Queue Managers are up.

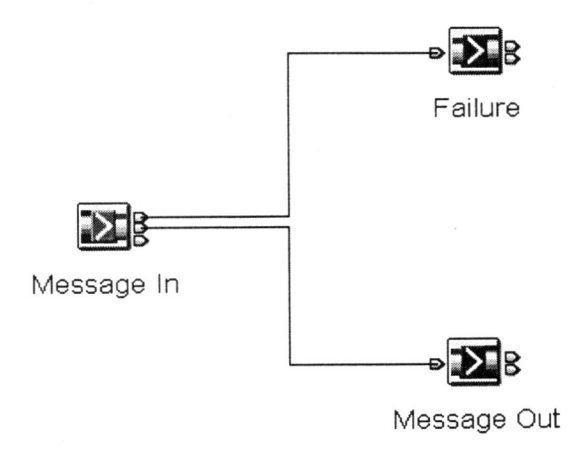

Figure 5-1   A simple message flow

## Deploy the message flow to the broker

Deploy the message flow to the WebSphere MQ Integrator Version 2.1 broker from the Control Center by creating an execution group on the broker and moving the message flow created above to this execution group (See Figure 5-2) in the Assignment tab. Complete the deployment and prepare to test your simple message flow.

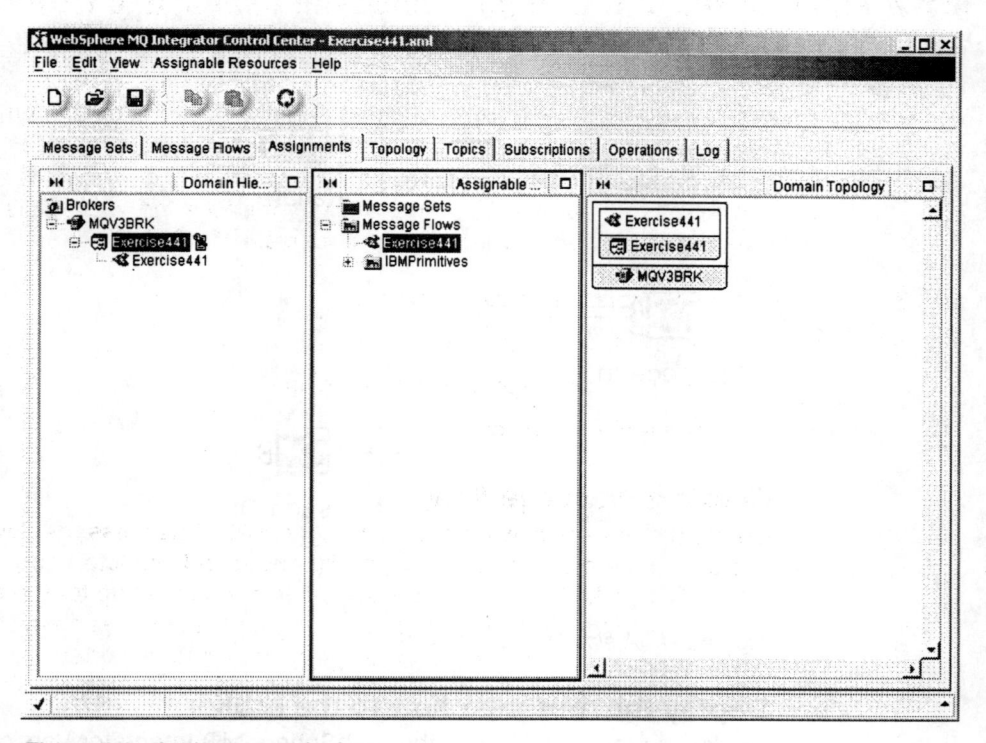

*Figure 5-2 Assignment tab view*

## Testing the message flow

Test the message flow with a generic XML message by creating a short message using the MQSeries Explorer for Windows NT or Windows 2000. Check that the message passes through the message flow and is found on the output queue. If it is not there, check the failure queue, dead letter queue or the Windows Application Log.

Check the Operations tab to verify that the broker is aware of the proper components in the broker domain (message flow and execution group).

## 5.1.2 Filter nodes and Compute nodes in a message flow

This sample message flow is an extension of the message flow created above. In this example, we create a message flow that reads in a message from an input queue, passes the message to a Filter node to check a value of the field called Version. If the verification result is true, the message is passed to the Compute node to alter the message based on the Complaint Type; from there the message is written to an output queue. If the result of a Filter node check is false, the message is written to another output queue.

In this example we do the following:

- Create the message flow
- Deploy the message flow to the broker
- Test the message flow

### Create a message flow

Create a message flow as shown in Figure 5-3. This message flow has, in addition to the previous example, a Filter node, a Compute node, and another MQOutput node. You should use the same queues set up for the previous example with the addition of a local queue for the false response from the Filter node. The ESQL code used for the Filter and Compute nodes can be very simple (refer to Figure 5-4 and Figure 5-5).

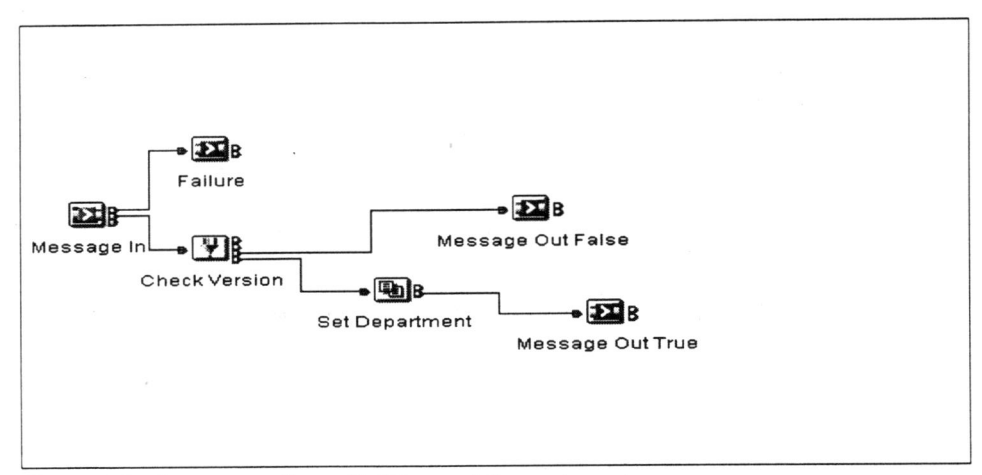

*Figure 5-3  A message flow with Filter and Compute nodes*

Chapter 5. WMQI operations on the z/OS platform    **93**

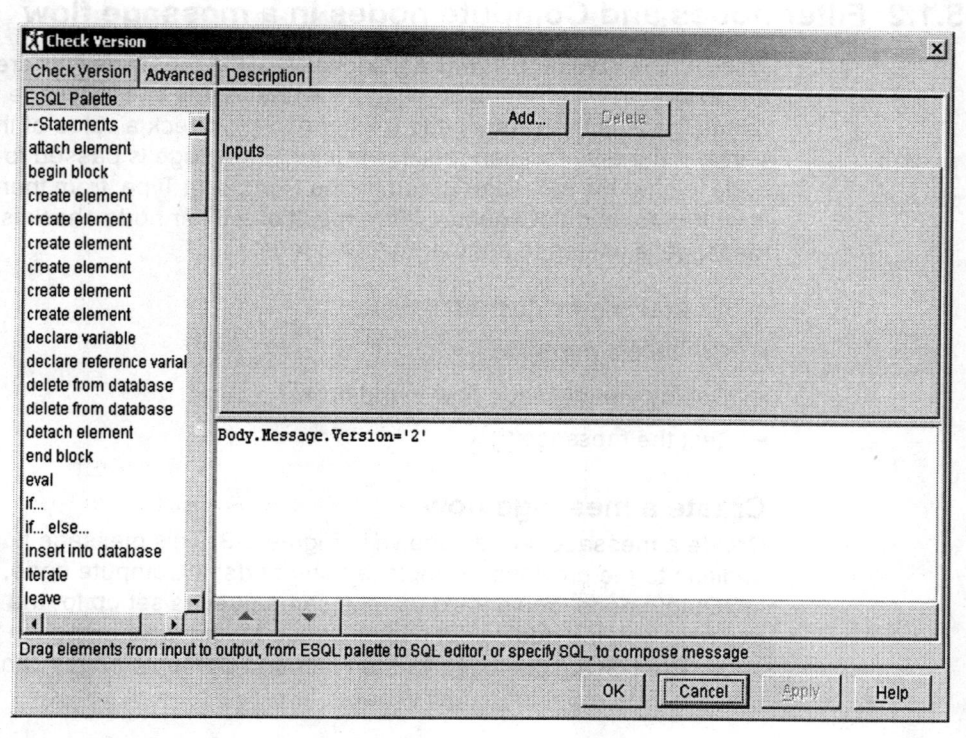

Figure 5-4  Sample ESQL code for Filter node property window

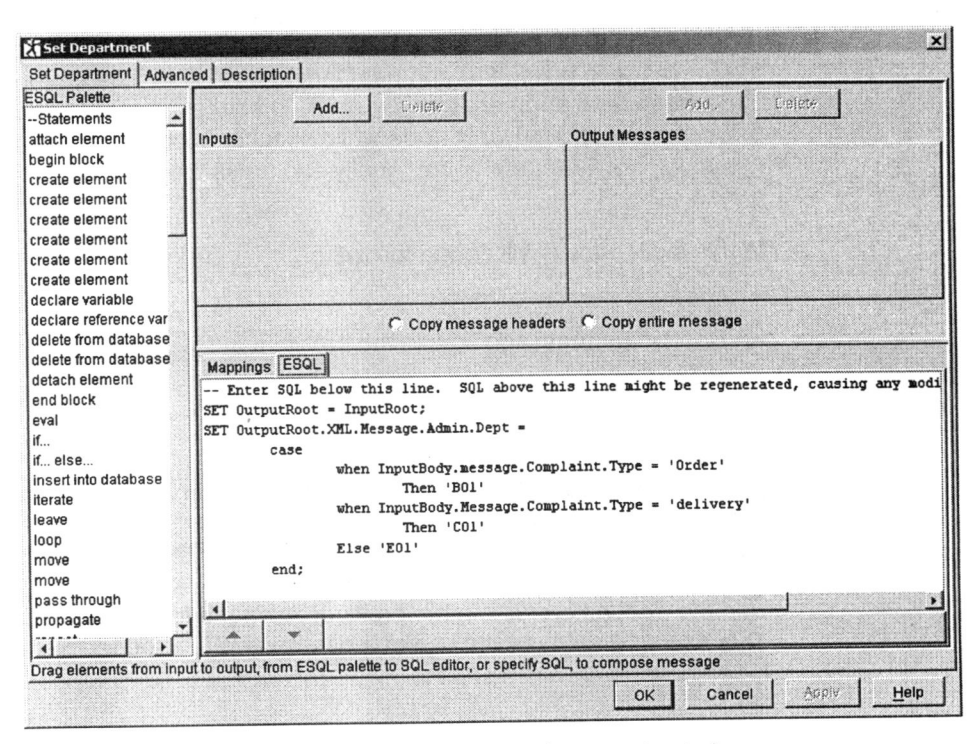

*Figure 5-5   Sample ESQL code for Compute node property window*

## Deploy the message flow

Use the instructions in "Deploy the message flow to the broker" on page 91 to deploy the message flow to the broker.

Other items for review are the Log tab and Operations tab to ensure that the broker domain is working normally.

## Test the message flow

Use the instruction from "Testing the message flow" on page 92 for details on testing the new message flow.

## 5.1.3 A simple database access example

This example is an extension of the exercise above and introduces some ESQL and database access from a WebSphere MQ Integrator Compute node. In this example, we read in a message from an input queue, pass this message to a Filter node to check the value of the field called Version. If false, the message, is written out to an MQSeries queue. If true, the message is passed to a Compute node to alter the message based on the Complaint Type field. Then the message is passed to another Compute node to add a Complaint ID to the message. Next, the message is passed to another Compute node to look up the manager of the department and augment the message. Then the message is passed back to the originator via an MQReply node while simultaneously being rewritten into a new message in a Compute node. Finally, the message is written out to an output queue.

In this example we will do the following:

- Create a message flow
- Deploy the message flow to the broker
- Test the message flow

## Create the message flow

Create a message flow as shown in Figure 5-6 on page 97. The enhancements to the message flow in the previous example are the addition of three Compute nodes and one MQReply node. Sample code for the Compute nodes is included in Figure 5-7 on page 98, Figure 5-8 on page 99, and Figure 5-9 on page 109. Use the queues created in the previous example to deploy the message flow. This example requires the use of a database. We used the SAMPLE database created when DB2 is installed.

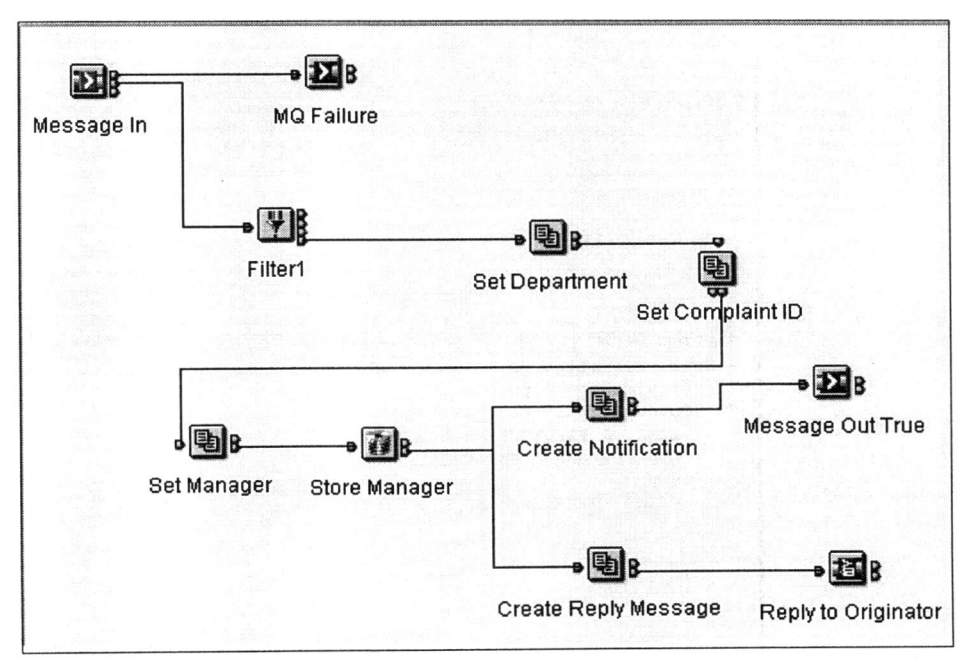

*Figure 5-6   Sample message flow of Database access*

*Example 5-1   Sample code for the Set ComplaintID Compute node*

```
SET OutputRoot=InputRoot;
declare FIN CHAR;
if ("InputBody"."Message"."Complaint"."Type" = 'Order') THEN
 SET FIN = 'O';
else
  if ("InputBody"."Message"."Complaint"."Type" = 'Delivery') THEN
    SET FIN = 'D';
  else
   SET FIN = 'X';
  end if;
end if;
Set "OutputRoot"."XML"."Message"."Admin"."ComplaintID" =
 'COM'||FIN;
```

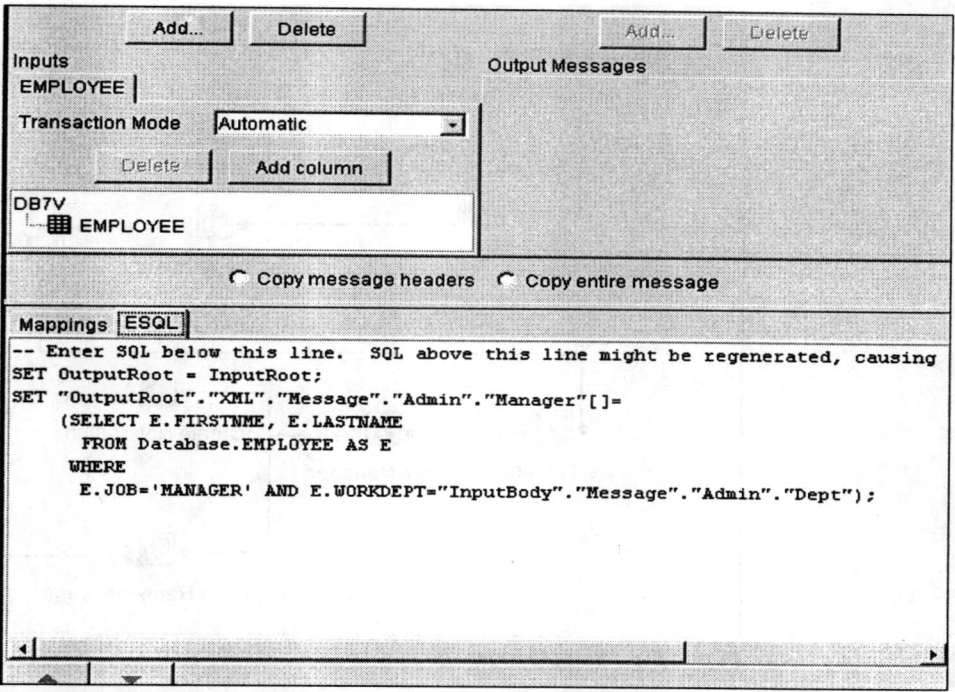

*Figure 5-7  Sample ESQL and DB2 code for the Set Manager Compute node*

*Example 5-2  ESQL code used for the Create Notification Compute node*

```
SET OutputRoot=InputRoot;
Set "OutputRoot"."XML"."Message"."Manager" =
    "InputBody"."Message"."Admin"."Manager"."FIRSTNME"||' '||
    "InputBody"."Message"."Admin"."Manager"."LASTNAME";
Set "OutputRoot"."XML"."Message"."Reference" =
    "InputRoot"."XML"."Message"."Admin"."ComplaintID";
Set "OutputRoot"."XML"."Message"."Text" = 'New Compliant Received';
```

*Example 5-3  ESQL code used for the Create Reply Message Compute node*

```
SET OutputRoot=InputRoot;
Set "OutputRoot"."XML"."Message"."Reply"."Text" = 'OK mate...';
```

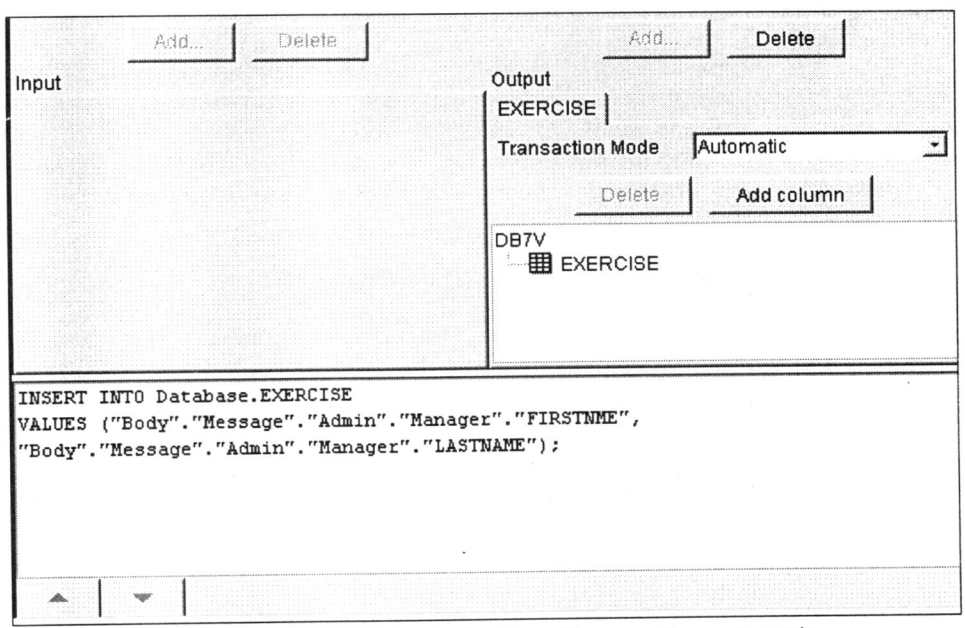

```
                Add...      Delete                          Add...      Delete
Input                                       Output
                                            EXERCISE
                                            Transaction Mode    Automatic         ▼
                                                         Delete      Add column
                                            DB7V
                                               ▦ EXERCISE

INSERT INTO Database.EXERCISE
VALUES ("Body"."Message"."Admin"."Manager"."FIRSTNME",
"Body"."Message"."Admin"."Manager"."LASTNAME");
```

*Figure 5-8   Sample ESQL and DB2 code for Store Manager Compute node*

**Note:** Consider the following if you use message flows with database nodes on z/OS:

► The database source name for the DB node (DB7V, in our case) refers to the DB2 LOCATION that corresponds to the DB2 SUBSYSTEM the flow is working with.

► When a node accessing a DB2 table is set to COMMIT, the source name (for example, DB7V) cannot be the same as that used in the other nodes. You should use mixed-case combinations (DB7V, db7V, Db7v, dB7V, etc.), if necessary, to keep sessions separated. It is advantageous to use mixed-case combinations if two database sessions (multiple threads) are desired.

► If the qualifier is not specified, the requested database object must exist associated to the creator that is the user ID of the broker started task.

### Deploy the message flow
Use the details from the above examples for deploying the message flow.

### Testing the message flow
Use the detail from the above examples for testing the message flow.

## 5.2 Common administrative tasks

Administration of the WebSphere MQ Integrator on z/OS consists mainly of proper installation and configuration (see Chapter 4, "Configuration of WMQI on z/OS and Windows platforms" on page 61) as well as periodic monitoring and adjusting the system to resolve a technical problem or achieve a performance gain. The areas we cover in this section are:

- Methods for executing console commands
- The most common commands and utilities

The information presented in this section is based on implementing tasks introduced in *WebSphere MQ Integrator Administration Guide*, SC34-5792, and *WebSphere MQ Integrator for z/OS Customization and Administration Guide*, SC34-5919.

### Stop and restart a component for command execution

On WMQI, the broker or User Name Server consists of a controller and a component. When the controller address space is started, the component is started automatically, although this behavior may change by modifying a parameter in the started task (changing 'AUTO' for 'MAN'). Some commands are used against the controller, and need to be executed when the component is *not* running. So, the component has to be stopped before the command is executed, and may be started after that.

Command to stop the component: `pc` or `stopcomponent`.

Command to start the component: `sc` or `startcomponent`.

If you do not stop the component, some commands, such as `changebroker`, produce an output like the following:

+(MQV3BRK) BIP8018E: Component running.

This means the command did not succeed because the component needs to be stopped.

> **Note:** If you get, as a result of the **changebroker** (or any other) command execution, an output like this:
>
> ```
> +(MQV3BRK) BIP8140E: Unable to find service userid ''
> ```
>
> review your customization process for the broker. You can check the content of the file ServiceUserId in the registry subdirectory of your component installation. If it is empty, a fast path to solve the problem is filling this file with the name of the broker's started task. Be careful to edit the file in such a way not to add an end-of-line character at the end. (For example, if the value you put in this file is MQV3BRK, the file size displayed by the **ls -l** command should be 7).

## Using OMVS or z/OS console commands for administration

Some of the WebSphere MQ Integrator for z/OS commands can be run in the OMVS from a TSO session, and others should run as a batch job, JCL, because they need access to the same environment as the broker, or User Name Server.

Commands that can be issued from the TSO OMVS are:

- mqsideletebroker
- mqsicreatebroker
- mqsicreateusernameserver
- mqsideleteusernameserver

For example:

```
mqsicreatebroker <broker name> -c <Component directory> -q <Queue Manager Name>
```

You operate the broker or User Name Server using the z/OS **START, STOP,** and **MODIFY** commands. You can issue commands, and get responses back from:

- The z/OS operator console
- The TSO CONSOLE facility
- The CONSOLE interface from REXX
- Products such as SDSF
- From z/OS automation products such as NetView

For example:

```
F MQV3BRK,CB
```

If you need to issue commands with mixed-case input, you can do so on z/OS using the REXX console interface, products such as SDSF, and NetView.

You can also submit commands using JCLs (batch jobs). For example:

```
//MI01CMD JOB MSGCLASS=H
// COMMAND 'f MQV3BRK, ct t=yes,e='default',l=debug,f='lowmfl''
//STEP1 EXEC PGM=IEFBR14
```

The remainder of this section discusses details for invoking the most common native MVS commands run on the z/OS.

## Start and stop WMQI brokers or User Name Servers

Start the broker or User Name Server using the `MVS START (S)` command. If you want to pass information to the broker or User Name Server while it is running, use the `MVS MODIFY (F)` command. For example:

- To start a broker use:

   `S MQV3BRK`

- To stop a broker use:

   `F MQV3BRK,stop`

- To change the trace characteristics of a broker, use:

   `F MQV3BRK,ct`

## Listing attributes of WMQI components

To list the execution groups, use the `list` command as follows:

`F <broker>,list.`

An example of this command is:

`F MQV3BRK,LIST`

This command produces output similar to the following:

```
F MQ09BRK,L
+(MQ09BRK) BIP8130I: EXECUTION GROUP: EFLOWTEST - 33751067
+(MQ09BRK) BIP8071I: SUCCESSFUL COMMAND COMPLETION
```

To list execution group details, use the list command as follows:

`F <broker>,list E='<execution group>'`

or

`F <broker>,L E=<EXECUTIONGROUP>`

An example of these commands is:

**F MQV3BRK,L E=FONE2ONE**

This command produces the following output:

```
F MQ09BRK,L E=FONE2ONE
+(MQ09BRK) BIP8131II: MESSAGEFLOW: myflow
+(MQ09BRK) BIP8071I: SUCCESSFUL COMMAND COMPLETION
```

### Resetting the broker

You might need to reset a broker to its initial state after customizing for the first time for situations where you have a corrupt database or you want to rededicate the broker to production service after using it for testing.

The job BIPJRSTC in the component PDSE resets the broker to the state it was after customizing for the first time and before any execution groups have been deployed. Note that this job deletes all rows in the DB2 tables associated with the broker. You lose all publish or subscriptions that your users have requested. Stop the broker before submitting the job. A summary of the effects of job BIPJRSTC are listed below:

- Deletes any contents of locks, log and errors directories.
- Resets the ENVFILE and DSNAOINI to its state after initial creation and customization: you will lose any changes you made to these files.
- Deletes all rows from the broker tables based on the brokerUID key. This includes any Publish/Subscribe subscriptions the applications might have made.
- Deletes all messages from the MQSeries queues.
- Resets internal files to their state after initial creation and customization. The output of this job is stored in ComponentDirectory/output/rstclog, Componentdirectory/output/rstcerr, and in the job output.

After submitting BIPJRSTC, you have to redeploy any flows and applications will have to resubmit their Publish/Subscribe requests.

### Deleting a broker

If you have to delete a broker, it is very important that you follow the steps in the order given. This ensures that you maintain network integrity.

To delete a broker, first use the Control Center to perform the following:

- Remove the broker from the configuration repository by deleting it from the Control Center Topology view.

- Deploy the complete configuration(all types) from the File menu on the Topology view. This removes the broker configuration data from the configuration repository.
- Check that the deployment has been successful (use the Log view). You have to expect a message saying the Broker has been succesfully removed from the Configuration Repository. For more information on the tasks involved through the Control Center, refer to *WebSphere MQ Integrator Using the Control Center*.
- On z/OS, stop the broker by stopping the started task.
- Submit the following delete jobs in your component PDSE to delete MQSeries and DB2 definitions:

| Delete Jobs | Description |
| --- | --- |
| BIP#MQ01 | Delete MQSeries broker queues and channels |
| BIP#DB01 | Drop the broker DB2 database |

- Invoke the **mqsideletebroker** command in your <INSTPATH>/bin directory. This command deletes directories and files in your component directory. The root directory is not deleted but will be empty. The command syntax is:

mqsideletebroker <brokername> -c <ComponentDirectory>

for example:

mqsideletebroker MQV3BRK -c /var/wmqi/MQV3BRK

- Delete all members from the component PDSE.

## Adding a User Name Server to a broker

If you want to use Publish/Subscribe topic-based security, you need to tell which Queue Manager the broker is to use. Use the **changebroker** command on MVS as follows. Do not forget to stop the broker's component before you execute the **changebroker** command. Restart the broker afterwards:

F <broker>,PC
F <broker>,CB S='<User Name Server Queue manager>'
F <broker>,SC

For example:

F MQV3BRK,PC
F MQV3BRK,CB S='MQV3'
F MQV3BRK,SC

> **Note:** To remove a User Name Server from a broker, follow the syntax for adding a UNS and substitute S=''.

For a complete explanation of all native MVS commands, refer to Chapter 5, "Console commands" in the *WebSphere MQ Integrator for z/OS Customization and Administration Guide,* SC34-5919.

## Reload New Era of Networks rules and formats

Use the command `reload` instead of the deprecated version `nrfreload` to force the broker to reaccess the New Era of Networks database. You must use this command if you make any changes to the database containing your new Era of Networks rules and formats definitions. You must issue this command for each broker that needs access to this database.

For example:

`F MQV3BRK,reload b=yes`

The deprecated version of the command, `nrfreload`, relates only to the New Era of Networks functionality provided by the NeonRules and NeonFormatter nodes, and the NEON domain message parser. It does not work with the New Era of Networks functionality provided by the NEONRulesEvaluation, NEONMap, and NEONTransform nodes, and the new NNSYMSG domain message parser.

Refer to Chapter 5 "Console Commands" in the *WebSphere MQ Integrator for z/OS Customization and Administration Guide* for complete details on the `reload` command.

## Using WMQI utility jobs

Utility jobs are provided with WebSphere MQ Integrator for z/OS to help perform other administrative tasks. These utilities can be invoked on MVS as well as in OMVS. Table 5-1 lists the utility jobs and the equivalent commands in OMVS.

*Table 5-1  Summary of WMQI utilities*

| JCL Name | Description | Command on OMVS |
|---|---|---|
| BIPJCMPS | Remove MQSeries Pub/Sub broker | `mqsiclearmqpubsub` |
| BIPJJMPS | Joins the WMQI broker to MQSeries Pub/Sub broker | `mqsijoinmqpubsub` |
| BIPJLMPS | Lists Pub/Sub neighbor broker | `mqsilistmqpubsub` |

| JCL Name | Description | Command on OMVS |
|---|---|---|
| BIPJLOG | Reads the WMQI trace and formats it to a text file | `mqsireadlog`<br>`mqsiformatlog` |
| BIPJRDMP | Generates XML file of WMQI unformatted dump | `mqsireaddump` |
| BIPJRSTC | Resets broker to a state the broker was in after creation | |

Follow these steps:

- Modify the parameters for the utilities according to the command descriptions in the *WebSphere MQ Integrator Administration Guide*.
- Submit the job on WebSphere MQ Integrator for z/OS.
- Check the job output and create files to ensure the job executed successfully.

Refer to the *WebSphere MQ Integrator Administration Guide* for further details.

## 5.3 Problem determination techniques

When you perform operations on the broker domain, problems may occur. These issues may range from simple to complex. This section discusses the most common technical issues that could occur and how to proceed to diagnose and resolve each. We discuss:

- Sources for proper problem determination
- Most common problems or errors on z/OS
- Deployment check lists

The information discussed in this section is based on implementation of tasks presented in *WebSphere MQ Integrator Problem Determination Guide* and *WebSphere MQ Integrator Using the Control Center*. Another important source of information is SupportPac IH01 - WebSphere MQ Integrator Problem Determination.

### 5.3.1 Sources for proper problem determination

Knowing where to look is as important as how to resolve a problem. When you start the broker on z/OS, the messages in the system log and the display of specific address spaces for WebSphere MQ Integrator indicate if the startup is complete. To decide if the startup is complete do the following:

- Check the messages in the system log.
- Display the address spaces.

The infrastructure main program bipimain is the first process in every address space. It starts either dipservice, bipbroker, DataflowEngine or bipuns as the second process in the same address space. For each execution group, an additional address space is started.

Below are resources used to capture problems or tools for isolating problems that happen in the course of operating the broker domain.

## Finding files on WMQI for z/OS

A broker or User Name Server puts files into the HFS. If you do not know where the files are for the broker, look at the started task procedure or job output and locate COHFS. This is set to a value such as /u/wmqi/MQV3BRK.

You should be careful to access the HFS on the correct system. If the HFS is not shared, there could directories with the same name on different MVS images. To be sure, you should log on to the system where the broker is running and access the file system. You can use the TSO `ISHell` command, or go into OMVS itself. Go to the directory specified and select the output directory. In this directory you find the following files: joberr, jobout, readlogerr, readlogout stderr, stdout, traceodbc.

Other files are stored in the home directory of the user ID of the started task. The MVS command `D A, jobname` displays the user ID of the job. The directory of the user ID is typically /u/userid but you should check with your systems programmer. or issue the TSO command `LU userid OMVS`. If you are authorized, this command displays text including the HOME statement. You should log on to the z/OS system where the started task is running when accessing the files, because the HFS might not be shared, and so you might use the wrong files if you are on a different z/OS.

## Message flow debugger utility

The Control Center offers a very useful utility for debugging complex message flows. This is a powerful problem determination tool when applying break points in strategic locations within the message flow. Refer to Appendix C, "Using the Control Center Debugger" on page 347 for more information.

## Dump and abend files

Dump files are created when a major exception occurs during the running of an application.

You should check for dumps and other diagnostic information. Information is stored in the following places:

- In the home directory of the started user ID. To display this information, an authorized user can issue the TSO command:

  `LU id OMVS`

- In the component directory in the /output subdirectory, for example, look for a broker called MQV3BRK in /var/wmqi/MQV3BRK/output.

When processes end abnormally, an abend file will be automatically created. An entry is made in the syslog. If there is more data to be written out than is appropriate for the log, a new file is created to contain it, and the log entry tells you the file name. The new file is called filename.abend in the /component_HFS/log directory. You may need to send the file to your IBM support center for analysis.

## MQSeries logs and events

WebSphere MQ Integrator components depend on MQSeries resources in many ways. You can learn some valuable information from the MQSeries logs and events.

All WebSphere MQ Integrator messages can be identified by the prefix BIP followed by a number string of four additional characters, which are a unique message identifier. *WebSphere MQ Integrator Messages* manual contains a detailed description of every message generated by WebSphere MQ Integrator, and provides information about any action required by you in response to each message. The destination of the messages for z/OS is either the system log file or the operator console, if those messages require some operator interaction. Messages issued by the command utilities can be found in the appropriate job log. Customization commands send messages to the OMVS session where they have been issued.

## Database logs and ODBC tracing

Database products used by WebSphere MQ Integrator can be a good source of information when performing problem determination for database issues. DB2 has a number of facilities that assist with problem diagnosis and recovery.

ODBC tracing can be activated in several ways. On z/OS, edit the /component_HFS/dsnaoini file to initiate an application trace for ODBC activity (APPLTRACE=1). You can use the db2trace utility to produce a formatted ODBC trace.

### Automation and recovery scenarios

You need to consider what you do in the event of operational problems. The following list details what you can do if, for example, a broker, a User Name Server, or an associated product including MQSeries, DB2, and OS/390 is not available.

- Use NetView or an equivalent product to automate starting the WebSphere MQ Integrator prerequisite products. For example, you can catch the MQSeries message notifying that the Queue Manager is available, and start the WebSphere MQ Integrator tasks.

- Use and MVS ARM facilities. Change the mqsicompcif file to activate ARM support and recustomize.

## 5.3.2 Most commons problems or errors

In this section we present some common problems you might encounter.

### Configuration Manager inaccessible from Control Center

This problem may occur if the information in the Configuration Manager is incorrect (Figure 5-9) or the Configuration Manager cannot access the MQSeries Java Bindings classes package com.ibm.mq.

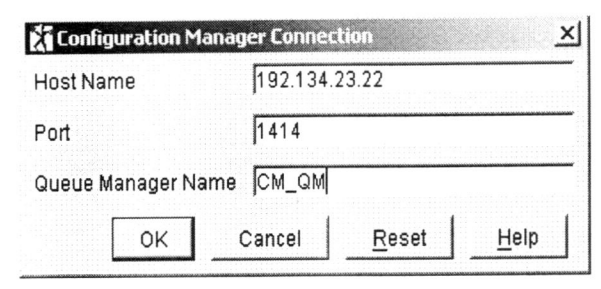

*Figure 5-9 Configuration Manager connection window*

To resolve, ensure that the information in the window is correct or stop the Configuration Manager, update your CLASSPATH variable to insert the MQSeries Java Bindings classes package path before the VisualAge for Java package path, and restart the Configuration Manager.

### The Control Center does not show z/OS or UNIX users

The likely cause is that the Configuration Manager has not registered with the User Name Server. To correct this issue do the following:

- Stop the Configuration Manager using the command **mqsistop configmgr**.

- Issue the command `mqsichangeconfigmgr` setting the -s to the correct User Name Server Queue Manager value.
- Restart the Configuration Manager using the command `mqsistart configmgr`.
- Check that the User Name Server is running.
- Check that all queues and channels between the Configuration Manager and the User Name Server have been created and are currently running.
- Restart the Control Center to refresh the displayed lists of users.

**Note:** On z/OS, if the User Name Server is running, and you have the above set correctly, but you are still not seeing z/OS users listed on the Control Center Topics tab, you should check that the z/OS users all have OMVS segments defined. They are not listed by the User Name Server if they do not.

### The Configuration Manager does not subscribe with a broker

Occasionally, when deploying changes to a broker, you may find a message in the WMQI log in the Control Center saying that the Configuration Manager is not able to subscribe with a broker for internal operations, meaning that the Operations Panel in the Control Center will not be up to date.

The Configuration Manager receives messages from the broker, for updating the operations panel, in a Pub/Sub fashion. If you do not have topic-based security, you will not encounter this problem.

But if you have set a broker to add a UNS, the broker might not be communicating with the UNS properly to get the user's information. Check that:

- The broker is provided with the correct information about the name of the User Name Server Queue Manager (see "Adding a User Name Server to a broker" on page 104).
- The service user ID for the Configuration Manager is defined in the system the UNS is running on, and it has an OMVS segment, so it is available for the UNS. Also check that this user ID belongs to the group MKBRKRS, which has special authority for WMQI internal subscriptions.

### Diagnostic messages when the broker fails to start on z/OS

Messages ICH4081E or BIP2048E can be generated when the broker fails to start. Diagnostic message ICH4081E is generated when the started task ID is not authorized to read, write, or execute files in a directory. The started task ID under which the broker runs needs to be in a RACF or UNIX System Services group that has rwx permissions on the broker directory. If the permissions are not set correctly, you get an error message written to the SDSF syslog.

Message BIP2048E indicates a database access error and usually issues a SQL State 58004. The SQL State value of 58004 reveals that a system error occurred. This might be due to a DB2 authorization problem. The ID under which the broker runs (the started task ID) needs the following DB2 authorizations to be granted:

- DELETE, INSERT, SELECT and UPDATE authorization on the broker tables
- EXECUTE authorization on plan DSNACLI
- SELECT authorization on table SYSIBM.SYSSYNONYMS
- SELECT authorization on table SYSIBM.SYSTABLES
- SELECT authorization on table SYSIBM.SYSDATABASE

If ODBC tracing is turned on you can get more details from the traceodbc file for the broker. To resolve, run batch job BIP$DB05 to grant the necessary authorizations on the broker tables. Other authorizations must be performed manually, for example using a SPUFI script.

### Unable to stop the broker after deleting broker database

The `mqsideletebroker` command checks for the broker database tables and raises this error because the database is not there.

You can work around this problem by creating a dummy database with the same name as the database you deleted. You must also recreate the ODBC connection. Reissue `mqsideletebroker`, and then delete the dummy database.

### Error message BIP2322E accessing DB2 on z/OS

This error message will occur when you are using a message flow in which a Database node, a Compute node, or a Filter node attempts to access a table on a DB2 data-sharing group other than the one the broker is using. The error message reads:

```
BIP2322E: DATABASE ERROR: SQL STATE '51002'; NATIVE ERROR CODE '-805'
```

This happens when the DSNACLI plan has not been bound in the correct way. See the section on DB2 planning in the *WebSphere MQ Integrator for z/OS Customization and Administration Guide*, and rebind following the instructions given there.

### Error message SQL1040N from DB2

The DB2 message:

```
"SQL1040N the maximum number of applications is already connected to the
database. SQLSTATE=57030"
```

indicates that the value of the DB2 database configuration parameter maxappls has been reached. DB2 has rejected the attempt to connect.

If this database is one of the defined broker databases, implying a broker thread connection request has failed, the broker is probably not functioning correctly.

To recover from this situation:

- Stop all brokers that connect to the affected database.
- Increase the value of the maxappls configuration parameter.

> **Note:** It is recommended that you determine the number of database connections required by a broker for capacity and resource planning purposes. On DB2, the default is to limit the number of concurrent connections to a database to the value of the maxappls configuration parameter. The default for maxappls is 40.
>
> The connection requirements for a single message broker are:
>
> - Five connections required by internal broker threads.
> - One connection required for each Publish/Subscribe neighbor.
> - One required for each message flow thread that contains a publication node.
> - One required for each message flow thread that parses MRM messages.
> - One required for each database access node to a separate ODBC data source name for each message flow thread (that is, if the same DSN is used by a different node, the same connection is used).
> - If you are using SCADA nodes with MQSeries Everyplace, add a further number depending on whether or not thread pooling is being used.

- Restart the DB2 database.

## z/OS broker startup fails with a device allocation error

A likely cause of this problem is that you do not have the correct permissions set on the component HFS, for the started task ID. Check the syslog; if the problem is caused by having incorrect permissions set for the started task ID, you often see a RACF authorization failure message (ICH408I). You can use this information to correct the permissions and then reissue the started broker request. This type of message is produced if the user issuing the command does not have the correct HFS permissions for the HFS component.

Another possible reason for authorization failures is inconsistencies in the RACF definitions for a user ID in the MVS image and the OMVS segment. You should also check with your system administrator that the RACF ID used on MVS has a corresponding OMVS image created.

## 5.3.3 Checklist for deployment problems

Here is a checklist to help you make smooth the deployment of your flows:

- Make sure the remote Queue Manager is running.
- Make sure the channels are running.
- Display the channel status to see if the number of messages sent increases.
- Check the channel from the remote end (Ping).
- Check that the channels are connected to the right Queue Manager.
- Check the Queue Manager name.
- Determine whether the channel is a cluster channel.
- Use the `mqsilist` command to check that the deployment was successful.

## 5.3.4 Using tracing to assist with problem determination

WebSphere MQ Integrator always records a minimum level of trace activity in the broker domain. You can choose to activate further traces of the major product components such as the Configuration Manager, the broker, or User Name Server. You can also trace execution groups and message flows you define in a broker. This section discusses the following topics.

- Displaying the status of a trace
- Collecting a user execution group trace

### Displaying the status of a trace

To display the status of a trace, we used the `reporttrace` command as follows:

```
F MQV3BRK,RT T=YES,E='FONE2ONE',F='MFFONE2ONE'
```

The E parameter specifies the label of the execution group for which a report is required. The F parameter specifies the label of the message flow for which a report is required.

This command produces the following results:

```
+BIP8098I MQV3BRK Trace level:none,mode:safe,size:4096 KB.
+BIP8071I MQV3BRK Successfully command completion.
```

> **Note:** Both names are case sensitive and you must include the names in single quotes if they contain mixed-case characters.

## Collecting a user execution group trace

To collect a user execution group trace, use the `collect trace` command as follows:

`F <broker>,ct u=YES,L=debug,E='default'`

When you have captured your trace, turn the trace off with:

`F <broker>,ct,u=YES,L=none,E='default'`

To format your trace:

- Edit your component PDSE and create a new member, for example EGTRACE. Copy in BIPJLOG.
- Search for `-t -b agent` and change it to `-u -e default`, where `default` is the name of your execution group.
- Search for format.log. This is where the output file is stored. Change the name if you want to have trace-specific names.

**Note:** If collecting a service execution group trace, follow the instruction above for user execution group tracing, substituting `-u` for `-t`.

# 6

# Overview of New Era of Networks support in WebSphere MQ Integrator

In this chapter, we describe the history of New Era of Networks (NEON) support in the MQSeries Integrator and WebSphere MQ Integrator products. We explain how the architecture enables WebSphere MQ Integrator functionality to be exploited with messages defined using the New Era of Networks graphical user interface (GUI).

The WebSphere MQ Integrator product is very different from MQSeries Integrator V1.11. In this chapter we discuss the main differences and new features in the New Era of Networks product code that customer should be aware of. Finally we present some of the issues that should be taken into consideration when planning to upgrade.

## 6.1 History of New Era of Networks support

In April 1999 IBM introduced MQSeries Integrator V1.0 as an additional part of its business integration family, complementing MQSeries and MQSeries Workflow, followed by MQSeries Integrator V1.1 two months later in June 1999.

The first versions of the product were fully compatible to NeoNet, a product developed by New Era of Networks, labeled by IBM with a different brand: MQSeries Integrator.

The architecture of the early V1.x products is completely different from the current V2.x products. MQSeries Integrator V1.x consists of the following development and runtime components (Figure 6-1).

- Formatter GUI
- Rules GUI
- Database (storing meta-data)
- Rules Daemon (also called Rules Engine).

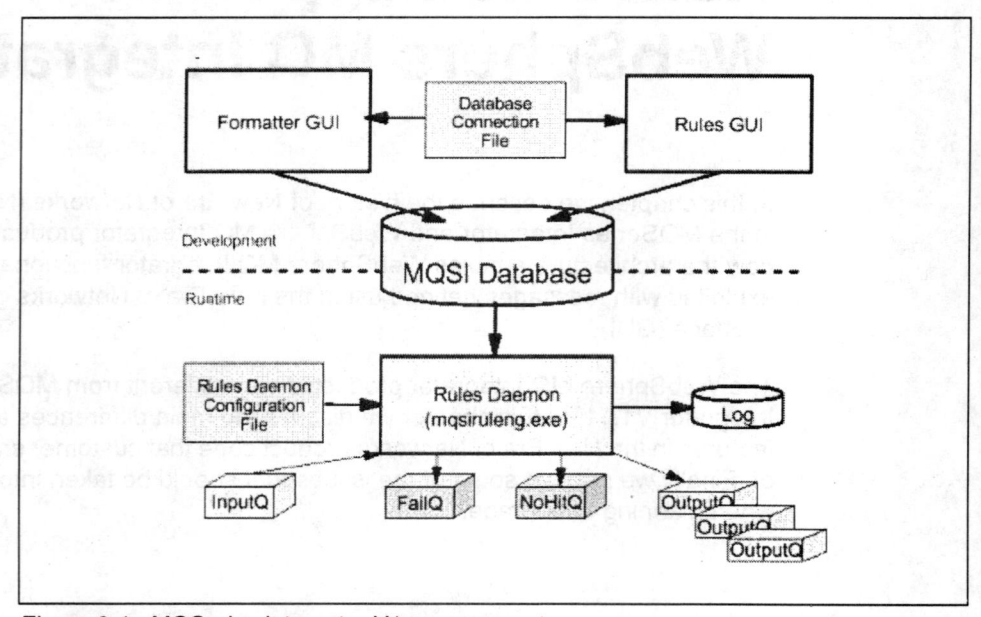

*Figure 6-1  MQSeries Integrator V1.x components*

MQSeries Integrator V2.x implements significant improvements. But the early versions did not offer a support for tagged and delimited messages, for example SWIFT, Siebel, EDI, SAP. These formats, however, were supported by using New Era of Networks and the integration of this product with MQSeries Integrator implements this functionality.

Tagged and delimited messages are now supported with WebSphere MQ Integrator. However, New Era of Networks is still supported for compatibility reasons.

Whereas IBM is carrying on with its own MQSeries Integrator architecture (now called WebSphere MQ Integrator), New Era of Networks proceeds with the development of e-Biz Integrator, which is the current product brand. However, the improvements to this product are continuously included with MQSeries Integrator and WebSphere MQ Integrator.

Table 6-1 gives a summary of the supported New Era of Networks versions with MQSeries Integrator/WebSphere MQ Integrator. The following sections give a brief overview of the enhancements that came with the versions.

*Table 6-1  MQSeries Integrator - NEON Compatibility Matrix*

| MQSeries Integrator/ WebSphere MQ Integrator | New Era of Networks |
| --- | --- |
| MQSeries Integrator V1.0 | New Era of Networks V4.0.1 |
| MQSeries Integrator V1.1, V2.0, V2.0.1 | New Era of Networks V4.1.1 |
| MQSeries Integrator V2.0.2 | New Era of Networks V5.2 |
| WebSphere MQ Integrator | New Era of Networks V5.6 |

## 6.2  WebSphere MQ Integrator with New Era of Networks

The integration of New Era of Networks support into the MQSeries Integrator product and later into WebSphere MQ Integrator was greatly improved with Version 2.02. Previously the fields and data in a New Era of Networks message were only visible to the New Era of Networks nodes and much of the functionality and power of MQSeries Integrator was unavailable.

Initial releases of MQSeries Integrator were delivered with four message domains: CWF, XML, BLOB and NEON. The NEON domain was restricted to a limited set of functionality. Customers using New Era of Networks messages could not exploit many of the nodes available to build message flows.

In recent releases, the NEONMSG domain has been introduced and much greater functionality is made available to it. The new domain enables much easier migration and opens up much more functionality to customers who have invested in MQSeries Integrator V1.1.

Customers can now use all the standard features in a message flow to manipulate messages that have been defined in the New Era of Networks GUI using the NEONMSG domain. Furthermore, they can use the WebSphere MQ Integrator graphical interface to build their flows and manipulate their messages using the standard nodes delivered with the product. Additionally Java or C built custom nodes can be used.

Figure 6-2 details the connections between the various components of WebSphere MQ Integrator to the New Era of Networks database of rules and formats.

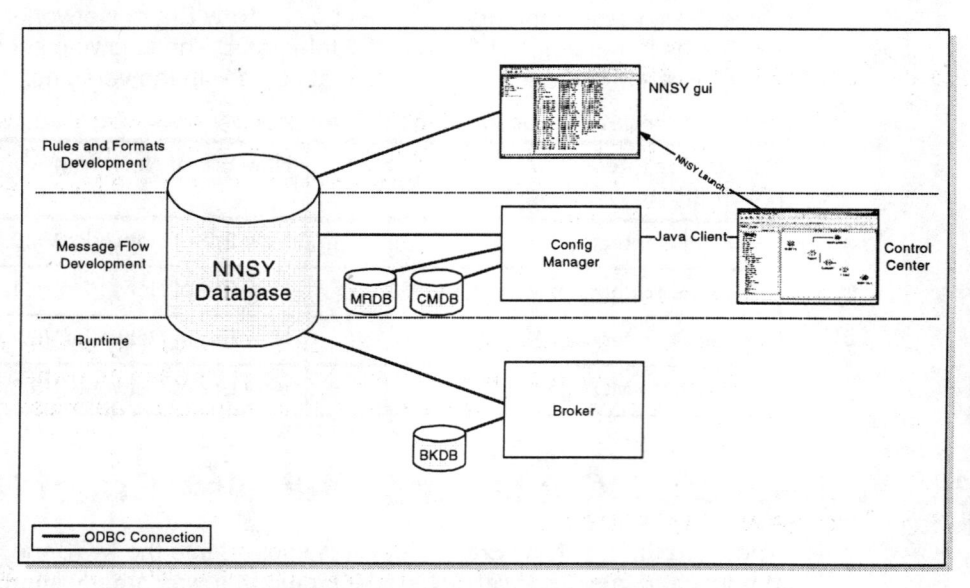

*Figure 6-2 New Era of Networks architecture in WebSphere MQ Integrator*

## 6.3 New Era of Networks new features

When you migrate from MQSeries Integrator V1.11 to WebSphere MQ Integrator V2.1, you jump from Version 4.1.1 to Version 5.6 of the New Era of Networks code. There is a huge list of new features and differences. This section deals with features that will be useful or you should be aware of when migrating and some of the significant implementation changes.

## 6.3.1 UNIX Systems Services

WebSphere MQ Integrator is installed in the UNIX Systems Services part of z/OS. Many of the support functions are therefore carried out as UNIX type functions, using shell programs with environment variables rather than by JCL submitted to MVS as would have been done with V1.11.

NNFie, NNRie, apitest, msgtest, ruletest and the consistency checker all run as UNIX System Services commands or from the developer workstation. There is no JCL provided with the product to run these tasks.

## 6.3.2 New parameter file

The MQSIRuleng parameter file is replaced by the nnsyreg.dat file with a different format. UNIX System Services environment variables point the broker to the location of this file.

## 6.3.3 The new Rules GUI

The GUI for defining and changing rules now uses the Microsoft Management Console (MMC) and looks completely different from the previous version. The look and feel is very similar to other products that use the MMC, for example MQSeries Explorer.

## 6.3.4 Format permissions

Formats now have permissions as well as rules. This may create problems initially when migrating, when all imported formats become owned by the user that ran the import utility. There is a utility to manipulate permissions, called PermUtil.

## 6.3.5 The new map function

A new folder in the format GUI is Maps. This folder allows you to define the mappings between input fields and output fields in map objects instead of in the output formats. By separating the field mapping into a separate object you can now reuse an output format for many input formats. The map function also decouples transformations from rules.

### 6.3.6 Binary literals

Literals can now be binary values or string. The default when creating a literal is binary. Because messages are sent across a channel from an ASCII platform to z/OS, you should ensure that literals that are meant to be string values are defined as such, and that the sender channel from the workstation specifies CONVERT(YES). Otherwise, message parsing will always fail.

### 6.3.7 NNFie -p option

Particularly for z/OS, the -p option on the NNFie import utility instructs it to import literals as strings. If you do not use this option with your import statement, your literals will be imported with the incorrect values and will need to be amended.

### 6.3.8 Reload Rules and Formats

You have to execute a new `F <brokername>,reload` command, if you wish the broker to clear its cache of rules and formats.

## 6.4 Migration planning

The migration process from MQSeries Integrator V1.11 to WebSphere MQ Integrator V2.1 is described in Chapter 8, "Migrating New Era of Networks Rules and Formats from MQSeries Integrator Version 1.11" on page 151. Initial experience indicates that the process is very straightforward and requires no change to existing applications. However with all major system changes to business critical applications, a cautious phased approach with comprehensive planning and testing is recommended.

Before starting migration, an organization should give additional consideration to the following:

- Software versions and maintenance level requirements, detailed in *WebSphere MQ Integrator Introduction and Planning*, GC34-5599.
- MQSeries Integrator V1.11 and WebSphere MQ Integrator are architecturally very different. At an early stage become familiar with the WebSphere MQ Integrator architecture and use.
- The Configuration Manager runs on Windows NT and requires a DB2 database on Windows NT. Additional hardware and skills may be required to support this.
- If you use New Era of Networks user exits in your formats, they will need to be recompiled. They are usually written in C and compiled on z/OS. You may need to plan to make sure these skills are available. Make yourself familiar

with SupportPac ID11 available from
`http://www.software.ibm.com/ts/mqseries/txppacs`.

- WebSphere MQ Integrator for z/OS is not supplied with PUTDATA and GETDATA programs. These were programs that put and got test data to and from queues. There are other, more useful utilities available, but you should carefully plan your testing strategy. Have a look at NNPutmsg and NNGetmsg utilities provided in $NNSY_ROOT/bin directory.

# 7

# Configuring New Era of Networks Support

In this chapter, we describe the steps to configure the New Era of Networks support to WebSphere MQ Integrator Version 2.1 on z/OS. This support is required by customers using MQSeries Integrator Version 1.1 wishing to migrate to the new version on z/OS. It will also be required by customers using more recent versions of MQSeries Integrator who have made use of New Era of Networks support.

We describe configuration of the three main WebSphere MQ Integrator components: the broker, Configuration Manager and the workstation running the Control Center and Rules and Formats GUI. We assume that the components are already installed and working and deal with the changes needed to implement the New Era of Networks functionality. The Configuration Manager and Control Center are dealt with as if running on separate platforms, which is the recommended approach although not a limitation.

In this chapter, we assume that you are familiar with the Control Center and building and deploying simple message flows.

The configuration steps are described in detail in *New Era of Networks Rules and Formatter Support for WebSphere MQ Integrator Systems Management Guide,* SC34-6083 and *Customizing and Administration Guide,* SC34-5919.

## 7.1 Broker configuration

The configuration process combines UNIX System Services tasks, such as running scripts and configuring environments, running batch JCL in native MVS and configuring the Windows environment. There are a number of steps that must be followed.

First you must ensure the broker was customized to include New Era of Networks support. If it wasn't it should be recustomized to build the appropriate environment.

The next step is to build the Rules and Formats database. To do this, you must amend configuration files in UNIX System Services, which are then used by scripts to build the correct JCL for your installation. You will need to review this JCL with your DB2 administrator to make sure it meets your installation standards before running them on native MVS.

Having built the Rules and Formats database you must build the configuration file used by the broker and other UNIX System Services utilities (NNFie, NNRie, apitest) to access it. The environment then needs to be modified so that the configuration file can be found. Getting the environment configured correctly is a very important step.

Once you have completed the broker configuration, you should continue with the workstation and Configuration Manager and build a simple flow to verify the New Era of Networks support and functionality.

### 7.1.1 Customizing the broker for New Era of Networks support

When you build your z/OS broker you must include New Era of Networks support. To do this you should add values described in Table 7-1 in the customization file mqsicompcif. When you run the **mqsicustomize** command this file is processed and amongst other thing produces an ENVFILE file. Do not directly edit ENVFILE. Instead amend the mqsicompcif file and rerun the **mqsicustomize** command.

> **Note:** Running **mqsicustomize** will rebuild your configuration JCL. If you have added job cards or directly edited it you may need to reapply your changes.

*Table 7-1  New Era of Networks Settings in mqsicompcif*

| Attribute | Value | Example |
|---|---|---|
| PATH | Append the NNSY bin directory nnsy/bin | :/usr/lpp/wmqi/nnsy/bin |

| Attribute | Value | Example |
|---|---|---|
| LIBPATH | Append the NNSY lib directory and the NNSY MIF lib directory | :/usr/lpp/wmqi/nnsy/lib:/usr/lpp/wmqi/nnsy/MIF/lib |
| LILPATH | Should include the NNSY MIF lib directory which contains lil files | /usr/lpp/mqi/nnsy/MIF/lib |
| NNSY_CATALOGUES | This is the path to the NNSY message catalog files | /usr/lpp/wmqi/nnsy/NNSY Catalogues |
| NN_CONFIG_FILE_PATH | This should be the path where you will keep the nnsyreg.dat file. | /usr/lpp/wmqi/nnsy |
| NNSY_ROOT | This is the root path where the NNSY files and directories were installed | /usr/lpp/wmqi/nnsy |

**Note:** The last three NN entries in Table 7-1 should be placed between the [ENVIRONMENTBEGIN] and [ENVIRONMENTEND] tags and should not have quotes around them.

If you are using shared HFS, do not place the nnsyreg.dat file in the $NNSY_ROOT directory. Put it into the component directory instead and specify NN_CONFIG_FILE_PATH accordingly.

### NNSY console messages

Copy the UNIX System Services file NEONMIF20.cat from $NNSY_ROOT/MIF/messages to the CONSOLE_NLSPATH path defined in mqsicompcif, which in our example was /usr/lpp/wmqi/messages/En_US.

## 7.1.2 Building the Rules and Formats database

Follow the steps described in Chapter 2 of *New Era of Networks Rules and Formatter Support for WebSphere MQ Integrator Systems Management Guide*, SC34-6083. After you successfully run the JCL, your database will have been built.

> **Note:** If you are migrating from DB2 UDB running on a distributed platform to DB2 on z/OS, it is important to understand the differences in connections. With UDB, an application connects to a database; with z/OS the application connects to the DB2 subsystem. Objects are identified by their name prefixed with their owner or schema, often determined by *currentsqlid*. Therefore on z/OS the database name becomes less significant, which is important when configuring New Era of Networks support on z/OS.

### 7.1.3 Configuring the broker UNIX System Services environment

The broker requires the nnsyreg.dat configuration file to locate its Rules and Formats database. This file in turn is found with the help of environment variables. A number of additional environment variables are required for the New Era of Networks utilities such as NNFie and NNRie. For completeness all New Era of Networks environment variables and configuration files are included in this section. You also need to set the NNSY environment variables in your .profile file, if you are going to use any of the NNSY utilities.

#### Environment variables

Table 7-2 shows the environment variables, what they are used for and an example value. These environment variables should be added to the profile for the broker user ID, normally with entries like:

```
export DSNAOINI=/var/wmqi/MQVSBRK/dsnaoini
```

With the exception of STEPLIB, these variables should already be used by the broker and set in the ENVFILE. Make sure your entries match those that are already set.

*Table 7-2   Example environment variables*

| Environment Variable | Value | Example |
|---|---|---|
| DSNAOINI | This is the fully qualified *filename* of the file 'dsnaoini' created when the broker was built with the mqsicustomize command | /var/wmqi/MQVSBRK/dsnaoini |
| LIBPATH | This should be prefixed with the NNSY and base wmqi library directory and the NNSY MIF lib directory | /usr/lpp/wmqi/nnsy/lib:/usr/lpp/wmqi/lib:/usr:/usr/lpp/wmqi/nnsy/MIF/lib:$LIBPATH |

| Environment Variable | Value | Example |
|---|---|---|
| NNSY_CATALOGUES | This is the path to the NNSY message catalog files | /usr/lpp/wmqi/nnsy/NNSY Catalogues |
| NN_CONFIG_FILE_PATH | This should be the path where you will keep the nnsyreg.dat file. | /usr/l/usr/lpp/wmqi/nnsy |
| NNSY_ROOT | This is the root path where the NNSY files and directories were installed | /usr/l/usr/lpp/wmqi/nnsy |
| PATH | This should be prefixed with the NNSY executables and base wmqi directory | /usr/lpp/wmqi/nnsy/bin:/usr/lpp/wmqi/bin:$PATH |
| STEPLIB | This variable should contain the name of the DB2 native MVS library where the DSNAOCLI module is | DB7V7.SDSNLOAD |

## nnsyreg.dat configuration file

The broker uses this configuration file, and the specific session entry MQSI_PLUGIN, to find its Rules and Formats database. It looks for the file using the following search order:

1. NNSY bin directory
2. Current working directory
3. Directory specified by $NN_CONFIG_FILE_PATH
4. Directory specified by $NNSY_ROOT

It is therefore important not to proliferate many copies of this file. Start by placing a single copy in $NNSY_ROOT and point NNSY_CONFIG_FILE_PATH to $NNSY_ROOT.

> **Warning:** Never place a copy of nnsyreg.dat in the NNSY bin directory. This takes precedence over all other locations for a number of New Era of Networks executables.
>
> As we already mentioned in "Customizing the broker for New Era of Networks support" on page 124, if you are using shared HFS, do not place the nnsyreg.dat file in the $NNSY_ROOT directory. Put it into the component directory instead and specify NN_CONFIG_FILE_PATH accordingly.

```
Session.MQSI_PLUGIN
     NNOT_SHARED_LIBRARY    = dbt26db250
     NNOT_FACTORY_FUNCTION  = NNSesDB2Factory
     NN_SES_SERVER          = DB7V
     NN_SES_DB_NAME         = MQV3BRK
```

*Figure 7-1  Example z/OS nnsyreg.dat session entry for the broker*

The parameter NN_SES_SERVER in Figure 7-1 points to the database server location. This will be known by your DB2 administrator or can be found out using the command **dis ddf** on the DB2 subsystem you are using for your Rules and Formats database.

The parameter NN_SES_DB_NAME in Figure 7-1 points to the schema or object owner name rather than the database name as described in the *System Management Guide,* SC34-6083. It should match the user ID you entered into the <auth-id> token when building the Rules and Formats database in the NnsyConfigFile.in file.

The session entries in Figure 7-1 show just the entry for the broker, MQSI_PLUGIN. Additional entries may be required for New Era of Networks tools such as NNFie, NNRie, and if you use them, apitest, msgtest and ruletest.

You also have to have a copy of the nnsyreg.dat file on your developer workstation and the Configuration Manager.

## 7.2 Setup of the Configuration Manager

Closer coupling of MQSeries Integrator with the New Era of Networks features was introduced in Version 2.0.2. This allowed some of the nodes in the Control Center to see the fields in a message type previously defined using the New Era of Networks GUI.

To achieve this functionality, the Configuration Manager must have access to the Rules and Formats database. To achieve this you must define an ODBC connection between the Configuration Manager platform and provide an nnsyreg.dat file. You must also configure the system environment variables that point to the nsyreg.dat, libraries and executables and then restart the Configuration Manager.

## 7.2.1 Defining the connection to the Rules and Formats database

On the Configuration Manager platform, define the Rules and Formats database to ODBC. There are many ways to achieve this but the next steps describe one way.

1. Click **Start -> Programs -> IBM DB2 -> Command Line Processor**

   Catalog the z/OS node and database. Example 7-1 shows how to do this.

   *Example 7-1   Cataloging a z/OS database on a Windows platform*
   ```
   catalog tcpip node DB7V remote wtsc66oe.itso.ibm.com server 33718 ostype mvs
   catalog dcs database MQV3NNSY as DB7V
   catalog database MQV3NNSY as MQV3NNSY at node DB7V authentication DCS
   connect to MQV3NNSY user MQV3BRK using xxxxxx
   ```

   In Example 7-1:
   - DB7V is our DDF location
   - wtsc66oe.itso.ibm.server is the host name
   - 33718 is the DRDA port used
   - MQV3NNSY is the Rules and Formats database name
   - MQV3BRK and xxxxxx are the user ID and password

2. Click **Start -> Programs -> IBM DB2 -> Client Configuration Assistant**.

3. Select your Rules and Formatter database and click the **Properties** button.

4. Check the **Register with ODBC** option. The **As a system datasource** should already be checked. Click the **OK** button.

## 7.2.2 Create the nnsyreg.dat

Like the broker, the Configuration Manager uses the nnsyreg.dat file to locate the Rules and Formats database. If you intend to run the Configuration Manager on its own platform without a broker or Control Center you will only need one session entry MQSI_CONFIG and one copy of the file. If you plan to run a broker or Control Center you will need to merge the entries in one file.

The same file search order holds true for the Configuration Manager, so we recommend initially that you put the file in NNSY_ROOT.

The entry is slightly different from the brokers. The Configuration Manager runs on a Windows platform and requires a user ID and password to connect to DB2 on z/OS. The broker is already running on z/OS and is already associated with a user ID and therefore does not require these values

> **Warning:** Never place a copy of nnsyreg.dat in the NNSY bin directory. This takes precedence over all other locations for a number of New Era of Networks executables.

```
Session.MQSI_CONFIG
        NNOT_SHARED_LIBRARY     = dbt26db250
        NNOT_FACTORY_FUNCTION   = NNSesDB2Factory
        NN_SES_SERVER           = MQV3NNSY
        NN_SES_DB_NAME          = MQV3BRK
        NN_SES_USER_ID          = MQV3BRK
        NN_SES_PASSWORD         = MQVGPASS
```

*Figure 7-2 Example z/OS nnsyreg.dat session for the Configuration Manager*

The parameter NN_SES_SERVER in Figure 7-2 should match the ODBC name you defined in 7.2.1, "Defining the connection to the Rules and Formats database" on page 129.

The parameter NN_SES_DB_NAME in Figure 7-2 points to the schema or object owner name rather than the database name as described in the *System Management Guide*, SC34-6083. It should match the user ID you entered into the <auth-id> token when building the Rules and Formats database in the NnsyConfigFile.in file.

### 7.2.3 Amending the system environment variables

The Configuration Manager must be able to find the New Era of Networks executables and the nnsyreg.dat file. It uses system environment variables for this. These are configured as follows:

1. Click **Start -> Settings -> Control Panel**
2. Select the **System** icon
3. Select the **Advanced** tab

4. Click the **Environment Variables...** button
5. Create new and amend existing values as detailed in Table 7-3

**Note:** These must be system and *not* user environment variables.

*Table 7-3  Configuration Manager System Environment variables*

| System Environment Variable | Value | Example |
|---|---|---|
| lib | This should include the NNSY library directory | .....;C:\Program Files\IBM\WebSphere MQ Integrator 2.1\nnsy\lib;... |
| NNSY_CATALOGUES | This is the path to the NNSY message catalog files | C:\Program Files\IBM\WebSphere MQ Integrator 2.1\nnsy\NNSYCatalogues |
| NN_CONFIG_FILE_PATH | This should be the path where you will keep the nnsyreg.dat file | C:\Program Files\IBM\WebSphere MQ Integrator 2.1\nnsy\ |
| NNSY_ROOT | This is the root path where the NNSY files and directories were installed | C:\Program Files\IBM\WebSphere MQ Integrator 2.1\nnsy\ |
| Path | This should include the NNSY executables directory | ...;C:\Program Files\IBM\WebSphere MQ Integrator 2.1\nnsy\bin;... |

## 7.2.4  Restart the Configuration Manager

Once you have completed the Configuration Manager steps you must stop and restart the broker and make sure that no errors or warnings are issued to the event log.

1. Click **Start -> Settings -> Control Panel**
2. Select the **Administration Tools** icon
3. Select the **Event Viewer** icon
4. Select the **Application Log** folder and check that there are no warnings or errors related to Configuration Manager startup

Figure 7-3 and Figure 7-4 show warnings in the Event Log where the Configuration Manager has found the nnsyreg.dat file but cannot access the database.

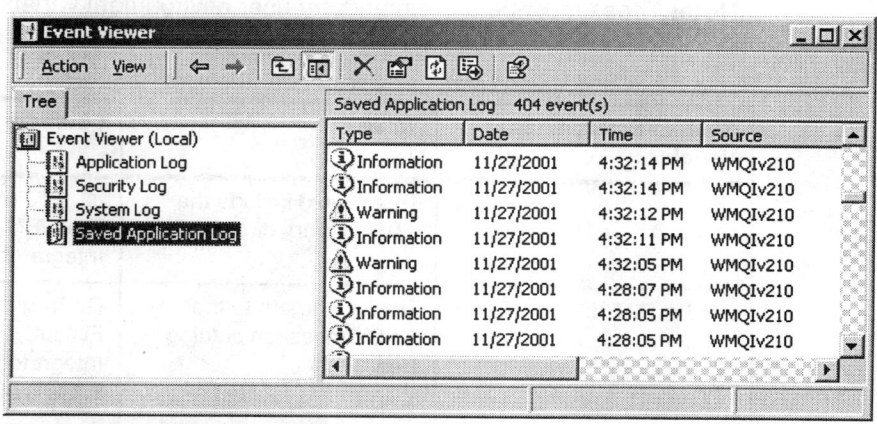

*Figure 7-3  Configuration Manager errors during startup*

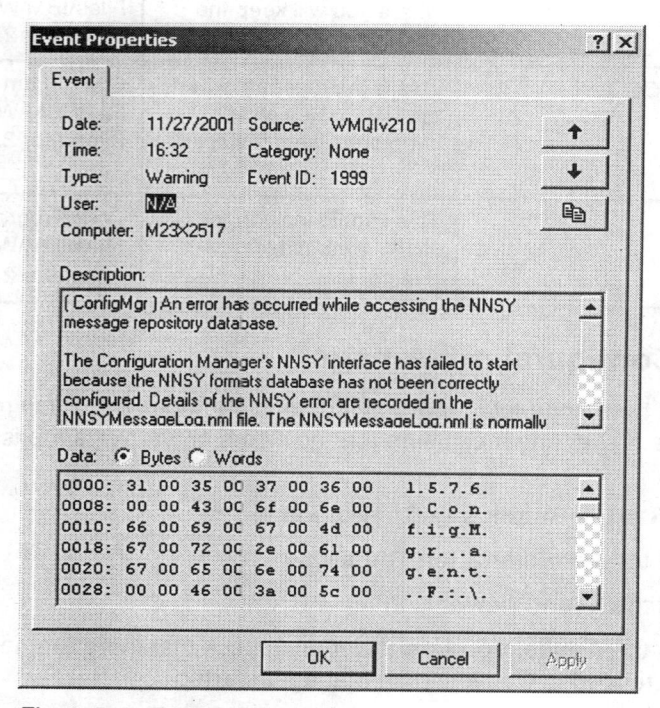

*Figure 7-4  Event log details*

## 7.3 Workstation configuration

The last configuration changes that are required are at the workstation where you run the Control Center and Rules and Formats GUI. First, ensure WebSphere MQ Integrator has been installed with the NNSY support option. This can be done by:doing the following:

1. Click **Start -> Settings -> Control Panel**
2. Select **Add/Remove Programs** icon
3. Check that you see the **New Era of Networks - NNSY Component Installer**

You must then configure the ODBC connect to the Rules and Formats database and check the system environment variables.

### 7.3.1 Defining the connection to the Rules and Formats database

Repeat the process of defining an ODBC connection from the workstation to the Rules and Formats database as detailed in 7.2.1, "Defining the connection to the Rules and Formats database" on page 129.

### 7.3.2 Creating the nnsyreg.dat file

This configuration file is only required if you are going to use the text utilities such as apitest, msgtest, ruletest, or export and import rules and formats. In our test we use a single session entry for all utilities and appended the session flag parameter flag with the command. When you have complex configurations or multiple databases, this encourages you to consider which database you are using.

```
Session.MQV3BRK
    NNOT_SHARED_LIBRARY= dbt26db250
    NNOT_FACTORY_FUNCTION= NNSesDB2Factory
    NN_SES_DB_NAME= MQV3BRK
    NN_SES_SERVER= MQV3NNSY
    NN_SES_USER_ID= MQV3BRK
    NN_SES_PASSWORD= MQVGPASS
```

*Figure 7-5   Windows nnsyreg.dat file for DB2*

### 7.3.3 Configuring the System Environment variables

The workstation needs two system environment variables which can be set as described in 7.2.3, "Amending the system environment variables" on page 130. They are:

▶ **NNSY_ROOT** should point to the root path where the New Era of Networks files and directories are stored. Details are similar for the Configuration Manager and are discussed in Table 7-3 on page 131.

▶ **NN_CONFIG_FILE_PATH** is required when you use the text-based command utilities apitest, msgtest and ruletest from the workstation. As in other sections, this must point to an nnsyreg.dat file which need an entry as shown in Figure 7-5 on page 133. Samples of this file are found in the <wmqi install>\nnsy\rulfmt56\examples.

## 7.3.4 Starting the Control Center and New Era of Networks GUI

Start the Control Center:

1. Click **Start -> Programs -> IBM WebSphere MQ Integrator -> Control Center**

    If the Configuration Manager Connection pane appears complete the Configuration Manager's host name, Queue Manager name and the port its Queue Manager is listening on.

2. Select the **Message Sets** tab and you should see that the menu bar items include Nnsy shown in Figure 7-6 on page 134. This pull-down accesses the New Era of Networks GUI.

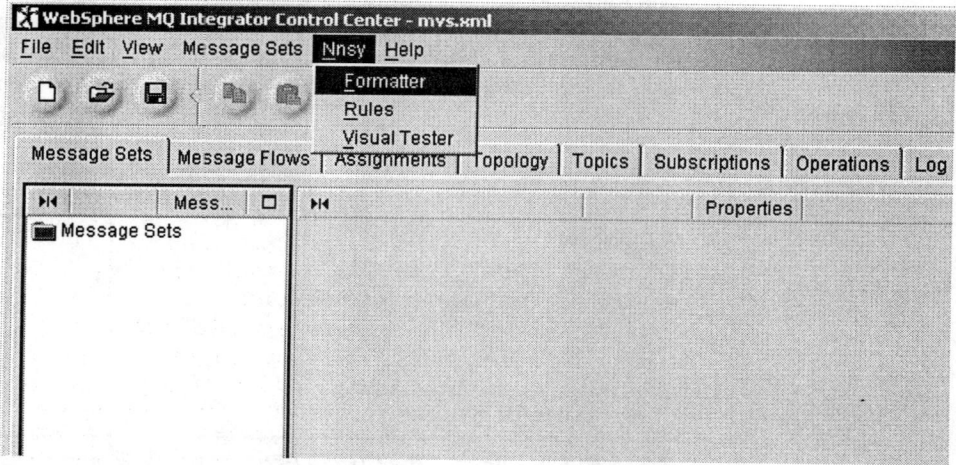

*Figure 7-6   WebSphere MQ Integrator Control Center Nnsy option*

3. Select **Formatter** and after a short delay the sign-on window shown in Figure 7-7 on page 135 should appear.

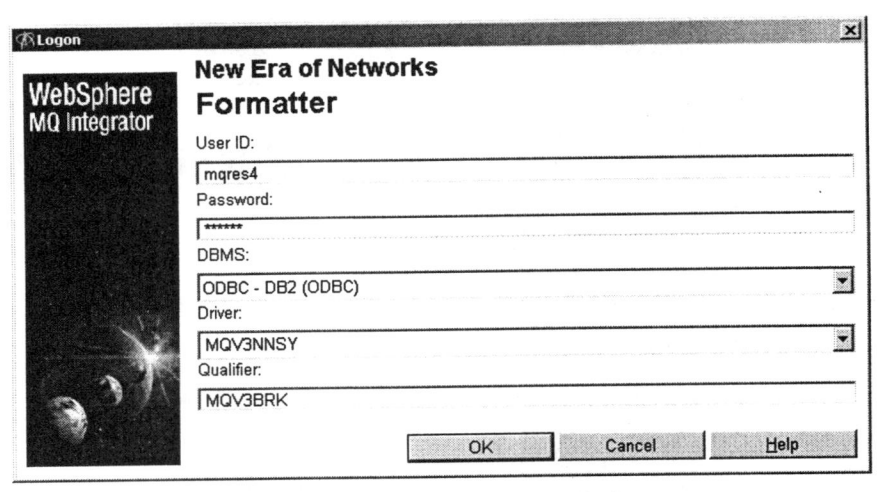

*Figure 7-7   New Era of Networks Formatter sign-on window*

An explanation of the values that should be entered is found in Table 7-4.

*Table 7-4   New Era of Networks GUI sign-on attributes*

| Attribute | Explanation | Sample Value |
| --- | --- | --- |
| User ID | Any user ID with read/update rights to the Rules and Formats database objects | MQRES4 |
| DBMS | DB2 is selected by using the ODBC DBMS type | ODBC - DB2(ODBC) |
| Driver | This should be the ODBC database name configured on your workstation as described in 7.3.1, "Defining the connection to the Rules and Formats database" on page 133 | MQV3NNSY |
| Qualifier | This is the database | MQV3BRK |

4. Return to the Control Center Message Sets tab and repeat the process for the Rules GUI (Figure 7-8 on page 136) entering the same values as you did for the Formatter.

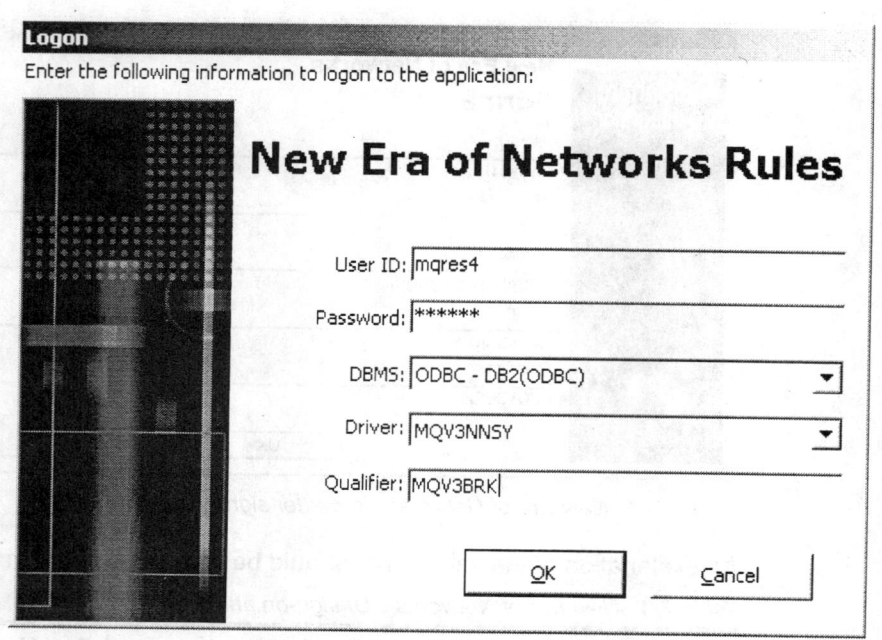

*Figure 7-8 New Era of Networks Rules sign-on window*

5. When signing on to Visual Tester select a DBMS value of **DB2 - OS/390**. Until you select this you will not see the Qualifier field shown in Figure 7-9 on page 137.

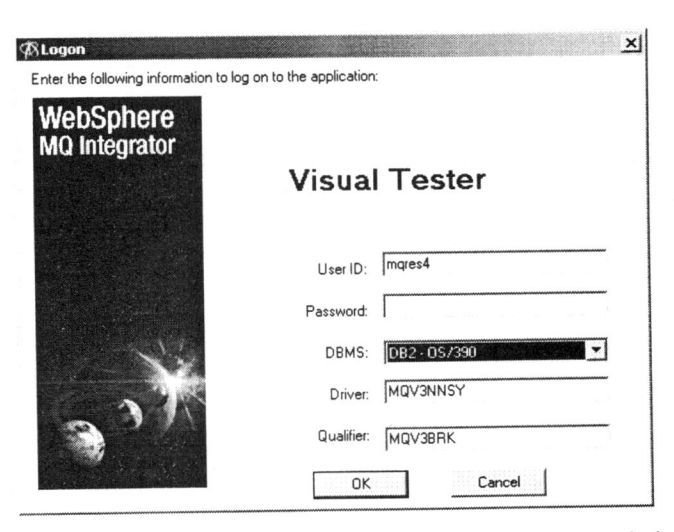

Figure 7-9   New Era of Networks Visual Tester sign-on window

## 7.4  Verification

Once you have built the environment, and before starting migration, it is useful to build a simple flat input and output format to verify the configuration. Building the formats is beyond the scope of this redbook. In our example in Figure 7-10 on page 138 we have built a two-field, comma-separated input (TwoFields) and an XML output format (NameAddressXML). You can import these formats from the file nnsy.exp in the additional materials described in Appendix D, "Additional material" on page 355.

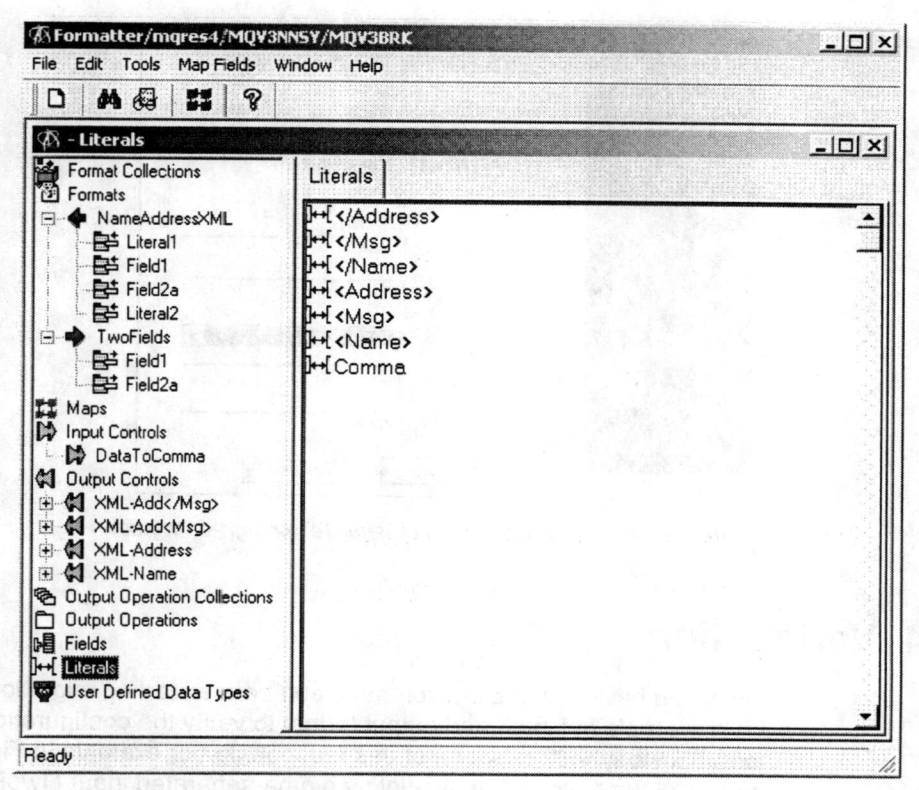

*Figure 7-10 Simple formats developed for verification*

## 7.4.1 Build a simple NEONTransform flow

Create a flow as shown in Figure 7-11 on page 139. This verification flow can be imported from the file NEONTransform Verification MsgFlow.exp.xml, found in the additional materials described in Appendix D, "Additional material" on page 355.

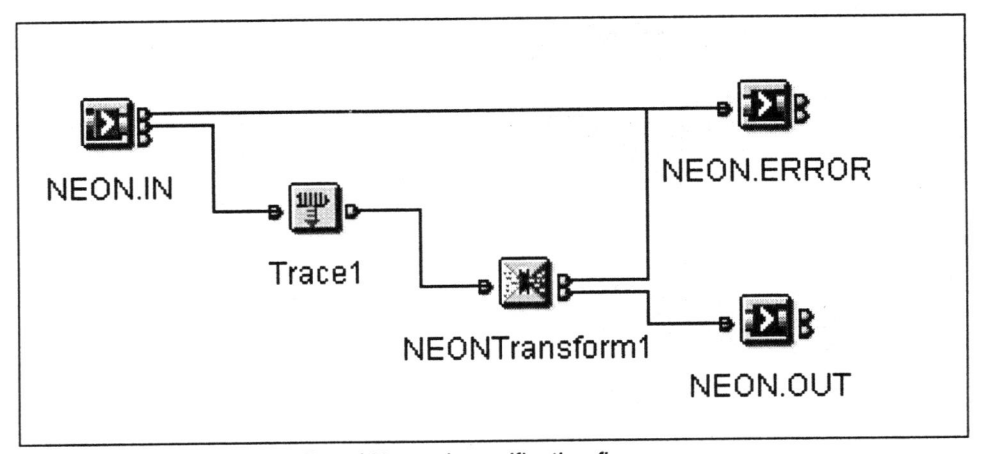

*Figure 7-11 Simple New Era of Networks verification flow*

## 7.4.2 Configure the node properties

Configure the nodes with properties as detailed.

### NEON.IN

This is an MQInput node. On the Basic tab configure Queue Name as the name of an input queue that will be the start of your flow (Figure 7-12).

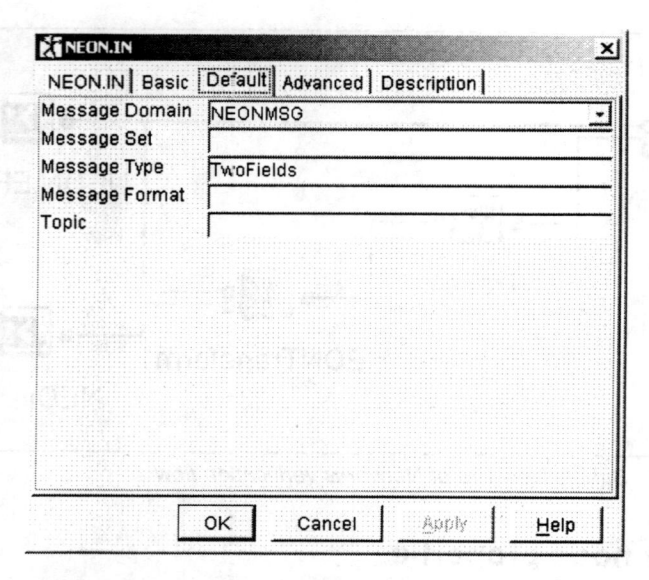

```
┌─────────────────────────────────────────┐
│ ✦ NEON.IN                            ×  │
├─────────────────────────────────────────┤
│ NEON.IN │ Basic │ Default │ Advanced │ Description │
│ Message Domain  │NEONMSG             ▼│ │
│ Message Set     │                     │ │
│ Message Type    │TwoFields            │ │
│ Message Format  │                     │ │
│ Topic           │                     │ │
│                                         │
│                                         │
│                                         │
│                                         │
│     OK      Cancel    Apply    Help     │
└─────────────────────────────────────────┘
```

*Figure 7-12 MQInput Node Default tab*

On the Default tab shown in Figure 7-12 on page 140 configure Message Domain as NEONMSG and Message Type as your simple Input Format that you have defined to verify the New Era of Networks functionality.

### Trace1

This is a Trace node. Configure it as shown in Figure 7-13 on page 141 using a File Path that the broker user ID will have access to.

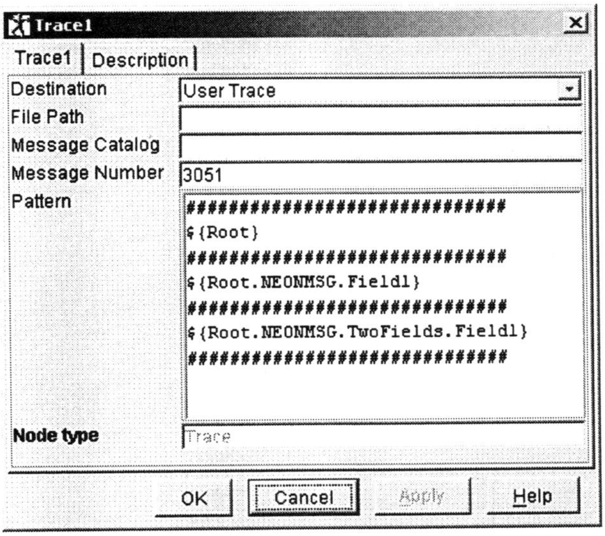

*Figure 7-13  Trace node properties*

## NeonTransform1

This is a NEONTransform node. Configure it as shown in Figure 7-14 on page 142. The Target Format is the name of the simple Output Format that you have defined to verify the New Era of Networks functionality. The Output Message Type is the name of your New Era of Networks Input Format.

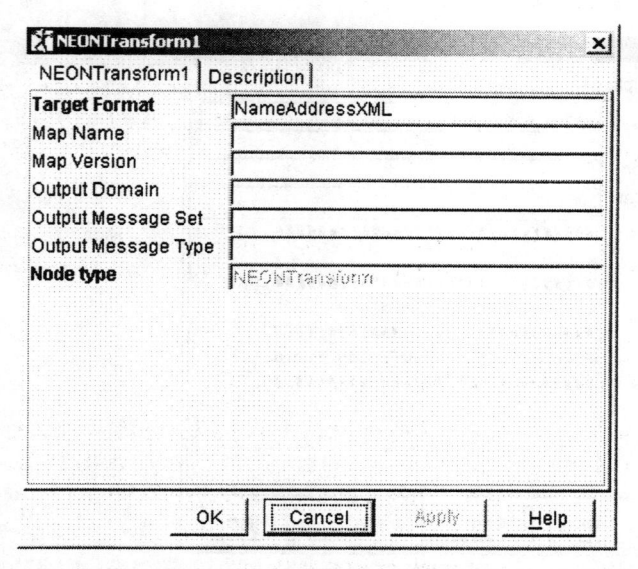

*Figure 7-14   NEONTransform node properties*

## NEON.ERROR and NEON.OUT

Both these nodes are MQOutput nodes. On the Basic tab of each configure a different Queue Name for each and leave the Queue Manager Name blank.

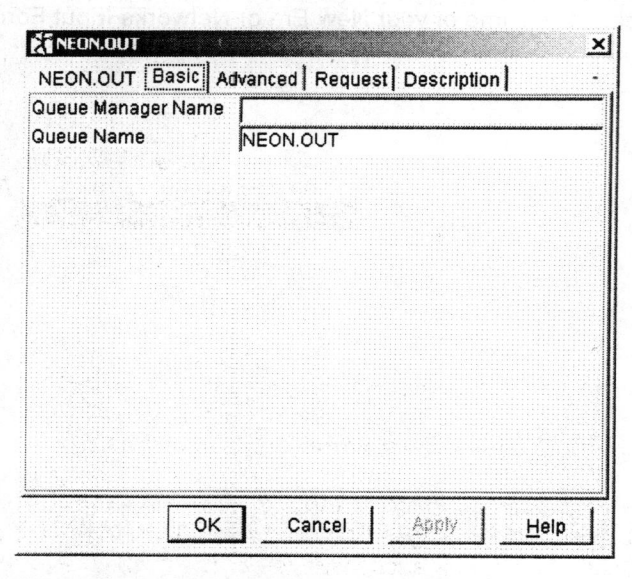

*Figure 7-15   MQOutput basic node properties*

## 7.4.3 Define queues

The flow we have defined uses three queues: one input queue and two output queues. In our example, we renamed the MQInput and MQOutput queues to match the queue names they use. This is good practice particularly with simple naming standards and during the early stages of working with WebSphere MQ Integrator.

Create these queues on your z/OS broker's Queue Manager. You will deploy and run the flow to this Broker and Queue Manager to verify the New Era of Networks support.

## 7.4.4 Deploy and test the message flow

Ensure that the flow is checked in. On the Assignments tab of the Control Center create a new Execution Group, or using an existing one, assign the flow to it and deploy the flow to the broker. This is shown in Figure 7-16.

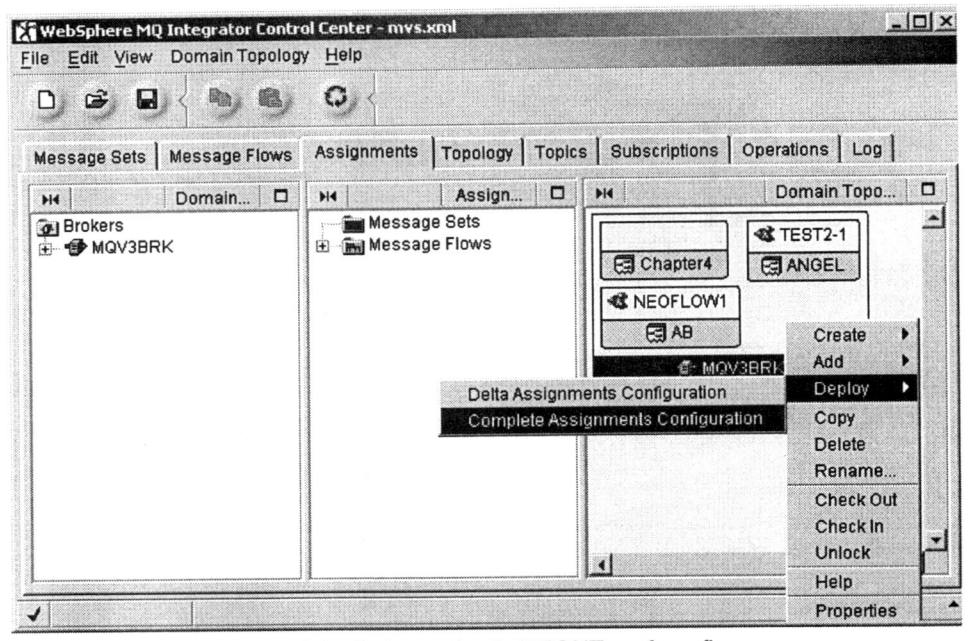

*Figure 7-16   Assigning and deploying a simple NEONTransform flow*

Check that the deployment has completed by refreshing and checking the Log tab. You should see two messages from the broker (BIP2056I) and the Execution Group (BIP4040I) indicating a successful deployment. Clear the log view of messages and then proceed to test the flow.

Generally, a successful deployment of a message flow to a broker using a New Era of Networks node indicates the broker is configured correctly. You can now use your favorite MQSeries utility to put a message on the message flow's input queue to test your reformat.

### 7.4.5 Verification of the Configuration Manager

The Configuration Manager should now be able to access the Rules and Formats database. To verify this:

1. Select the **Message Sets** tab in the Control Center.
2. Right-click **Message Sets**
3. Select **Add to Workspace, Message Set...** (as shown in Figure 7-17)

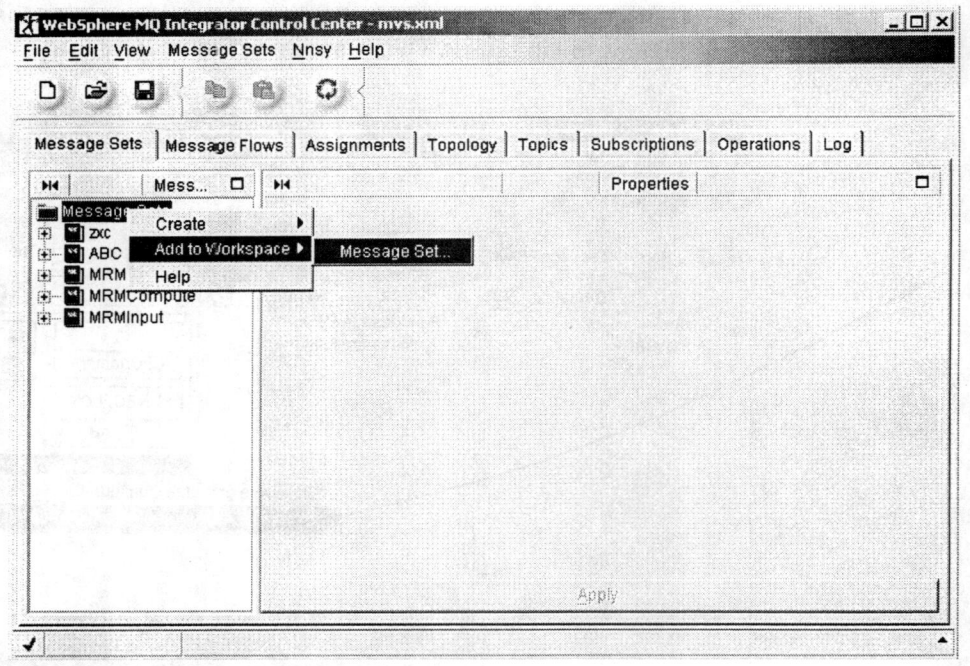

*Figure 7-17  Adding a message set to the Control Center*

4. Select the **NEON Message Set** as shown in Figure 7-18 on page 145 and click **Finish**.

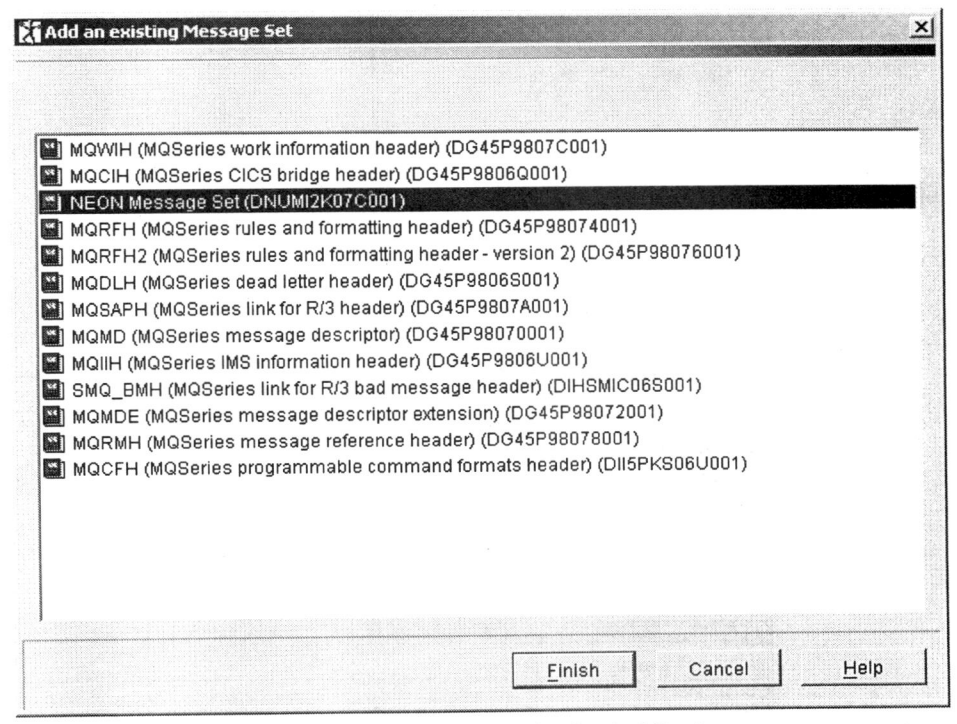

*Figure 7-18   Adding the NEON message set to the Control Center*

5. Once you have added the NEON Message Set to the Control Center, select the **Message Flows** tab and create a new message flow. Add a single Compute node to it and open up the properties view.

6. The Compute node properties divided left and right for Inputs and Output Messages. Above the Inputs pane on the left, click the **Add** button and an Add Message or Table pop-up box should appear as shown in Figure 7-19 on page 146.

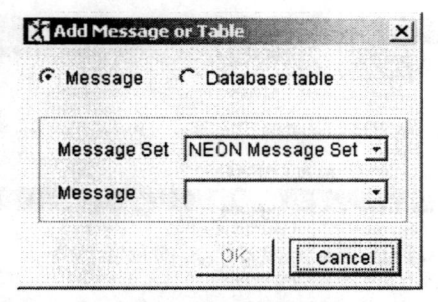

*Figure 7-19   Adding a NEON message set in a Compute node*

7. Select **NEON Message Set** from the Message Set scroll-down.
8. Type the name of your input format into the Message scroll-down, in our example it is TwoFields. The scroll list will not list your New Era of Networks formats.
9. Click the **OK** button and you should see your message name added to the Compute node as shown in Figure 7-20.

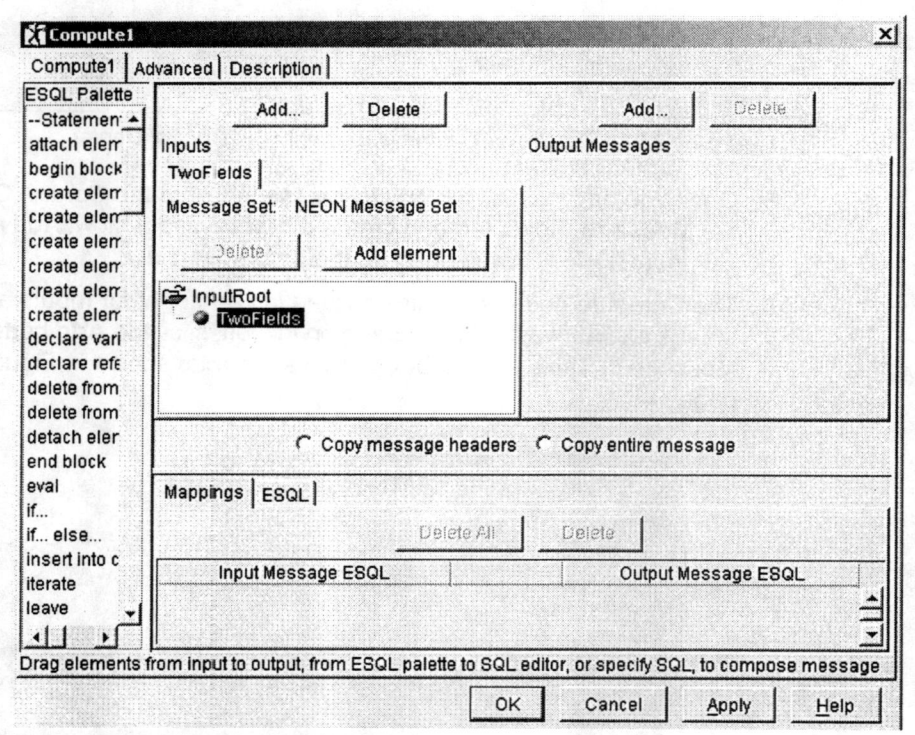

*Figure 7-20   New Era of Networks input format in a Compute node*

**146**  WebSphere MQ Integrator for z/OS V2.1 Implementation Guide

10. Now click **Add Element**. After a short delay while the Configuration Manager retrieves data from the Rules and Formats database you should see an Element pop-up box with all the format fields. Select only your input format (Figure 7-21) and click **OK**.

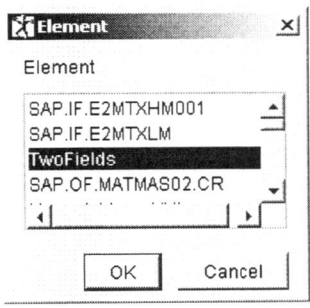

*Figure 7-21   Adding a New Era of Networks input format to a Compute node*

11. Expand the input format and you should be able to view the fields that make up your New Era of Networks message format.
12. Above the right pane click **Add** and an Add Message or Table pop-up box should appear. Again select the **NEON Message Set** in the Message Set pull-down and type the name of the output format (in our example NameAddressXML) in the Message window (Figure 7-22). Again the scroll down will not list your NEON output formats.

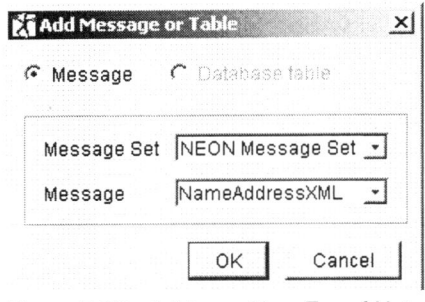

*Figure 7-22   Adding a New Era of Networks output format to a Compute node*

13. Again click **Add Element** and after another short delay you should see the list of formats. Select only your output format (in our example NameAddressXML).
14. Select **OK** and you should now have an input format on the left and an output format on the right as shown in Figure 7-23 on page 148.

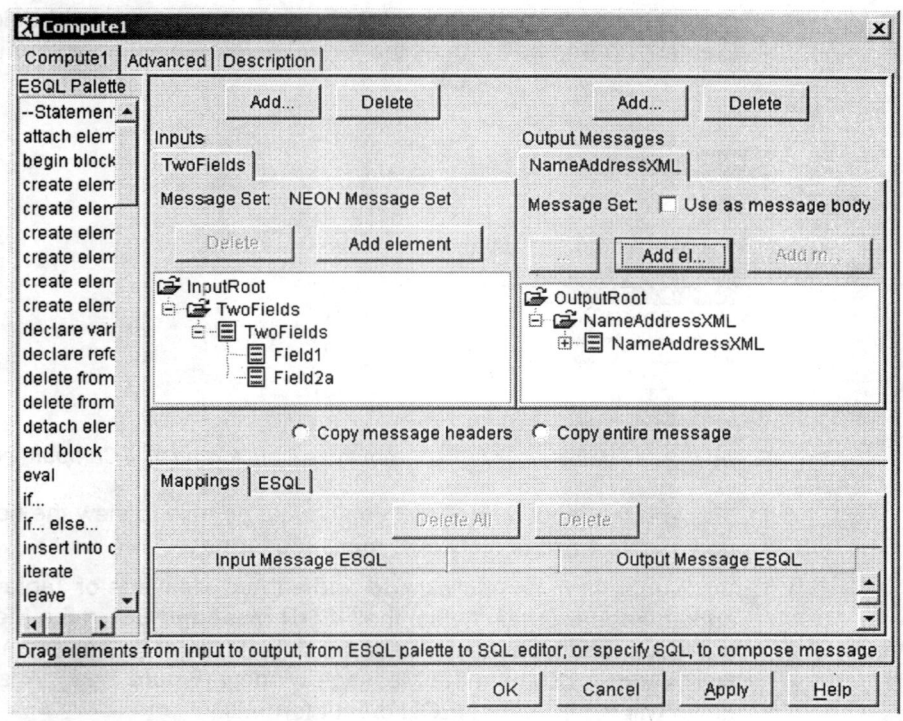

*Figure 7-23   Ready to be dragged and dropped*

15. You can now drag and drop the fields from the input format to the output format. By selecting the **Copy message headers** button and dragging Field1 and Field2 in the input pane onto their appropriate output fields the Compute node will build up a graphical picture of your reformat. In the ESQL tab as shown in Figure 7-24 on page 149 you can see the ESQL code that will be used to build the output message.

```
DECLARE I INTEGER;
SET I = 1;
WHILE I < CARDINALITY(InputRoot.*[]) DO
   SET OutputRoot.*[I] = InputRoot.*[I];
   SET I=I+1;
END WHILE;
SET "OutputRoot"."NEONMSG"."NameAddressXML"."Field1" =
"InputBody"."TwoFields"."Field1";
SET "OutputRoot"."NEONMSG"."NameAddressXML"."Field2a" =
"InputBody"."TwoFields"."Field2a";
-- Enter SQL below this line.  SQL above this line might be regenerated,
causing any modifications to be lost.
```

*Figure 7-24  Sample ESQL code built by a Compute node*

This Compute node you have built could replace the NEONTransform1 node in the verification flow shown in Figure 7-11 on page 139 that you built earlier. There are a number of ways of achieving the same results, but successfully viewing the input and output fields in a Compute node verifies the Configuration Manager is certainly communicating with the Rules and Formats database.

### 7.4.6 Configuration problem determination

During setup and configuration of the New Era of Networks components, there will invariably be some problems. There are a number of places to look for help in understanding, diagnosing and resolving these issues. This section briefly discusses the first steps in diagnosing any problems. It only considers the New Era of Networks components and access to them.

#### Broker

The broker writes messages to the MVS syslog and to UNIX System Services files NNSYMessageLog.nml, stderr and stdout. These files can be found in your broker configuration directory and its subdirectories, /var/wmqi/<brokername> and /var/wmqi/<brokername>/output.

Additional information can be found by running an ODBC trace. To do this, you can temporarily amend the dsnaoini file pointed to by environment variable DSNAOINI by specifying APPLTRACE=1 to set ODBC tracing on. Remember to change it back and restart the broker after you have resolved any problems.

## Configuration Manager

The Configuration Manager will record an event, which can be viewed with the Windows Event Viewer, when it cannot access the Rules and Formats database, but has an nnsyreg.dat file.

If it doesn't record an event, but doesn't give you access from the Control Center to the Rules and Formats database, it is likely it can't find the nnsyreg.dat file. Check your environment variables and perhaps try temporarily placing a copy in the WebSphere MQ Integrator bin directory (do not leave it there).

If it records an event, there is likely to be additional information in the NNSYMessageLog.nml in the WebSphere MQ Integrator bin directory.

It is useful to stop the Configuration Manager, clear out the Events, delete the NNSYMessageLog.nml file, and restart the broker. This will minimize the output you have to deal with.

Additionally, you can run an ODBC trace. This trace is configured from the Windows ODBC setting from the Control Panel in the Advanced options, under the Service tab. Remember to switch it off once you have diagnosed the problem.

## Control Center NNSY GUI program startup

Check the NNSY component was installed on the workstation. Check the network connection between your workstation and the database and ensure you can connect and log into the DB2 database using a DB2 Command Line processor.

Starting the New Era of Networks GUI programs, rely on the NNSY_ROOT environment variable and the PATH being set up correctly. Additional error information may be recorded in the NNSYMessageLog.nml file in one of the folders in $NNSY_ROOT/gui.

## Workstation NNSY utility problems

These utilities require NN_CONFIG_FILE_PATH to be defined and point to a nnsyreg.dat with an appropriate definition. An error log NNSYMessageLog.nml is created in the directory the utility is run from. There are also some notes in the Readme file that should be reviewed.

# Migrating New Era of Networks Rules and Formats from MQSeries Integrator Version 1.11

In this chapter, we describe the migration process from MQSeries Integrator V1.11 on z/OS to WebSphere MQ Integrator V2.10. This is the process of taking your existing Rules and Formats and configuring them to run in the new environment, with your existing applications unchanged.

Existing MQSeries Integrator implementations may be complex with many Rules Engine (RULENG) processes running, processing very many different types of messages and reading from many input queues. We take a simple example and then discuss how it can be extended to cater for more complex implementations.

We review the new New Era of Networks nodes introduced in MQSeries Integrator 2.02, particularly the NEONRulesEvaluation node. This is the node we recommend you use when you migrate from MQSeries Integrator Version 1.11.

We also introduce some of the other features available in WebSphere MQ Integrator V2.10 and the underlying New Era of Networks code that will help you in migration. We also look at configuring your environment so that you can use the New Era of Networks systems management utilities, particularly NNFie and NNRie.

## 8.1 Migration overview

To migrate your Rules and Formats from MQSeries Integrator V1.11 to WebSphere MQ Integrator V2.10, you should first become familiar with the new product. You should be able to build simple message flows and diagnose and resolve problems. Familiarity with the New Era of Networks utilities NNFie and NNRie is beneficial.

The traditional Rules Engine (RULENG), in Version 1.11, which enriches, routes and processes your message, is replaced by the broker and execution groups. These brokers and execution groups run your message flows, taking your messages, evaluating the rules and reformatting them using a new Rules and Formats database.

Your existing rules and formats need to be migrated from the current Version 1.11 database into a new one for Version 2.1. The old utilities such as NNFie and NNRie are replaced by similar code from the WebSphere MQ Integrator product.

The steps to achieve a successful migration are:

1. Consistency-check and export all your existing rules and formats using the MQSeries Integrator V1.11 utilities.
2. Back up all your existing Rules and Formats databases for security.
3. Install WebSphere MQ Integrator 2.1, including New Era of Networks support as described in Chapter 7, "Configuring New Era of Networks Support" on page 123.
4. Copy the export files from step 1 to the UNIX System Services file system, import them into the new Rules and Formats database created in step 3 and consistency-check them.
5. Create message flows, including a NEONRulesEvaluation node, to provide your MQSeries Integrator 1.11 functionality.
6. Deploy and test your new flow.

Steps 1, 2, 3, and 6 have already been dealt with earlier in this redbook, or as a customer running MQSeries Integrator, you should be familiar with. We therefore focus on the remaining steps to complete the migration.

You should refer to the Readme file and the *New Era of Networks Rules and Formatter Support for WebSphere MQ Integrator Systems Management Guide,* SC43-6083 for further information.

## 8.2 Copying your export files to UNIX System Services

Having exported your formats from the Rules and Formats database to native MVS data sets you must copy these to a UNIX System Services file system. The facilities to do this are discussed in Chapter 2, "z/OS UNIX System Services" on page 31.

The simplest way is to use **OPUT** from the TSO command line as in the following example:

**OPUT 'MQRES3.RULES' '/u/mqres4/rules111.exp'**

> **Note:** Check that your UNIX System Services file is in readable text. If you have transferred it as a binary file it will be unreadable in EBCDIC format and will not import.

## 8.3 Importing your rules and formats

In this section we document how to import rules and formats with appropriate utilities.

### 8.3.1 Configuring NNFie and NNRie

Importing of rules and formats is achieved by using the NNFie and NNRie New Era of Networks utilities in your UNIX System Services environment. The executable *must* be the version shipped with WebSphere MQ Integrator V2.1. These are usually in /usr/lpp/wmqi/nnsy/bin. We used a telnet window from a Windows workstation.

Before executing NNFie and NNRie make sure you have set up your user ID with the environment variables discussed in "Environment variables" on page 126. The path NN_CONFIG_FILE_PATH should point to an nnsyreg.dat file with an entry similar to Figure 8-1. The values of each parameter are discussed in "nnsyreg.dat configuration file" on page 127.

```
Session.MQV3BRK
        NNOT_SHARED_LIBRARY      = dbt26db250
        NNOT_FACTORY_FUNCTION    = NNSesDB2Factory
        NN_SES_SERVER            = DB7V
        NN_SES_DB_NAME           = MQV3BRK
```

*Figure 8-1  Sample nnsyreg.dat entry for NNFie and NNRie*

**Tip:** In the example nnsyreg.dat shown in Figure 8-1, we avoid using the default session entries nnfie and nnrmie. By using the session entry MQV3BRK we force the user of NNFie or NNRie to decide where the import is going. This is useful when you have multiple environments.

Verify the version of both utilities by using the -V option of the commands as shown in Figure 8-2 on page 154. Only part of the output produced by NNFie has been included.

```
MQRES4 @ SC66:/u/mqres4>NNRie -V
Rules Import / Export utility (NNRie)
@<%> NNSYRF_Version   R5_20:src:Fri Jan 05 10:42:41 MST 2001
Copyright (c) 2000   New Era of Networks, Inc.
All Rights Reserved.


MQRES4 @ SC66:/u/mqres4>NNFie -V
Formatter Import / Export utility (NNFie)
Version: @<%> NNSYRF_Version   R5_20:src:Fri Jan 05 10:42:41 MST 2001
Copyright (C) 1996-2000, New Era Of Networks, Inc.
All Rights Reserved.
usage:
NNFie ((-C <command file name>)
       (-i <import file name> [-T] [ -o|-g|-n|-4|-p ] [-s <session name>]
        [-c <database configuration file name>])
       (-e <export file name> [-m <format name>+] [-q "comment"]
        [-Q <Comment file name>] [-w <number>] [-s <session name>]
```

*Figure 8-2  NNFie and NNRie verification*

## 8.3.2 Importing formats

Import your formats using NNFie. In our example in Figure 8-3 on page 155 we are importing to an empty database schema. We therefore do not need to worry about overwrite conflicts where objects of the same name already exist. If you have had failed imports or are repeating the import process, refer to the command options in the *Systems Management Guide,* SC34-6083 to deal with the situation.

**Note:** The -p option is required with z/OS when importing MQSI 1.11 formats. It ensures your literals are imported as string literals. Without this option your literals are imported as their binary value.

Refer to NNFie in the *Systems Management Guide,* SC34-6083, if your formats use Data-using output operation collections'.

Refer to the NNSY Readme file for a list of literal values that cannot be imported or exported to or from an NNSY formats database.

You should see the familiar Working: message at the bottom of your screen until the message no errors found indicates a successful completion.

```
MQRES4 @ SC66:/u/mqres4>NNFie -i  format111.exp -p -s MQV3BRK
Working: |

NNFie complete: no errors found
MQRES4 @ SC66:/u/mqres4>
```

*Figure 8-3  NNFie import running*

Once you have imported the formats start the Formatter GUI from the Control Center to verify success.

In the New Era of Networks Formatter in WebSphere MQ Integrator 2.1 you will see ownership permissions for formats. These are similar permissions to those that Rules had in MQSeries Integrator 1.11. Initially the owner will be set to the user that runs the import. You can see this in Figure 8-4.

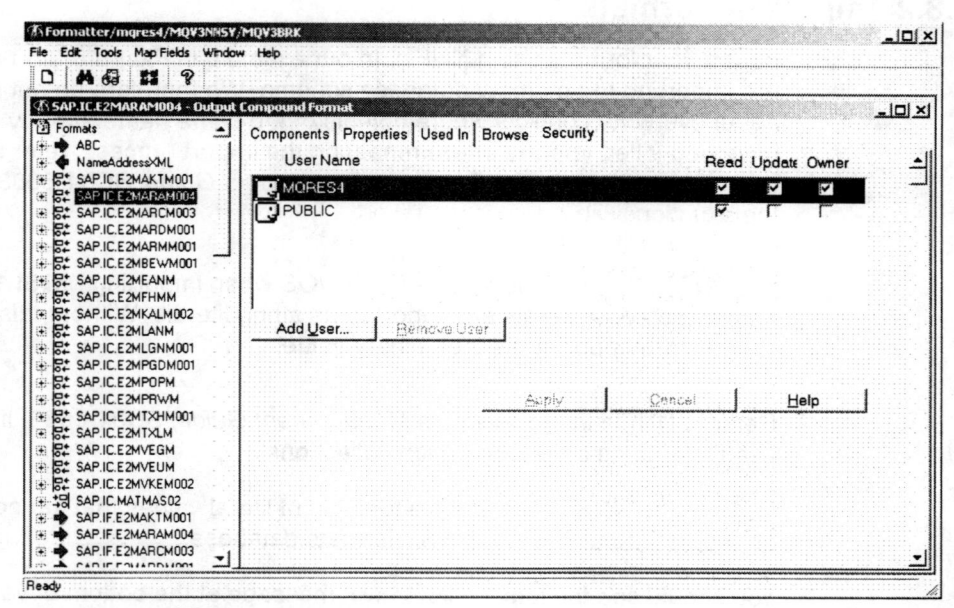

*Figure 8-4   Security permissions in the Formatter GUI*

Ownership and permissions is discussed in the *System Management Guide*, SC34-6083 and can be amended with the `PermUtil` command.

## 8.3.3 Importing rules

Import your rules using NNRie. In our example in Figure 8-5, we are again importing to an empty database schema. We therefore do not need to worry about overwrite conflicts where rules or subscriptions of the same name already exist. If you have had failed imports or are repeating the import process, refer to the command options in the *Systems Management Guide,* SC34-6083 to deal with the situation.

```
MQRES4 @ SC66:/u/mqres4>NNRie -i rules111.exp -s MQV3BRK
Rules Import / Export utility (NNRie)
@<%> NNSYRF_Version  R5_20:src:Fri Jan 05 10:42:41 MST 2001
Copyright (c) 2000  New Era of Networks, Inc.
All Rights Reserved.
Import / export / inventory is set to "importing"?
Import / export file is "rules111.exp"
Database session tag is "nnrmie"
Importing from file to database+
AMscppcpSCPPCPnnRnnel


Number of Apps       3
Number of Msg Types  5
Number of Rules      7
Number of Subs       15
All done.
```

*Figure 8-5   NNRie import running*

Once complete, start the Rules GUI from the Control Center to verify success. You may notice the GUI is considerably different from the GUI in MQSeries Integrator V1.11. However, it is intuitive enough to validate success of the import. For further information on using the GUI refer to the *New Era of Networks Rules and Formatter Support for WebSphere MQ Integrator User's Guide,* SC34-6084.

## 8.4 Running the consistency checker

The consistency checker for rules, formats and permissions is executed in three steps. They are run through JCL from the SBIPJCL library built when you ran the **NNInstallDriver.sh** command. The members are MAINFCC, MAINRCC and PERMCC. They are detailed in *New Era of Networks Rules and Formats Support for WebSphere MQ Integrator Systems Management Guide,* SC34-6083.

## 8.5 Creating your migration message flow

The NEONRulesEvaluation node is the core node in a message flow that allows it to behave similarly to the Rules Engine process. In the example shown in Figure 8-6 on page 158, we have a simple NEONRulesEvaluation node surrounded by MQInput and MQOutput nodes. The properties of each are discussed below.

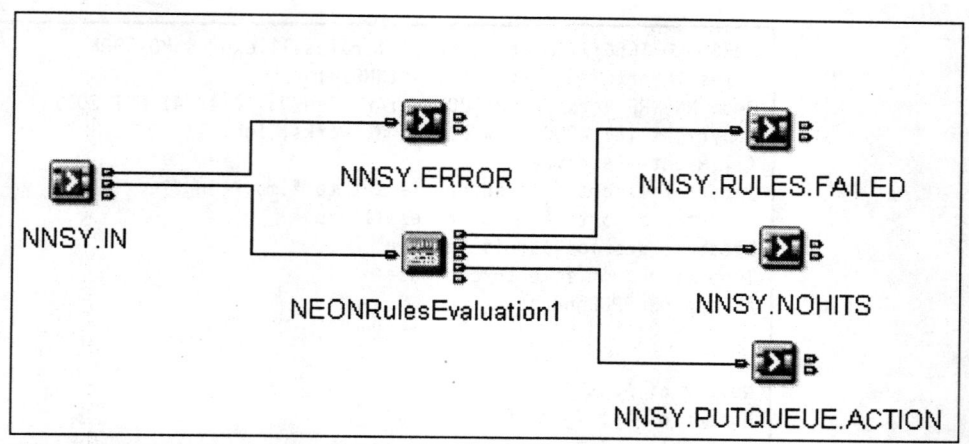

Figure 8-6   Migration message flow

## 8.5.1 NNSY.IN

The MQInput node provides much of the information that was formerly in your Rules Engine (RULENG) parameter file with MQSeries Integrator V1.11. On the Basic tab we have the Queue Name (Figure 8-7). This obviously equates to InputQueueName.

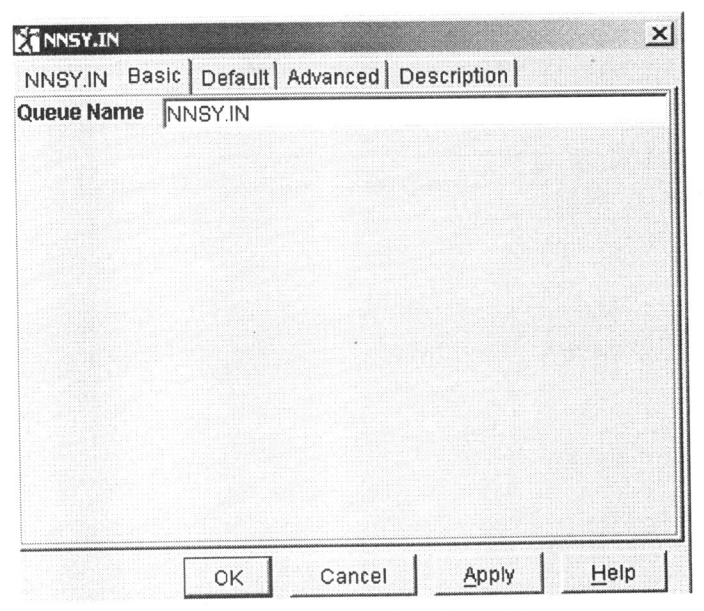

*Figure 8-7  MQInput Node Properties, Basic tab*

The Default tab provides information on how to process the message if it does not have an MQRFH (or the newer MQRFH2 header). The Message Set field equates to DefaultAppGroup and the Message Type equates to the DefaultMsgType that was formerly in the Rules Engine (RULENG) parameter file.

The Message Domain should be defined as NEONMSG from the pull down menu (Figure 8-8).

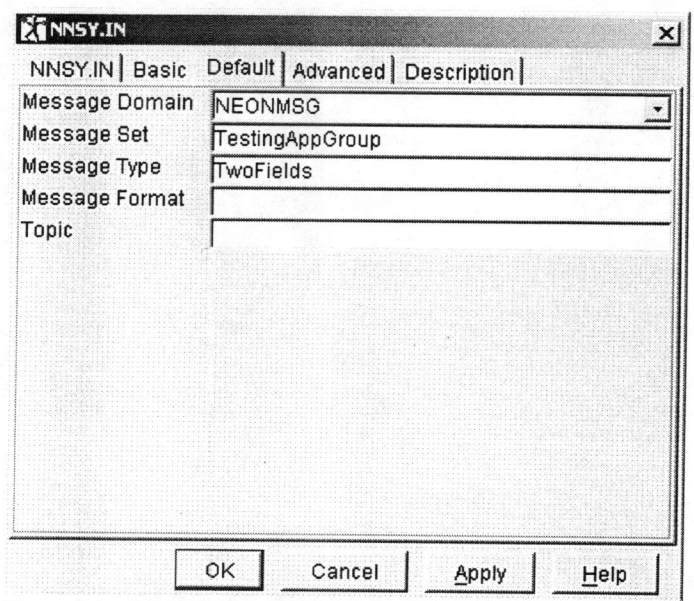

*Figure 8-8 MQInput Node Properties, Default tab*

### Using an MQRFH or MQRFH2 header

There should be no reason to change your existing applications when using WebSphere MQ Integrator. If you already use an MQRFH header then it will be correctly passed in the NEONMSG domain against the Message Type and Application Group within the header. None of the fields on the Default tab on the MQInput node will be used.

If you are building new applications it is recommended that you use the MQRFH2 header and preferably messages defined in the MRM. If however you are writing a new application using an old messages format defined with the New Era of Networks GUI, you may use the MQRFH2 header. In this instance you must define the domain as NEONMSG, using the <msd> field in the <mcd> folder.

The MQRFH2 is detailed in the *WebSphere MQ Integrator Programming Guide*, SC34-5603.

## 8.5.2 NEONRulesEvaluation1 node

The NEONRulesEvaluation node has no properties set. It has five output terminals which are discussed in 8.7.1, "NEONRulesEvaluation node terminals" on page 165. In the example shown in Figure 8-6 on page 158, we have connected up the FAILED, NOHIT and PUTQUEUE terminals.

### 8.5.3 NNSY.RULES.FAILED and NNSY.NOHITS

These nodes are both MQOutput nodes with just Queue Name configured on the Basic tab. Once again we have named the nodes to match the queues we are using. The Queue Manager property on the Basic tab is left blank. This value defaults to the broker's Queue Manager name.

#### Routing errors to a remote Queue Manager

If you centralize your error handling you may want to route these errors to a different Queue Manager. You can use a remote queue name in the Queue Name field on the MQOutput node. Alternatively, if you do not use remote queue definitions you can use the Queue Name together with the Queue Manager name fields on the MQOutput node. WebSphere MQ Integrator will attempt to resolve this to a transmission queue. Refer to your MQ Systems Administrator on how your definitions are configured.

### 8.5.4 NNSY.PUTQUEUE.ACTION

This node is also an MQOutput node but is configured differently so that your rules and subscriptions can decide where your output message goes.

The Basic tab is left blank with no Queue or Queue Manager name.

The Advanced tab is configured with Destination Mode = Destination List from the pull-down. When a rule results in a putqueue action WebSphere MQ Integrator passes the queue name internally in the message (In the LocalEnvironment folder) for the MQOutput node to process. Refer to Figure 8-9).

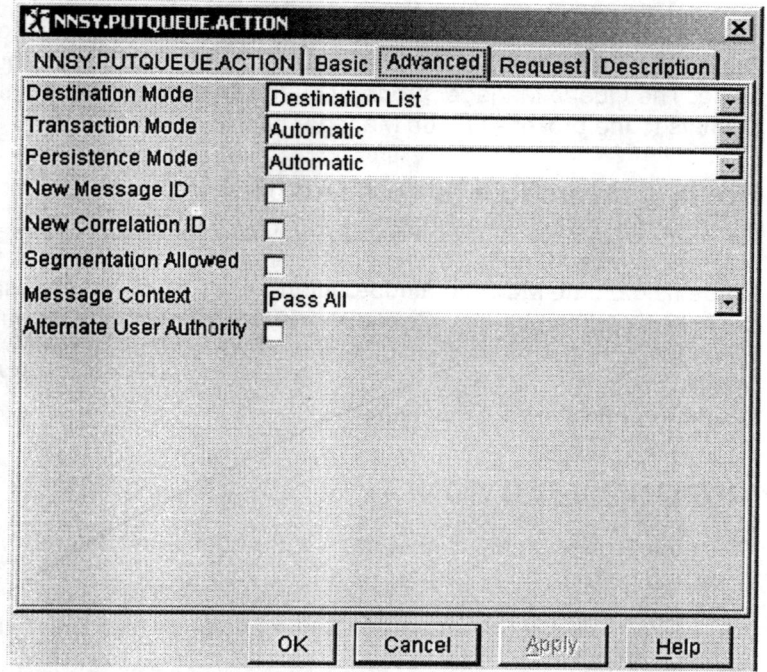

*Figure 8-9 MQOuput node properties for New Era of Networks support*

## 8.6 Other migration considerations

The basic flow described in 8.5, "Creating your migration message flow" on page 157 when deployed to a broker replaces your Rules Engine (RULENG). However, there are a number of other considerations to ensure that all MQSeries Integrator V1.11 functionality is correctly configured in WebSphere MQ Integrator V2.1.

### 8.6.1 Configuring WMQI to match your Rules Engine

You need to consider how you have configured your existing Rules Engine (RULENG) to behave and how the equivalent can be configured with WebSphere MQ Integrator. Table 8-1 on page 163 discusses the various configuration options and how that behavior can be configured in WebSphere MQ Integrator.

*Table 8-1  Rules Engine (RULENG) parameter file values in WebSphere MQ Integrator*

| Rules Engine Parameter | WebSphere MQ Integrator Configuration equivalent |
|---|---|
| CredentialsEnabled | This is configured on all the MQOutput nodes. The default action of an MQOutput node is to put using the authority of the broker, which resolves to CredentialsEnabled=0. If you have configured CredentialsEnabled=1 then you should check the Alternate User Authority box in the Advanced tab on the MQOutput nodes. |
| QueueManagerName | The Queue Manager name is configured when you build a broker. If you have more than one MQSIRuleng running against different Queue Managers you will need more than one broker. |
| MaxBackoutCount | This parameter is configured on the input queue (BOTHRESH), together with a backout queue name (BOQNAME). If the broker tries to process a message that exceeds the backout count it will put it on the backout queue. To emulate MQSIRuleng behavior the backout queue name should match the RulesEvaluate failure queue. |
| InputQueueName | This is configured with the Queue Name on the MQInput node. You can have multiple input queues using multiple MQInput nodes. |
| NoHitQueueName | This is configured by attaching the Nohit terminal of the NEONRulesEvaluation node to an MQOutput node with the Queue Name configured on the Basic properties. |
| FailureQueueName | This is configured by attaching the failure terminal of the NEONRulesEvaluation node to an MQOutput node with the Queue Name configured on the Basic properties. |
| DefaultAppGroup | This is configured on the Message Set parameter of the Default tab on the MQInput node. You must also specify the domain as NEONMSG. |
| DefaultMsgType | This is configured on the Message Type parameter of the Default tab on the MQInput node. You must also specify the domain as NEONMSG. |
| MaxHandles | The number of MQSeries queue handles used by the broker is managed internally and is not configurable. |

| Rules Engine Parameter | WebSphere MQ Integrator Configuration equivalent |
|---|---|
| LogFileName | Errors are written to the console and to stderr, stdout and NNSYMessageLog.nml files. |
| LogLevel | This is configured in the brokers nnsyreg.dat file as follows:<br>Broker.Logging<br>    LogLevel=0 |
| ServerName | Configured in the brokers copy of nnsyreg.dat with the NN_SES_SERVER parameter |
| UserId | The user ID and password comes from the broker started task and is not configured in a parameter file |
| Password | The user ID and password come from the broker started task and are not configured in a parameter file. |
| DatabaseInstance | Configured in the brokers copy of nnsyreg.dat with the NN_SES_DB_NAME parameter. |
| DatabaseType | DB2 is the only supported database type for a z/OS broker. It is implied in the brokers copy of the nnsyreg.dat file from the NNOT_SHARED_LIBRARY and NNOT_FACTORY_FUNCTION values. |

### 8.6.2 User exits

In this release of WebSphere MQ Integrator, references to NEON (a shortened reference to NeoNet from New Era of Networks and not NEON Systems Inc.) have been changed to NNSY. To reflect this, a number of other name changes have been made to header files, directory structures, and environment variables. There is also a new set of libraries delivered with the product.

Any user exits should be recompiled against the new libraries, taking into consideration the name changes detailed in the Readme file.

Refer to SupportPac ID11 for details about restrictions that apply when you run UNIX System Services.

### 8.6.3 Multiple databases and Rules Engines

A single broker can only use one Rules and Formats database schema. Furthermore, a single Queue Manager can only run one broker.

Although more widespread on the distributed platforms, some customers may have created many Rules Engines (RULENG) accessing Rules and Formats in different database schemas and reading different input queues. This might be for a number of reasons such as workload separation, performance or change management. If each database schema contain only a subset of the Rules and Formats used by the organization, then you will need to plan your implementation carefully.

### Additional input queues

If all the Rules Engines (RULENG) access the same databases, but use different input queues this is simply achieved by adding additional MQInput nodes in your flow or creating separate flows. If the additional Rules Engine (RULENG) instance was for performance then WebSphere MQ Integrator can be configured with additional execution groups. These execution groups equate to additional z/OS processes and each can run the same or different flows.

### Additional brokers

If you can justify the additional overheads you can run more than one broker on a single z/OS image. Each broker requires its own Queue Manager and can be configured to use a separate Rules and Formats database schema.

### Merging database schema

Rules and formats can be merged into a single database schema, provided your object names do not conflict with each other. To do this you will need to export all Rules and formats from your existing schemas and import them into a single schema using NNFie and NNRie. This is the preferred method and offers the greatest flexibility when using WebSphere MQ Integrator features.

## 8.7 Other New Era of Networks features

This section introduces some of the other features and functionality that can be utilized with New Era of Networks messages in WebSphere MQ Integrator. These features are not required for migration from MQSeries Integrator V1.11 but might be useful in providing additional benefits to a customer.

### 8.7.1 NEONRulesEvaluation node terminals

This is the most important of the New Era of Networks nodes for migration purposes. We have shown how the Failure, Nohit and Output terminals of a NEONRulesEvaluation node behave. These are the normal terminals used for the purpose of migrating.

There are two more terminals to this node, which enable additional WebSphere MQ Integrator functionality to be used against your existing messages formatted in New Era of Networks GUI tools. The propagate terminal and the route terminal require additional rules and subscription changes and more complex flows. Although not required for migration they do add the considerable power and functionality of WebSphere MQ Integrator.

## The propagate terminal

Within the New Era of Networks rules subscriptions there is a new propagate action. This action passes the message out on the propagate terminal of the NEONRulesEvaluation node rather than the Putqueue terminal. You might use this if you want to do additional processing in other nodes in the flow before writing it out to a queue. These additional nodes will need to provide a destination queue for the message.

A simple example, shown in Figure 8-12 on page 169, demonstrates the use of this. For a particular message type, we want our normal existing Rules and Formats functionality, but additionally we want to store some of the message content in a database and keep the message on an audit queue for 24 hours. We achieved this as follows:

1. In the Rules GUI, build an additional rule for our audit case. In our example shown in Figure 8-10 on page 167, we add a rule called "AuditCase" for anyone with a first name of Steve.

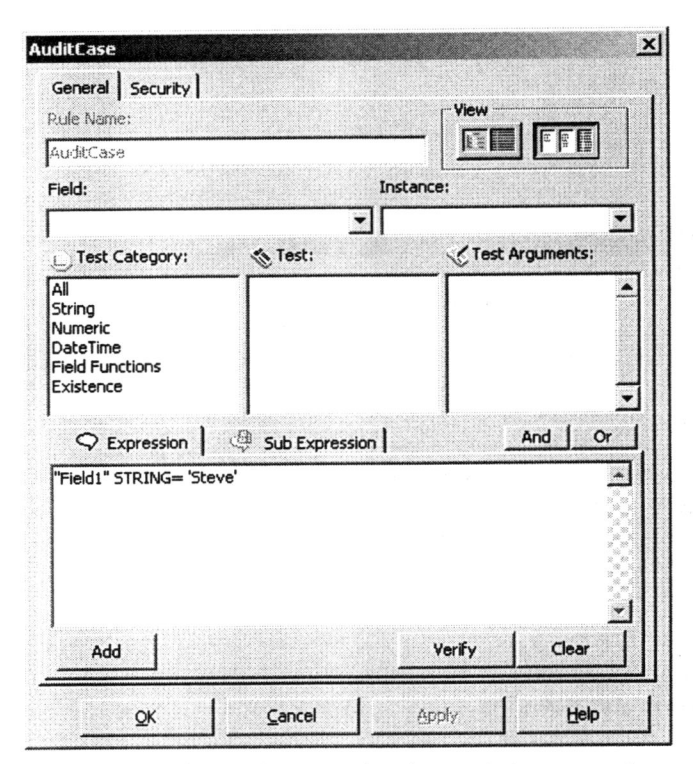

*Figure 8-10   Sample Rule used to demonstrate propagate*

2. Next create a subscription to propagate the message. You may choose to transform the message depending on how you want to process it later in your flow. In our example shown in Figure 8-11 on page 168, we transform it using the new "transform" option, which works similar to the deprecated reformat function. This is followed by a propagate action that sends the message to the propagate terminal.

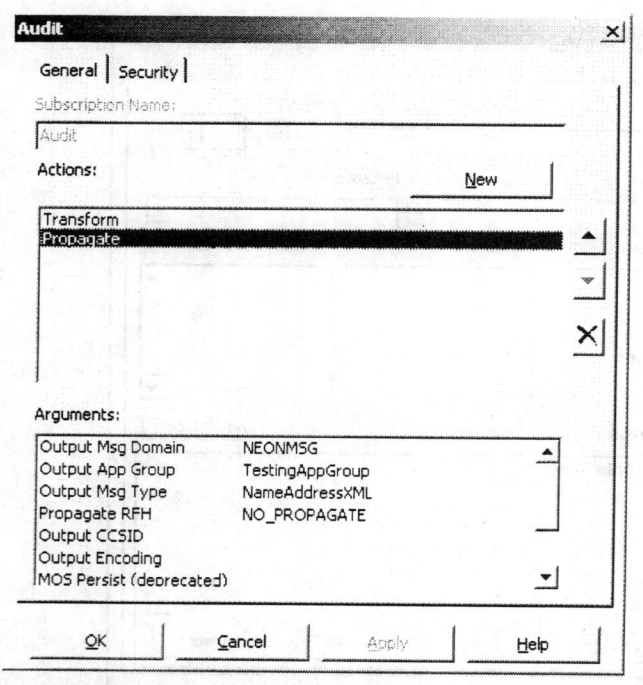

*Figure 8-11 Transform and Propagate Subscription*

3. The message flow continues from the propagate terminal with a database node called StoreInDB to store the data in a database

4. A Compute node called SetExpiry adds an expiration time to the message by setting OutputRoot.MQMD.Expiry.

5. An MQOutput node puts the message on a named queue configured in the node properties.

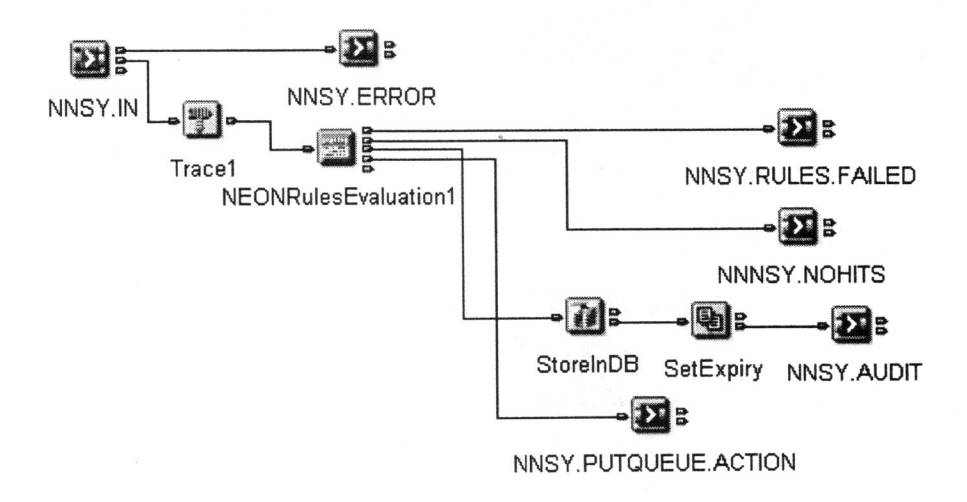

*Figure 8-12   Using the NEONRulesEvaluation propagate terminal*

### The route terminal

The route terminal is similar to the propagate terminal in that it allows us to extend WebSphere MQ Integrator functionality to a New Era of Networks message type. New Era of Networks subscriptions can have a route action. In the route action, we define a label name that should correspond to a label in the message flow.

In Figure 8-13 on page 170 we attach the NEONRulesEvaluation propagate terminal to a RouteToLabel node called RouteToSpecicalCase. There are no configuration options on the RouteToLabel node.

We have two Label nodes, called SpecialCase1 and SpecialCase2. These nodes are configured with a LabelName that must match the Label Name defined on the route action on the subscriptions in the Rules GUI.

When a rule is hit with a route subscription, the broker populates the LocalEnvironment data held internally in the message. When the message reaches the RouteToLabel, the broker checks the LocalEnvironment folder for information on where in the flow to pass control to.

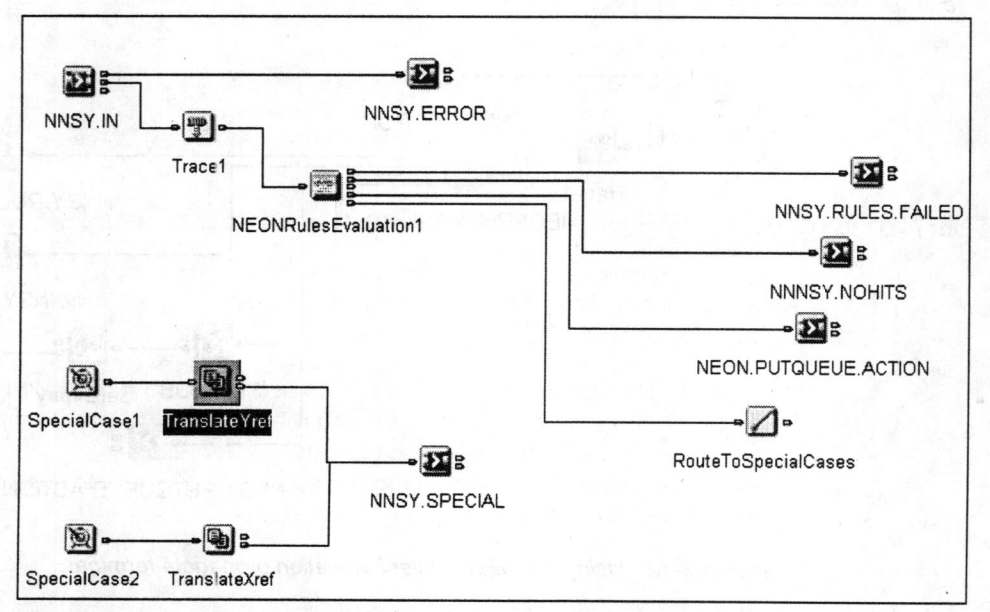

*Figure 8-13 Using the NEONRulesEvaluation route terminal*

## 8.7.2 NEONMap node

Among many new features introduced in the New Era of Networks code are the map functions. These functions are defined in the Formatter GUI and map input fields to output fields. This means you can define the output format with output field names and the input format with input field names. You can then create a map definition that details which field is populated from where. The NEONMap node makes use of this feature, but *does not* apply any of the output operations or controls associated with the map definition.

## 8.7.3 NEONTransform node

This node simply instructs the broker to reformat the incoming message from its current format to the one defined in the node properties. It does not execute any rules. The reformat is explicitly stated in the properties. A simple example of this is shown in 7.4, "Verification" on page 137.

## 8.7.4 NeonRules and NeonFormatter nodes

These nodes are included for compatibility with MQSeries Integrator V2.0. It is recommended that customers migrating from MQSeries Integrator V1.11 to WebSphere MQ Integrator V2.1 *not use them*. NEONRulesEvaluation and NEONTransform nodes are more powerful and should be used.

## 8.7.5 Exploiting ESQL with New Era of Networks messages

Closer coupling of the New Era of Networks support and MQSeries Integrator was advanced in V2.02 and can be exploited with WebSphere MQ Integrator V2.1 using ESQL.

We demonstrated in 7.4.5, "Verification of the Configuration Manager" on page 144 how we can graphically add a New Era of Networks message into a Compute node. This same process can be used in all the database nodes including the Warehouse node and the Filter node. We can further extend the functionality by using ESQL in our message.

In "Building XML" on page 171, we show how to address the fields of a New Era of Networks message using ESQL. In this example we build an XML record from the input message. However, ESQL unlocks much more than this simple example demonstrates and can be exploited in many of the other nodes.

### Building XML

In the next examples we take an input message defined within the formats database and build an XML message using ESQL. These examples demonstrate how to address the elements of a New Era of Networks message. It builds dynamic XML rather than XML defined in the MRM.

To demonstrate this we use a simple flow as shown in Figure 8-14 on page 172. The MQInput nodes and MQOutput nodes are configured with just queue names and renamed to match there queue names. When testing this we used an RFH header and therefore did not configure the basics of the MQInput. The NNSYtoXML node is a Compute node and in the examples we show the ESQL code and the NNSY format.

In the examples we look at addressing simple flat formats, repeating formats and alternate formats.

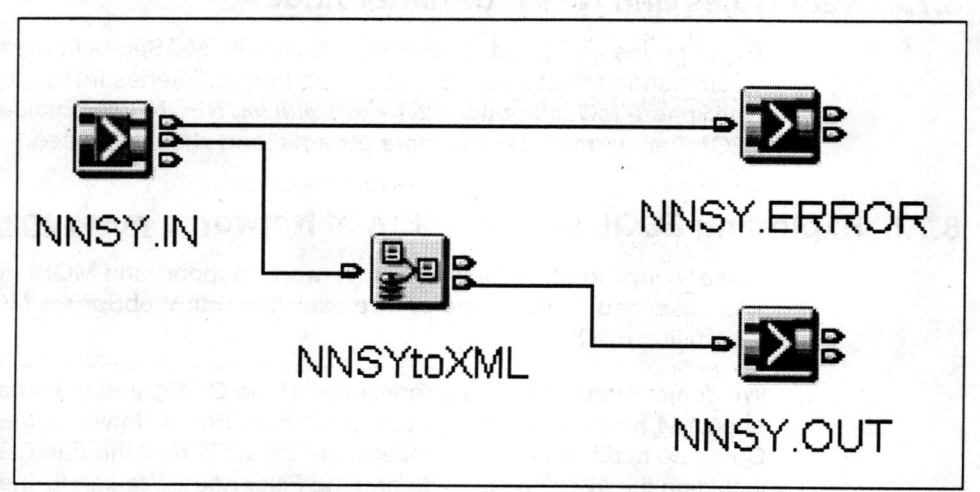

*Figure 8-14   Message flow to translate New Era of Networks message to XML*

## A simple flat format

In this example we use an incoming variable length message with four comma-delimited fields representing Name, Last Name, Address and Postcode.

The input format name is FourFields, shown in Figure 8-15 on page 173.

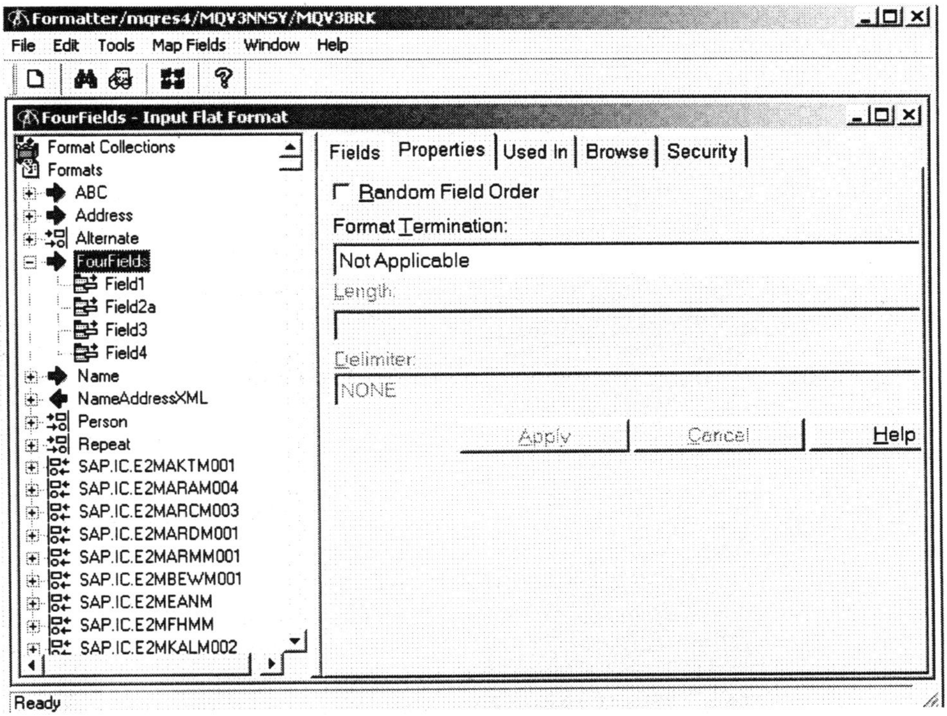
Formatter/mqres4/MQV3NNSY/MQV3BRK
File Edit Tools Map Fields Window Help
FourFields - Input Flat Format
Format Collections
Formats
ABC
Address
Alternate
FourFields
Field1
Field2a
Field3
Field4
Name
NameAddressXML
Person
Repeat
SAP.IC.E2MAKTM001
SAP.IC.E2MARAM004
SAP.IC.E2MARCM003
SAP.IC.E2MARDM001
SAP.IC.E2MARMM001
SAP.IC.E2MBEWM001
SAP.IC.E2MEANM
SAP.IC.E2MFHMM
SAP.IC.E2MKALM002
Fields
Properties
Used In
Browse
Security
Random Field Order
Format Termination:
Not Applicable
Length:
Delimiter:
NONE
Apply
Cancel
Help
Ready

*Figure 8-15 Simple New Era of Networks flat input format*

The ESQL code in Example 8-1 on page 174 is generated by clicking the **Copy message headers** button and then entering the ESQL below the comment line to generate the XML. Notice that we do not address the format name, just the fields.

From an input message shown in Figure 8-16:

```
John,Doe,Apt 523 Waterford Village Durham,NC27713
```

*Figure 8-16 Simple input message*

We generate an XML output message, shown in Figure 8-17 on page 174.

> **Note:** The XML output has been formatted for easier reading in all the examples shown.

```
<People>
  <Person>
    <Name>
      <FirstName>John</FirstName>
      <LastName>Doe</LastName>
    </Name>
    <Address>
      <Line1>,Apt 523 Waterford Village Durham</Line1>
      <PostCode>NC27713</PostCode>
    </Address>
  </Person>
</People>
```

*Figure 8-17  XML output message*

*Example 8-1  Compute node ESQL to create XML from flat FourFields format*

```
DECLARE I INTEGER;
SET I = 1;
WHILE I < CARDINALITY(InputRoot.*[]) DO
   SET OutputRoot.*[I] = InputRoot.*[I];
   SET I=I+1;
END WHILE;
-- Enter SQL below this line.  SQL above this line might be regenerated,
causing any modifications to be lost.
SET OutputRoot.XML.People.Person.Name.FirstName = InputRoot.NEONMSG.Field1;
SET OutputRoot.XML.People.Person.Name.LastName = InputRoot.NEONMSG.Field2a;
SET OutputRoot.XML.People.Person.Address.Line1 = InputRoot.NEONMSG.Field3;
SET OutputRoot.XML.People.Person.Address.PostCode = InputRoot.NEONMSG.Field4;
```

## A repeating format

In this example we have a simple repeating compound input format called "Repeat", shown in Figure 8-18 on page 175. The compound format Repeat contains a repeating flat format called "Twofields". We are expecting an input message with pairs of firstname and lastnames, comma delimited, as shown in Figure 8-19 on page 175.

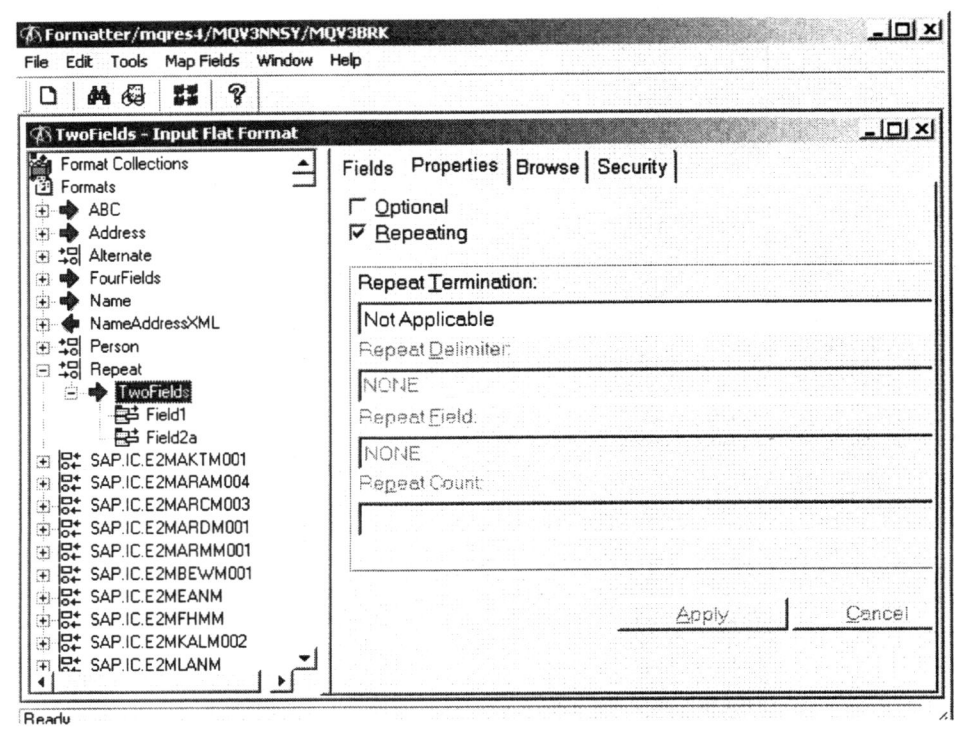

*Figure 8-18 Simple New Era of Networks repeating format*

To distinguish between different instances of a repeat format we use square brackets with an index number to represent the specific instance. This can be seen in the Compute node ESQL in Example 8-2 on page 176.

```
John,Doe,Joe,Bloggs
```

*Figure 8-19 Simple input message*

The input message shown in Figure 8-19 is reformatted to XML shown in Figure 8-20 on page 176.

```
<People>
  <Person>
    <Name>
      <FirstName>John</FirstName>
      <LastName>Doe</LastName>
    </Name>
  </Person>
  <Person>
    <Name>
      <FirstName>Joe</FirstName>
      <LastName>Bloggs</LastName>
    </Name>
  </Person>
</People>
```

*Figure 8-20   XML output from repeating message*

The while loop in Example 8-2 on page 176 checks to see if the first field Field1 has a value for each instance of TwoFields in the input message. When it reaches InputRoot.NEONMSG.TwoFields[3].Field1, the third instance which does not exist, NULL is returned and the loop is exited.

*Example 8-2   Compute node ESQL to create XML from a repeat format*

```
DECLARE I INTEGER;
SET I = 1;
WHILE I < CARDINALITY(InputRoot.*[]) DO
   SET OutputRoot.*[I] = InputRoot.*[I];
   SET I=I+1;
END WHILE;
-- Enter SQL below this line.  SQL above this line might be regenerated,
causing any modifications to be lost.
DECLARE J INTEGER;
SET J = 1;
WHILE InputRoot.NEONMSG.TwoFields[J].Field1 is not NULL DO
SET OutputRoot.XML.People.Person[J].Name.FirstName =
InputRoot.NEONMSG.TwoFields[J].Field1;
SET OutputRoot.XML.People.Person[J].Name.LastName =
InputRoot.NEONMSG.TwoFields[J].Field2a;
SET J=J+1;
END WHILE;
```

## An alternate format

In this example we have a simple alternate format called "Alternate", shown in Figure 8-21. It is expecting either a simple TwoFields firstname and lastname record or an alternate firstname, lastname, address, postcode record. A separate termination character was put on each of the two flat formats to distinguish which alternate was present in the compound format "Alternate".

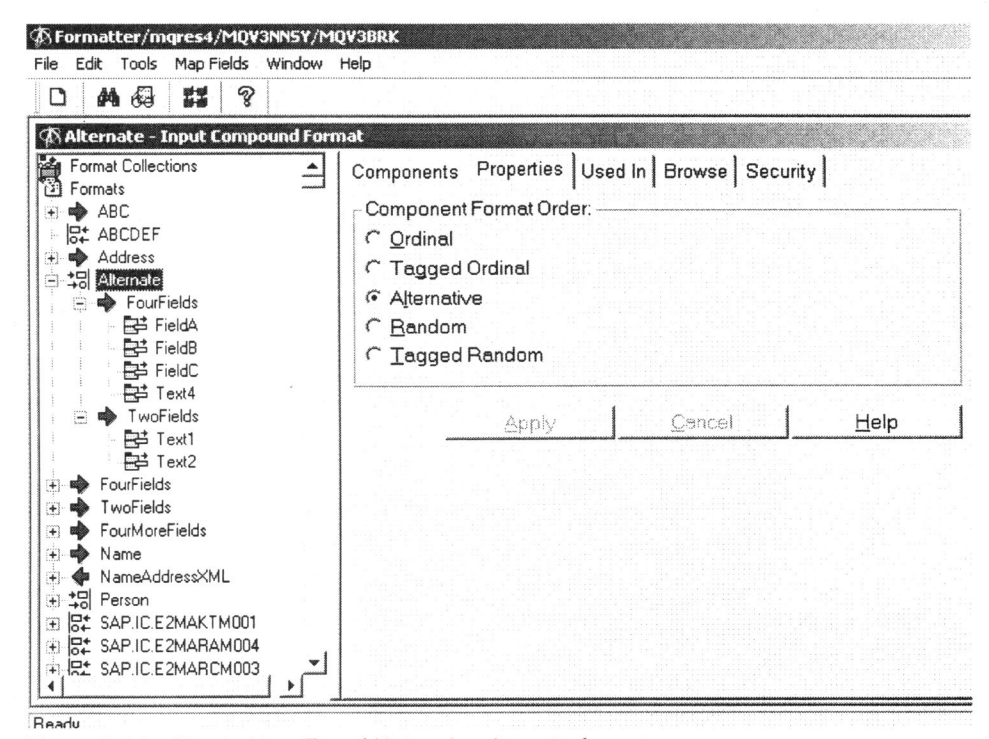

*Figure 8-21 Simple New Era of Networks alternate format*

If we use the record in our first example, shown in Figure 8-16 on page 173, with just FirstName and LastName, we expect the same results as we got previously. However, if we have four fields we expect the additional fields Address and Postcode to be written to the output XML.

In our ESQL we always copy the first two fields over because whether it is a TwoFields or FourFields alternate the fields are always FirstName and LastName. Rather than fully addressing the elements by name, we address them by relative position. The following lines of ESQL code achieve this goal:

```
SET OutputRoot.XML.People.Person.Name.FirstName = InputRoot.NEONMSG.*[3].*[1];

SET OutputRoot.XML.People.Person.Name.LastName = InputRoot.NEONMSG.*[3].*[2];
```

To understand why we address the third element of NEONMSG, we have to understand how the message is parsed. This is shown with a trace, an extract of which is shown in Figure 8-22. When the message is parsed by the broker it appends two folders, MessageType and Format, before the data content.

```
(0x1000000)NEONMSG     = (
   (0x7000000)MessageType = 'Alternate'
   (0x7000000)Format      = 'Content'
   (0x1000000)TwoFields   = (
      (0x3000000)Text1 = 'Joe'
      (0x3000000)Text2 = 'Of no addresss'
   )
)
```

*Figure 8-22   Sample trace showing parsing of NEONMSG*

Having copied the first two fields, the ESQL checks that the third field is present and if it is, it copies the additional Address and PostCode elements (Example 8-3).

*Example 8-3   Compute node ESQL to create XML from an alternate format*

```
DECLARE I INTEGER;
SET I = 1;
WHILE I < CARDINALITY(InputRoot.*[]) DO
   SET OutputRoot.*[I] = InputRoot.*[I];
   SET I=I+1;
END WHILE;
-- Enter SQL below this line.  SQL above this line might be regenerated,
causing any modifications to be lost.

SET OutputRoot.XML.People.Person.Name.FirstName = InputRoot.NEONMSG.*[3].*[1];
SET OutputRoot.XML.People.Person.Name.LastName = InputRoot.NEONMSG.*[3].*[2];

if InputRoot.NEONMSG.FourFields.*[3] is not NULL then
 SET OutputRoot.XML.People.Person.Name.Address =
InputRoot.NEONMSG.FourFields.*[3];
 SET OutputRoot.XML.People.Person.Name.PostCode =
InputRoot.NEONMSG.FourFields.*[4];
end if;
```

This way of addressing the fields of a New Era of Networks message with ESQL can be extended to much more complex messages. This technique helps to integrate existing messages with the advanced functionality of WebSphere MQ Integrator.

**Note:** An alternative way to create XML formats from New Era of Networks messages is to use a NEONTransform or NEONMap nodes and set the output domain to XML. This technique converts the data to XML encapsulating the data in XML tags matching their field names in the output format. It is useful only if your field names match your XML tag requirements and you have no literals in the output format.

# 9

# Migration from distributed platforms to WMQI for z/OS

If you already have production systems on earlier releases of WMQI, they run on one of supported distributed platforms. To migrate those flows to WMQI for z/OS, you can follow one of the following two paths:

- Migrate to WMQI V2.1 on your distributed platform and then migrate to WMQI for z/OS
- Migrate directly from WMQI on a distributed platform on an earlier release to WMQI for z/OS V2.1

You should prefer, whenever possible, the first path. Thus, you will deal with release-to-release migration and platform migration separately. In the course of this project, we did not encounter particular problems deploying flows developed on a Windows platform to WMQI for z/OS. We identified, however, some areas that should be given special consideration.

We discuss these considerations and describe the tasks that must be performed. The topics we cover are:

- General migration considerations
- Migration from Version 2.0.2
- Migration from Version 2.0.1
- Migration from Version 2.0

> **Note:** If you need to migrate from MQSeries Integrator Version 1 or Version 1.1 on z/OS, refer to the *WebSphere MQ Integrator for z/OS Customization and Administration Guide* and to "Migrating New Era of Networks Rules and Formats from MQSeries Integrator Version 1.11" on page 151 of this book.

The material discussed in this chapter is based on tasks introduced and implemented in *WebSphere MQ Integrator Administration Guide* and *WebSphere MQ Integrator for z/OS Customization and Administration Guide*.

## 9.1 Considerations for migration

WebSphere MQ Integrator introduces some significant changes over previous releases of MQSeries Integrator. As you start your migration process following the instructions in the *WebSphere MQ Integrator Administration Guide* and *WebSphere MQ Integrator for z/OS Customization and Administration Guide*, most of the changes are handled for you automatically. Pay attention to the following issues:

- Refer to the Readme.txt to ensure that you have access to the latest information available for migration and related topics.

- If your message flow accesses databases, the first question you have to ask yourself is whether to migrate those databases to DB2 for z/OS. If the database that you use on your distributed platform is DB2 Universal Database (UDB), you can probably leave your data there and access it from your message flows on z/OS using capabilities provided by the DB2 UDB environment. If this database is not DB2 UDB, you would need an IBM Data Joiner product to access this data. In this case, you would probably prefer to migrate this relational data to DB2 on z/OS.

- Database Source Name

    In a message flow that uses database accesses in a distributed environment, an ODBC source name will have been used in the Database Source name in the message flow node. This value should be the DDF location name when the broker runs on z/OS. You might have to make this change in your message flow.

- In earlier releases of WMQI, you could define an invalid XML format that later in the flow would be corrected.

    For example:

    SET OutputRoot.XML.Customer.Name.FirstName='John';

    SET OutputRoot.XML.MetaData.ProcessOption='NO';

This is no longer supported and any code written in this way will not work.

- Because all flows on z/OS are globally coordinated, you might observe a different transactional behavior of your message flow when you migrate it to WMQI for z/OS. On z/OS you can also mix a database commit in the middle of a flow while maintaining the global transaction. On distributed platforms you can *not* mix Commit and Automatic options when running under a global transaction. Refer to "Transactional support" on page 48 for more information.
- It is recommended that you upgrade your components in the following order: Configuration Manager, Control Center, Broker.
- You might consider migrating your distributed environment to V2.1 first, because of the significant enhancements in the MRM and the changes in its underlying structure. Migrate and exercise your message sets and associated flows on the distributed V2.1 that you are familiar with to insure they are working. Then deploy to z/OS V2.1, which has proven very straightforward in the examples developed for this book.

## 9.2 Migrating from MQSeries Integrator V2.02

To successfully migrate from Version 2.0.2 to Version 2.1, you must perform the following tasks:

- Upgrade the Configuration Manager to the new version.
- Upgrade the Control Center to the new version.
- Upgrade the broker to WebSphere MQ Integrator V2.1.

**Note:** The User Name Server is not required to be upgraded on any platform.

### 9.2.1 Upgrading your MQSeries Integrator V2.02 Configuration Manager

This section focuses on migration of the Configuration Manager from Version 2.0.2 to 2.1. The steps to perform are:

- Check in all message flows and message sets.
- Preserve the existing configuration data.
- Delete and recreate the Configuration Manager.

## Preserving the existing configuration data

It is strongly recommended that you preserve your existing configuration data when you delete the Configuration Manager.

To keep your existing configuration data, use the command `mqsiimpexpmsgset` to preserve your message set definitions as follows:

```
mqsiimpexpmsgset -e -s <MessageSetName> -l <MessageSetLevel> -n
<MRMDataSourceName> -u <MRMDataSourceUserID> -p <MRMDataSourcePassword>
-f <XMLFileName>
```

For example:

```
mqsiimpexpmsgset -e -s "Accounts Payable" -l 1 -n MQSIMRDB -u mqsiuid -p
mqsipwd -f acctpay.mrp
```

This command exports the message sets stored in the message repository into a file that you can import after reinstallation. If you do not perform this step to preserve your configuration data, you will lose all your message sets.

## Delete and recreate the Configuration Manager

You must delete and recreate the Configuration Manager to pick up new and changed IBM-supplied nodes, and to incorporate modifications to tables. Follow the steps below to complete this properly:

1. Delete the Configuration Manager and queues on its local Queue Manager using the command `mqsideleteconfigmgr` without specifying the -n and -m flags (not specifying the -n and -m flags preserves the configuration repository and message repository, respectively, in the existing tables).

    For example:

    ```
    mqsideleteconfigmgr -q [-w]
    ```

    **Note:** Be very careful in specifying the -n and -m flags. The configuration repository and message repository contain the configuration data for the whole broker domain, not just data internal to the Configuration Manager itself. Deleting these repositories therefore destroys all information pertinent to the broker domain, and requires that you destroy every resource within it to recover the broker domain.

2. Remove the Version 2.0.2 Integrator software on the system.
3. Install WebSphere MQ Integrator V 2.1 software on the Windows platform.
4. Open a DB2 command window with `db2cmd` command.
5. From the DB2 command window issue the following command:

```
mqsimrmdroptables <MRMDataSourceName> <MRMDataSourceUserID>
<MRMDataSourcePassword>
```

This command drops the tables that are contained in the message repository. You must therefore ensure that you specify the correct values for <MRMDataSourceName>, <MRMDataSourceUserID>, and <MRMDataSourcePassword>.

6. From the DB2 command window issue the following command:

   ```
   mqsimigrateconfigmgr <DataBaseName> <DataBaseUserID>
   <DataBasePassword>
   ```

   This command updates the tables that are contained in the configuration repository. You must therefore ensure that you specify the correct values for <DataBaseName>, <DataBaseUserID>, and <DataBasePassword>.

7. From the Windows command line, issue the following command to create and Configuration Manager:

   ```
   mqsicreateconfigmgr -i <ServiceUserID> -a <ServicePassword> -q
   <QueueManager> -n <DataBaseName> -u <DataBaseUserID> -p
   <DataBasePassword> -m <MRMDataSourceName> -e <MRMDataSourceUserID>
   -r <MRMDataSourcePassword> -s <UserNameServer QueueManagerName> -w
   <workpath>
   ```

   For example:

   ```
   mqsicreateconfigmgr -i mqsiuid -a mqsipw -q CM_MQ -n MQSICMBRK -m
   MQSIMRBRK -s MQV3
   ```

   You must specify the same values for the parameters <DataBaseName>, <DataBaseUserID>, and <DataBasePassword> on this command as those you used on the mqsimigrateconfigmgr command. If you do not do so, the Configuration Manager is unable to access the configuration data that you preserved.

8. Use the mqsiimpexpmsgset command to import the message sets you exported as follows:

   ```
   mqsiimpexpmsgset -i -s <MessageSetName> -l <MessageSetLevel> -n
   <MRMDataSourceName> -u <MRMDataSourceUserID -p
   <MRMDataSourcePassword -f <XMLFileName>
   ```

   For example:

   ```
   mqsiimpexpmsgset -i -s "Accounts Payable" -l 1 -n MQSIMRDB
   -u mqsiuid -p mqsipwd -f acctpay.mrp
   ```

   The import action automatically converts your message sets to the new format supported by WebSphere MQ Integrator 2.1.

### 9.2.2 Upgrading your MQSeries Integrator V2.02 Control Center

To upgrade the Control Center, do the following tasks:

1. Check in the message flows prior to upgrading the Configuration Manager to WebSphere MQ Integrator Version 2.1.
2. Uninstall the earlier version software.
3. Install WebSphere MQ Integrator Version 2.1.

> **Note:** When you upgrade the Control Center to WebSphere MQ Integrator Version 2.1, you must upgrade the Configuration Manager to the same version (the Configuration Manager and Control Center must always be at the same version level). The brokers can be upgraded later.

### 9.2.3 Upgrading your MQSeries Integrator V2.02 brokers

Upgrading the broker to WebSphere MQ Integrator Version 2.1 does not technically have to happen at the same time you upgrade the Configuration Manager and Control Center, but there is no business advantage to delaying this migration. It is strongly recommended that you migrate the brokers to the newer version after completing the migration of the Configuration Manager and Control Center.

To upgrade the broker, perform the following tasks:

1. Stop the broker(s) that are running on the system using the `mqsistop` command.
2. Back up the broker database tables.
3. Back up your user data contained in directories /var/mqsi and /opt/mqsi, if applicable.
4. Uninstall the Integrator software.
5. Install the newer version of Integrator.
6. Migrate each database used by the broker(s) to the Version 2.1 level.
7. Migrate each instance of the database associated with each user ID.

> **Note:** It is very important that you successfully complete this task: If you do not do so, the broker generates runtime errors when it interacts with a database that has not been migrated.

To ensure successful completion of migration of the database and user IDs to the WebSphere MQ Integrator 2.1 do the following:

1. Create a new temporary broker, with any convenient name, specifying the name of the database with the -n flag and the appropriate database user ID with the -u flag on the `mqsicreatebroker` command.

   For example:

   ```
   mqsicreatebroker MQV3BRK -c <DatabaseName> -n <Database Name> -u <User ID>
   ```

   This causes new database tables introduced in WebSphere MQ Integrator 2.1 to be created for this user ID.

2. Delete the temporary broker that you have just created using the `mqsicreatebroker` command.

> **Note:** You must start brokers that use a particular database and user ID only after you have carried out the above steps for the database and user ID.

### 9.2.4 Migrating New Era of Networks Rules and Formats from V2.02

If you plan to migrate your New Era of Networks Rules and Formats from MQSeries Integrator V2.02 to WebSphere MQ Integrator V2.1 for z/OS, pay attention to the following limitation. You cannot FTP an NNFie export file from Windows to z/OS and import it using the z/OS version of NNFie. You must use the Windows version of NNFie with an ODBC connection to the DB2 z/OS database.

## 9.3 Migrating from MQSeries Integrator V2.0.1

Follow the steps outlined in "Migrating from MQSeries Integrator V2.02" on page 183 for migrating the Configuration Manager, Control Center, and broker from MQSeries Integrator Version 2.0.2 to WebSphere MQ Integrator Version 2.1. You should follow those tasks for a successful migration from Version 2.0.1 as well. In this section, we discuss some coexistence issues.

### Coexisting with MQSeries Integrator V2.0.1 brokers

If you want to continue working with one or more brokers in your broker domain at MQSeries Integrator Version 2.0.1 level after you have migrated your Configuration Manager and Control Center to WebSphere MQ Integrator Version 2.1, you must install a migration library on each relevant broker system. This library is supplied with WebSphere MQ Integrator Version 2.1.

To use earlier version brokers do the following:

1. Copy the migration loadable implementation library (LIL) file imbdfmignd.lil from <install_dir> to the /bin directory within the MQSeries Integrator Version 2.0.1 product directory, or the /lil directory.
2. Ensure that the file ownership and permissions on the broker system are set to the same value as those in the Version 2.1 system.
3. Restart the broker.

If you do not install this migration library, when you deploy to a MQSeries Integrator Version 2.0.1 broker from the WebSphere MQ Integrator Version 2.1 Control Center, errors BIP2087E, BIP4041E, and BIP2241E are generated and the operation fails.

## 9.4 Migrating from MQSeries Integrator V2.0

The steps necessary to migrate the Configuration Manager and Control Center from MQSeries Integrator Version 2.0 to WebSphere MQ Integrator Version 2.1 have been described in "Migrating from MQSeries Integrator V2.02" on page 183. You should follow those tasks for a successful migration. There are some additional considerations when you want to migrate a broker from MQSeries Integrator Version 2.0 to WebSphere MQ Integrator Version 2.1. For example, you can not use the Control Center for the Version 2.1 to work with Version 2.0 brokers. In this section we discuss the tasks to upgrade the Version 2.0 broker to Version 2.1.

### Upgrading your MQSeries Integrator V2.0 brokers

Upgrading the Version 2.0 broker has to be done at the same time that the Configuration Manager and Control Center is upgraded. You will not be able to communicate with the broker otherwise. To upgrade the Version 2.0 broker you should do the following:

- Back up your broker database tables.
- Stop the broker(s) using the **mqsistop** command.
- Uninstall the Version 2.0 software.
- Install WebSphere MQ Integrator Version 2.1 on the system.

After you have the new version software installed, you must migrate each different database used by the brokers on this system to the version 2.1 level. The databases created for the broker are associated with the user ID that you specified on the -u flag of the **mqsicreatebroker** command, or that you later modified using the **mqsichangebroker** command. You must therefore migrate each instance of the database associated with each user ID to complete the migration.

For each database you must perform the following:

1. Use the DB2 Control Center or issue **db2cmd** to open a DB2 command window.
2. Run the following command for each database and user ID:

   **mqsimigratebroker db2 <DataSourceName> <DataSourceUserID> <DataSourcePassword>**
3. Create a new temporary broker, with any convenient name, specifying the name of the database with the -n flag and the appropriate database user ID with the -u flag on the **mqsicreatebroker** command.

   **Note:** This step is important because it causes new database tables required by WebSphere MQ Integrator 2.1 to be created for this user ID, and existing tables are automatically upgraded.

4. Delete the temporary broker that you have just created using the **mqsideletebroker** command.

You must start brokers that use a particular database and user ID only after you have carried out the last two steps above.

# 10

# WMQI in a Parallel Sysplex environment

In this chapter, we describe possible configurations of WMQI in a z/OS Parallel Sysplex, and considerations to be taken into account for working with this architecture. It explains how to set up and configure the brokers, User Name Servers, Queue Managers and their elements, and how to deploy message flows to these brokers when high availability is desired.

We also cover transactional message flow behavior on a Parallel Sysplex and publishing and subscribing applications.

For a discussion regarding performance aspects of WMQI execution in a z/OS environment, refer to SupportPac IP11 - WebSphere MQ Integrator for z/OS V2.1 Performance report.

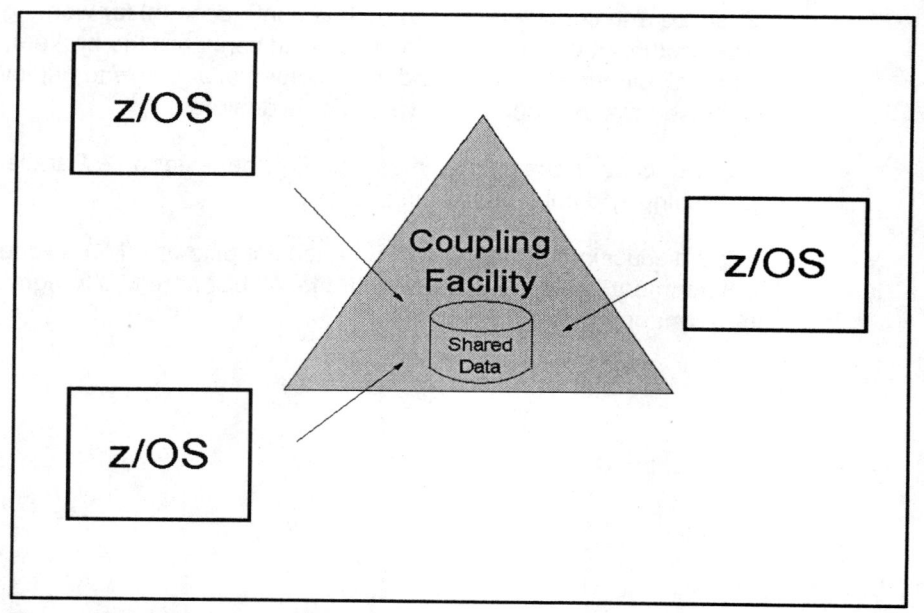

## 10.1 The Parallel Sysplex concept

A Parallel Sysplex is a group of two or more z/OS (or OS/390) computer systems operating as one computer system. Its purpose is to allow users to combine the processing capability of more than one z/OS while appearing as one large computer system (a single-system image) to both the administrators and the system operators.

The Parallel Sysplex enables its components to work as a single system, by synchronizing their time references and allowing data to be shared while ensuring data integrity. This is achieved while offering a single image for operations, and its main benefit is continuous availability. Other features of this architecture are dynamic load balancing and data sharing and integrity across multiple processors.

Data sharing is made possible by the Coupling Facility. It provides locking, caching and message list services among processors. The Coupling Facility may be executed in a logical partition (LPAR), or supported by a separate processor, within the sysplex, but always outside any of its z/OS images. Typically it is configured to run in a separate device, and made resilient to software failures and also to hardware and power failures, making its stored information highly available.

Figure 10-1 illustrates the Parallel Sysplex concept.

*Figure 10-1  The Parallel Sysplex concept*

> **Note:** Although a single Coupling Facility is used in this chapter's charts and explanations, the Coupling Facility in production environments *is usually duplicated* to ensure high availability.

## 10.2 MQSeries message sharing

In this topic we describe how MQSeries makes use of the features of a Parallel Sysplex. These mechanisms are fundamental to an understanding of the behavior of WMQI message flows in a Parallel Sysplex architecture.

This topic is based on parts of the *MQSeries for OS/390 Concepts and Planning Guide,* GC34-5650.

### 10.2.1 Queue-sharing groups

We introduce in this section some concepts pertinent to a queue-sharing environment.

#### Definition

A queue-sharing group consists of several Queue Managers, running in a sysplex, that are able to access the same objects and data concurrently. The shareable object definitions are stored in a shared DB2 database, and message data held in at least one Coupling Facility.

#### Message data shareability

Message data is available for all Queue Managers in the sharing group, and may be retrieved by applications connected to any of them, if it is held in a shared queue. Message data may be stored in local queues as well, becoming available only for applications connected to the Queue Manager those local queues belong to.

#### Shared objects

The shared objects are defined from any of the Queue Managers in the group, becoming available for the whole group. Once a shared object has been defined, no object can be defined locally, in any of the Queue Managers in the group, with the same name as the existing shared object.

## Peer recovery

MQSeries is able to detect if another Queue Manager has disconnected from the Coupling Facility abnormally, and back out its in-flight units of work, leaving the information available for processing by the applications connected to any other Queue Manager in the group. This feature is known as *peer recovery*.

Figure 10-2 illustrates application access to shared queues from z/OS images.

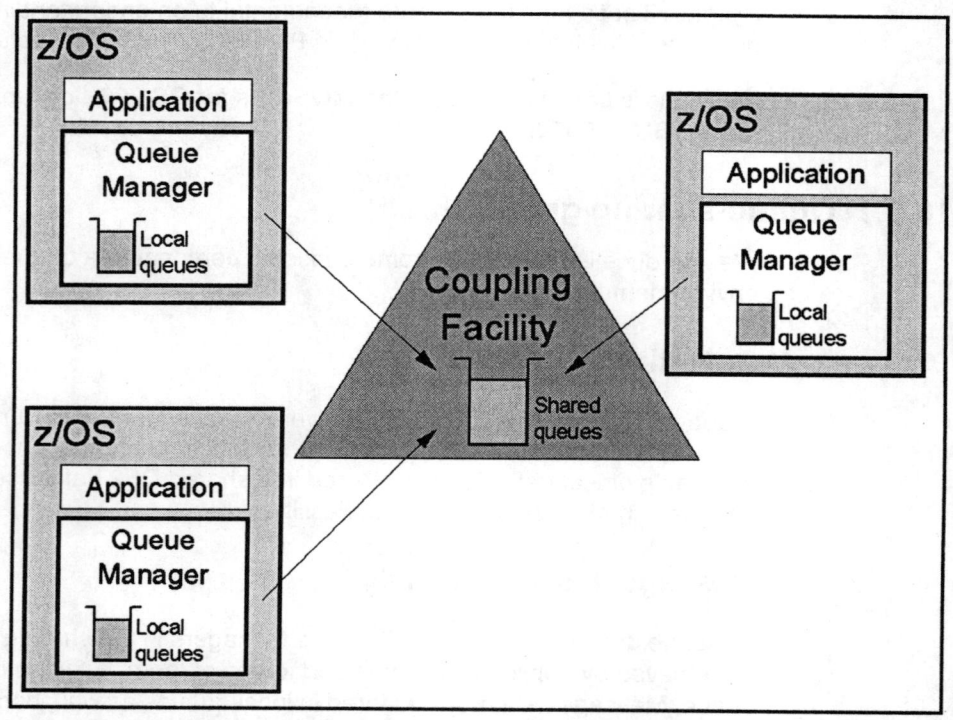

*Figure 10-2  Applications working with Queue Managers in a queue-sharing group*

### 10.2.2 Shared objects

In a Parallel Sysplex environment, queues and channels can be shared between Queue Managers running on different MVS images.

#### Shared queues

A *shared queue* is a local queue defined as shared by any of the Queue Managers in the queue-sharing group. A message can be put to a shared queue using any given Queue Manager, and accessed through any other.

The messages held in a shared queue are stored in the Coupling Facility, making them available for all the Queue Managers in the group.

For storing messages, the Coupling Facility *list structures* are used, which need to be defined before a shared queue can be defined. The name of the structure is provided when defining the shared queue. The length of a message in the shared queue is limited to 63 Kb.

Shared queues do not support message persistence. Anyway, the messages in shared queues are stored in the Coupling Facility, what makes them highly available. A Queue Manager receiving a message set as persistent for putting into a shared queue will send it to the Dead Letter queue.

The Coupling Facility storage is limited. This has to be taken into account when working with these queues, to prevent them from becoming full. Also queue indexing is limited because of this fact.

### Shared channels

VTAM Generic Resources and also TCP/IP Domain Name System (DNS) are the technologies used by channel initiators to achieve inbound network requests balancing among servers. Server failures can thus be hidden from the network. To take advantage of the capabilities of shared queues, shared channels are also defined with the help of these components.

- Inbound channels.

  An additional listener is started by the channel initiator in the queue-sharing group, listening on a *generic port*. The request coming through the generic port is dispatched to any of the listeners in the queue-sharing group.

- Outbound channels.

  An outbound channel takes messages from a shared transmission queue. It is started by any channel initiator within the queue sharing group, and restarted by any other channel initiator in the group if the Queue Manager or the channel initiator itself fails.

  Given that outbound channels read from shared queues, the maximum message length supported by one of these channels is 63 Kb, a limitation imposed by use of the Coupling Facility.

## 10.2.3 Remarks

- All Queue Managers in a queue-sharing group share queues and channels.
- The messages present in a shared queue are available for all the Queue Managers in the group.

- A Queue Manager is able to back out an unfinished unit of work of another Queue Manager that has disconnected abnormally from the Coupling Facility.
- The maximum message length for a shared queue, and also for a shared sender channel, is 63 Kb.
- Message persistence is *not* allowed for shared queues.

Figure 10-3 shows system components involved in queue and channel sharing.

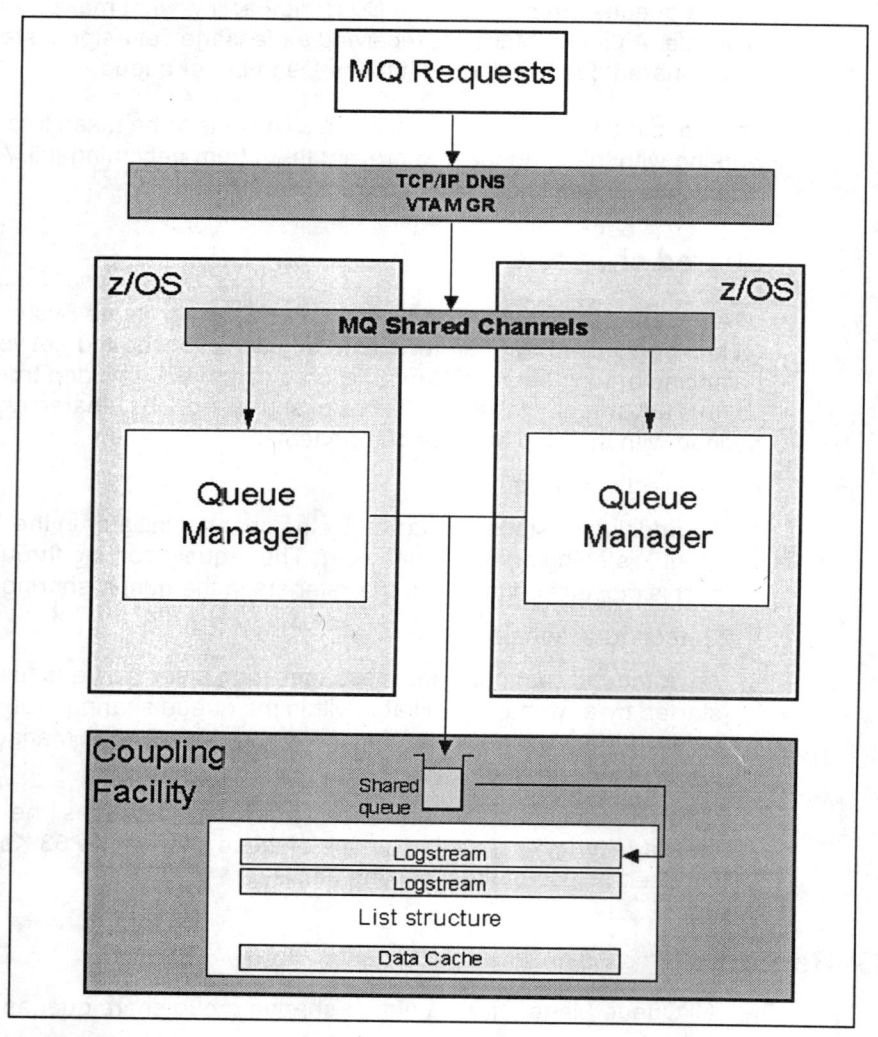

*Figure 10-3 Different components involved in the MQ shared objects usage*

## 10.3 WMQI configuration in a Parallel Sysplex

In this section we discuss configuration considerations for WMQI in a Parallel Sysplex environment.

### 10.3.1 Introduction

The high availability features of WebSphere MQ Integrator in a Parallel Sysplex environment rely upon base MQSeries support discussed in the previous section. A WMQI broker is an MQSeries application. It is connected to a specific Queue Manager and executes message flows. Our goal is to achieve high availability for these message flows.

### 10.3.2 Overview

Figure 10-4 depicts a configuration with multiple brokers in a Parallel Sysplex.

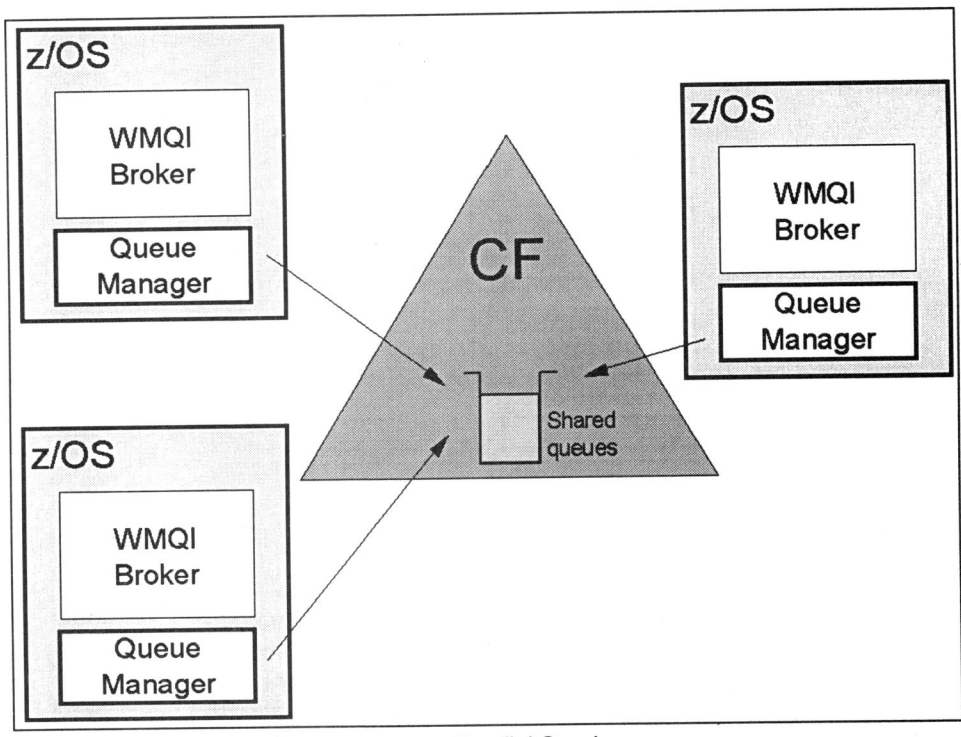

*Figure 10-4 Multiple WMQI brokers in a Parallel Sysplex*

Improved availability of WMQI message flows can be achieved if they are deployed to several brokers. The Queue Managers these brokers are connected to share the queues involved in those message flows. That means that the data present in any of these shared queues is available to any broker. In case of a failure of one of the systems, unfinished units of work are backed out, so the backed-out messages are available for the rest of the brokers in the sysplex.

> **Note:** Other resources involved in a given unit of work of a message flow, such as DB2 resources, should be shared as well, so that consistency is maintained if a transaction is backed out and restarted in another system.

### 10.3.3 WMQI sample architecture

The WebSphere MQSeries Integrator architecture used in the test cases for this chapter is based on three z/OS systems in a Parallel Sysplex, with a Queue Manager in each of them, in a queue-sharing group. The WMQI Configuration Manager is running in a Windows 2000 server, with a local Queue Manager (see Figure 10-5).

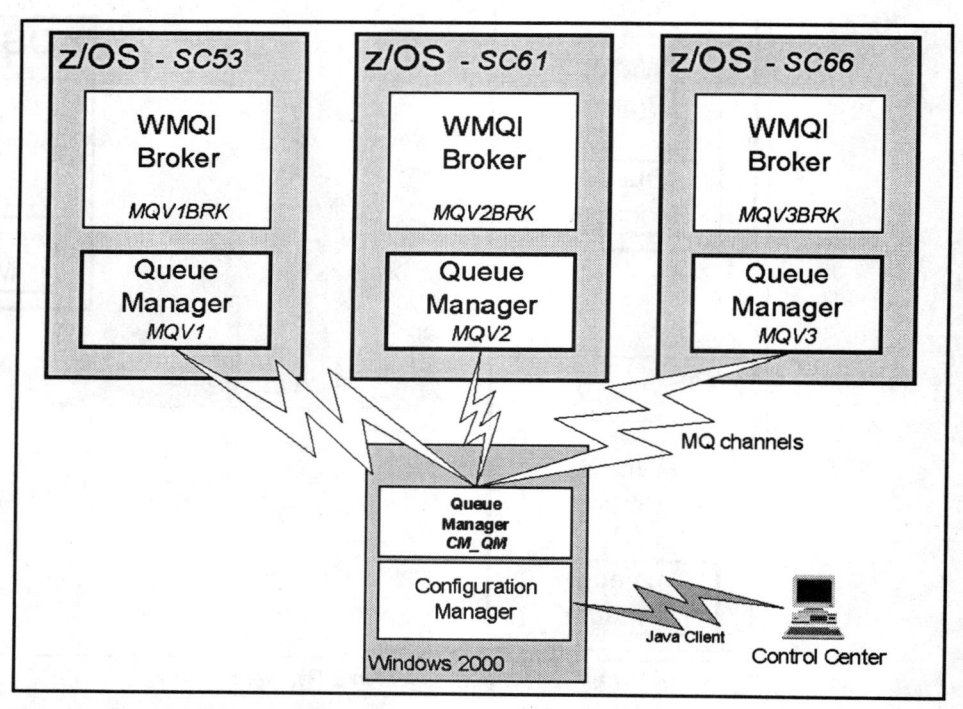

*Figure 10-5   The WMQI architecture used for this chapter*

The WMQI network is based on connections among the different Queue Managers. These connections are achieved using the corresponding channel pairs, transmit queues and initiated processes.

Refer to Chapter 4, "Configuration of WMQI on z/OS and Windows platforms" on page 61 for a discussion of:

- A relation of elements needed to connect two Queue Managers
- The necessary steps to be taken to configure and run a broker in a z/OS environment

## WMQI topology

Once all the brokers in the sysplex have been defined and started in their corresponding environments, they have to be defined in the Configuration Manager's topology. This action is performed in the Control Center, by specifying the broker name and the Queue Manager's name for each broker. When this is done, the brokers will be ready to receive deployment messages and to execute the deployed message flows.

Figure 10-6 shows the Configuration Manager Topology tab with three brokers.

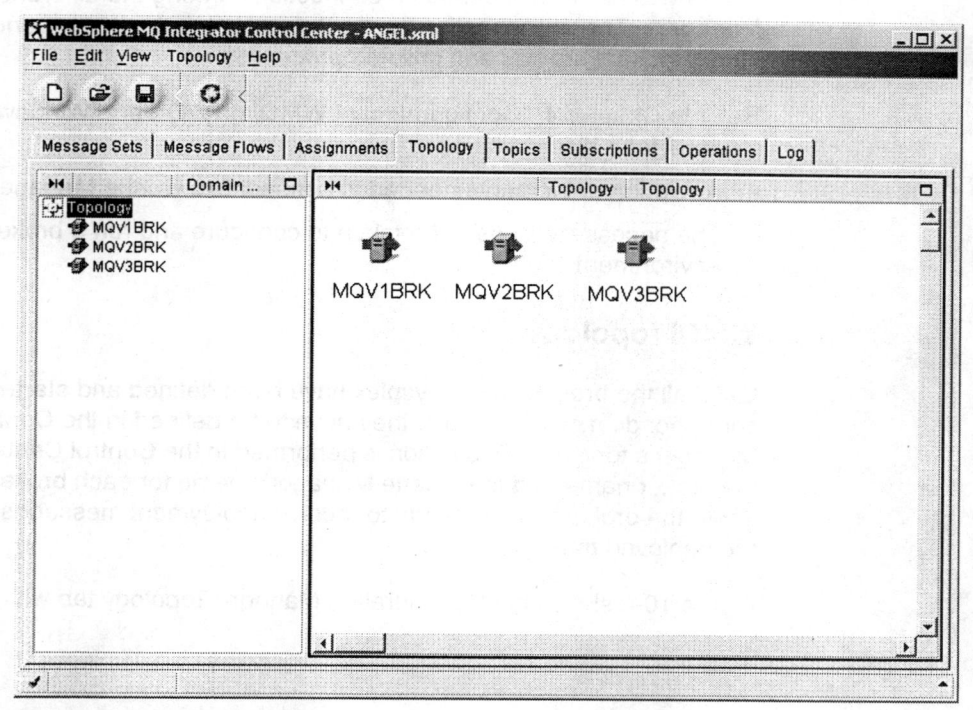

*Figure 10-6   Configuration Manager topology tab with three brokers*

## Message flow deployment

The way to achieve high availability for message flows is to run them in several brokers in the Parallel Sysplex.

The message flow has to be built with the Control Center, and deployed from the Configuration Manager to the brokers, resulting in the assignments shown in Figure 10-7.

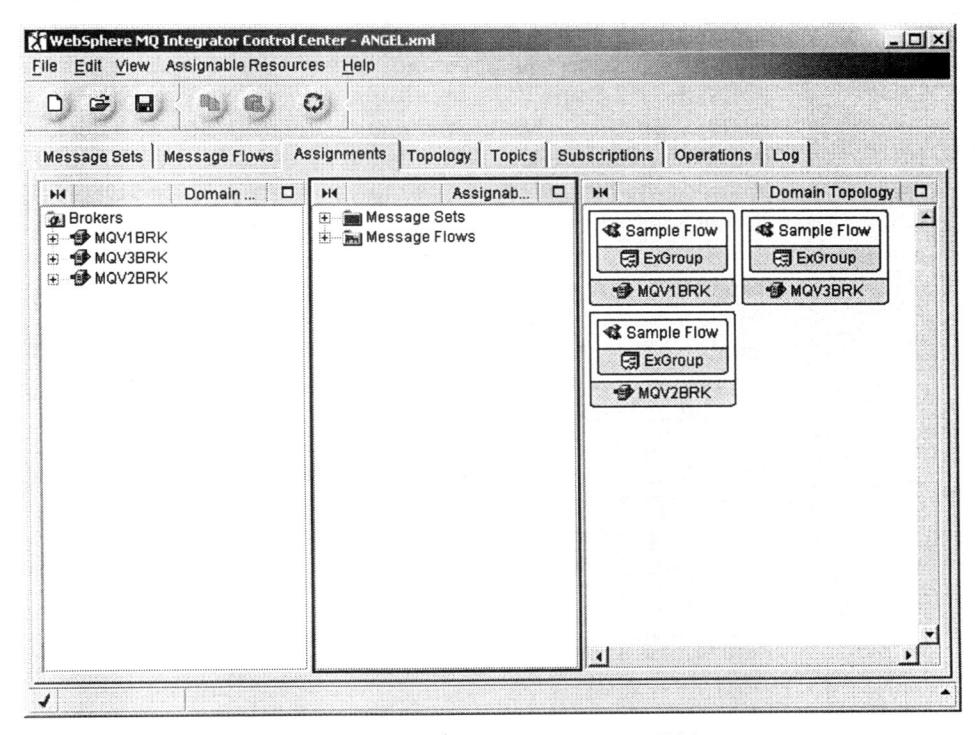

*Figure 10-7 Message flow assignment to execution groups in all three brokers*

After deploying the whole configuration, the message flow is ready for execution in all the brokers.

> **Note:** A message flow may be deployed to all the brokers if it does not contain any feature that is particular for a broker. For instance, if it does not specify the Queue Manager name of the queue in an output node (and that Queue Manager is not known to any broker), this would result in an execution error in runtime. A flow that has features particular to a given broker can only work properly in that broker. In this case we can say that the flow has an affinity to a certain broker.

## 10.3.4 Execution of message flows in the sysplex

A possible way to take advantage of the Parallel Sysplex architecture in WMQI is to run the message flows in brokers running continually on the systems in the sysplex, on Queue Managers sharing the message flow queues. This way, an incoming message to a flow is taken by any one of the brokers to process it following the flow rules. You cannot know which of the brokers is going to process the message.

### The Put sample program

A sample program, called Put, has been used for all test cases in this chapter. It is a program running on Windows NT-2000, where an MQ Client has been installed. It is able to put the contents of a file, as a message, in a given queue. It is also able to put the contents of all the files in a directory, each one as a single message, in a given queue, with the time delay desired between puts. The persistence of the messages is MQPER_PERSISTENCE_AS_Q_DEF, which means that the messages will be persistent if that is the default setting for the queue. Also the Code Character Set ID for the messages can be set to a desired value.

Figure 10-8 shows the window from which the Put program is launched.

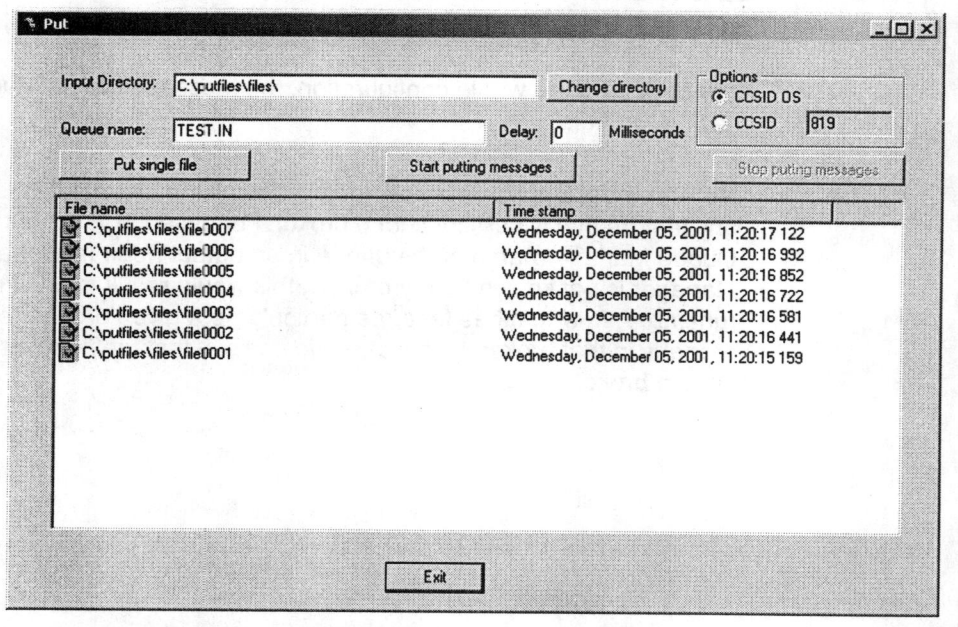

*Figure 10-8 The Put program operations window*

## Simple message flow execution

To check that the sysplex broker architecture works properly, the first test performed executes a very simple message flow, like the one shown in Figure 10-9, called "Sample Flow". The flow has been deployed to all the brokers in the sysplex.

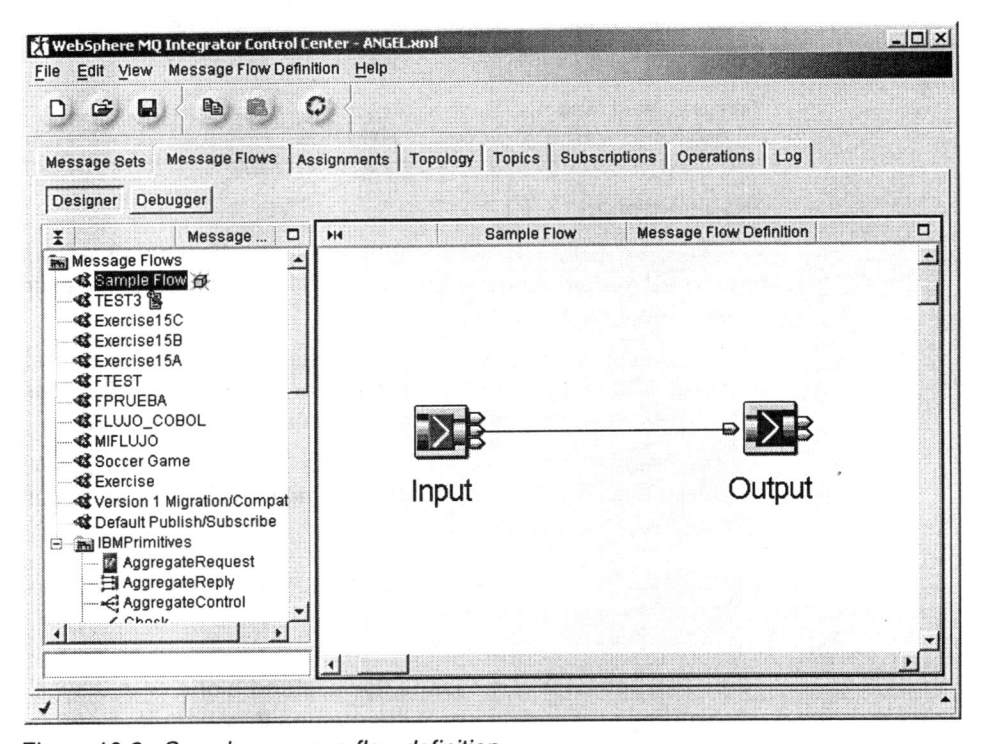

*Figure 10-9 Sample message flow definition*

This flow uses two queues, called "SYSPLEX.INPUT" and "SYSPLEX.OUTPUT". The SYSPLEX.INPUT queue is a shared queue. Example 10-1 shows the definition parameters of the shared input queue.

*Example 10-1 Parameters for the definition of the SYSPLEX.INPUT queue*

```
Queue name  . . . . . . . . . . SYSPLEX.INPUT
Disposition . . . . . . . . . : SHARED
Description . . . . . . . . . : Shared queue for input to the
                                group
Put enabled . . . . . . . . . : Y   Y=Yes,N=No
Get enabled . . . . . . . . . : Y   Y=Yes,N=No
Usage . . . . . . . . . . . . : N   N=Normal,X=XmitQ
Storage class . . . . . . . . : DEFAULT
```

```
CF structure name . . . . . : APPLICATION1
Creation method . . . . . . : PREDEFINED
Default persistence . . . . : N    Y=Yes,N=No
Default priority  . . . . . : 0    0 - 9
Message delivery sequence . : P    P=Priority,F=FIFO
Permit shared access  . . . : Y    Y=Yes,N=No
Default share option  . . . : S    E=Exclusive,S=Shared
Index type  . . . . . . . . : N    N=None,M=MsgId,C=CorrelId,T=MsgToken
Maximum queue depth . . . . : 9999       0 - 999999999
Maximum message length  . . : 4096       0 - 104857600
 . . . .
Backout Reporting
   Backout threshold  . . . : 999999999
```

Pay attention to:

▶ The maximum message length and the default persistence when defining a shared queue. Also the queue depth has to be carefully estimated because of storage limitations.

▶ The permit shared access and default share option parameters have to be taken into account for concurrency and message order considerations (see "Message sequence order and serialization" on page 207).

▶ The backout threshold for the queue is very important for WMQI to take decisions in case of message flow failures. See "Transactional behavior" on page 210 for details.

The CF structure name to be used has to refer to an already existing CF when defining a shared queue.

**Tip:** The behavior of message flows, stand-alone or in a sysplex, is very dependent on the settings of the queues they handle. Read carefully the details about the parameters highlighted here when designing these queues, to make sure they match the features needed for the behavior you desire, and plan the queue characteristics carefully before their creation. This approach saves time and effort.

### Preliminary test

In a preliminary test, both SYSPLEX.INPUT and SYSPLEX.OUTPUT are defined in the same way, as shared queues. We put a message in SYSPLEX.INPUT and observe that any of the message flows processes it and places it on the output queue.

Figure 10-10 shows the setup with shared input and output queues.

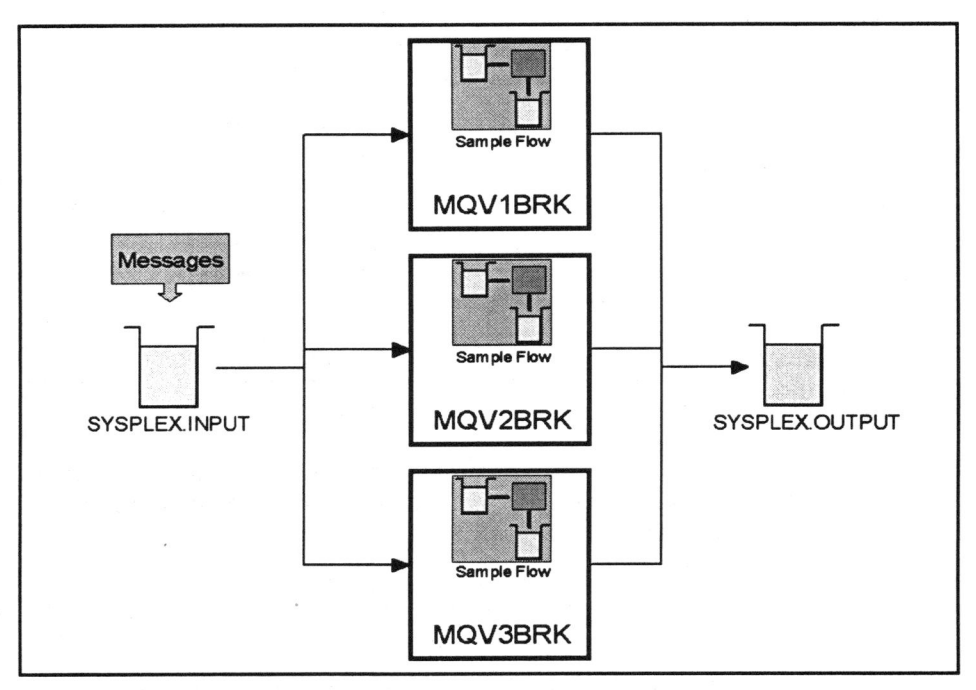

*Figure 10-10   Path followed by a message put to the input queue in a preliminary test*

When we put a batch of messages at a high speed into the input queue, we find them all in the output queue after being processed by the message flow. But this test demonstrates only that at least one of the brokers is working as expected.

### Checking that all brokers are executing the deployed message flow

Although the most logical configuration for the sample flow is the one described above, because sharing both the input and the output queue is the way to make the messages in both queues available for all the Queue Managers in the sysplex, the best way to test if all the brokers in the sysplex are working as expected is to separate the output queues, so that it is possible to find out how many of the incoming messages have been processed by each broker.

Figure 10-11 shows the setup with shared input and separate output queues.

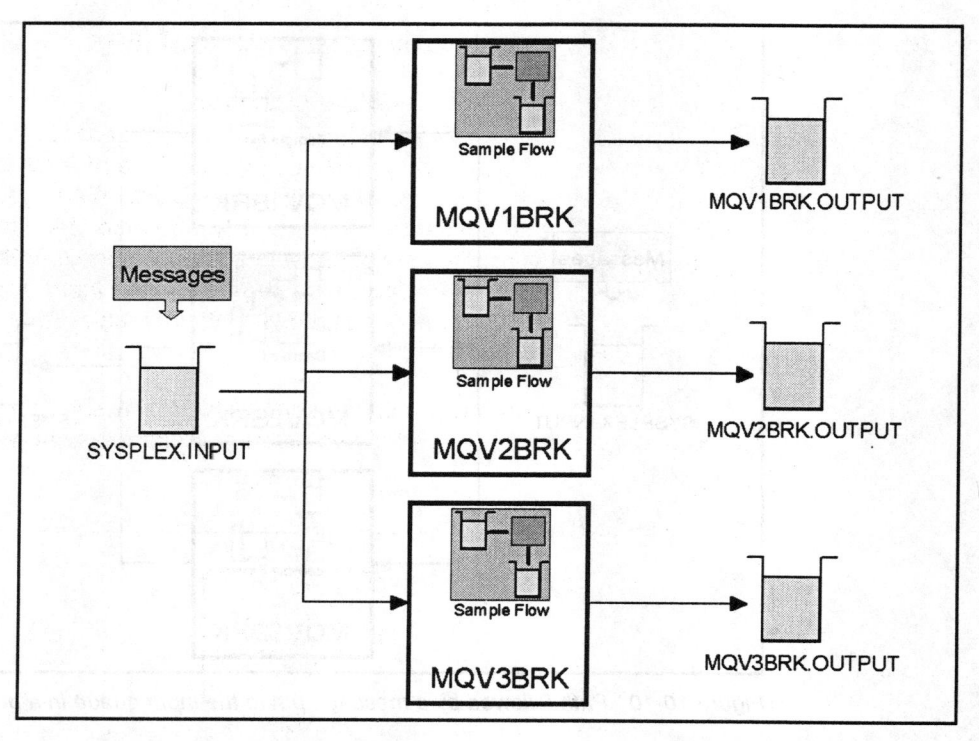

*Figure 10-11 Path followed by a message in a test of all the brokers in the sysplex*

> **Note:** The output queues in the figure have different names only to make it understandable that they are different queues, and local to the Queue Manager of the corresponding broker. But all of them must have the same name if it is desired to make the message flow deployment from the Control Center a single operation for all the brokers in the domain, rather than having different flows for doing the same operation.

So, when you put a batch of messages in the input queue, a different number of messages appear in each output queue. The number of messages in each output queue, that is the number of messages picked up and processed by each broker, depends on the load level of each system, and it is not guaranteed to be the same.

In a test made with the sample flow in the sysplex environment described, putting a batch of 30 messages in the SYSPLEX.INPUT queue has resulted in:

- 9 messages present in the output queue for MQV1BRK.

- 14 messages present in the output queue for MQV2BRK.
- 7 messages present in the output queue for MQV3BRK.

### Message sequence order and serialization

In a configuration like that shown in Figure 10-10 on page 205, all messages are received in the same queue and processed by any of the brokers watching it, and it is not possible to know which broker will get a specific message. The result is an improvement of the message flow availability, and also of the performance in the message processing. But it is not possible to guarantee that the order of the messages in the output queue will be the same as in the input queue. That is because there may be different conditions of work in each system, depending on how busy the systems are.

A test to illustrate the behavior may be done with two flows reading and writing in the same queues, and deployed to two different brokers, as shown in Figure 10-12.

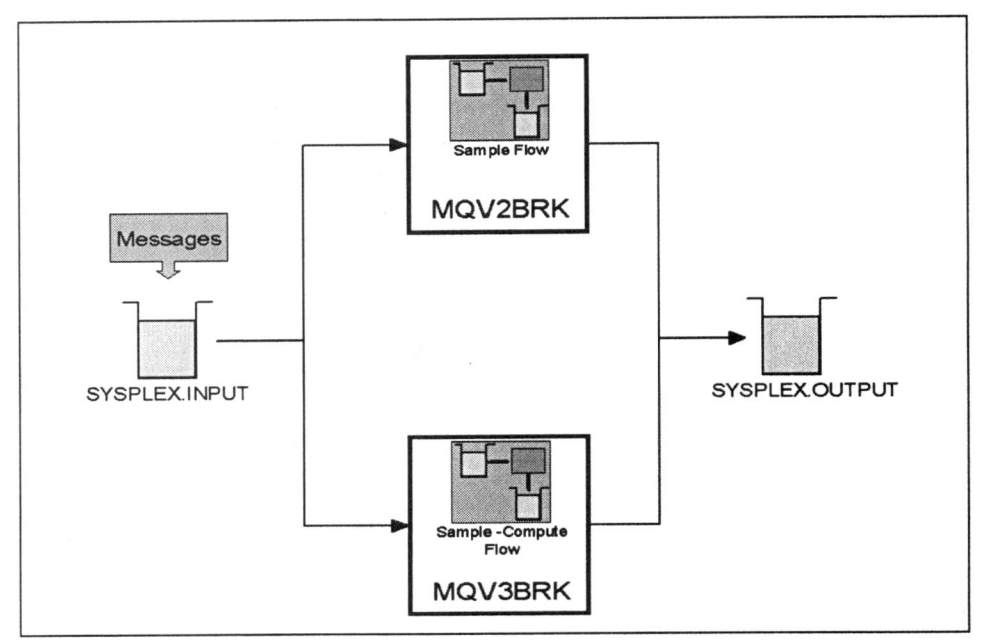

*Figure 10-12 Configuration for testing messages order*

Notice that in the shown configuration, two different message flows are used, rather that using the same flow, which is the most logical issue. The purpose of doing this is to simulate different work conditions in both systems, forcing one of the flows to take more time than the other to process a single message.

Figure 10-13 shows a message flow with a Compute node.

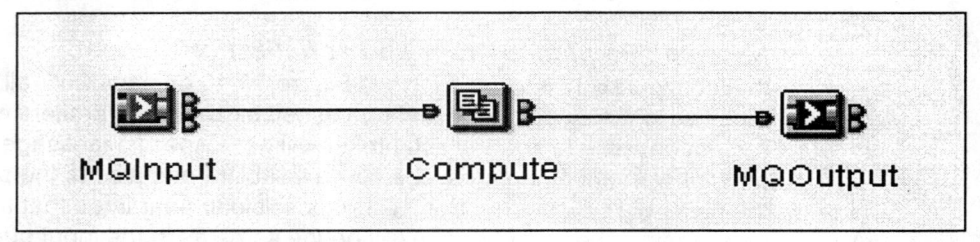

*Figure 10-13   Sample Compute node flow*

The second message flow adds a Compute node containing a loop within its ESQL code, as shown in Figure 10-14.

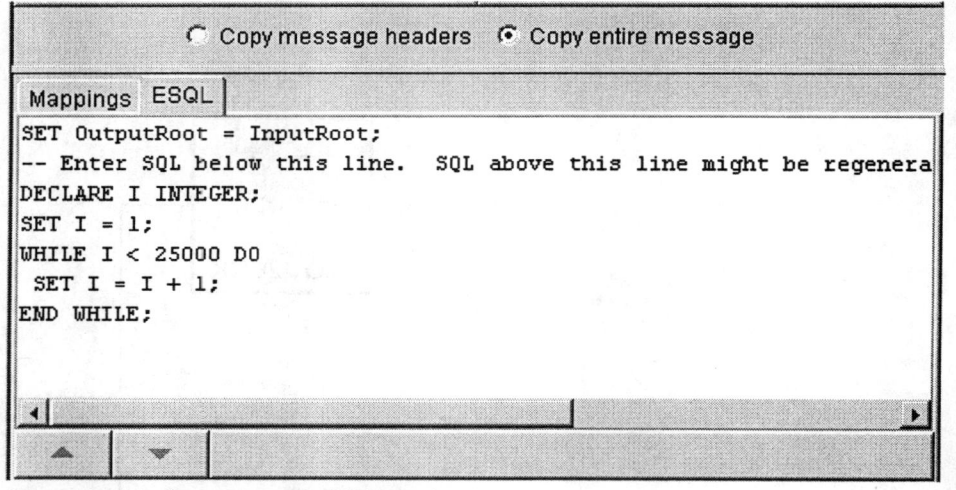

```
SET OutputRoot = InputRoot;
-- Enter SQL below this line.  SQL above this line might be regenera
DECLARE I INTEGER;
SET I = 1;
WHILE I < 25000 DO
  SET I = I + 1;
END WHILE;
```

*Figure 10-14   Compute node ESQL code*

A simple test case may consist of putting a batch of 20 messages in the input queue, read by both message flows. The order of the messages in the output will now, more probably, not be the same.

In some cases, this may be inconvenient for certain application processes, in which, for any reason, you would prefer to receive the broker-processed messages in a given order. The way to achieve such a behavior is setting the queues to be accessed in *exclusive mode*.

When defining a shared queue (see Example 10-1 on page 203), the parameters have to be set in the following way for the different brokers to access that queue in shared mode (notice these parameters are about *access mode*, not about the queue shareability among the Queue Managers):

```
Permit shared access    . . . : Y  Y=Yes,N=No
Default share option    . . . : S  E=Exclusive,S=Shared
```

Switching these values so that they do not permit shared access will force the queue to be accessed in exclusive mode:

```
Permit shared access    . . . : N  Y=Yes,N=No
Default share option    . . . : E  E=Exclusive,S=Shared
```

If a shared queue is defined in this way, the first broker opening it will keep it open in exclusive mode, and will process all incoming messages. This guarantees that all messages are sent to the output queue in the same order they were put for input.

Example 10-2 shows the output of tests performed with a configuration like that described in Figure 10-12 on page 207.

*Example 10-2   Output message sequence with shared (left) and exclusive (right) input queue*

```
C:\>AMQSGETC SYSPLEX.OUTPUT        C:\>AMQSGETC SYSPLEX.OUTPUT
Sample AMQSGETO start              Sample AMQSGETO start
message <file0002>                 message <file0001>
message <file0001>                 message <file0002>
message <file0003>                 message <file0003>
message <file0004>                 message <file0004>
message <file0005>                 message <file0005>
message <file0006>                 message <file0006>
message <file0008>                 message <file0007>
message <file0007>                 message <file0008>
message <file0009>                 message <file0009>
message <file0011>                 message <file0010>
message <file0010>                 message <file0011>
message <file0013>                 message <file0012>
message <file0012>                 message <file0013>
message <file0014>                 message <file0014>
message <file0016>                 message <file0015>
message <file0015>                 message <file0016>
message <file0018>                 message <file0017>
message <file0017>                 message <file0018>
message <file0019>                 message <file0019>
message <file0020>                 message <file0020>
no more messages                   no more messages
Sample AMQSGETO end                Sample AMQSGETO end
```

Accessing queues in exclusive mode prevents the messages for a message flow from being processed in parallel, but ensures message serialization. This setup can be useful for some applications.

> **Note:** High availability is ensured regardless of whether exclusive or shared access is performed by the brokers on shared queues. If a broker stops for any reason, the others continue to work. If the broker had a queue open in exclusive mode, other broker continues working, opening also the queue in exclusive mode, and ensuring the order of the messages in the output. No message is lost in these operations. See Transactional behavior for details about ensuring transactional behavior in a sysplex environment.

> **Tip:** When you plan that some message flows have to access a shared queue in exclusive mode, define that shared queue as exclusively accessed from the very beginning. Otherwise, altering the queue afterwards could be ignored by MQSeries, when it is a shared queue, as we observed in our tests.

### 10.3.5 Transactional behavior

In this section, we discuss the broker transactional behavior in a Parallel Sysplex environment.

#### Backout procedure performed by a broker

To understand the transactional behavior of brokers in a sysplex, we should first recap what the broker does when a message flow reaches a failure for any reason.

The resources are backed out by the z/OS Resource Recovery Services (RRS) including all MQ and DB2 resources involved in the unit of work that is being backed out. If a broker stops abnormally, all resources handled by in-flight transactions are backed out by RRS, regardless of whether the flows are set to transactional or not.

When a message flow is not able to completely succeed in its process between getting a message from the input queue and putting it into the output queue (and there is no abnormal termination of the flow or the broker), what the flow will do depends on whether the flow has been set as transactional. If it has not, the message is disposed by the flow (the different cases of this behavior are listed in Table 3-1 on page 58).

> **Important:** A message flow is processed as a transaction if it is set as transactional in its input node. Notice that it is possible to establish that property as Automatic, so the message flow will be processed as a transaction if the incoming message is persistent. Shared queues *do not permit* putting persistent messages, so when a message flow reads from a shared queue, its Transaction Mode has to be explicitly set to Yes, if it is desired that the flow behaves as a transaction.

When a flow, set as transactional, is not able to completely succeed in its process between getting a message from the input queue and putting it into the output queue, it proceeds in this sequence:

- The whole process is backed out. All MQ and DB2 resources included (if no node accessing DB2 resources is set explicitly to Commit). The message subject for the process is again put into the input queue. The backout count property for that message is increased by 1.
- If the backout count for the message *is less* than the backout threshold property of the input queue, the message is available for new processing by the message flow (or any other instance of the message flow, that is in a Parallel Sysplex environment). The message flow will take it again and retry the process.
- If the backout count for the message *equals or exceeds* the backout threshold property of the input queue, then the message flow proceeds as follows:
    - If the Failure terminal of input node in the message flow is connected to an output node (Failure node), as shown in Figure 10-15, the message is put into the queue determined by the Failure node.

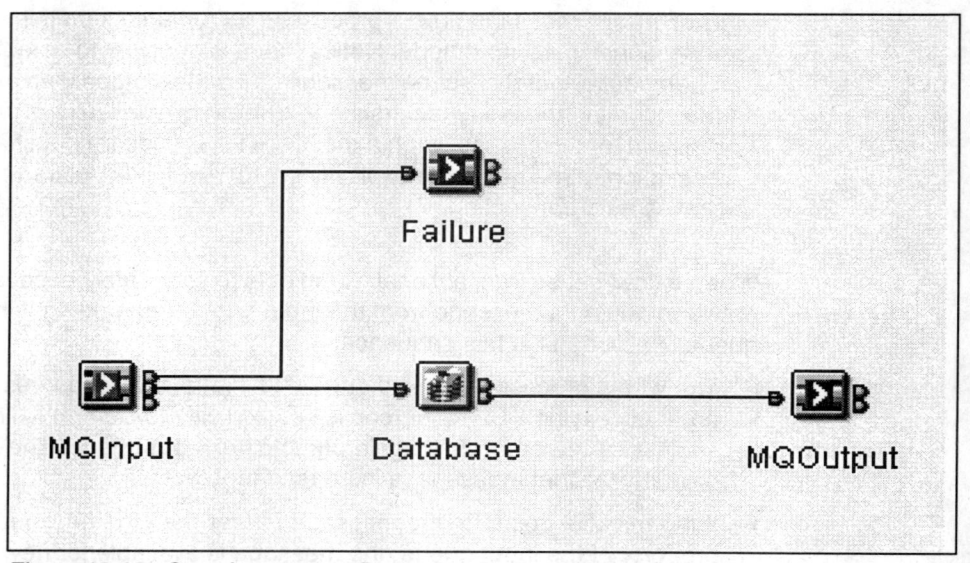

*Figure 10-15 Sample message flow with a Failure node connected to the input node*

- If there is no Failure node, the flow checks if any Backout queue name is specified in the input queue properties. If it is, the message is put into the Backout queue.

- If there is no Failure node and no Backout queue, the flow sends the message to the Dead Letter queue specified in the Queue Manager properties.

- If there are no Failure node, Backout queue and Dead Letter queue, the flow will keep trying to put the message in any of these three places endlessly, incrementing the backout count for the message every time it fails doing this, until any of these places is available to place the message into.

Take into account that a message the backout count of which has already exceeded the backout threshold for the input queue *is not available* anymore for successful processing by the flow, regardless the conditions that made the flow fail processing the message are already solved or not. If a flow holds a message looping in its search for Failure-Backout-Dead Letter queue and then the failing conditions are solved, it does not mean that message will be successfully processed.

**Important:** If the backout threshold for an input queue in a message flow is set to 0 (zero), any message failing while being processed will not be available for retrying even once. It will be set for sending to Failure-Backout-Dead Letter queue immediately after the first backout, and the flow (or any other instance of the flow) will not retry to process it again. This has to be taken into account if it is desired that any other instance of the flow (in a sysplex) gets the message for retrying the successful process with it.

## Transactional behavior in a sysplex

When a broker stops for any reason, the changes of any in-flight message flow are backed out. Also, if a Queue Manager disconnects abnormally from the Coupling Facility, other Queue Manager will back out any in-flight transaction, because of the peer recovery property of MQSeries (see "Queue-sharing groups" on page 193). In both cases, the messages that were the subject of a backed-out transaction are left available to be processed by any other broker.

### Input queue related settings: the backout threshold

The messages that were the subject of a backed-out transaction are left available to be processed by any other broker. What the broker newly processing a backed-out message will do depends on the backout count for the message.

As described in "Backout procedure performed by a broker" on page 210, if the backout count for the message is *less* than the backout threshold for the input queue in the message flow that is processing the message, then the flow will try to process the message again. Otherwise, the message flow will send the message to the first available queue in Failure Node-Backout-Dead Letter queue, or will keep the message trying to be put into to any of these until available, preventing the message from being processed again.

Take into account that the default backout threshold for a newly defined queue is 0 (zero). If this setting is kept as the default, the message will not be available for new processing after the first backout. So, if, for instance, a broker shuts down abnormally, a message being processed will be taken by other broker in the sysplex, and backed out. If the backout threshold of the input queue is zero, the condition not to process the message is *already* reached, and the message will not be processed. So the backout threshold has to be changed to prevent this from happening.

*Example 10-3   Backout threshold sample value for message re-processing by a second message flow instance*

```
Backout Reporting
   Backout threshold  . . . : 999999999
```

This behavior has nothing to do with the message serialization already described in previous topics. If the input queue is accessed exclusively by a flow and the broker fails, the flow in another broker may continue the transaction, opening the queue also in exclusive mode, keeping the message order.

### Sample test of transaction recovery

A simple test case may be done for checking this behavior, by using a message flow with a Database node, as shown in Figure 10-16. The Database node is just a node inserting a row in a DB2 table. Its ESQL code is shown in Figure 10-17.

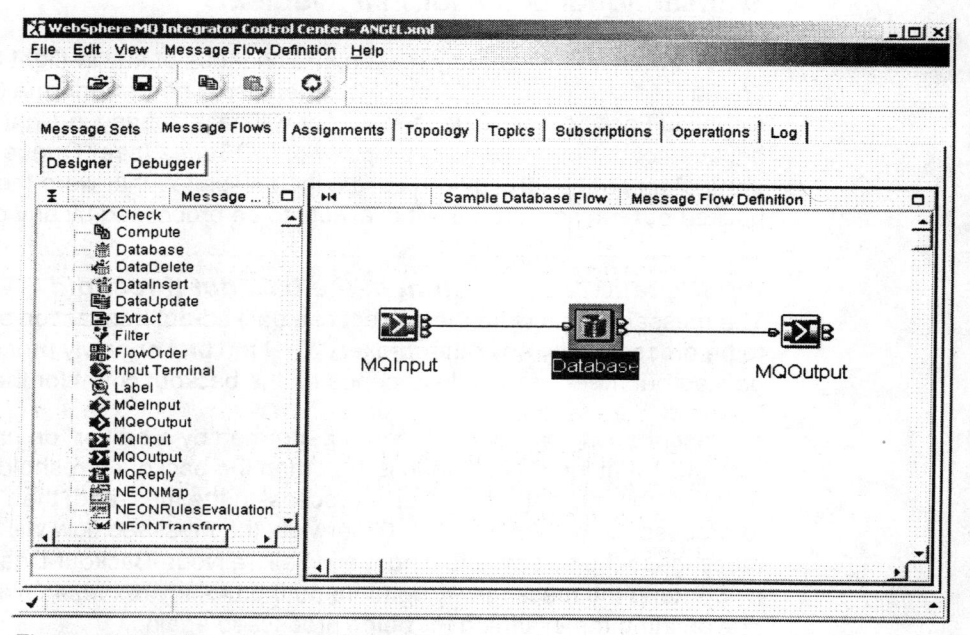

*Figure 10-16   Message flow with a Database node*

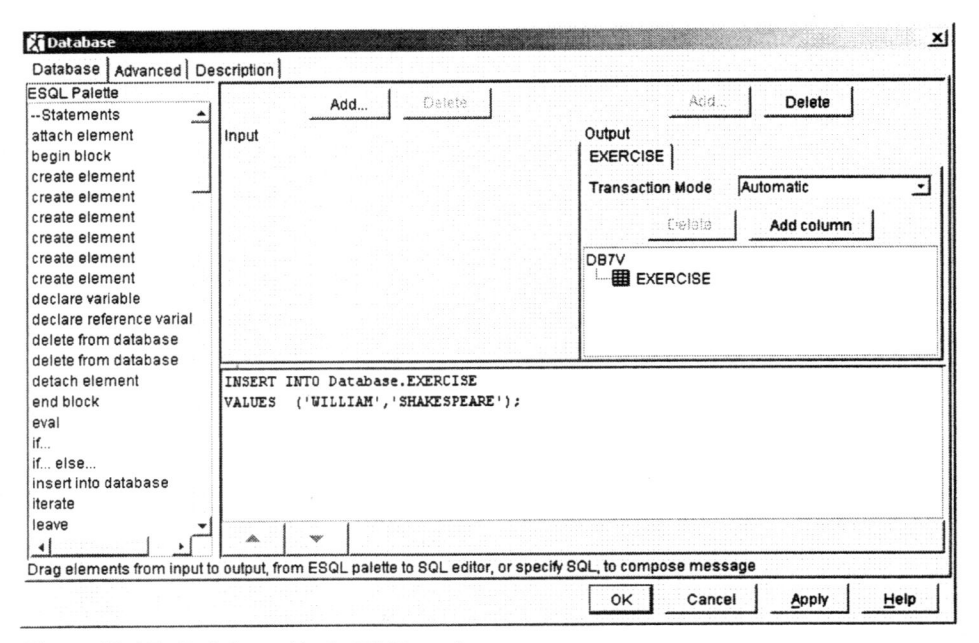

*Figure 10-17   Database Node ESQL code*

The procedure for doing the transaction recovery test case is as follows:

► Deploy the sample database flow to two brokers. The input and output queues are shared queues, and their backout threshold is set to 999999999. It does not matter whether shared or exclusive access mode is applied to the queues.

► Start the message flow only in one of the brokers, to be sure which broker is executing the incoming message.

► Using other tool, such as SPUFI, insert a record in the table with the same values the message flow uses in the Database Node ESQL code (notice that the DB2 table has to be defined with a unique index for those values). The record has to be inserted, but *not* committed (if you have used separate databases for doing the test, rather than a shared one, do this operation in the database accessed by the currently started flow).

► Put a message into the input queue, so that the message flow gets it.

► Notice that the message does not appear in the output queue. That means that the message flow is waiting. The time the message flow will be waiting depends on the DB2 installation. After the timeout period, if nothing is done, the message flow will get a DB2 SQL error (SQL code -911, deadlock).

- Notice that while the message flow is waiting, if the record inserted with SPUFI is committed, the message flow will get a DB2 SQL error (SQL code -803, duplicate key). If it is rolled back, the message flow will succeed inserting the DB2 record and will put the message into the output queue.
- While the message flow is waiting, start it in another broker it has been deployed to, and stop the broker currently processing the message, by canceling the broker started task job.
- Roll back the record insertion with SPUFI.
- The message will appear in the output queue. This means the changes made by the first broker were backed out, and the message was taken and successfully processed by the second broker. Also the DB2 record has had to be inserted by the flow. If you have used separate databases for doing the test, rather than a shared one, you'll see the record in the database accessed by the second started broker.

We followed the steps exactly as described to test the transaction recovery capabilities of WMQI in a Parallel Sysplex environment.

If you do not succeed getting the message in the output queue, review:

- The input queue for the message flow has its backout threshold set to 0 (zero). This means that the message is set not to be processed after the first backout. So, the second broker, when getting the message:
  - Has sent the message to the Failure node queue, if there is a node connected to the failure terminal of the input node.
  - Has sent the message to the Backout queue, if such queue is defined in the input queue settings.
  - Has sent the message to the Dead Letter queue for the Queue Manager accused by the second broker, if no Failure terminal and nor Backout queue are being used.
  - Is still in the input queue, incrementing continually its backout count, if none of these queues are being used.
- The input queue for the message flow does *not* have its backout threshold set to 0 (zero). Check the Failure, Backout, Dead Letter and Input queues anyway. The error may come from other issue, such as DB2 SQL error or unavailability of the output queue. Trace the flow to find out what the problem is.

## 10.3.6 Automatic Restart Management (ARM) planning

All the considerations discussed so far in this chapter about WMQI running in a Parallel Sysplex took into account that brokers were running simultaneously in several systems. An alternative to provide WMQI message flows with high availability capabilities is registering brokers in ARM.

Automatic Restart Management (ARM) handles application or subsystem failures within a sysplex. It is intended to reduce the downtime of critical applications by restarting them automatically when failures are detected.

Notice that all considerations discussed in this chapter about transactional behavior of brokers in a sysplex, or about message serialization are also valid when brokers are registered to ARM. If a broker stops abnormally and is automatically restarted, all in-flight transactions are restarted (by the same broker after restarting or by any other broker already running, if it has been deployed with the same message flows). Refer to "Transactional behavior in a sysplex" on page 213 for details.

So, using ARM is an alternative for parallel execution of brokers when, for system-load reasons, you cannot run multiple instances of your message flows.

A broker registered with ARM may be restarted in the same system in the sysplex, in case of abnormal termination. To enable automatic restart, you have to:

- Customize the broker to register with ARM at startup.
- Implement the ARM policy for the component to be restarted.

**Note:** You should not set a broker to register with ARM if the broker is running flows in a development-testing environment. Restarting the broker could also restart the problem that caused the failure.

### Customization of a broker for using ARM

For customizing the broker to use ARM, you have to provide the appropriate settings in the customization input file, and to customize the broker (see "Customizing brokers" on page 65 for details about the customization procedure).

The values concerning ARM, already referred to in Table 4-1 on page 68, are:

| Attribute | Value | Example |
|---|---|---|
| USE_ARM | Automatic Restart Management switch (see note below) | YES |
| ARM_ELEMENTNAME | Element Name used by ARM | MQV3BRK |
| ARM_ELEMENTTYPE | ElementType used by ARM | SYSWMQI |

**Note:** ARM_ELEMENTNAME is 8 characters long. WMQI adds the prefix SYSWMQI, so the name to be defined in the ARM policy is SYSWMQI_MQV3BRK.

**Tip:** In Table 4-1 on page 68, the sample value specified for USE_ARM is NO. A broker may be customized without ARM settings, as described in Chapter 4, "Configuration of WMQI on z/OS and Windows platforms" on page 61. If, later, it is planned for the broker to use ARM, it is possible to change these values and recustomize the broker.

### ARM policy implementation

To implement the policy, you need:

- To set up an ARM couple data set and ensure that it is available to all systems in the sysplex that are to participate in automatic restart management. Refer to *OS/390 Setting up a Sysplex* for details.
- To define an ARM policy, with the automatic actions you want to be taken when restarting.
- To start the ARM policy.

#### Define the ARM policy

To define an ARM policy, use the IXCMIAPU utility. Refer to *OS/390 Setting up a Sysplex* for details.

Given that the broker is uniquely attached to a Queue Manager, it is convenient to group both of them for restarting. Example 10-4 shows a policy for restarting both the Queue Manager and the broker.

*Example 10-4   ARM policy for restarting a Queue Manager and a broker*

```
DATA TYPE(ARM) REPORT(YES)
```

```
       DEFINE POLICY NAME(ARMPOL06) REPLACE(YES)

   RESTART_GROUP(MQV2)
     TARGET_SYSTEM(SC61)
     RESTART_PACING(20)
     ELEMENT(SYSMQMGRMQV2)
       RESTART_ATTEMPTS(3,300)
       RESTART_TIMEOUT(120)
       TERMTYPE(ALLTERM)
       RESTART_METHOD(BOTH,STC,'-mqv2 start qmgr')
     ELEMENT(MQV2BRK)
       RESTART_ATTEMPTS(3,300)
       RESTART_TIMEOUT(120)
       TERMTYPE(ALLTERM)
       RESTART_METHOD(BOTH,STC,'S MQV2BRK')
```

The policy in this example restarts a Queue Manager and a broker in system SC61, with a maximum of three attempts to restart each of them. All of those attempts must occur within 300 seconds to succeed. The command needed to restart both components is also provided.

### *Activating the policy*
Once the policy is defined, it has to be started, by using the **SETXCF** command:

**SETXCF START,POLICY,TYPE=ARM,POLNAME=ARMPOL06**

This is the output expected for the command execution:

```
IXC805I ARM POLICY HAS BEEN STARTED BY SYSTEM SC61.
POLICY NAMED ARMPOL06 IS NOW IN EFFECT.
```

### *Checking broker restart by ARM*
It is possible to check that the broker will be restarted by ARM in case of failure. To do so, cancel the broker started task with the option ARMRESTART as follows:

**C MQV2BRK,ARMRESTART**

The expected output in the system log on successful ARM restarting of the broker is shown in Example 10-5.

*Example 10-5  System log output when ARM restarts the broker MQV2BRK*

```
S MQV2BRK
IXC812I JOBNAME MQV2BRK, ELEMENT SYSWMQI_MQV2BRK FAILED.
THE ELEMENT WAS RESTARTED WITH OVERRIDE START TEXT.
IXC813I JOBNAME MQV2BRK, ELEMENT SYSWMQI_MQV2BRK
WAS RESTARTED WITH THE FOLLOWING START TEXT:
S MQV2BRK
```

```
THE RESTART METHOD USED WAS DETERMINED BY THE ACTIVE POLICY.
$HASP100 MQV2BRK  ON STCINRDR
IEF695I START MQV2BRK  WITH JOBNAME MQV2BRK  IS ASSIGNED TO USER
MQV2BRK , GROUP SYS1
$HASP373 MQV2BRK  STARTED
IEF403I MQV2BRK - STARTED - TIME=14.03.16 - ASID=0097.
```

### 10.3.7 Configuration for publishing and subscribing in a sysplex

If you plan to use publish/subscribe facilities of WebSphere MQ Integrator in a Parallel Sysplex, you should look at some other issues in addition to those already discussed in this chapter.

In a sysplex, the WMQI components are configured sharing resources in a way that provides message flows with the high availability capabilities of the sysplex. The behavior of brokers when publish/subscribe is used needs special attention to achieve this purpose. This is the subject of the following sections.

#### Basic publish/subscribe

The basic publish/subscribe model involves an application publishing messages, a broker and an application subscribing to messages. Figure 10-18 shows this model and the participating components.

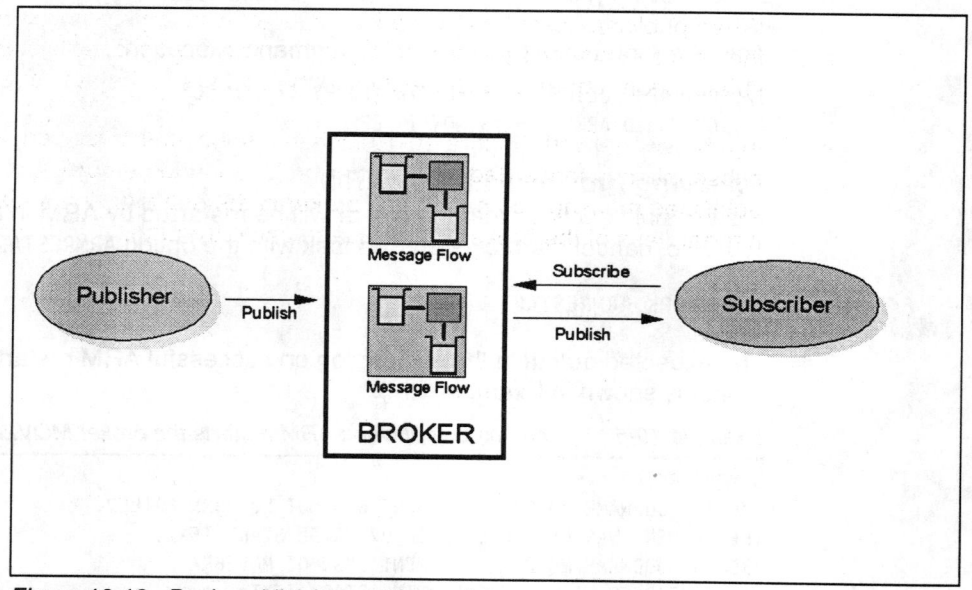

*Figure 10-18  Basic publish/subscribe model*

The publish/subscribe model works as follows:

- An application, the *subscriber*, sends to the broker a request to *subscribe* to messages of a given *topic*. In that message, the subscriber provides the name of an input queue where it expects to receive the messages.
- The broker registers the subscription for the user and topic.
- An application, the *publisher*, sends a message with contents to be published. The message also contains a topic and a request for the broker to publish the message.
- The broker checks that there already exists a registered subscription for that topic.
- The broker puts the published message in the input queue specified by the subscriber.

Many subscribers may subscribe to a given topic, each of them specifying their own destination for the published messages (the destination is a unique combination of Queue Manager name-queue correlation ID). Also many publishers may publish messages of the same topic, and their messages will be sent to the subscribers that are registered in the broker at the moment of the publication (it is also possible to retain publications;see the *Introduction and Planning* manual).

## Broker networks

When publish/subscribe applications interact with a given number of brokers, they have to be configured in a *broker network*, so that publishing and subscription requests take effect in all the brokers of the network.

In a broker network (Figure 10-19), when a subscription request is received, that subscription is forwarded to the other brokers in the network. So, when a published message comes to any broker in the network, the subscriber receives it regardless of the broker the message came through.

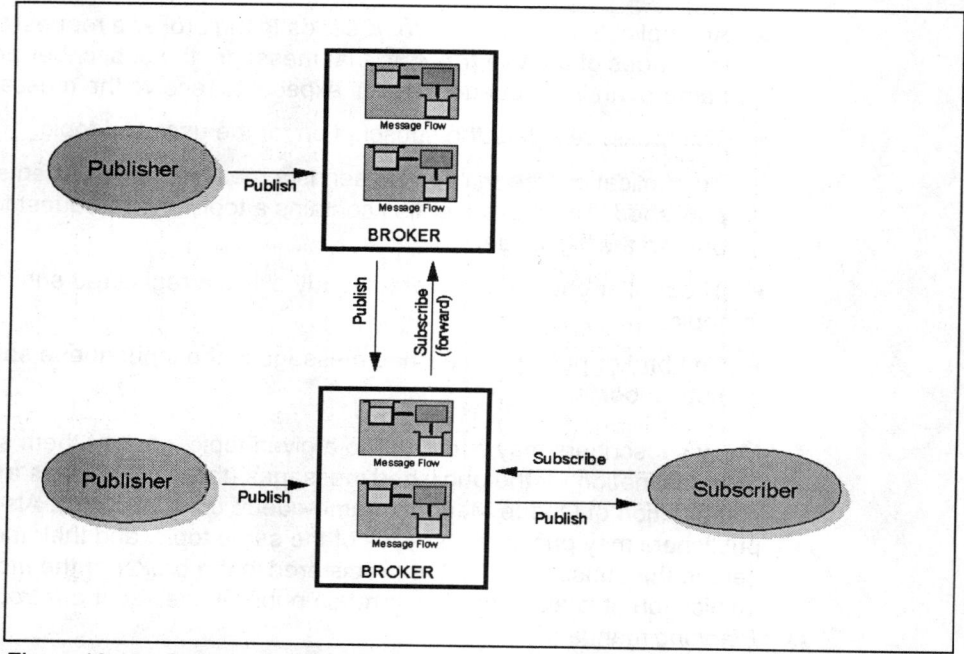

*Figure 10-19 Subscription forwarding in a broker network*

The mechanism to achieve this behavior is for the *forwarded* brokers to register a subscription to send the published messages to that broker registering the subscription with the subscriber. When this occurs, in the subscriptions window of the Control Center you can see:

- The subscription registered by the subscriber for a topic in a broker, and
- The subscription registered by that broker with each of the others for the same topic, so that it will receive the messages of that topic (for sending them to the subscriber).

In order to arrange a set of brokers in a network, you need to define the corresponding MQ communication resources among them, in addition to those already defined between each broker and the Configuration Manager.

Those MQ communication resources are the corresponding channel pairs, transmission queues and channel-initiating triggered processes.

Figure 10-20 on page 223 illustrates the connections among Queue Managers needed in a broker network.

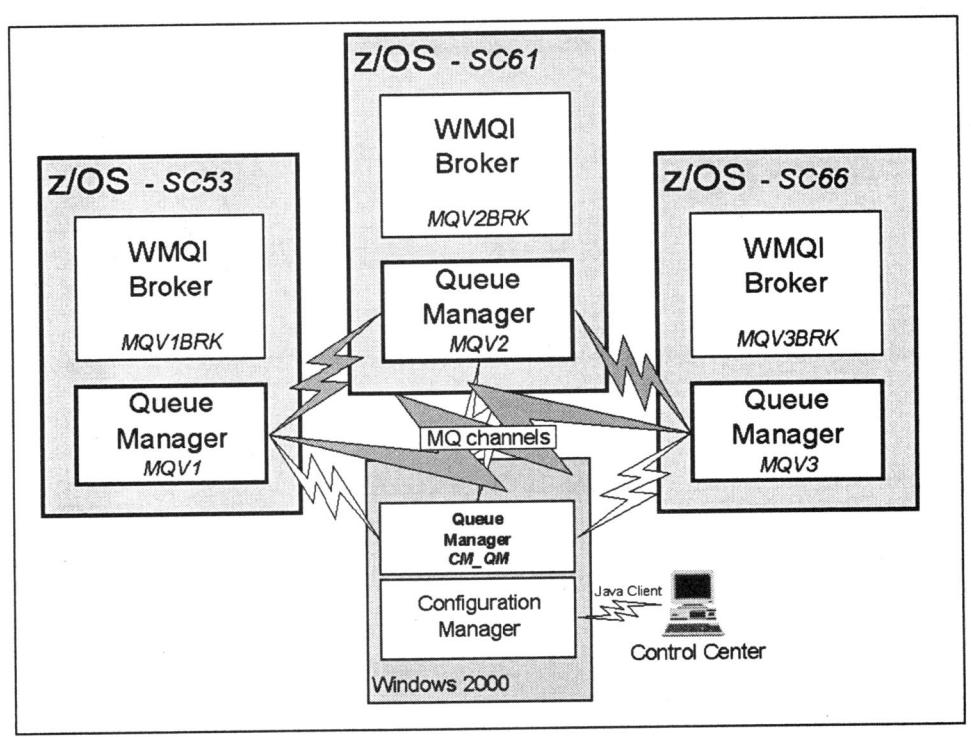

*Figure 10-20   MQ connections in a broker network*

## Collectives

Grouping brokers in collectives (Figure 10-21) is the easiest and most effective way to organize brokers in a network for publish/subscribe.

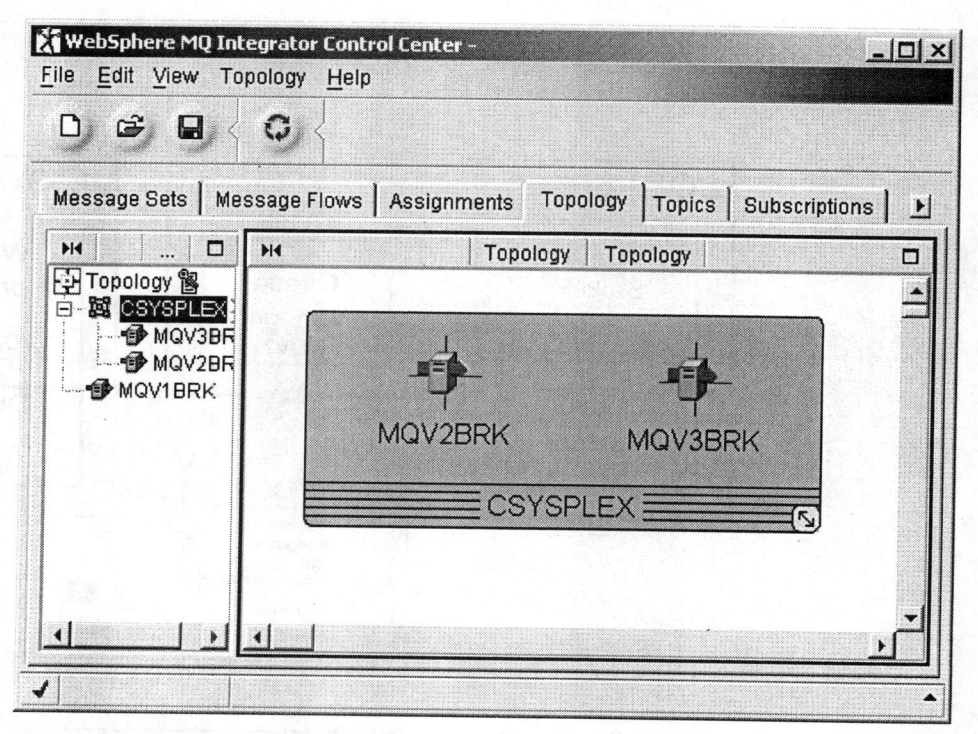

*Figure 10-21 Brokers MQV2BRK and MQV3BRK grouped in the collective CSYSPLEX*

## Publishing and subscribing in a sysplex

When publish/subscribe is performed in a sysplex, there are some additional considerations to be taken into account.

In a sysplex, the brokers are, in most cases, deployed with the same message flows and sharing all those message flow resources, queues and databases, so that each incoming message to a flow may be processed by any broker (if the input queue for the flow is not open in exclusive mode by any broker; see "Message sequence order and serialization" on page 207). This configuration is taken to provide the flows with high-availability capabilities.

So, because of this, if the message flows for publishing and subscribing are sharing resources among brokers, it happens that:

- ▶ When a subscription request comes to the sysplex, any broker in the sysplex may take the message and register that subscription.
- ▶ The broker registering the subscription forwards that subscription to the other brokers in the sysplex.

- Any published message that affects that subscription, coming to the sysplex, may be taken by any broker in the sysplex. If that broker is not the broker registering the subscription, the published message has to be sent to that broker.
- The broker registering the subscription sends the published message to the subscriber.

## Sample configuration of brokers in a sysplex for publish/subscribe

A simple configuration of brokers to support publish/subscribe in a sysplex involves two brokers, that is MQV2BRK and MQV3BRK. To set them into a broker network, they are grouped into a collective using the Control Center.

The brokers have to communicate with the Configuration Manager and between them. This is achieved by defining the appropriate elements of communication among Queue Managers, which include:

- A transmission queue
- A sender channel
- A triggered process that starts the channel
- A receiver channel

Once these elements are defined, and the brokers grouped in a collective, very simple flows like those shown in Figure 10-22 on page 226 and Figure 10-23 on page 226 may be used for testing the publish/subscribe capabilities of the brokers configuration:

- A flow for subscribing, that gets any incoming message and, after adding to it a topic and a subscribing request, puts it into the broker control queue.
- A flow that takes any incoming message and adds to it a topic and a publish request.

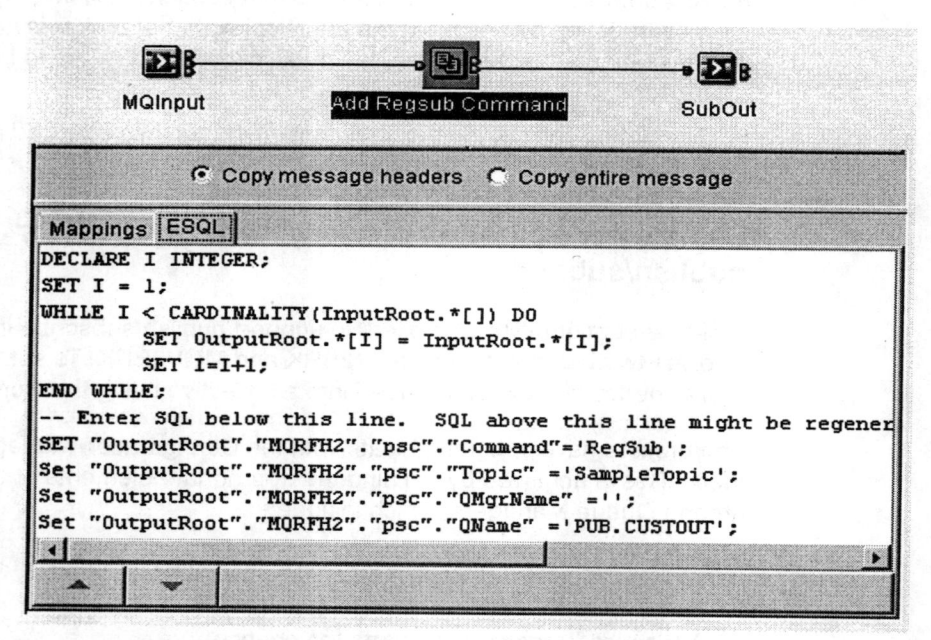

*Figure 10-22   Schema and source code for the subscribing flow*

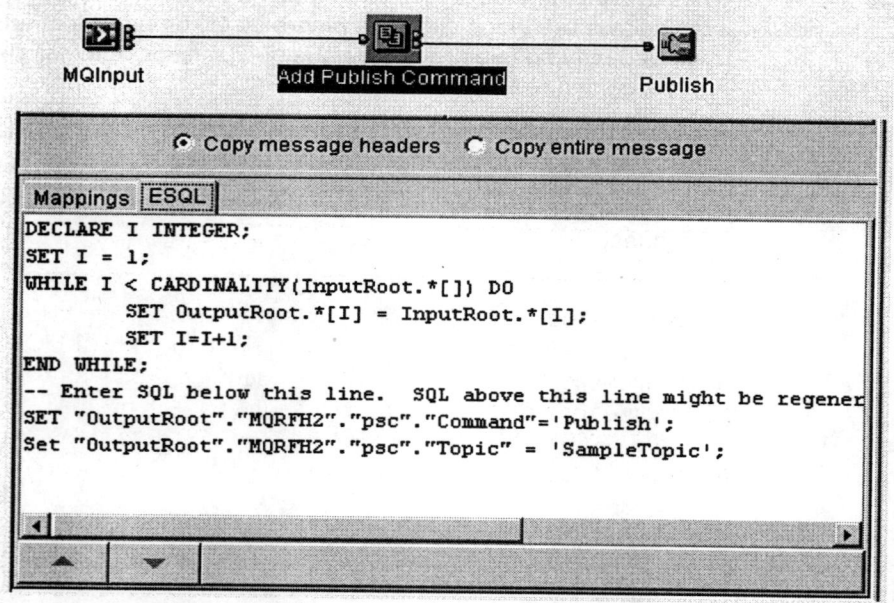

*Figure 10-23   Schema and source code for the publishing flow*

To have both flows deployed in both brokers, the following resources are defined:

- A queue for input to the subscribing flow, defined as *shared*, with *shared access* and 999999999 for backout threshold (see previous topics in this chapter to understand these settings).
- A queue for input to the publishing flow, with the same characteristics.
- The subscribing flow output queue has to be SYSTEM.BROKER.CONTROL.QUEUE. Make sure that you do not supply the Queue Manager name in the output node for this flow (any broker may register a subscription).
- As seen in the source code for the subscribing flow, the desired queue to receive the publications through is PUB.CUSTOUT. The Queue Manager name, on the other hand, is intentionally set to blanks. This way, the ReplyToQmgrName property of the subscribing message is set as destination Queue Manager for the publications. So, in both Queue Managers of the brokers in the collective you have to define:
  - A remote queue definition called PUB.CUSTOUT.
  - The needed communication elements with the Queue Manager the subscription requests will come from, if they are not defined yet (transmission queue, triggered process and the channels pair).

Once these definitions are made, you can check (see Table 10-1) that any incoming message to the input queue of the subscription flow registers a subscription with the topic called "SampleTopic" in both brokers. One of them corresponds to the subscriber with a broker, the other to the broker registering that subscription with the other broker.

*Table 10-1  Information about subscriptions displayed for both brokers*

| Topic | broker | Client |
|---|---|---|
| SampleTopic | MQV2BRK | MQV3:SYSTEM.BROKER.INTERBROKER.QUEUE |
| SampleTopic | MQV3BRK | EXTQMGR:PUB.CUSTOUT |

In the table above, a subscription message comes from the Queue Manager EXTQMGR, and registers a subscription with the broker MQV3BRK to receive publications in the queue PUB.CUSTOUT. This broker forwards the subscription to the other broker, MQV2BRK, whose destination for the publications is the queue SYSTEM.BROKER.INTERBROKER.QUEUE in the Queue Manager of the broker MQV3BRK, that effectively registered the subscription.

Notice that these subscriptions may take place in any order in the sysplex. In this case, MQV3BRK registered the subscription and forwarded it, but it could be the other broker that performs this operation.

Once the subscription is done, you can put messages to the input queue of the publishing flow and check that the messages are effectively sent to the subscriber. If the subscriptions are registered by the other broker, there is no change in message publishing to the subscriber.

### Availability of subscriptions

When a subscriber sends a subscripting request to the sysplex for a given topic:

- The broker processing the message registers the subscription for the subscriber to that topic
- The broker processing the message subscribes with the other brokers, to receive the messages belonging to that topic

This setup ensures that publications coming through any broker in the sysplex will be sent to the subscriber. As long as the broker that registered the subscription is up and running, publications are forwarded properly to the subscriber. If the broker that has registered the subscriber stops, the messages subject for that subscription are not sent to the subscriber anymore.

The solution for this is to configure the brokers to register with ARM. Then in case of failure, the broker will be restarted, thus ensuring the availability of the subscriptions it registered. See "Automatic Restart Management (ARM) planning" on page 217) for details about configuring brokers for using ARM.

So, in a sysplex running more than one broker, it is advisable to register those brokers with ARM, in addition to sharing the queues used in their message flows, when publish/subscribe applications are used, to ensure high availability for publications.

## 10.3.8 Topic-based security in a Parallel Sysplex environment

If you are going to use publishing and subscribing applications, probably you want to add topic-based security to your system, in addition to the security already provided on MQ queues. The User Name Server is responsible for providing the WMQI system with information about users and groups.

See "Customizing the User Name Server (UNS)" on page 75 for details about UNS roles and the customization procedure for a UNS. Also see "Adding a User Name Server to a broker" on page 104 for details about configuring the brokers to communicate with UNS.

## The UNS in a broker domain

The UNS may be:

- Unique for the whole broker domain, which means that all the brokers and also the Configuration Manager are attached to the same UNS, or
- Each component may be attached to its own UNS. Given that, in a sysplex, the users and groups information comes from the z/OS security subsystem (RACF in most cases) the UNS for the Configuration Manager has to be in z/OS as well, so the Configuration Manager can just share the UNS with one of the brokers.

Table 10-24 shows a multiple-UNS configuration, with each broker interacting with its own UNS. The Configuration Manager shares a UNS with one of the brokers.

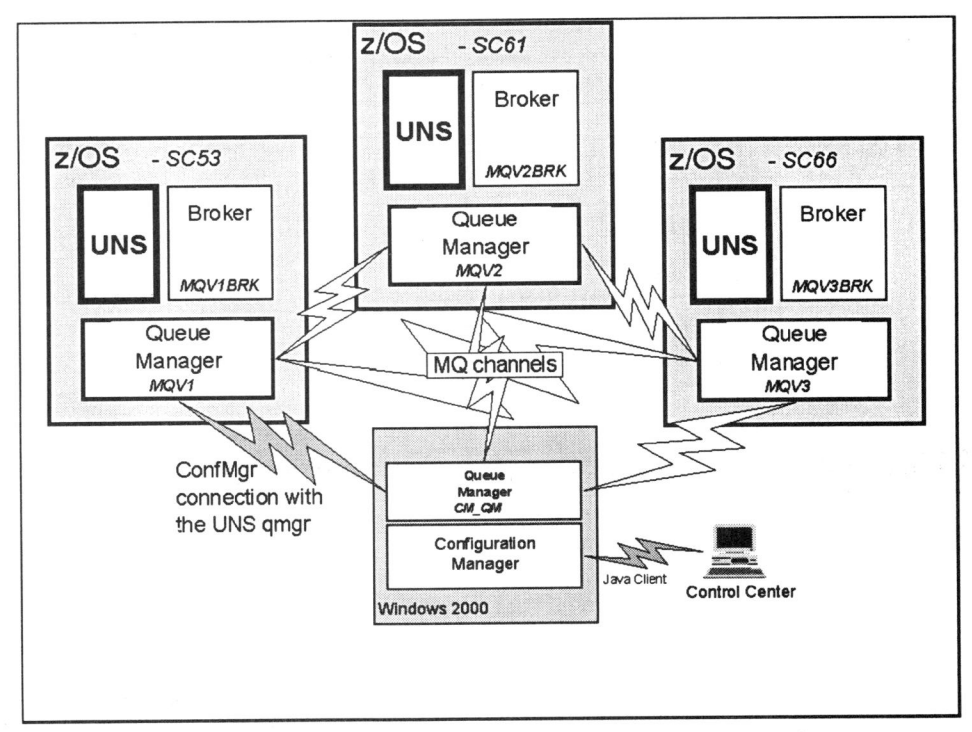

*Figure 10-24 Multiple-UNS configuration*

There are circumstances when you might decide to create more than one UNS, for example performance reasons. If you have a large number of brokers in your system, their requests to the UNS will be handled more quickly. Also high-availability reasons may be taken into account in such a case.

Take into account that, in such a configuration, all UNSs in the sysplex must have access to the same users and group database, or the different databases need to have the same data, in order to prevent inconsistency in the security policy appliance.

In Figure 10-24 on page 229, each broker interacts with its own UNS, and the channels among Queue Managers are set to build the broker network required for publish/subscribe applications to forward subscriptions (see "Configuration for publishing and subscribing in a sysplex" on page 220 for details about broker networks and subscription forwarding).

### Single UNS configuration

You are strongly recommended to configure a single User Name Server in your broker domain, as shown in Figure 10-25, for ease of use, and administration. All brokers and also the Configuration Manager interact with the same UNS.

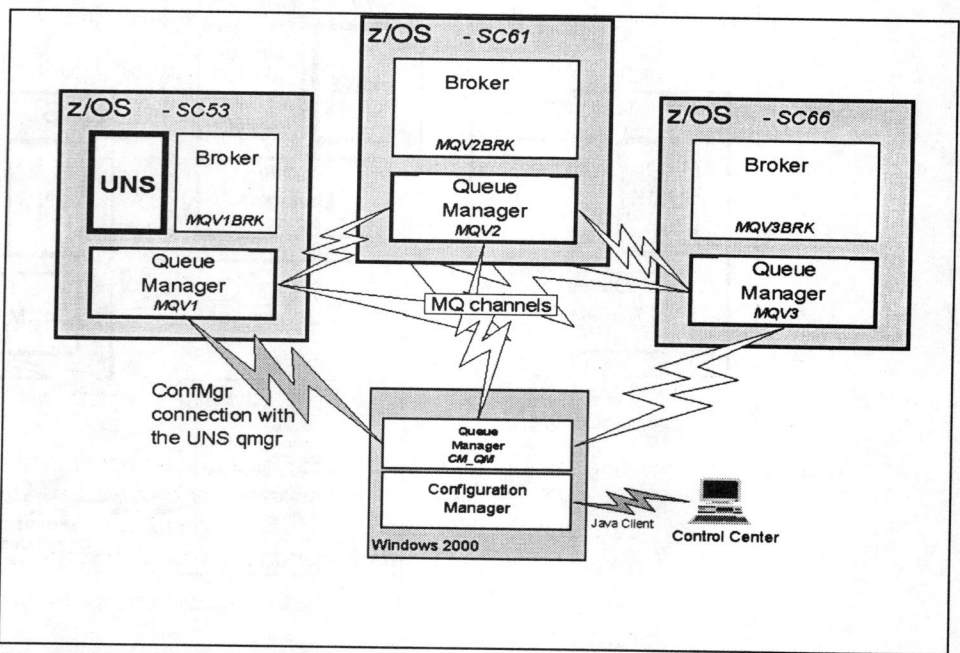

*Figure 10-25   Single User Name Server in the broker domain*

In Figure 10-25, all brokers interact with the same UNS, and the channels among Queue Managers are set to permit this communication, and also to build the broker network required for publish/subscribe applications to forward subscriptions (see "Configuration for publishing and subscribing in a sysplex" on page 220 for details about broker networks and subscriptions forwarding).

### High availability of the UNS

Take into account that high availability for the UNS is not as critical as it is for the brokers in a domain. The brokers cache user and group information. The UNS sleeps according to a refresh interval established when the UNS was created (see "Customizing the User Name Server (UNS)" on page 75 for details). After each refresh interval expires, the UNS rereads user and group information, looking for changes. If nothing has changed, the UNS falls asleep again. Only when something has changed does the UNS send a complete refresh of users and groups information to registered clients: the Configuration Manager and the brokers.

Given the role and the behavior of the UNS, its availability is critical only in environments in which frequent changes on the user/group information are expected for any reason in a given moment. If frequent changes are not expected, brokers may work without refreshing this information for some time without consequences in the topic-based security. So the UNS is not critical enough to have several of them running in parallel. It is advisable to have only one for the broker domain, ensuring the minimal downtime for it.

The downtime for the UNS should be minimized by configuring the UNS to register with ARM. See "Automatic Restart Management (ARM) planning" on page 217 for details about configuring a UNS to register with ARM at start time. Keep in mind that the steps described to set up a broker for using ARM are exactly the same for configuring a UNS to ARM.

When configuring a UNS for using ARM, take into account:

► The UNS is uniquely attached to a Queue Manager, which has a given fixed name. That Queue Manager has to be started in the system the UNS will run in. So the Queue Manager must be defined in each z/OS image on which that Queue Manager might be restarted, with a sysplex-wide, unique 4-character subsystem name.

► Restarting the Queue Manager in other system might mean a change in its IP address or VTAM name. Shared channels should be used for other Queue Managers (the Configuration Manager, Queue Manager, and all the brokers' Queue Managers) to be able to continue to communicate with this one.

► The UNS uses resources that have to be available in the new system. Those resources are:

– Users and groups information retrieved from the Security Subsystem database, typically RACF. The same database must be available in the target system after restart, or the same data has to be stored in the new database to prevent inconsistency in the ACL information security.

– HFS files (Hierarchical File System files) that correspond to the UNIX System Services files used by the UNS.

These resources have to be available in the target system of the restarting process, or in all systems in the sysplex, if it is desired to restart the UNS in any system available. The UNS must be defined and customized in those systems with the same name in all of them.

A possible ARM policy for the UNS is to include it in the same group as its Queue Manager, and, if it shares the Queue Manager with a broker, then to include the three of them in the group (see "Define the ARM policy" on page 218 for details).

# Part 3

# Advanced features

# 11

# New MRM and XML features

WebSphere MQ Integrator V2.1 introduces enhanced support for a much wider range of message types within its own message repository, the MRM. Tagged and delimited messages are now supported and WMQI now has the ability to import an XML document type definition (DTD).

This chapter introduces the new support, showing examples of how to define the new message types and import the DTDs using the Control Center. We assumes that you already have the Control Center, the broker and the Configuration Manager installed and working.

It also demonstrates manipulation of XML messages, including changing field orders, adding attributes and amending the system tags.

Finally, we take a look at generic XML and a new ESQL feature to help you reference your data in a message.

Notice that there are a number of SupportPacs available from http://www.software.ibm.com/ts/mqseries/txppacs that help you deal with MRM and with tagged and delimited messages. Of particular interest are:

- ID05 - WebSphere MQ Integrator - Tagged/delimited message examples
- ID06 - WebSphere MQ Integrator - MRM utilities

## 11.1 Put, get, and view MQSeries messages

To demonstrate and test the features illustrated in this chapter we used IBM SupportPac IHO3 available from the MQSeries Web site at:

http://www.software.ibm.com/ts/mqseries/txppacs

Our z/OS system was configured with MQSeries Client Access Facility (CAF), which enabled us to connect using MQClient from a Windows 2000 workstation. By using IH03 and the client rfhutilc program we could directly put messages onto and get messages from mainframe queues. We then created local text files to be read in as the source for messages.

If your system does not have the CAF facility, there are a number of options to put, get, and view messages from z/OS Queue Manager queues. If you wish to use IH03, you could use your Configuration Manager's MQSeries Queue Manager as follows:

- For each MQInput node, define a local queue on the broker's Queue Manager. Define a remote queue on the Configuration Manager's Queue Manager pointing to it, through the broker's transmission queue.

- For each MQOutput node, define a local queue on the Configuration Manager's Queue Manager. Define a remote queue on the broker's Queue Manager pointing to it, through the Configuration Manager's transmission queue. Use this remote queue name in the MQOutput node and do not specify a Queue Manager name.

- Define a SVRCONN channel on the Configuration Manager's Queue Manager

- Define the MQSERVER environment variable on the Windows 2000/NT workstation you wish to use IH03 from

You can then use the MQSeries Client and rfhutilc to access the queues on the Configuration Manager's Queue Manager to send messages to the broker and receive the results from your flow.

With rfhutilc, the figures in this chapter show XML messages with a data format of XML. All other messages are shown with a data format of Character. In our testing, we did not provide an RFH header but we configured the default properites of the MQInput node to provide message details. This could as well be done specifying an RFH2 header in rfhutilc.

> **Tip:** When using rfhutilc, open up three windows, one each for the input, output and error queues. This avoids retyping queue names when you switch from putting a message on a queue to checking the results.

## 11.2 Testing the MRM in a message flow

To test the MRM, we configured a flow shown in Figure 11-1.

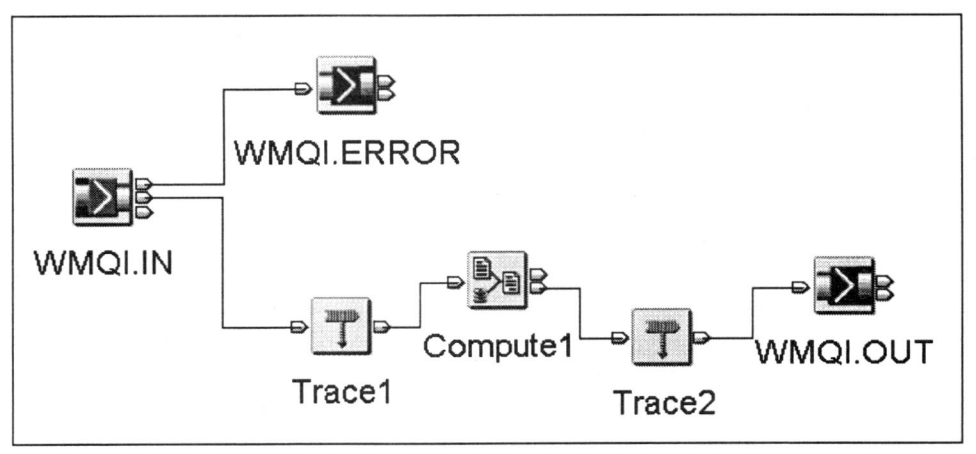

*Figure 11-1 Sample testing message flow*

> **Note:** It is assumed that the reader has a basic familiarity with the Control Center and with developing message flows. If you do not, refer to *Using the Control Center,* SC34-5602.

The flow consists of the following nodes:

- **WMQI.IN** - This is an MQInput node configured with a queue name on the Basic tab of WMQI.IN. During the tests we changed the Default tab of this node to use the message sets, message types and message formats we created.
- **Compute1** - This is a Compute node. We changed the properties in this node throughout the testing of our message sets to show features of the MRM and WebSphere MQ Integrator.
- **WMQI.ERROR** - This is an MQOutput node with WMQI.ERROR configured as the queue name on the Basic tab. The Queue Manager defaults to the Queue Manager name of the broker that runs the flow.
- **WMQI.OUT** - This is an MQOutput node with WMQI.OUT configured as the queue name on the Basic tab. Again the Queue Manager defaults to the Queue Manager name of the broker that runs the flow.

**Trace1 & Trace2** - These trace nodes were configured to print ${Root} to the usertrace logs. This is useful in debugging the flow and checking the message content before and after transformation. For further details refer to Appendix A, "Running a message flow trace" on page 321.

There are three examples that are shown in this chapter. They are revisited in the last section so we recommend that you create a new message flow and a new message set for each. Once you have built one flow, you can duplicate it for each new test. To do this:

- Right-click the message flow in the Message Flows tab of the control center and click **Copy**.
- Right-click the folder message flows and click **Paste**.
- You can now rename the flow by right-clicking it and selecting **Rename**.

Throughout the tests we refer to this flow and the changes that need to be made to the MQInput node and the Compute node. We put messages onto the input queue WMQI.IN and get the results from the output queue WMQI.OUT using rfhutilc described previously.

> **Problem Resolution:** In this chapter we discuss some advanced features. Refer to Appendix A, "Running a message flow trace" on page 321 and Appendix C, "Using the Control Center Debugger" on page 347 when things do not go according to plan: It is not uncommon!

The message set export files are also available in the additional materials described in Appendix D, "Additional material" on page 355.

## 11.3 Defining delimited messages

In this example, we define an MRM message to parse a comma-delimited message, commonly referred to as a comma-separated variable (CSV) message. To demonstrate, this we convert it to XML, which again we will define in the MRM.

In our example we use a message with four fields: first_name, last_name, email_address and location. The incoming message looks as shown in Figure 11-2.

```
Joe,Bloggs,Joe.Blogss@somewhere.co.uk,London
```

*Figure 11-2  Sample delimited message*

By defining the XML format in the MRM, we can demonstrate the drag-and-drop features within a Compute node. However, it is just as simple to use generic XML, which is built up by your statements in a Compute node, rather than to use the MRM.

The steps to achieve this are:

1. Build the message set
   a. Create a new message set
   b. Add the physical formats to the message set
   c. Create some string elements
   d. Create a new compound type and add the elements
   e. Creatie the new message using the compound type
2. Create and deploy a new message flow
   f. Configure the MQInput and MQOutput nodes
   g. Configure the Compute node to transform the message
   h. Deploy the message set and flow
3. Test the flow with a CSV message

## 11.3.1 Building the message set

There are a number of steps to build the message sets. The steps in "Creating the new message set" on page 239 and "Adding the physical formats to the message set" on page 242 will be repeated by each MRM example we discuss.

### Creating the new message set

- In the Control Center, select the **Message Sets** tab.
- Right-click the **Message Sets** part of the navigation tree to bring up the context menu.
- Select **Create -> Message Set...**

This is illustrated in Figure 11-3 on page 240.

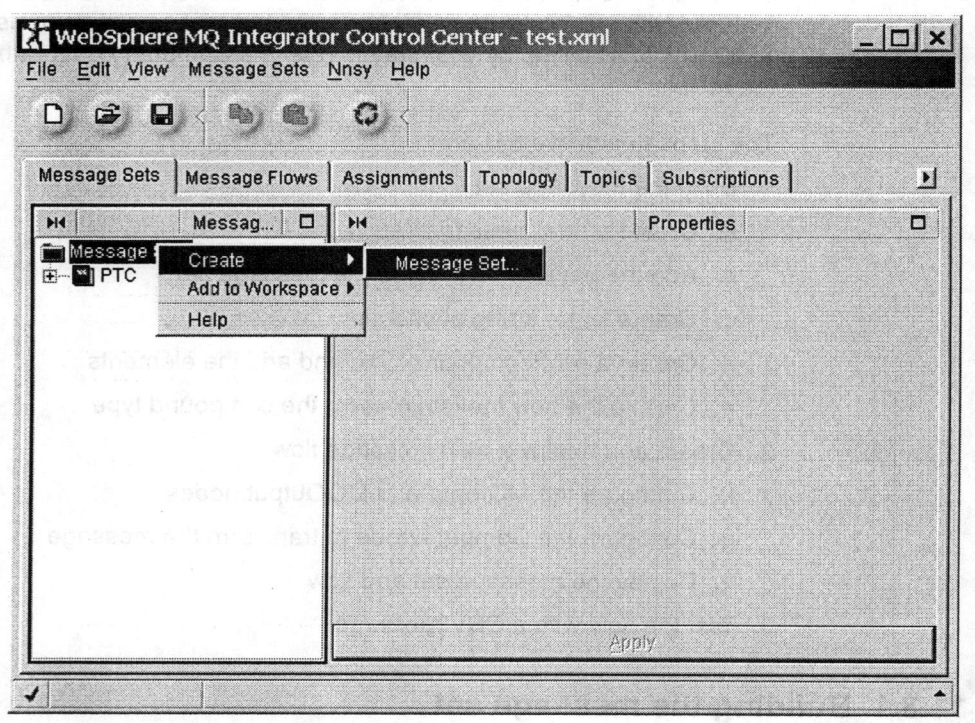

*Figure 11-3 Creating a new message set*

- Complete the Name field (in our example we used DLM_TEST)

  **Note:** The message set name needs to be unique within the Configuration Manager. It is a good idea to include message set names in a set of naming standard for your organization.

- Leave the other fields as their default (Figure 11-4 on page 241) and click **Finish.**

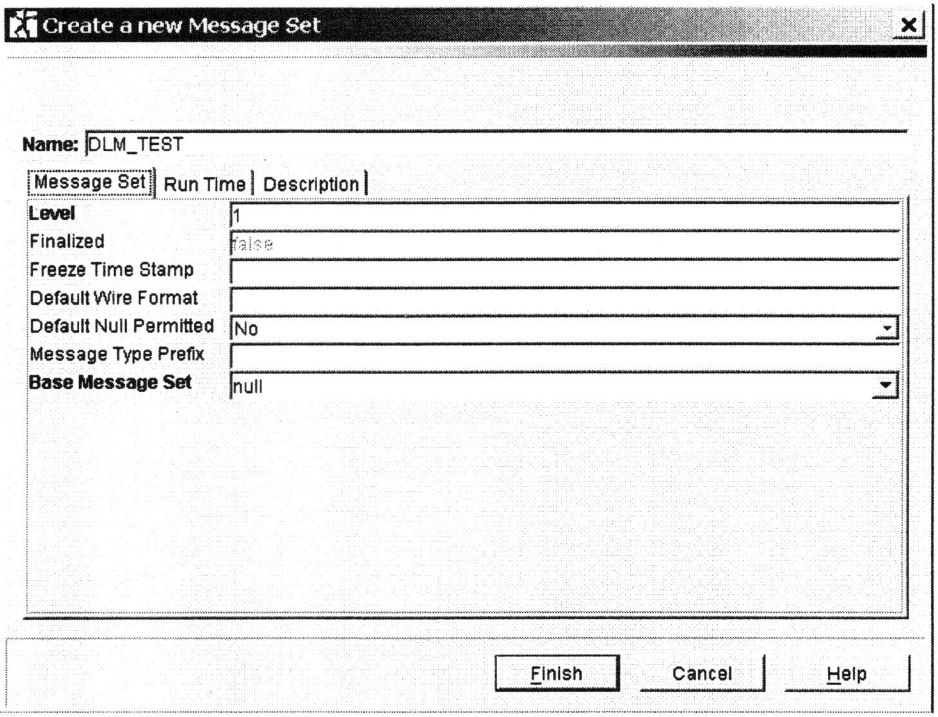

*Figure 11-4 Naming the new message set*

- Select the new message set as shown in Figure 11-5 on page 242.
- Make a note of the message set Identifier for use in later steps.

**Note:** The message set is allocated a unique identifier by the Configuration Manager. You can see this value, DNTBFL807M001, in Figure 11-5 on page 242. Initially a Configuration Manager varies the last few bytes of identifiers it allocates, so take special care to use the correct value.

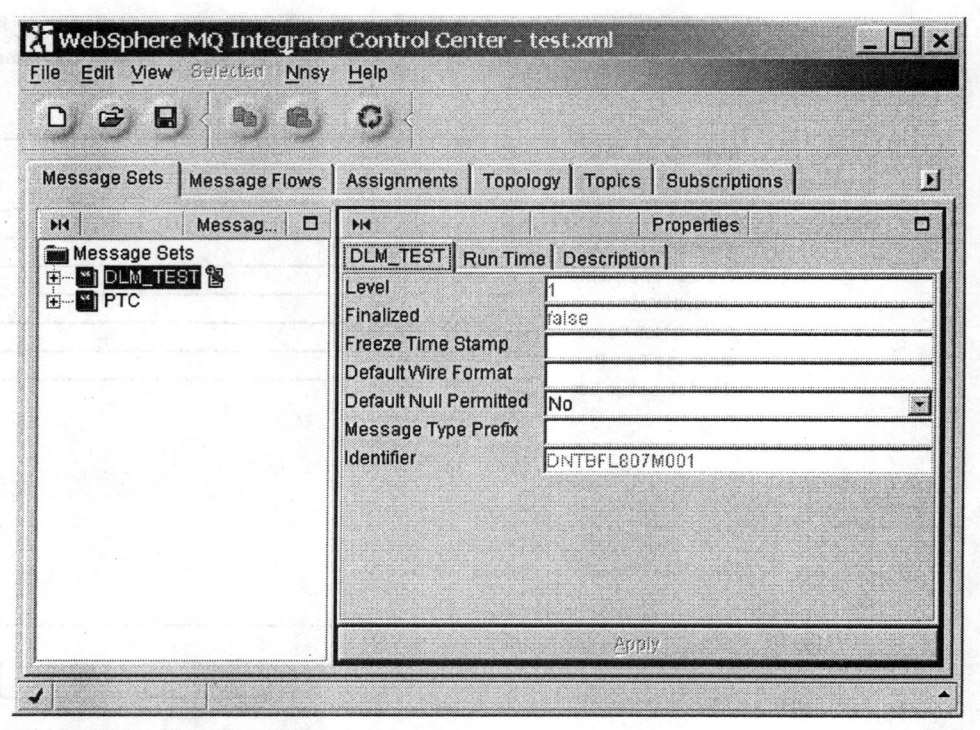

*Figure 11-5   The newly created message set*

If you click the **Run Time** tab, you see that the Parser value is set to MRM (see Figure 11-6). This is the default and indicates that this message set will use the MRM. It is important to make the distinction between MRM-defined XML and generic (or self-defining) XML. This example uses MRM-defined XML, which allows the MRM to perform most of the work required for message transformation.

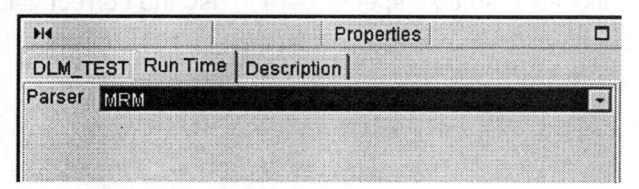

*Figure 11-6   Parser value is MRM*

## Adding the physical formats to the message set

The next step is to add the physical formats (Figure 11-7), starting with the tagged/delimited format.

- Right-click your message set, then select **Add -> Physical Format -> Tagged/Delimited Format**.

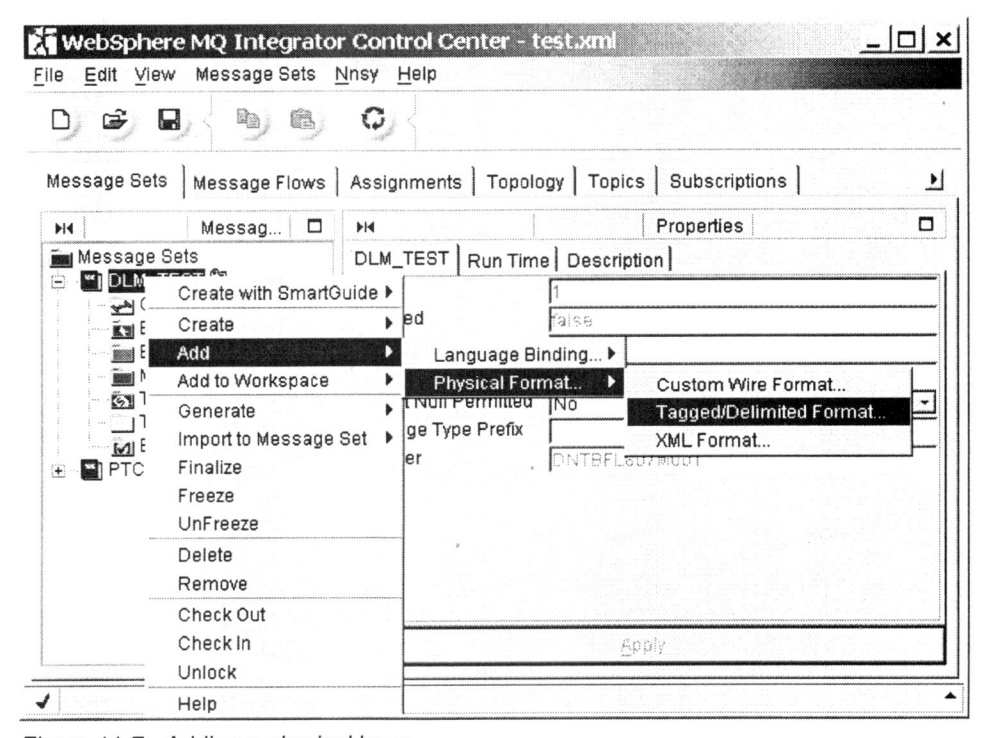

*Figure 11-7 Adding a physical layer*

- Complete the Name field (In our example TDS1) and select **Finish.**

You should now see a new physical layer tab appear on the message set with the name you have just supplied.

- Select the physical layer tab you have just added.
- Change the TDS Wire Format Identifier to match the name you gave the physical layer.

**Note:** We recommend that you keep the name and identifier the same to avoid confusion.

- Enter the delimiter character (a comma) in the Delimiter field.
- Click the **Apply** button at the bottom of the physical layer tab.

Chapter 11. New MRM and XML features    **243**

The messaging standard (see Figure 11-8) defaults to UNKNOWN. This is correct, since we are not using one of the predefined industry-standard formats (such as SWIFT) in this example.

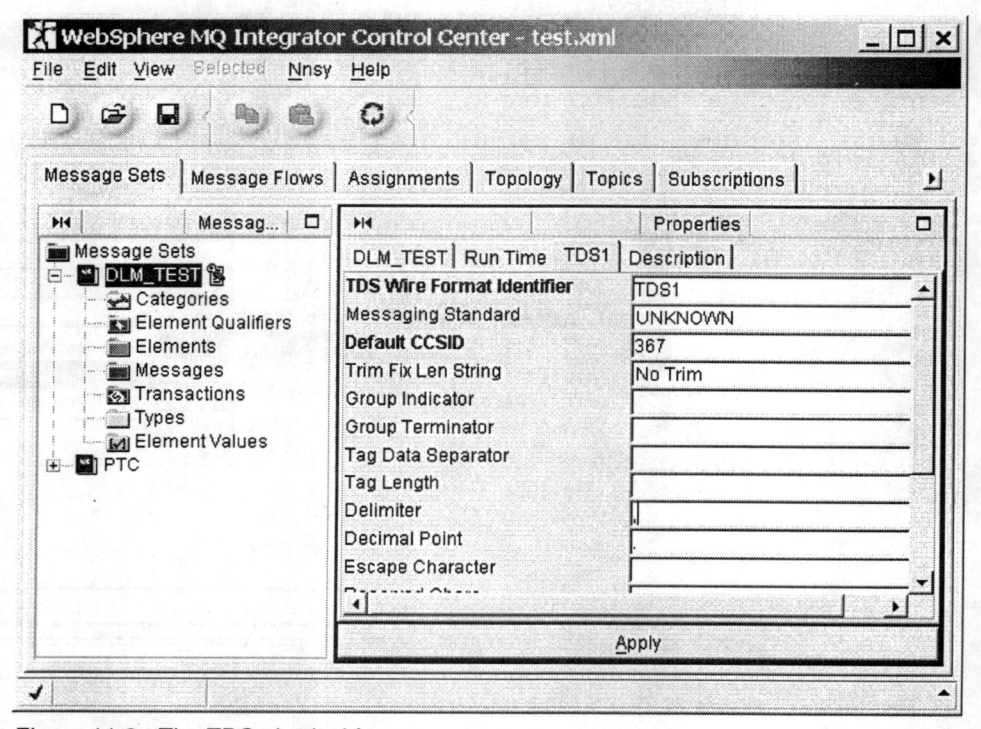

*Figure 11-8   The TDS physical format*

▶ Repeat this step to add an XML physical layer format with the name XML1 (see Figure 11-9 on page 245). Take care to choose appropriate format names, since once they are added, formats cannot be deleted from the message set.

**Note:** You could name and identify your XML physical format as XML if you wish. This is suggested as a good installation standard, so that if you have existing MRM messages that specify XML as their RFH2 format, then they will pick up the new XML physical format. However, the use of XML1 here illustrates that we are specifying an identifier (which we set) and not simply selecting XML from a predefined Control Center list of formats.

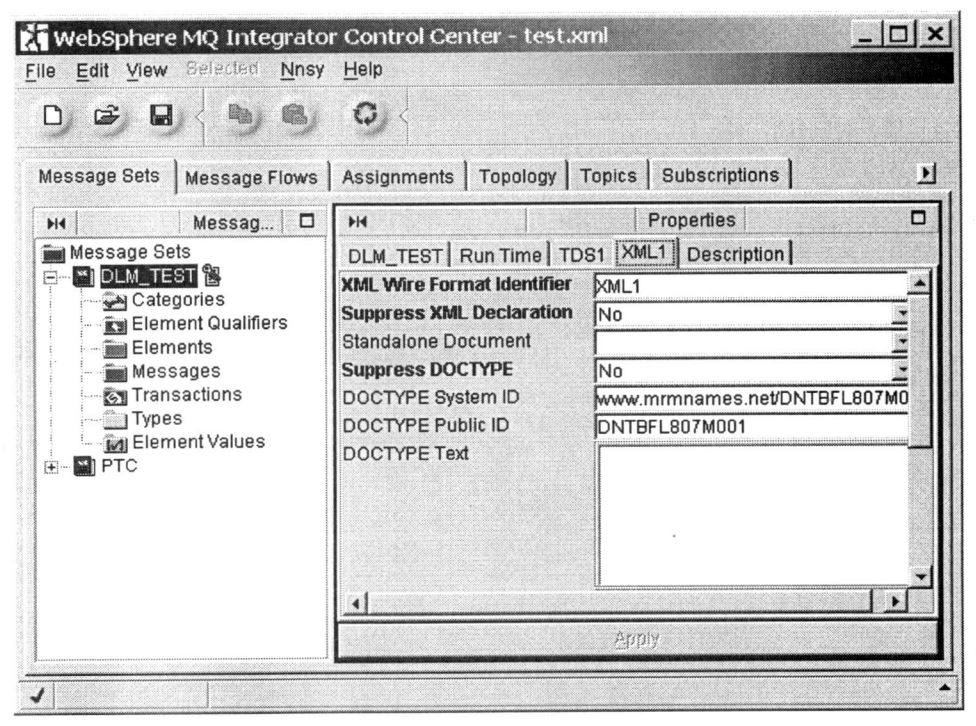

Figure 11-9   The XML format in the MRM

## Creating message elements
The next step is to create the elements that make up the fields in your message.

- Expand your Message Sets tree folder in the left pane of the Message Sets tab.
- Right-click the **Elements** section and select **Create -> Element.**
- Enter the name of the first field in your message (FIRST_NAME) in the Name and Identifier fields and select **STRING** from the Type pull-down menu as shown in Figure 11-10 on page 246.

> **Note:** Again for simplicity we recommend keeping element names and identifiers the same.

- Click the **Finish** button.
- Repeat for all the fields in your message (FIRST_NAME, LAST_NAME, EMAIL_ADDR and LOCATION).

It is not necessary to specify a length value for the element, since we are parsing variable length delimited messages in this example.

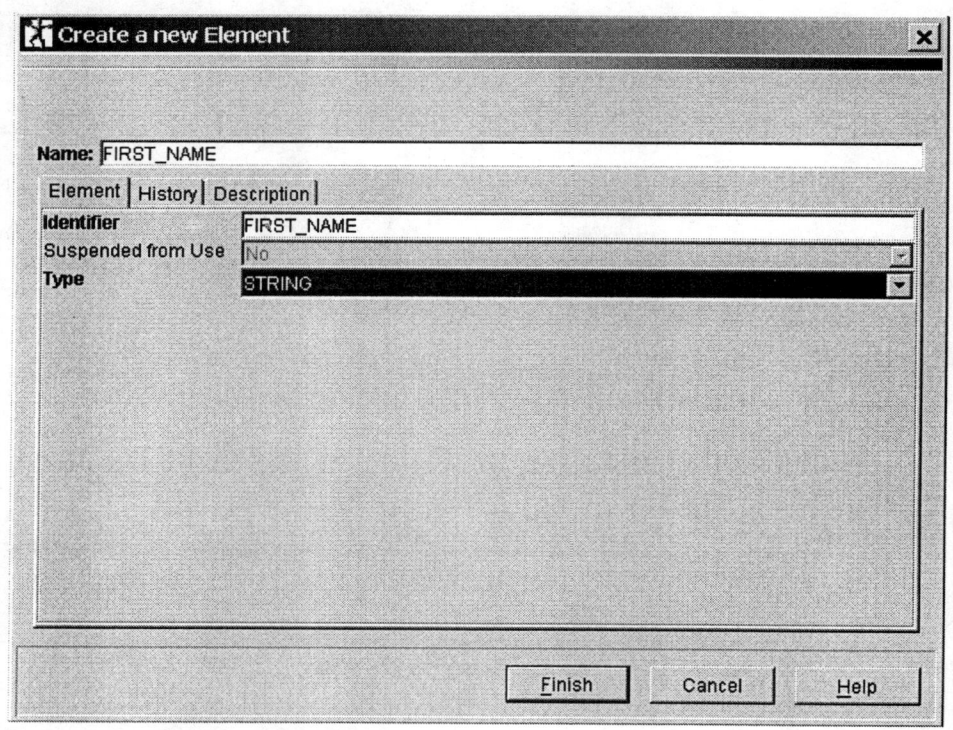

*Figure 11-10   Creating an element*

When you have added all four elements, your message set should look like Figure 11-11 on page 247.

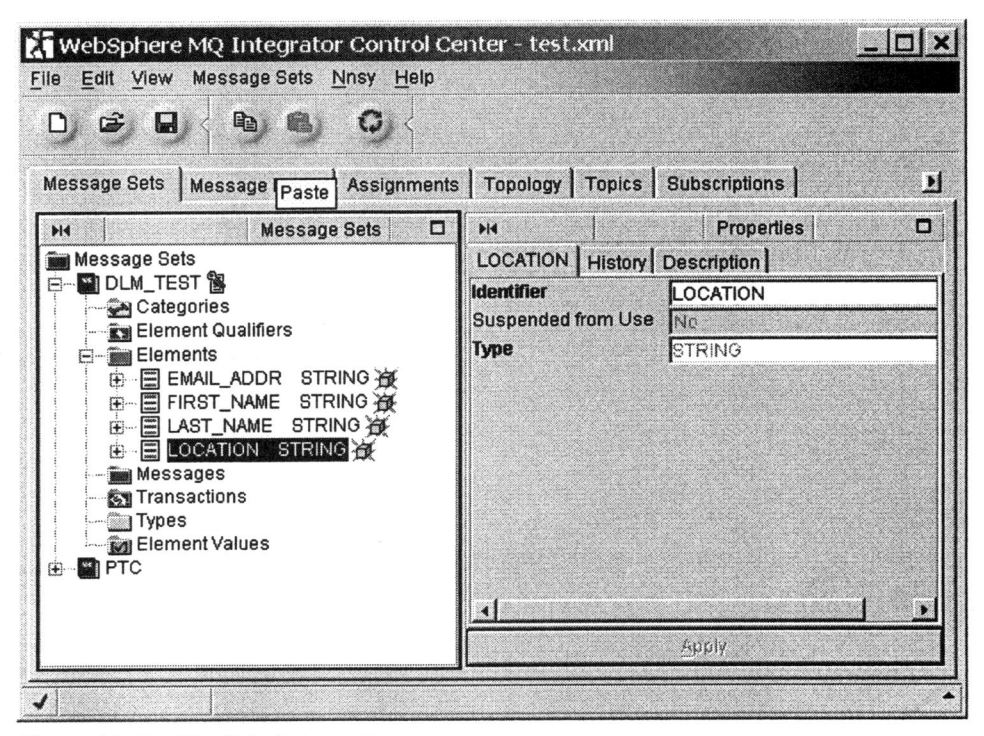

Figure 11-11  The list of elements

## Create the message type

Now we create a type that we can use to define our message. This type must include the elements that make up the message. Complex messages can be defined from many compound types. In our example (Figure 11-12 on page 248) we just use a very simple compound type which we call "LIST".

- Right-click **Types** folder and select **Create -> Compound Type**.

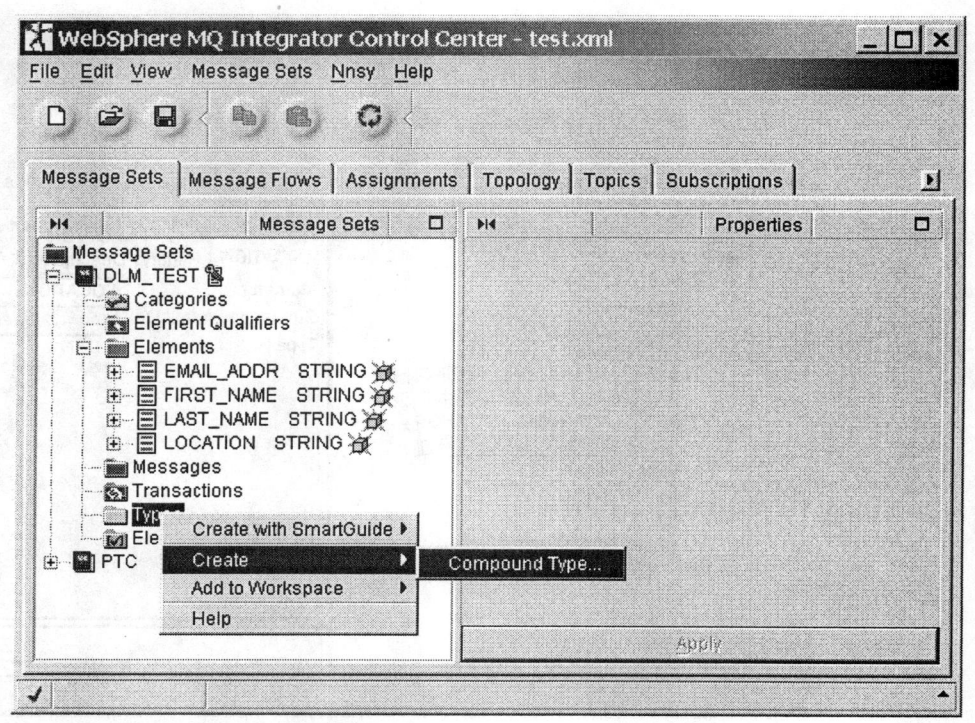

*Figure 11-12   Create compound type*

- Enter LIST, the name we will use for our compound type, in the Name and identifier fields.
- Change the Type Content to closed from the pull-down menu.

    This means that all fields in the message must be defined in the message set.
- Select **Finish** to create the message type, shown in Figure 11-13 on page 249.

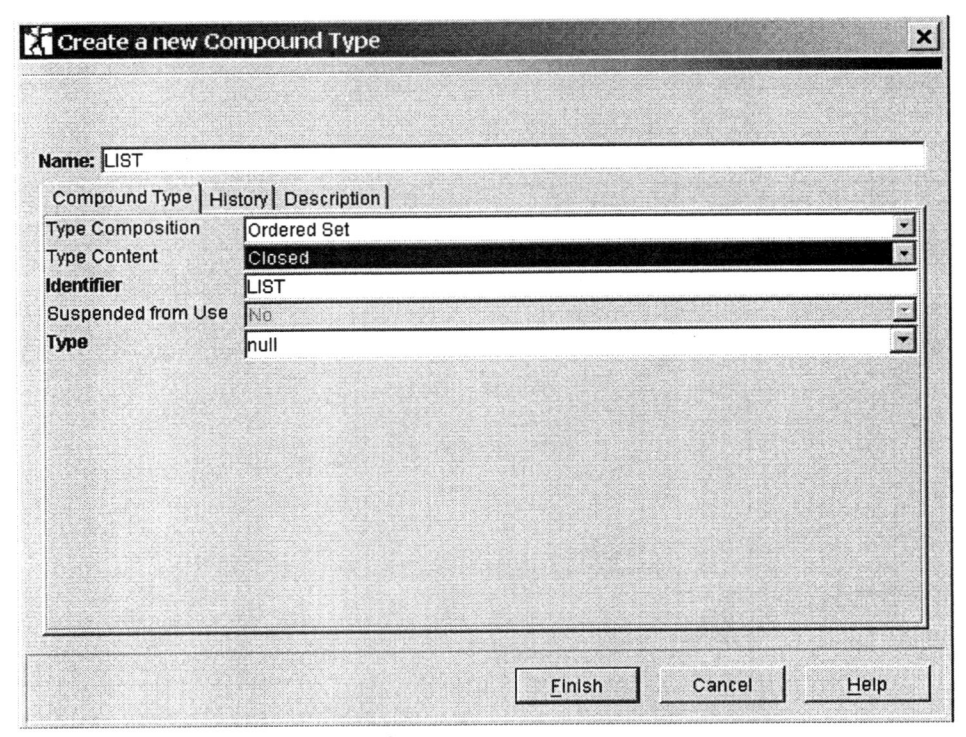

*Figure 11-13  Name the compound type*

The next step is to add the elements to the compound type we have created.

- Right-click the new compound type LIST in the right pane as shown in Figure 11-15 on page 250 and select **Add -> Element...**

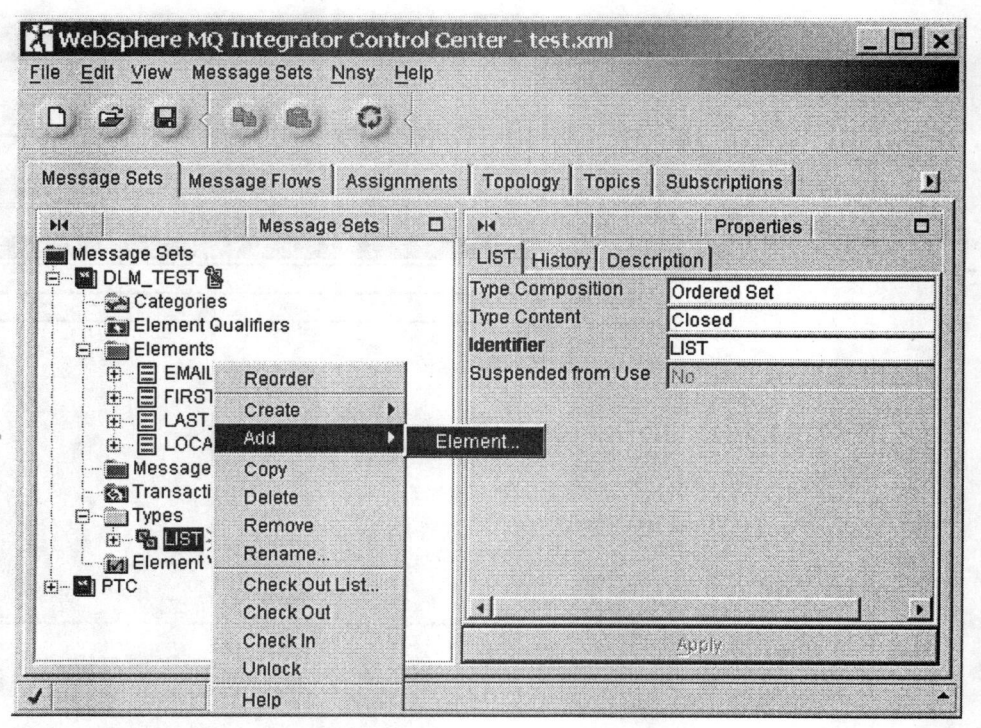

*Figure 11-14   Adding elements to type*

The elements previously created are displayed.

- Select all four of the elements (see Figure 11-15) (hold the Ctrl key down while selecting each row in turn) and click **Finish**.

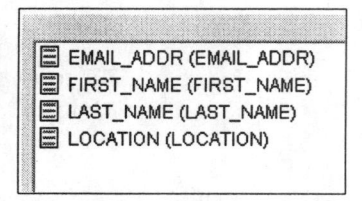

*Figure 11-15   Element names*

Your new message set should look as shown in Figure 11-16 on page 251.

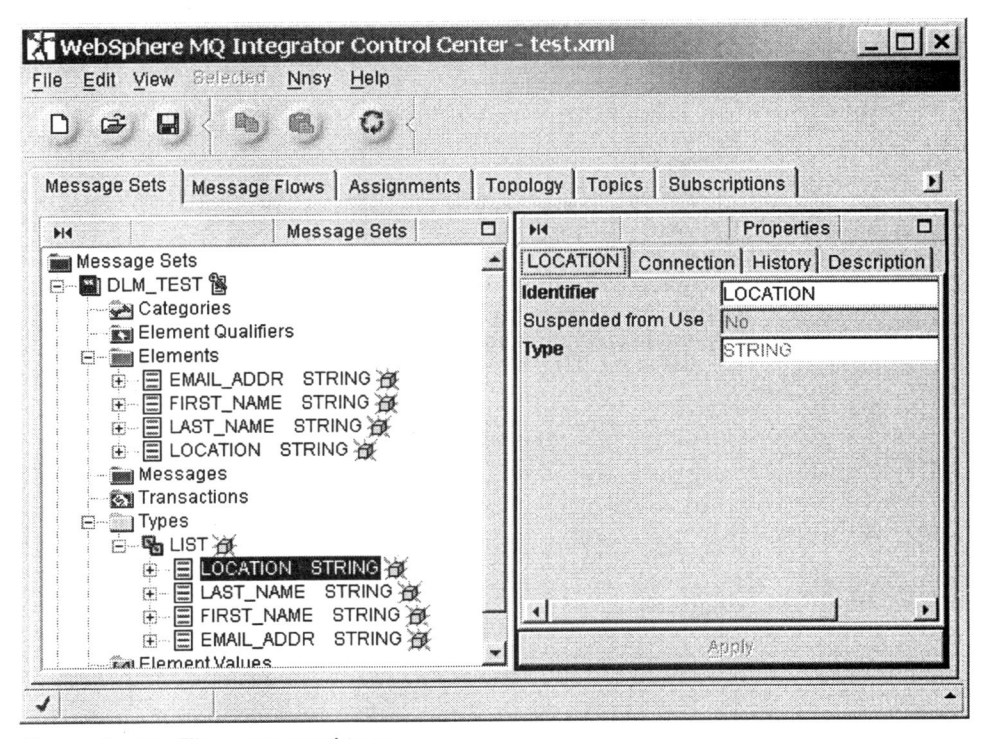

*Figure 11-16   The compound type*

## Creating a message using the compound type

Next we create a message based on the compound type we have just created. In our example, we call the message "TEST".

- Right-click **Messages** folder in the left pane and select **Create -> Message**.
- Enter the message Name (TEST) and again the same in the Identifier field.
- Select the compound type you have just created (LIST) from the Type drop-down menu (Figure 11-17 on page 252) and click the **Finish** button.

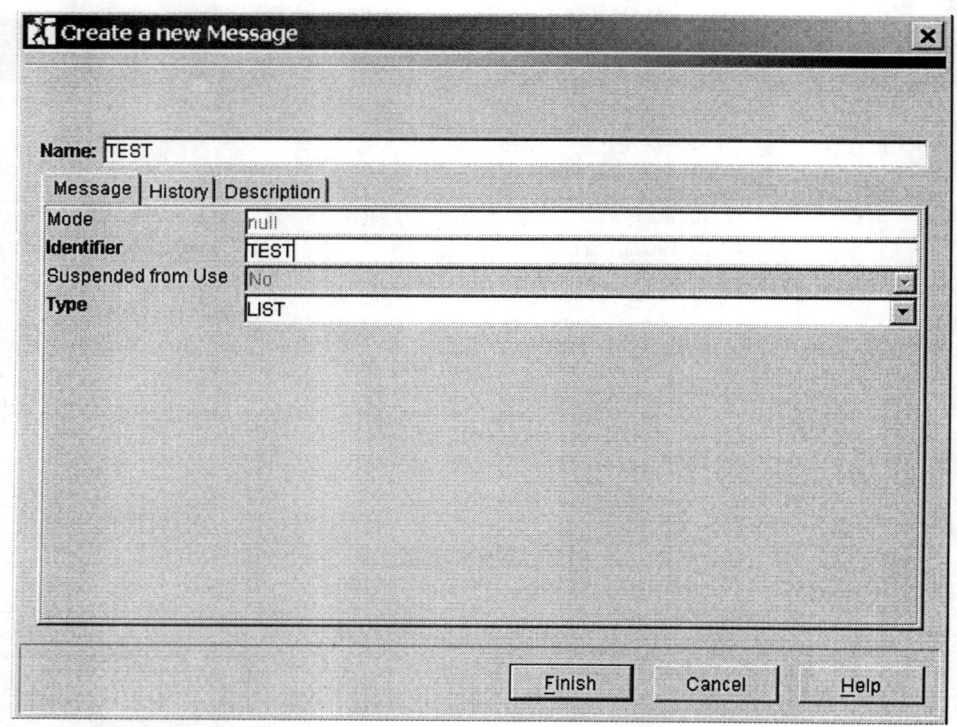

*Figure 11-17 Creating the message*

At this point, you should check in the elements and types of the message set.

- Right-click one of the new elements and select **Check In**.

When you check in one element, the Control Center checks in the other elements and the new type for you. After this, you see tabs for the new physical formats when you select elements or types.

We now want to define the message as containing variable length fields (such as you might have if you exported a spreadsheet to a CSV file).

- Right-click our message type (LIST) and select **Check Out**.
- Select our delimited physical layer tab **TDS1**.
- Change the Data Element Separation field to Variable Length Elements Delimited.
- Set the delimiter to a comma and click **Apply** as shown in Figure 11-18 on page 253.

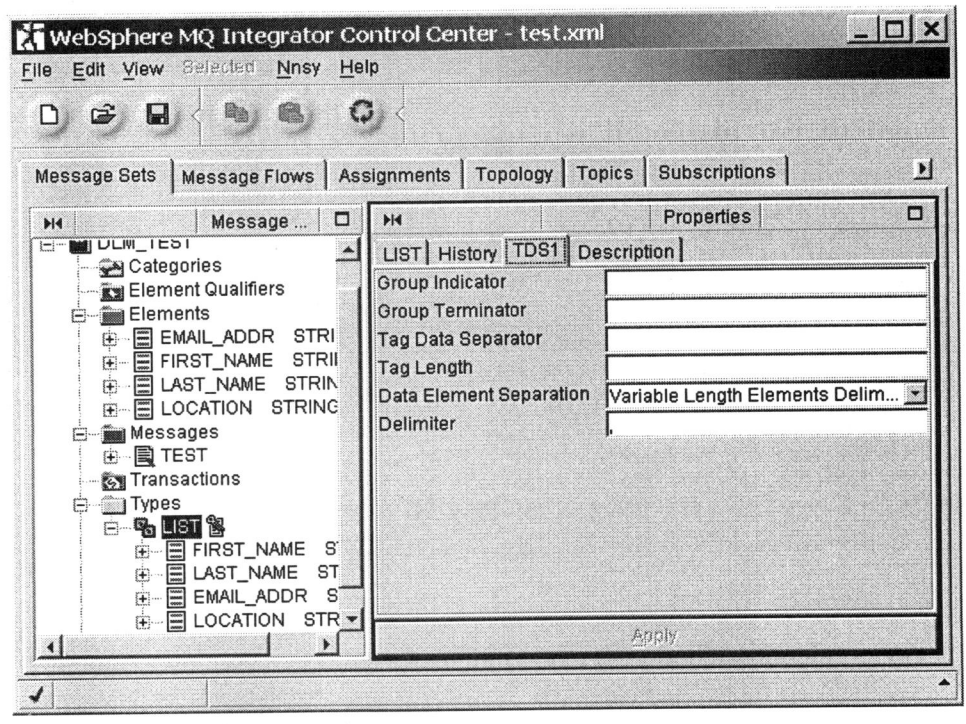

*Figure 11-18  Modifying the type TDS1*

If the elements are not in the correct order for your message, you can reorder them. To do this:

- Right-click your new type and select **Reorder**.
- Select an element in the Reorder Elements pane shown in Figure 11-19 on page 254 and move it up or down using the arrow keys to top and bottom right of the pane. Repeat until all elements are in the appropriate position and click **Finish**.

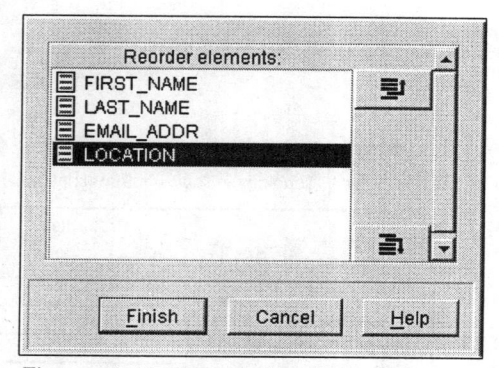

*Figure 11-19  Reordering elements*

- Check in the type again and the message set (if needed).

## 11.3.2 Creating a message flow to convert CSV to XML

Using 11.2, "Testing the MRM in a message flow" on page 237 as a guide, build a message flow to test the new message set.

### Configuring the MQInput node

Select the properties Default tab and complete the fields very carefully as shown in Table 11-1.

> **Warning:** The MQInput node gives you a pull-down list on the Default tab for message format. The list shows the format names and *not* the required identifiers. If you do not keep the physical format identifier and name the same and rely on the default settings on the MQInput, you will have problems. You can, however, complete the field correctly by typing the identifier in it.

*Table 11-1  MQInput node properties*

| Property Name | Example Value | Description |
| --- | --- | --- |
| Message Domain | **MRM** | Message Domain (and the parser to use). |
| Message Set | **DNTBFL807M001** | Use the identifier for *your* message set here. |
| Message Type | **TEST** | The identifier of the message (*not* the compound type). |

| Property Name | Example Value | Description |
| --- | --- | --- |
| Message Format | TDS1 | The identifier of the physical format. |

With this configuration of the MQInput node, when a message is taken from the input queue with no RFH header WebSphere MQ Integrator parses the message using the MRM. If the parsing is successful, it creates an MRM message tree, in this case with four string elements which are named FIRST_NAME, LAST_NAME, EMAIL_ADDR and LOCATION.

## Configuring the Compute node

The Compute node can now be configured to transform the message to XML by specifying the new Message Format for its output message. Compute nodes are the only type of nodes that modify the message. They construct an output message, which can be based on some or all of the input message.

The output refers to the output of the Compute node and is not necessarily the final output message from the flow. The actions of the Compute node are performed by ESQL statements. These actions can be coded manually or generated by selecting options on the properties window, or a mixture of both.

In our example we give you two options to configure the Compute node. The first is the simplest and is the normal way to configure such a simple example. However, the second option shows how we can use the graphical drag-and-drop facility in a Compute node, one of the advantages of defining a message to the MRM. In this second option we choose to select only three of the four incoming fields.

### Option 1

1. Select **Copy entire message** in the Compute node properties.
2. Select the **ESQL** tab in the Compute node properties and add this one additional statement:

   ```
   Set OutputRoot.Properties.MessageFormat = 'XML1';
   ```

   This command instructs the MRM (which is the default message domain) to construct the output message (from the Compute node) using the message format XML1 (which we defined in our message set as an XML physical layer).

3. Select **OK**.

### Option 2

1. Select **Copy message headers** in the Compute node properties.

Now we add the message layouts to both the input and output areas (Figure 11-20) in order to be able to use the MRM definitions to provide a drag-and-drop way to create ESQL statements.

2. Click **Add...** on the top left half of the Compute node properties pane. Select your previously defined Message Set and Message from the pull-down list.
3. Click **Add...** on the top right half of the Compute node properties pane. Once again select your previously defined Message Set and Message from the pull-down list.

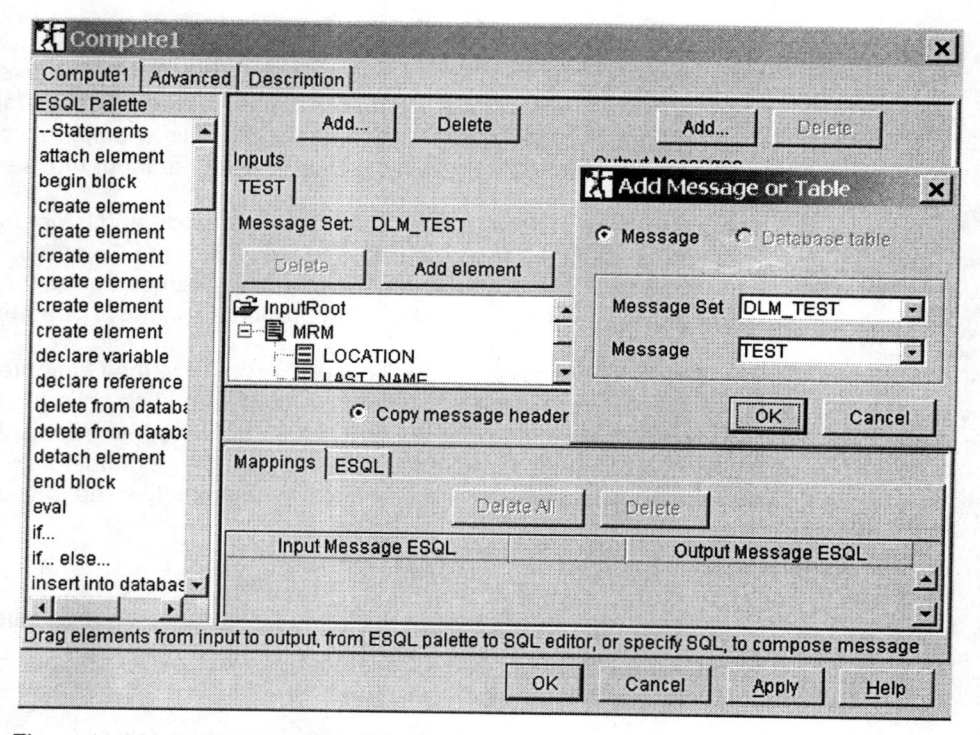

*Figure 11-20  Adding message to Compute node*

4. Select **Use as message body** button towards the top right of the properties pane. This option causes generation of an ESQL statement to copy over the message set identifier and message type identifier.
5. Drag three of the input fields (shown in the left pane) onto three of the matching output fields (shown on the right pane).

In our example, we dragged the fields FIRST_NAME, LAST_NAME and EMAIL_ADDR. For each drag operation a line should appear below on the Mappings tab. If you do not cleanly drag one field right on top of the other, the map operations may not work, so check the lines that are generated.

The result should look like Figure 11-21 on page 257.

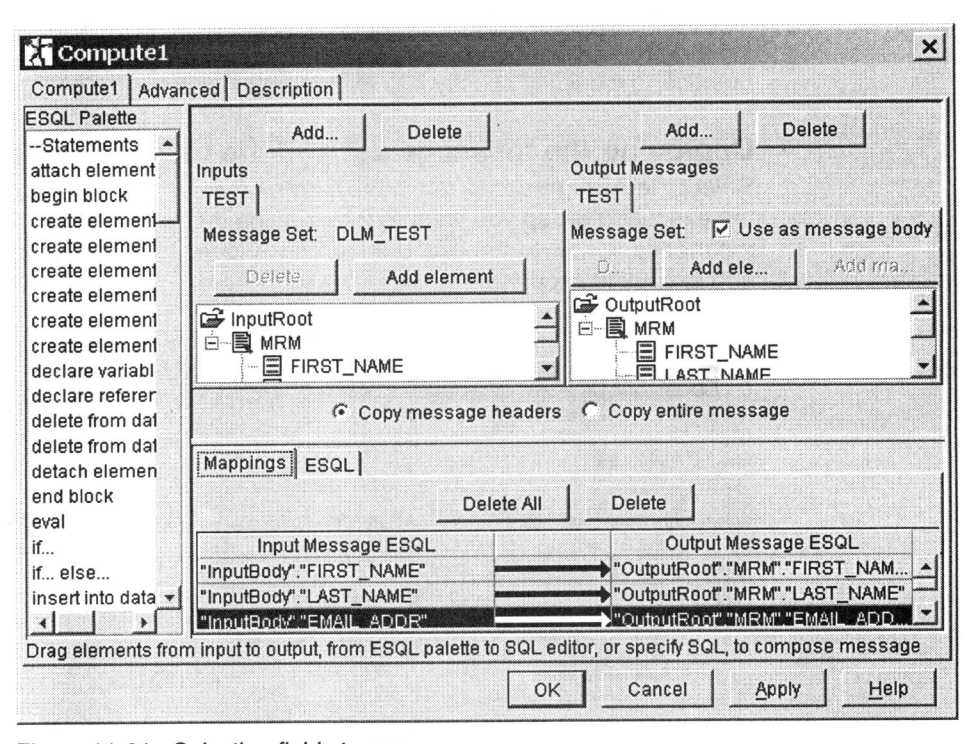

*Figure 11-21   Selecting fields to copy*

6. Click the **ESQL** tab to manually add the two statements at the end of the ESQL code sequence, as shown in the last lines in Example 11-1.

*Example 11-1   Compute Node ESQL to transform fields to XML with the MRM*

```
DECLARE I INTEGER;
SET I = 1;
WHILE I < CARDINALITY(InputRoot.*[]) DO
   SET OutputRoot.*[I] = InputRoot.*[I];
   SET I=I+1;
END WHILE;
SET "OutputRoot"."MRM"."FIRST_NAME" = "InputBody"."FIRST_NAME";
SET "OutputRoot"."MRM"."LAST_NAME" = "InputBody"."LAST_NAME";
SET "OutputRoot"."MRM"."EMAIL_ADDR" = "InputBody"."EMAIL_ADDR";
```

```
SET OutputRoot.Properties.MessageSet = 'DNTBFL807M001';
SET OutputRoot.Properties.MessageType = 'TEST';
-- Enter SQL below this line.  SQL above this line might be regenerated,
causing any modifications to be lost.
Set OutputRoot.Properties.MessageFormat = 'XML1';
Set OutputRoot.Properties.MessageDomain = 'MRM';
```

The Message Format refers to the physical format in the message set, which we called XML1. The message domain would default to MRM, but it is a good practice to explicitly specify it to avoid confusion with the generic XML domain.

### Deploying the message set and the message flow

Select the **Assignments** tab in the Control Center and *check out* the broker and the execution group you want to use. Assign the message set to the broker and the message flow to the execution group (Figure 11-22). *Check in* the broker and execution group.

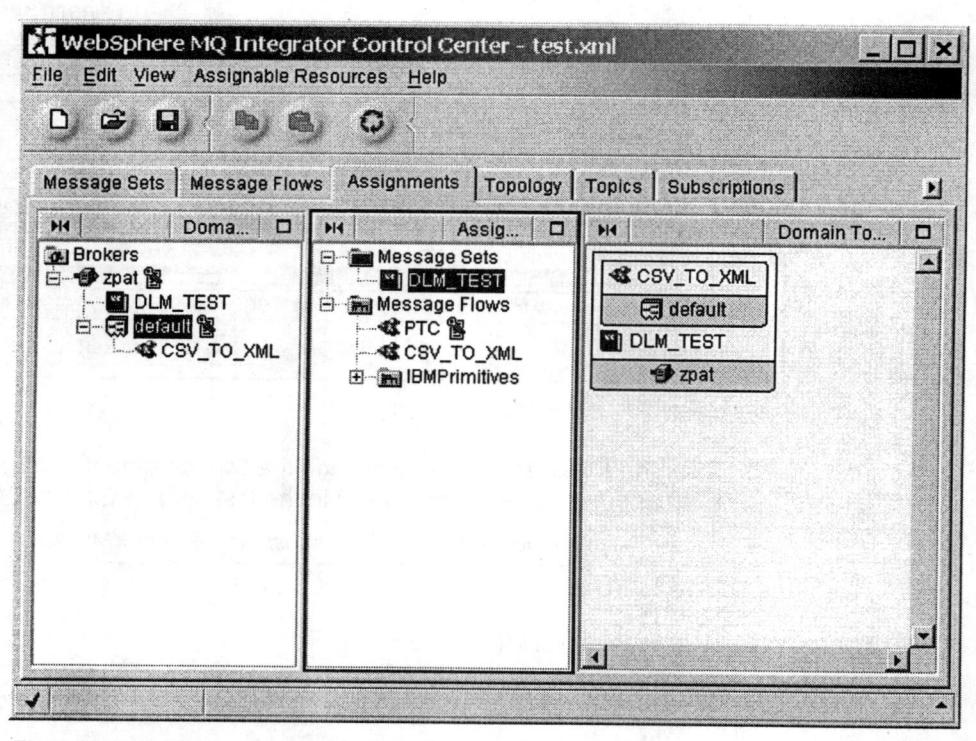

*Figure 11-22 The assigned message flow and set*

Deploy the changes to the broker (either a Delta or a Complete deploy).

> **Note:** We recommend that when you deploy a message set, you do a *Delta deploy*. This avoids unnecessary processing and is generally quicker. However on occasions during our testing it was necessary to do a *Complete deploy* to successfully send our message set updates to the broker.

Check the Log tab in the Control Center to determine when the deployment has completed successfully.

If you have made any mistakes in your development so far, the deploy operation may not be successful. The log view on your Control Center or the Windows Event Viewer on the Configuration Manager host should help you locate the cause of any problems (which tend to be omissions of a message set fields). When an error is detected in a tagged/delimited format, the error is recorded in a file named TDS1.log, which is in the log directory of WebSphere MQ Integrator on the Configuration Managers system.

The message flow is now running in the broker. If you have not already done so, create some MQSeries queues. You can create extra queues that can be used to send failure messages to (by connecting the failure nodes to MQOutput nodes which use these queues).

The input count on the WMQI.IN queue should now be at least one (see Figure 11-23). This is due to the message flow having opened this queue for input.

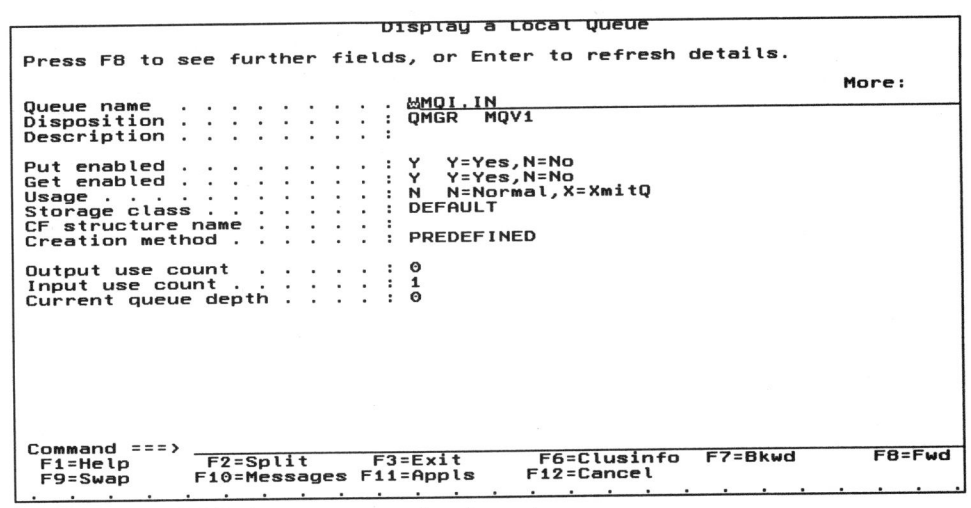

```
                        Display a Local Queue
Press F8 to see further fields, or Enter to refresh details.
                                                                   More:
Queue name  . . . . . . . . . : WMQI.IN
Disposition . . . . . . . . . : QMGR      MQV1
Description . . . . . . . . . :

Put enabled . . . . . . . . . : Y    Y=Yes,N=No
Get enabled . . . . . . . . . : Y    Y=Yes,N=No
Usage . . . . . . . . . . . . : N    N=Normal,X=XmitQ
Storage class . . . . . . . . : DEFAULT
CF structure name . . . . . . :
Creation method . . . . . . . : PREDEFINED

Output use count  . . . . . . : 0
Input use count . . . . . . . : 1
Current queue depth . . . . . : 0




Command ===>
 F1=Help      F2=Split      F3=Exit      F6=Clusinfo    F7=Bkwd     F8=Fwd
 F9=Swap      F10=Messages F11=Appls     F12=Cancel
```

*Figure 11-23  MQSeries queue open input count*

## 11.3.3 Testing the message flow

Generate a test message to test your flow. In our case, we created a text file (Figure 11-24) and using rfhutilc (from IH03) put this file directly onto the broker's input queue WMQI.IN.

*Figure 11-24  Delimited input message*

There should now be an output message on WMQI.OUT that looks like Figure 11-25. The message has been formatted as XML by selecting the **Data Format** as **XML** in the top right of the rfhutilc utility.

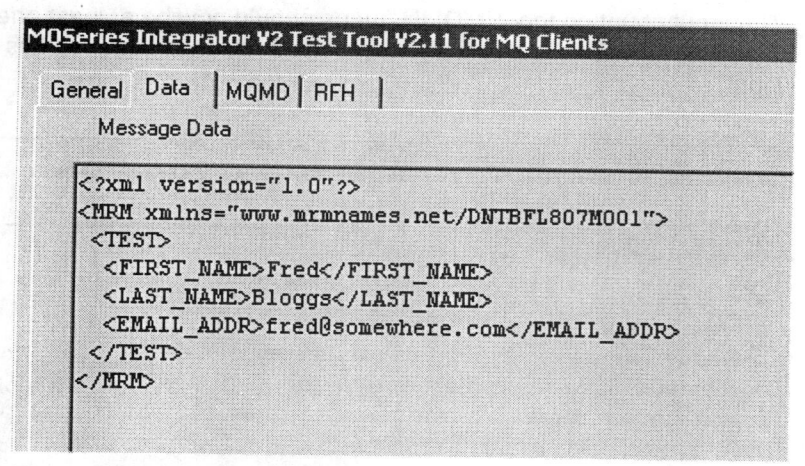

*Figure 11-25  XML1 output message*

You have now transformed a comma-delimited message into XML using the MRM. In "Additional XML MRM features" on page 284 we explore further how to manipulate the XML message produced by a message flow.

## 11.4 Building tagged messages

In this example we demonstrate how to transform a tagged message into XML. We use a message that uses an equals sign as the tag and a semicolon as a delimiter so our data might look as it is shown in Figure 11-26.

```
Given=John,Surname=Doe,Email=jdoe@nowhere.com;Location=Earth
```

*Figure 11-26   Sample tagged message*

The process is similar to 11.3, "Defining delimited messages" on page 238 so only the differences are shown. You could also just modify the message set and flow created for the CSV transformation rather than create a new one as we do.

### 11.4.1 Build the message set

Using the same procedures as the 11.3.1, "Building the message set" on page 239:

- Create a new message set (TAGGED_TEST)
- Add physical formats for tagged/delimited(TAG) and XML with names that match their identifiers
- Create the same four string elements
- Create a compound type (LIST)
- Add elements to the new compound type
- Create a message using the new compound type
- Reorder the elements

Check in the message set, elements and types. We are now ready to configure the message set to process the tagged data correctly.

#### Configuring a message set for tagged data

Check out the new compound type. Change the type composition setting to unordered set. This option allows the tags to occur in any order. It can be left as an ordered set if the tags must be in order and you want an error to be generated if they are not. Set type content to open (this option permits message fields other than the ones defined in the message set to exist without causing errors). This is shown in Figure 11-27 on page 262.

> **Tip:** The Control Center online help is the best place to find more detailed explanations of the various message set fields.

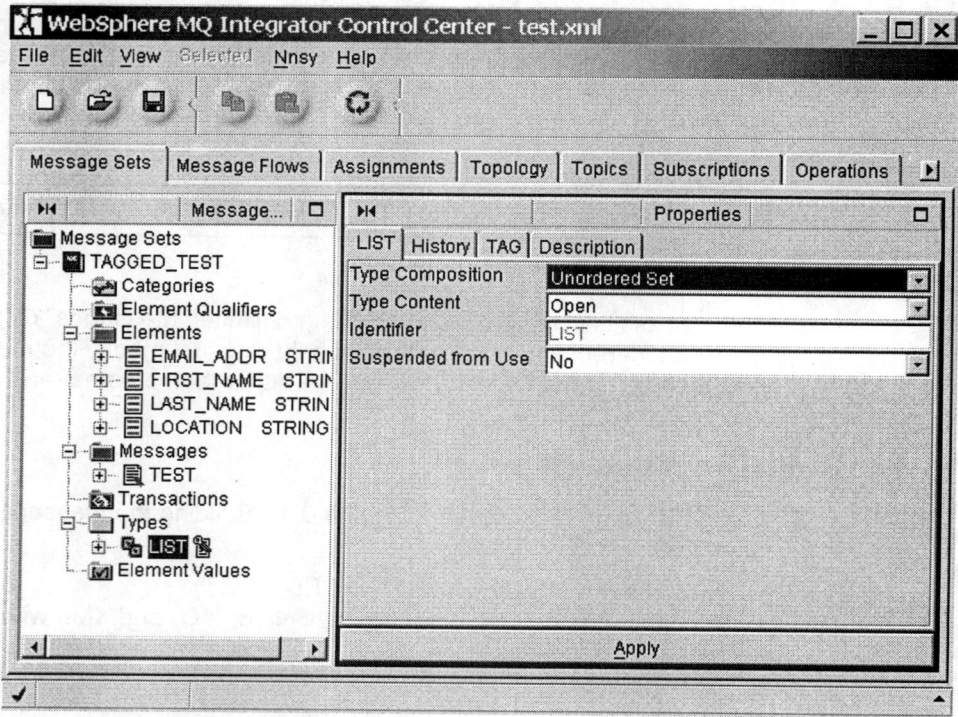

*Figure 11-27  Changing the LIST type settings*

Now click the TAG tab as in Figure 11-28 on page 263 and set the Tag Data Separator to = (an equals sign), the Data Element Separation to Tagged Delimited and the Delimiter to ; (a semicolon). Be careful not to add any spaces after the delimiter, unless you wish these spaces to become part of the delimiter string. Apply the changes.

This action configures the message set to process tagged data with a delimiter (rather than fixed length fields) and with a separator between the tag and the data. An equals sign separates each tag from its data. Each tagged field is delimited with a semicolon from the next field.

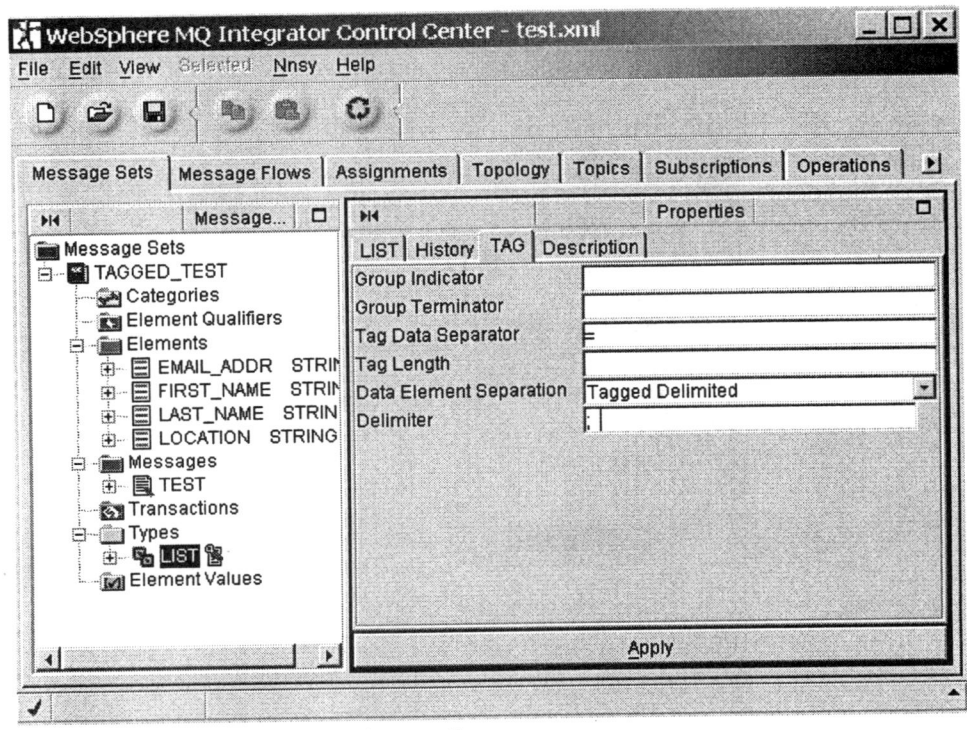

*Figure 11-28 Setting the tagged properties*

Now expand the LIST type to show the elements within it and check out each element in turn. For each element, click the **TAG** tab to set the tag names (Figure 11-28).

We set the XML and tag names as shown in Table 11-2.

*Table 11-2 Element values*

| Element | Tag | XML Name |
| --- | --- | --- |
| FIRST_NAME | Given | First |
| LAST_NAME | Surname | Last |
| EMAIL_ADDR | Email | Email_Address |
| LOCATION | Location | Location |

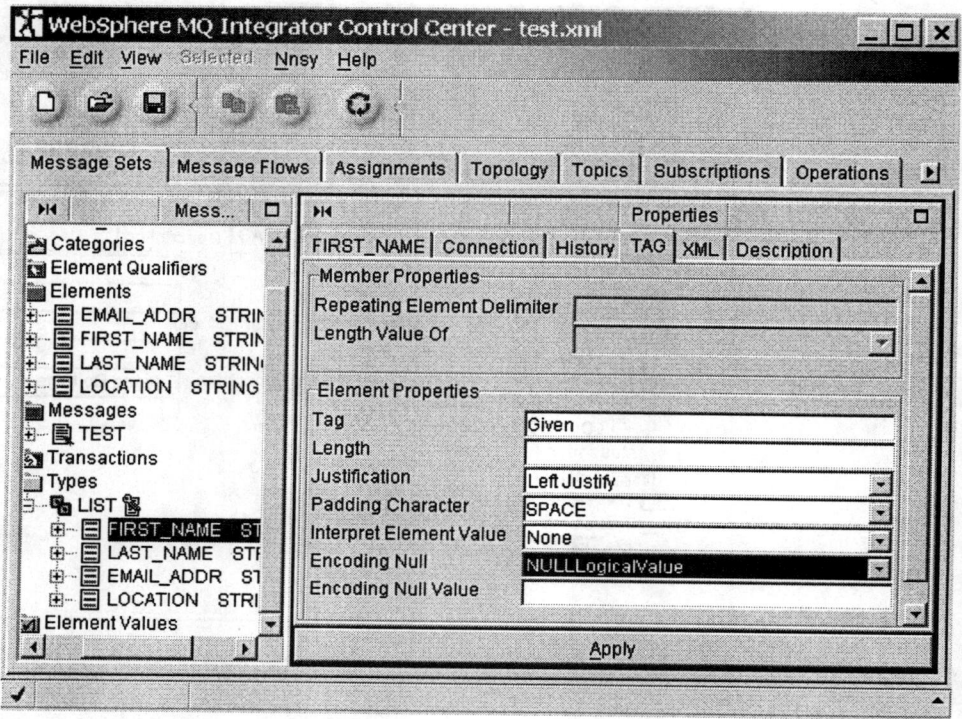

*Figure 11-29 Setting the tag values*

Click the **XML** tab to set the XML names as shown for FIRST_NAME in Figure 11-30 on page 265.

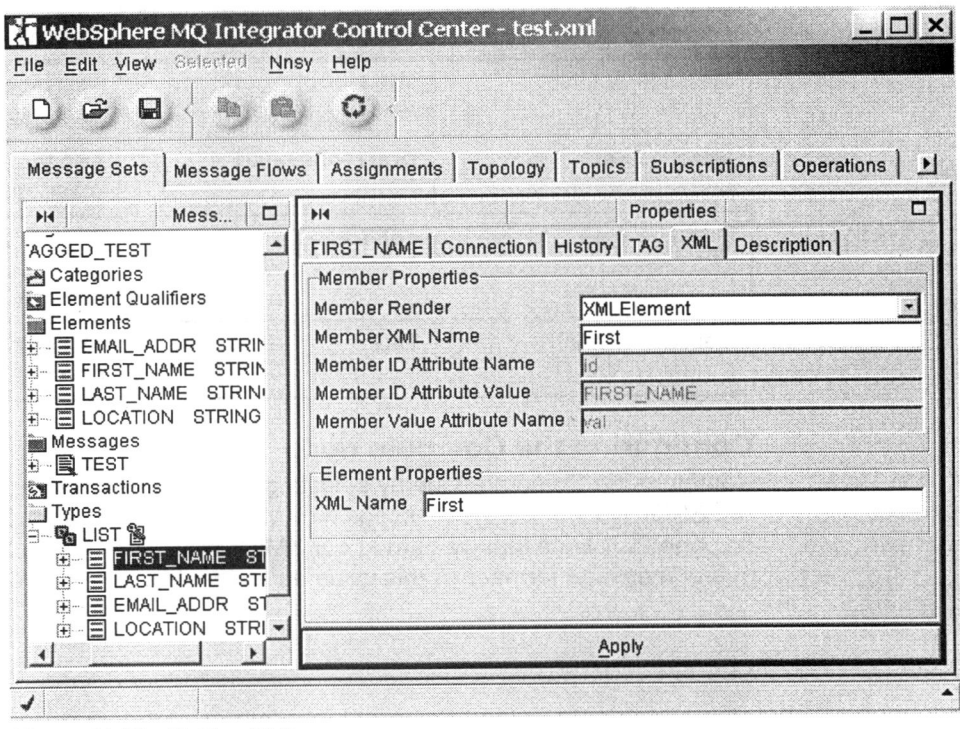

*Figure 11-30 Setting XML names*

Check in all the elements and the compound type.

## 11.4.2 Creating a message flow to convert tagged messages to XML

Using 11.2, "Testing the MRM in a message flow" on page 237 as a guide, build a message flow to test the new message set.

### Configuring the MQInput node

Select the properties Default tab and complete the fields very carefully as detailed in Table 11-3 on page 266.

> **Warning:** The MQInput node gives you a pull-down list on the Default tab for message format. This list shows the format names and *not* the required identifiers. If you do not keep the physical format identifier and name the same and rely on the default settings on the MQInput, you will have problems. You can, however, complete the field correctly by typing the identifier in it.

Chapter 11. New MRM and XML features **265**

*Table 11-3   MQInput node properties*

| Property Name | Example Value | Description |
|---|---|---|
| Message Domain | MRM | Message Domain (and the parser to use). |
| Message Set | DO5T44S070001 | Use the identifier for *your* message set here. |
| Message Type | TEST | The identifier of the message (*not* the compound type). |
| Message Format | TAG | The identifier of the physical format. |

## Configuring the Compute node

Configure the Compute node by selecting **Copy entire message** and add the two ESQL lines to set the message format and domain as shown in Figure 11-31 on page 267. Note that we named our XML physical layer "XML" this time, so the output message format has this value as an identifier.

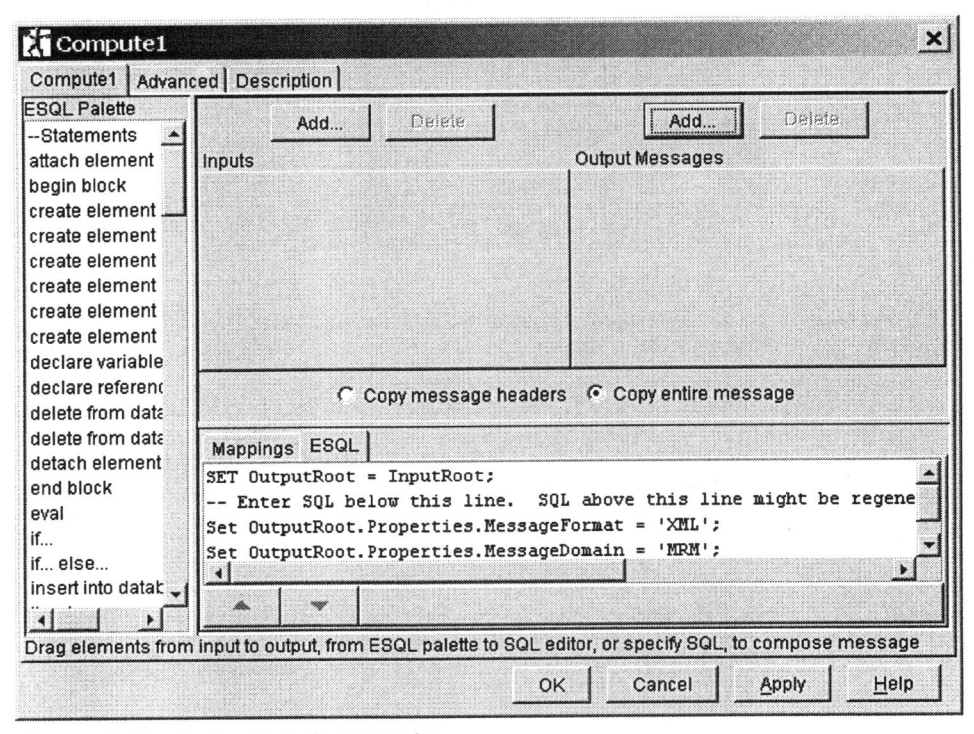

*Figure 11-31   Compute node properties*

Assign the new (or modified) message set to the broker, along with the flow to an execution group, and deploy. Make sure you do not have more than one message flow using a particular queue as an input queue.

### 11.4.3  Test the message flow

Generate a test message, shown in Figure 11-32 on page 268, to test your flow.

Try changing the order of the tags in the input message and you see that it still works correctly because we specified an unordered set. If we had specified an ordered set, then changing the input tag order would generate an error.

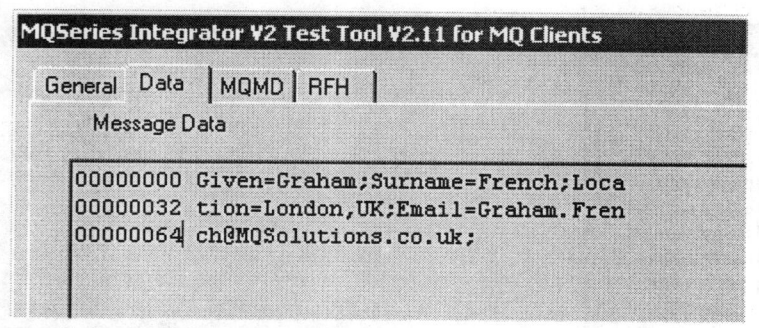

```
00000000  Given=Graham;Surname=French;Loca
00000032  tion=London,UK;Email=Graham.Fren
00000064  ch@MQSolutions.co.uk;
```

*Figure 11-32   Tagged input message*

There should now be an output message on WMQI.OUT that looks like Figure 11-33 on page 268. This message has been formatted as XML by selecting the Data Format as XML in the top right of the rfhutilc utilit.y.

```xml
<?xml version="1.0"?>
<MRM xmlns="www.mrmnames.net/D05T44S070001">
 <TEST>
  <First>Graham</First>
  <Last>French</Last>
  <Location>London,UK</Location>
  <Email_Address>Graham.French@MQSolutions.co.uk</Email_Address>
 </TEST>
</MRM>
```

*Figure 11-33   XML output message*

Notice the element order in the output reflects the input order. If you want to predetermine the output order, you can change the Compute node to select fields individually. The order of assignment in the ESQL code will determine their order in the resulting XML message.

Figure 11-34 on page 269 shows the Compute node properties that generate the XML tags in a fixed order regardless of their input order.

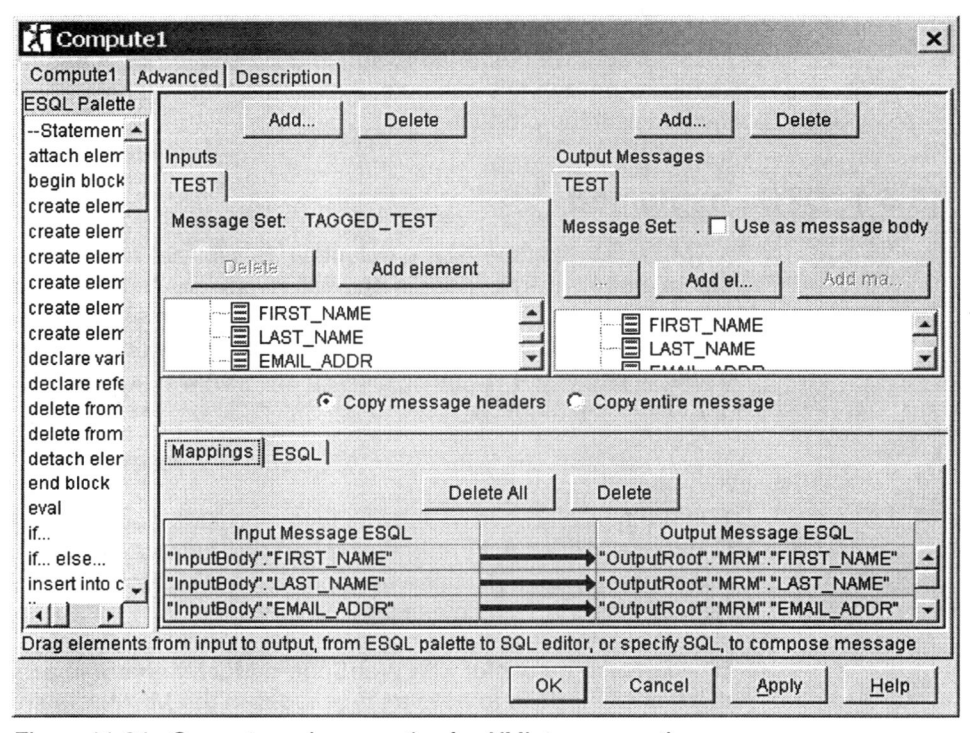

*Figure 11-34   Compute node properties for XML tag generation*

You can change the top level XML tag, <MRM> in our output, by amending the message set. On the XML tab of the message set you will see the Root Tag Name fields. Try to change it and check the results.

There is also a Suppress DOCTYPE option on this tab. This option removes the <?xml version="1.0"?> from your output.

We have now transformed a tagged message into XML format using the MRM.

## 11.5 Importing an XML DTD

In this section, we create an example DTD and import it into the MRM. Before you follow through this example, make sure that you have read the readme file provided with the product.

### 11.5.1 DTDs explained

An XML DTD (document type definition) is a formal statement that specifies which elements may appear in an XML message. A DTD lists all the elements, attributes and entities that the XML document (or message) uses, and the context in which it uses them. DTDs can be hugely complex, but in our example we take a simple one. Extensive information on DTDs is available on the Internet. A good starting point is:

http://www.xml.com/pub/a/98/10/guide2.html#DOCTYPEDEF

DTDs are typically used to validate incoming XML documents, but WebSphere MQ Integrator does not currently support this function. However, you can create MRM message set definitions by importing a DTD, which WebSphere MQ Integrator can then use to validate the message.

DTDs can also be useful with WebSphere MQ Integrator in providing a faster, non-graphic interface to building messages in the MRM. It is sometimes faster to create a DTD in a text editor and import it to build your message set, rather than use the Control Center.

An example DTD is shown in Example 11-2 to demonstrate the import facility.

*Example 11-2   Example DTD*

```
<!ELEMENT people (person)+>
<!ELEMENT person (name, email*)>
<!ATTLIST person location CDATA #REQUIRED>
<!ATTLIST person age CDATA #IMPLIED>
<!ELEMENT name (first,last)>
<!ELEMENT first (#PCDATA)>
<!ELEMENT last (#PCDATA)>
<!ELEMENT email (#PCDATA)>
```

This DTD defines the *people* element as consisting of one or more *person*s. Each person has a name and zero or more e-mail addresses. *Location* is an attribute of person and is required. *Age* is an attribute of person and is optional. Each name consists of first and last (in that order). The *first, last* and *email* elements are PCDATA (Parsed Character Data).

Attributes are associated with elements and appear in the same XML tag as the element. They can be used for values that occur only once per element. They are an alternative to using child elements, and XML designers have to choose which method to use. Example 11-3 shows a valid XML message that conforms to this DTD.

*Example 11-3*

```
<?xml version="1.0"?>
<people>
 <person location="London" age="35">
  <name>
   <first>Fred</first>
   <last>Bloggs</last>
  </name>
  <email>fred@nowhere.com</email>
 </person>
</people>
```

## 11.5.2 Importing the DTD

Before we can start, we need a message set to import the DTD into and it will need an XML physical layer. The steps are described in 11.3.1, "Building the message set" on page 239. In our example in Figure 11-35 on page 272, we created a message set named CONTACTS and added a physical layer named XML. Having completed this:

1. Right-click the message set name and select **Import to Message Set -> DTD** as shown in Figure 11-35 on page 272.

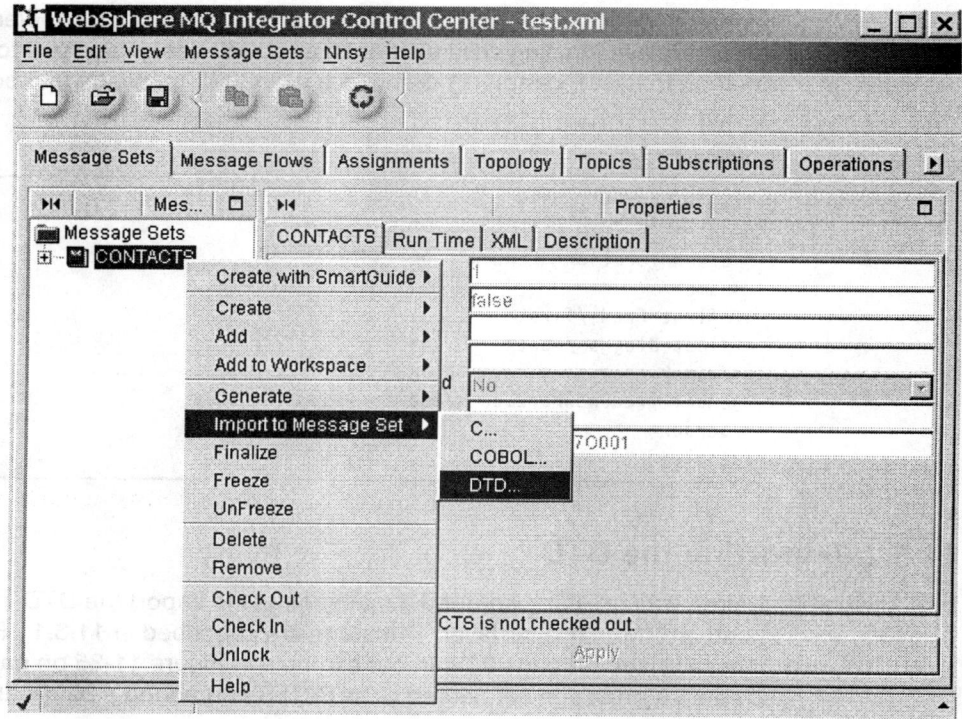

*Figure 11-35   Importing a DTD*

2. Enter the fully qualified filename of the DTD file that you want to import.

> **Tip:** If you choose to click the **Browse** button to locate the file, you must click the **>>** arrows when you have selected the file to add it to the right half of the browse pane before clicking **OK**.

You should now see the name of your DTD in the Source File pane as shown in Figure 11-36 on page 273.

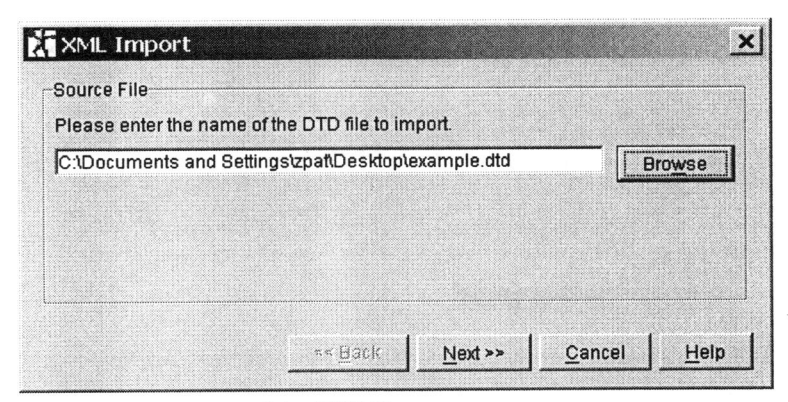

*Figure 11-36   Name of the DTD file*

3. Click **Next >>** to make the importer parse the DTD.

   Any basic syntactical errors in the DTD cause an error message window to display and the import operation to terminate. Correct any errors and try again.

   Assuming the file is parsed correctly, the importer displays a list of the elements contained in the DTD. All these elements are imported as elements into the message set. However, you can select any of the listed elements to be imported as messages. In our example, we will use the *people* element.

   This element is chosen because it is the top-level element in the XML tree. This corresponds to the MRM message type. Selecting the top-level element to add as a message is an essential step when importing a DTD.

4. Select the **people** element as shown in Figure 11-37 on page 274

5. Click **>>** to add people as a MRM message.

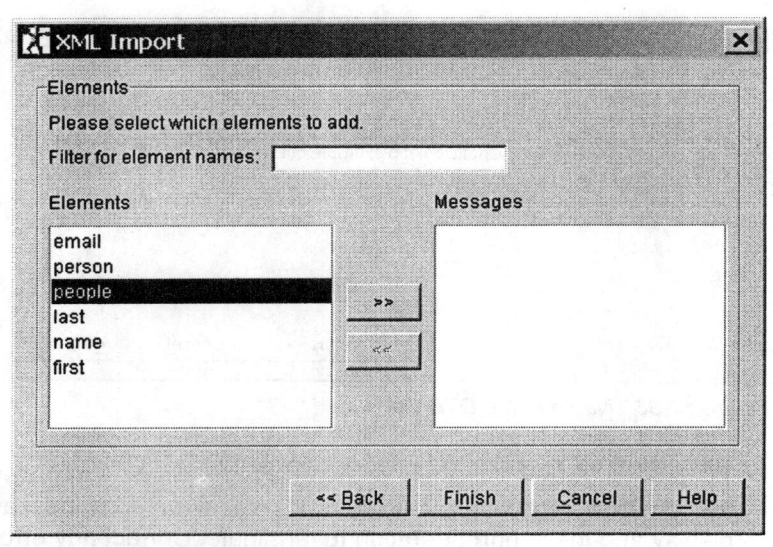

*Figure 11-37   List of elements*

6. When *people* is displayed in the right pane as in Figure 11-38 on page 274, click the **Finish** button.

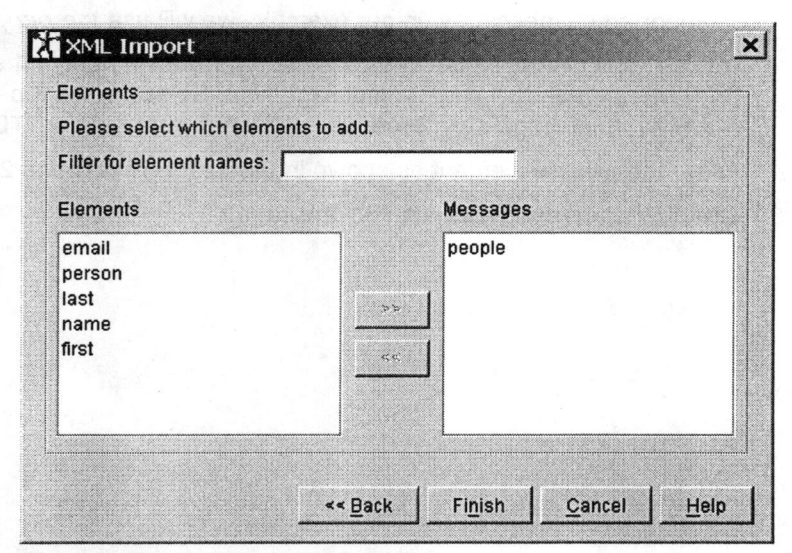

*Figure 11-38   Selecting people as message*

An XML Model Building Progress window, shown in Figure 11-39 on page 275, should now appear, which shows the stages in importing the DTD. In our simple example the process is relatively quick. Larger DTDs may take some time.

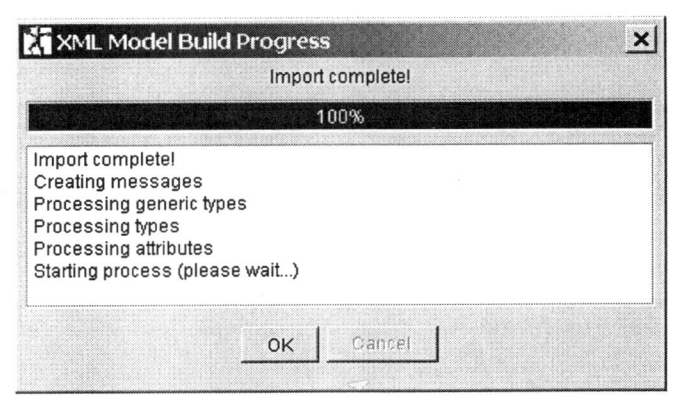

*Figure 11-39   Completed import*

7. Click **OK** to close the progress window.

   Your message set should now look similar to Figure 11-40.

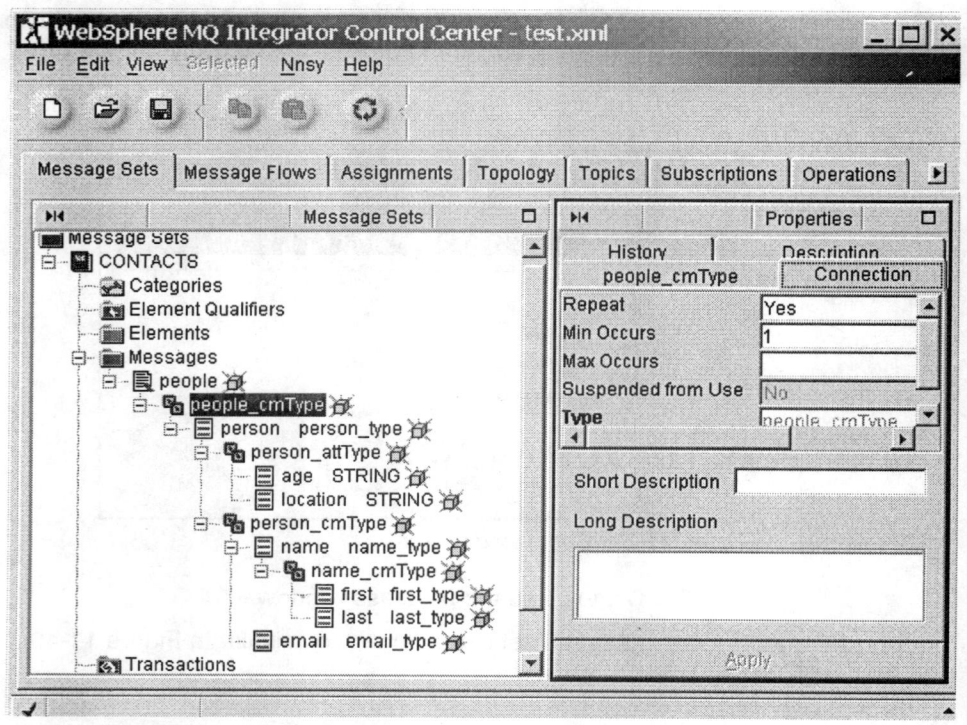

*Figure 11-40   DTD imported message set definition*

8. Check in the new message. The Configuration Manager checks in the other elements and types as a result.

    This step is important because it checks that all the element names and identifiers are acceptable to the MRM. If any duplicates have been created, you have to manually amend these until you are able to check in the message. This problem will not happen with our small example DTD, but may happen when you start to build bigger and more complex message sets.

### Amending the XML names the DTD importer created

**Attention:** Some of the XML names generated from a DTD import in early releases of WebSphere MQ Integrator V2.1 may need amending to match your requirements. If you have installed the latest CSD, this step should not be required.

1. Check out the new message *people*. On the XML tab change the XML Name to match its name and click **Apply**.

2. Add all the new elements to the workspace by right-clicking **Elements** and selecting **Add to Workspace --> Element..**
3. Select all elements by holding down the Shift key and clicking the first and last element in the list. When all elements are highlighted click **Finish**.
4. Check the XML Name given to each element on the on the XML tab. In our example the DTD importer created incorrect XML tag names for the two atrtibutes' *age* and *location*. Amend them and click **Apply** and check the elements back in.

In our example, we changed just the *age* and *location* elements and the *people* type. This is shown in Figure 11-41.

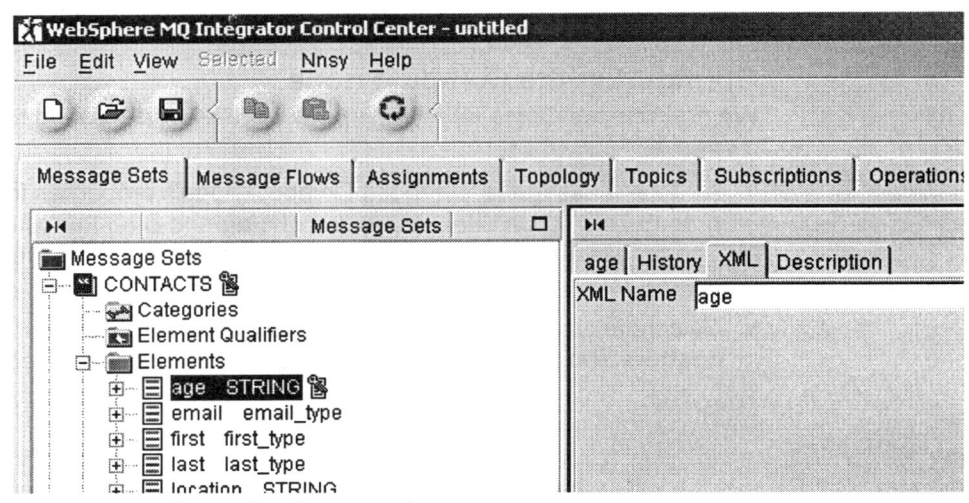

*Figure 11-41 Renaming the age xml name*

## 11.5.3 Creating a message flow to test the DTD import

Using 11.2, "Testing the MRM in a message flow" on page 237 as a guide, build a message flow to test the new DTD imported message set.

In this example we first configure a flow to test the DTD import and then further amend it to change the location attribute from Texas to Dallas.

### Configuring the MQInput node

Select the properties Default tab and complete the fields very carefully as detailed in Table 11-4 on page 278.

Table 11-4   MQInput node properties

| Property Name | Example Value | Description |
| --- | --- | --- |
| Message Domain | **MRM** | Message Domain (and the parser to use). |
| Message Set | **DO5T44S074001** | Use the identifier for *your* message set here. |
| Message Type | **people** | The identifier of the message (*not* the compound type). |
| Message Format | **XML** | The identifier of the physical format. |

## Configuring the Compute node

We now use the Compute node to pass the elements through to the output message.

1. Add the message layout to the Compute node's properties for input and output. This action enables the use of drag-and-drop to manipulate elements. The results are shown in Figure 11-42 on page 279 .The message set name is *contacts* and the message name is *people*.

2. Select the check boxes **Use as message body** and **Copy message headers**.The properties page now looks like Figure 11-42 on page 279.

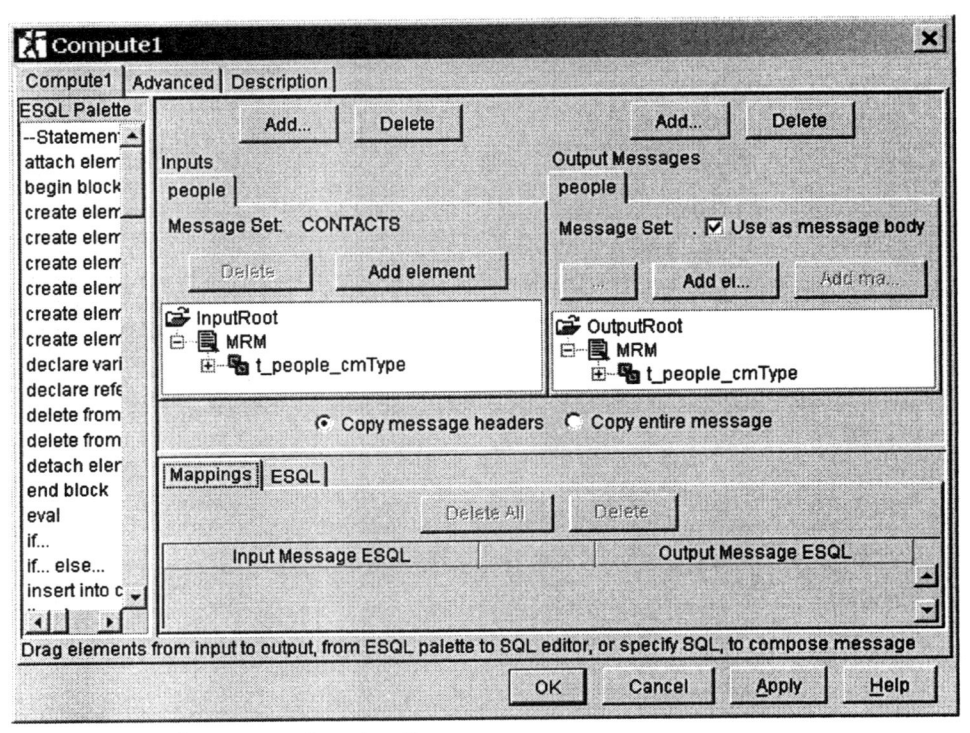

Figure 11-42   Compute node properties

3. Expand the message tree on the input and output side as shown in Figure 11-43 on page 280.

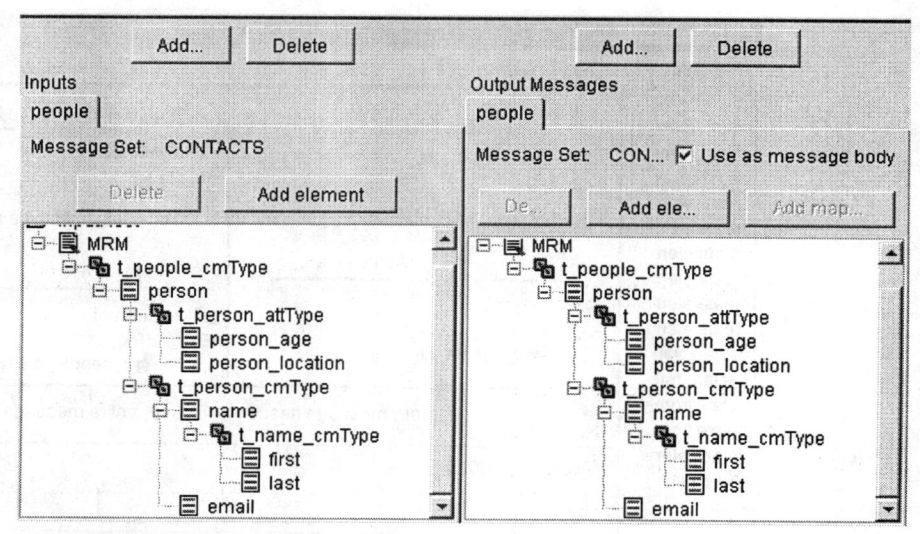

*Figure 11-43 The message tree*

4. Drag and drop the following elements *in this sequence* from the input side to the output side (to the same element/attribute name):

   – person_age

   – person_location

   – first

   – last

   – email

   This sequence matches the order that the elements were defined in the DTD and therefore the order of the elements in the message set. When constructing the output message, the MRM expects to process the elements in the same order.

   The Compute node properties should now look as shown in Figure 11-44 on page 281.

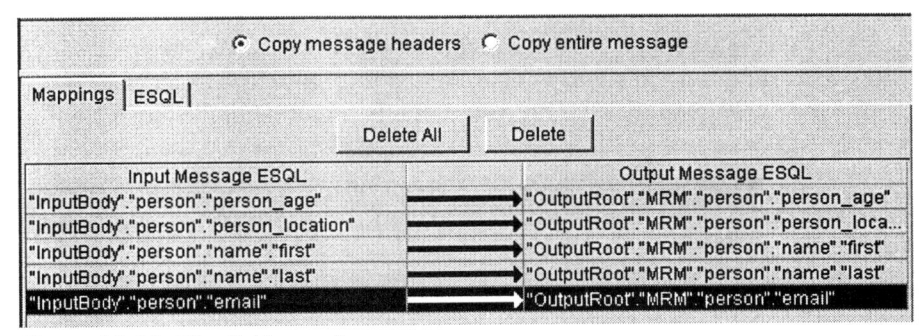

*Figure 11-44  The field mappings*

The drag-and-drop operation generates ESQL code (which includes copying the message header) shown in Example 11-4.

*Example 11-4  Generated ESQL code*

```
DECLARE I INTEGER;
SET I = 1;
WHILE I < CARDINALITY(InputRoot.*[]) DO
  SET OutputRoot.*[I] = InputRoot.*[I];
  SET I=I+1;
END WHILE;
SET "OutputRoot"."MRM"."person"."person_age" =
"InputBody"."person"."person_age";
SET "OutputRoot"."MRM"."person"."person_location" =
"InputBody"."person"."person_location";
SET "OutputRoot"."MRM"."person"."name"."first" =
"InputBody"."person"."name"."first";
SET "OutputRoot"."MRM"."person"."name"."last" =
"InputBody"."person"."name"."last";
SET "OutputRoot"."MRM"."person"."email" = "InputBody"."person"."email";
SET OutputRoot.Properties.MessageSet = 'D05T44S074001';
SET OutputRoot.Properties.MessageType = 'm_people';
-- Enter SQL below this line.
```

5. Add these additional lines manually at the bottom of the ESQL (these commands specify the message domain and format for the output message):

    `Set OutputRoot.Properties.MessageFormat = 'XML';`

    `Set OutputRoot.Properties.MessageDomain = 'MRM';`

6. Check in and deploy the message set and message flow.

    The ESQL code shown in this example will not modify the message contents, but it is advisable to test everything developed so far.

### 11.5.4 Testing the message flow

Create a test XML message with no additonal white space or carriage returns and read this into rfhutilc. Additonal characters are invalid and will cause problems with the message parser. Figure 11-45 shows our input message.

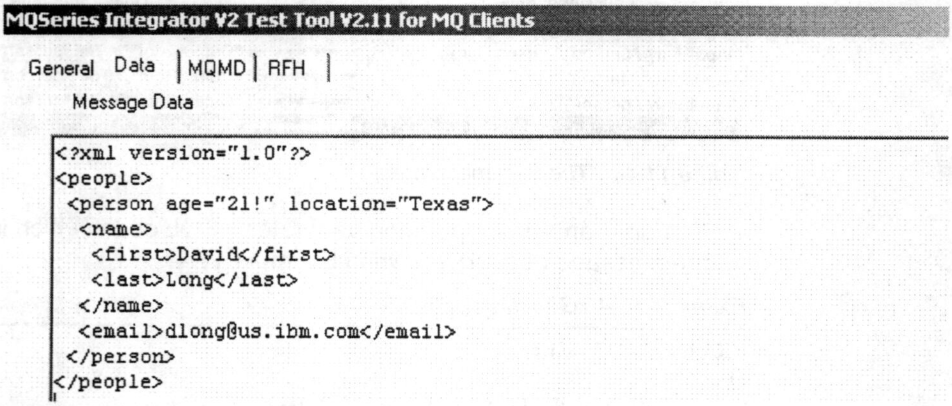

```
MQSeries Integrator V2 Test Tool V2.11 for MQ Clients
General  Data  | MQMD | RFH |
    Message Data

<?xml version="1.0"?>
<people>
 <person age="21!" location="Texas">
  <name>
   <first>David</first>
   <last>Long</last>
  </name>
  <email>dlong@us.ibm.com</email>
 </person>
</people>
```

*Figure 11-45   XML dtd test input message*

The output should look like Figure 11-46.

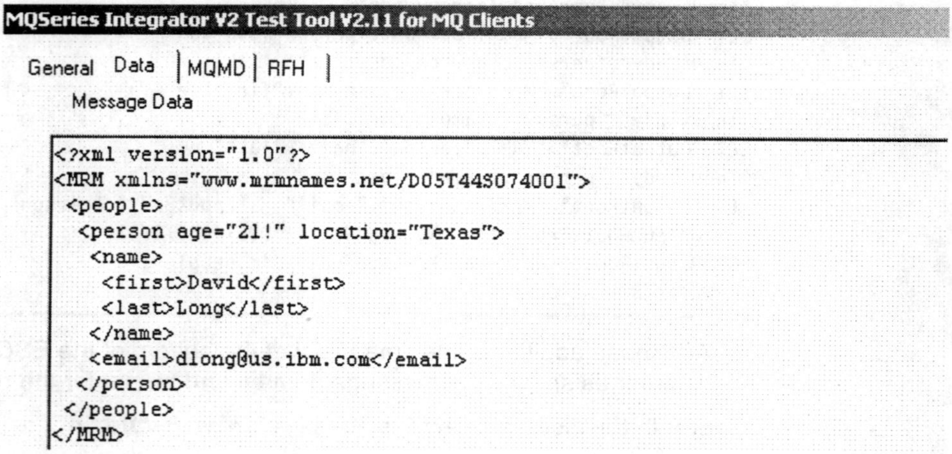

```
MQSeries Integrator V2 Test Tool V2.11 for MQ Clients
General  Data  | MQMD | RFH |
    Message Data

<?xml version="1.0"?>
<MRM xmlns="www.mrmnames.net/D05T44S074001">
 <people>
  <person age="21!" location="Texas">
   <name>
    <first>David</first>
    <last>Long</last>
   </name>
   <email>dlong@us.ibm.com</email>
  </person>
 </people>
</MRM>
```

*Figure 11-46   XML dtd output message*

Notice the MRM tags in the output message that have been added by WebSphere MQ Integrator. In 11.6, "Additional XML MRM features" on page 284 we discuss how to remove or manipulate these tags.

## 11.5.5 Modifying the location attribute in a Compute node

Check out the message flow and open up the Compute node properties. Add these three lines of ESQL code at the bottom of the window opened by the ESQL tab.

```
If "InputBody"."person"."person_location" = 'Texas' then
   Set "OutputRoot"."MRM"."person"."person_location" = 'Dallas';
end if;
```

You can drag the statements from the left of the pane and drag the field names from above into the ESQL window to build up your statements without keying them in.

Check in the message flow and test it again with the example message.

The output message shown in Figure 11-47 now has the location set to Dallas. Test it again with a different location set in the input message to make sure the conditional logic is working correctly.

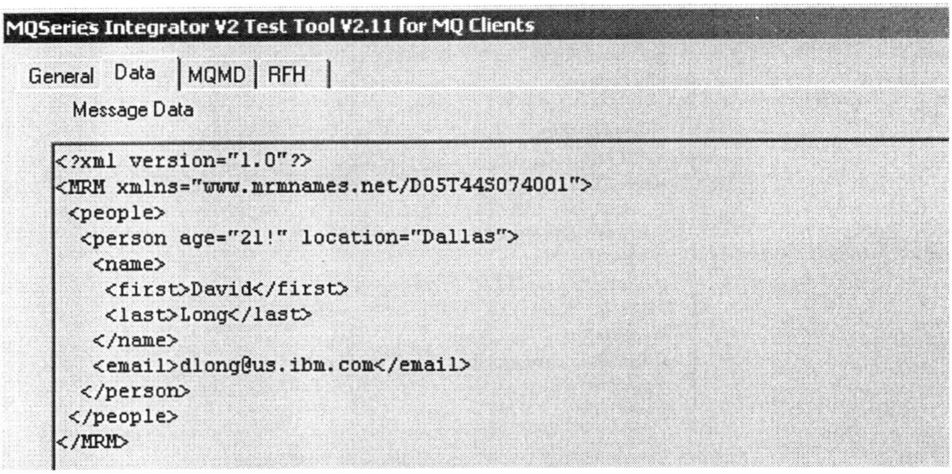

```
<?xml version="1.0"?>
<MRM xmlns="www.mrmnames.net/D05T44S074001">
 <people>
  <person age="21!" location="Dallas">
   <name>
    <first>David</first>
    <last>Long</last>
   </name>
   <email>dlong@us.ibm.com</email>
  </person>
 </people>
</MRM>
```

*Figure 11-47   Amend location attribute*

We have now created a message set from a DTD and used it to process and manipulate an XML message, with the MRM parsing the input and generating the output message.

## 11.6 Additional XML MRM features

Having demonstrated some of the new features, we now take a look at some additional features. These show us how to change the MRM definition to create the XML message we want. These examples build on the flows we have created earlier.

### 11.6.1 Multiple XML entities

Our DTD in 11.5, "Importing an XML DTD" on page 270 specified that there could be multiple person elements in *people*. So our input message might look as shown in Figure 11-48.

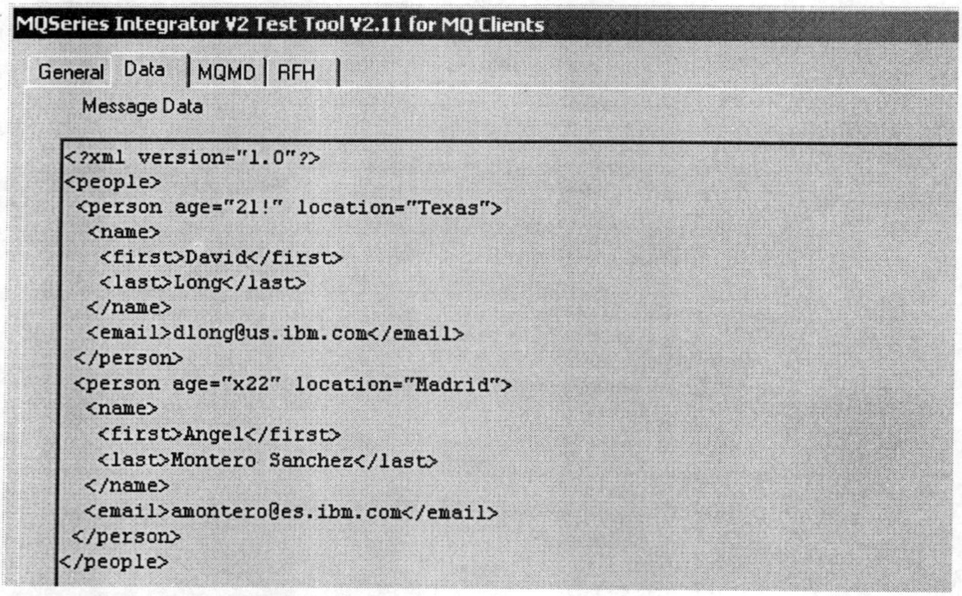

```
<?xml version="1.0"?>
<people>
 <person age="21!" location="Texas">
  <name>
   <first>David</first>
   <last>Long</last>
  </name>
  <email>dlong@us.ibm.com</email>
 </person>
 <person age="x22" location="Madrid">
  <name>
   <first>Angel</first>
   <last>Montero Sanchez</last>
  </name>
  <email>amontero@es.ibm.com</email>
 </person>
</people>
```

*Figure 11-48  Multi person people xml message*

However, our Compute node is not coded to cope with this. By default, when we reference an element in a message, we reference the first instance of that element. By appending the element name with [n], we can directly address the nth instance of that element. Our Compute node would therefore copy the first instance over and no more.

We can therefore change the Compute node ESQL to cater for multiple occurences as shown in Example 11-5. The Compute node will iterate through multiple occurences of the *person* element and the output message therefore will also contain multiple *person* elements. You can see where the variable J has been used as an array subscript.

The first loop is generated by WebSphere MQ Integrator when **Copy the message header** is clicked (but this loop does not copy the body). Then clicking the **Use as message body** option generates the assignments for the message set ID and message type. Then we set the output message format and domain and then iterate through the *person* elements, performing our processing on each one in turn.

This iteration is within a single message. The flow would be invoked again for multiple MQSeries messages.

*Example 11-5   Processing multiple person elements*

```
DECLARE I INTEGER;
SET I = 1;
WHILE I < CARDINALITY(InputRoot.*[]) DO
    SET OutputRoot.*[I] = InputRoot.*[I];
    SET I=I+1;
END WHILE;
SET OutputRoot.Properties.MessageSet = 'D05T44S074001';
SET OutputRoot.Properties.MessageType = 'm_people';
-- Enter SQL below this line.  SQL above this line might be regenerated,
causing any modifications to be lost.
Set OutputRoot.Properties.MessageFormat = 'XML';
Set OutputRoot.Properties.MessageDomain = 'MRM';
DECLARE J INTEGER;
DECLARE K INTEGER;
SET J =1;
SET K = CARDINALITY("InputBody".*[]);
WHILE J <= K DO
  SET "OutputRoot"."MRM"."person"[J]."person_age" =
"InputBody"."person"[J]."person_age";
  SET "OutputRoot"."MRM"."person"[J]."person_location" =
"InputBody"."person"[J]."person_location";
  SET "OutputRoot"."MRM"."person"[J]."name"."first" =
"InputBody"."person"[J]."name"."first";
  SET "OutputRoot"."MRM"."person"[J]."name"."last" =
"InputBody"."person"[J]."name"."last";
  SET "OutputRoot"."MRM"."person"[J]."email" = "InputBody"."person"[J]."email";
  If "InputBody"."person"[J]."person_location" = 'Texas' then
     Set "OutputRoot"."MRM"."person"[J]."person_location" = 'Dallas';
  end if;
  SET J = J + 1;
```

```
END WHILE;
```

You can generate separate output messages for each loop of an input person element, using the new PROPAGATE statement. This causes the message tree to be immediately sent on the out terminal (without the node terminating). The message tree is then cleared (and so needs to be fully set up in each loop). Two MQSeries messages will be produced from our example message in Figure 11-48 on page 284.

When using propagate you would normally end the node ESQL with RETURN FALSE; to suppress the automatic send of the message tree at the end of the node. It's actually good practice to explicitly code RETURN TRUE; at the end of the ESQL code in all the Compute nodes when you do not explicitly code PROPAGATE.

*Example 11-6   Generating multiple messages*

```
-- Enter SQL below this line.  SQL above this line might be regenerated,
causing any modifications to be lost.DECLARE I INTEGER;
DECLARE J INTEGER;
DECLARE K INTEGER;
SET K = CARDINALITY(InputRoot.*[]);
SET J=1;
WHILE J <= K DO
  SET I = 1;
  WHILE I < K DO
    SET OutputRoot.*[I] = InputRoot.*[I];
    SET I=I+1;
  END WHILE;
  SET OutputRoot.Properties.MessageSet = 'DO5T44S074001';
  SET OutputRoot.Properties.MessageType = 'm_people';
  SET OutputRoot.Properties.MessageDomain = 'MRM';
  SET OutputRoot.Properties.MessageFormat = 'XML';
  SET "OutputRoot"."MRM"."person"."person_age" =
"InputBody"."person"[J]."person_age";
  SET "OutputRoot"."MRM"."person"."person_location" =
"InputBody"."person"[J]."person_location";
  SET "OutputRoot"."MRM"."person"."name"."first" =
"InputBody"."person"[J]."name"."first";
  SET "OutputRoot"."MRM"."person"."name"."last" =
"InputBody"."person"[J]."name"."last";
  SET "OutputRoot"."MRM"."person"."email" = "InputBody"."person"[J]."email";
  PROPAGATE;
  SET J = J + 1;
END WHILE;
RETURN FALSE;
```

## 11.6.2 Mixing MRM and generic XML

The new MRM features and the DTD import relate to MRM-defined XML. However, you can still use generic XML. You might want the input message to be MRM-defined but the output message to be generic XML. In this case, you do not need to specify an output message set or format, just the message domain as XML.

In this case, we build the XML structure by the ESQL statements we execute. We take the person records and build customer records. To set this up, delete the Compute node in your flow and drag a new one in. Select the **Copy message headers** button only and start constructing your ESQL.

*Example 11-7 ESQL code for generic XML output*

```
DECLARE I INTEGER;
SET I = 1;
WHILE I < CARDINALITY(InputRoot.*[]) DO
   SET OutputRoot.*[I] = InputRoot.*[I];
   SET I=I+1;
END WHILE;
-- Enter SQL below this line.  SQL above this line might be regenerated,
causing any modifications to be lost.
Set OutputRoot.Properties.MessageDomain = 'XML';
SET OutputRoot.XML.(XML.XmlDecl)='';
SET OutputRoot.XML.(XML.XmlDecl).(XML.Version)='1.0';

DECLARE J INTEGER;
DECLARE K INTEGER;
SET K = CARDINALITY("InputBody".*[]);
SET J =1;
WHILE J <= K DO
  SET OutputRoot.XML.People.Customer[J].(XML.attr)age =
InputBody.person[J].person_age;
  SET OutputRoot.XML.People.Customer[J].(XML.attr)location =
InputBody.person[J].person_location;
  SET OutputRoot.XML.People.Customer[J].name.first =
InputBody.person[J].name.first;
  SET OutputRoot.XML.People.Customer[J].name.last =
InputBody.person[J].name.last;
  SET OutputRoot.XML.People.Customer[J].email = InputBody.person[J].email;
  SET J = J + 1;
END WHILE;
```

The results are shown in Figure 11-49 on page 288.

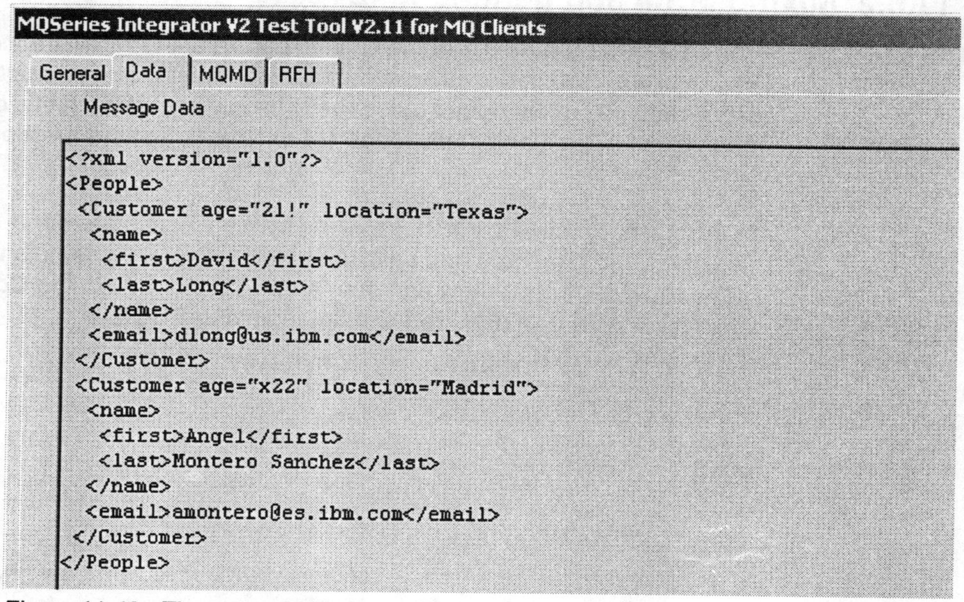

```
MQSeries Integrator V2 Test Tool V2.11 for MQ Clients
General  Data  MQMD  RFH
   Message Data

<?xml version="1.0"?>
<People>
 <Customer age="21!" location="Texas">
  <name>
   <first>David</first>
   <last>Long</last>
  </name>
  <email>dlong@us.ibm.com</email>
 </Customer>
 <Customer age="x22" location="Madrid">
  <name>
   <first>Angel</first>
   <last>Montero Sanchez</last>
  </name>
  <email>amontero@es.ibm.com</email>
 </Customer>
</People>
```

*Figure 11-49   The output XML data*

It's worth contrasting the way the XML attributes are generated in MRM XML and generic XML.

With MRM-defined XML, an attribute is set with ESQL code like this:

```
SET "OutputRoot"."MRM"."person"[J]."person_age" =
"InputBody"."person"[J]."person_age";
```

The MRM knows that age is an attribute of person and will process it accordingly. However, when you create an attribute in generic XML, you need to specify it as an attribute; otherwise, the broker will just create another element for you.

```
SET OutputRoot.XML.People.Customer[J].(XML.attr)age =
InputBody.person[J].person_age;
```

If you use XML headers and declarations, you must also explicitly generate them with this code:

```
SET OutputRoot.XML.(XML.XmlDecl)='';
SET OutputRoot.XML.(XML.XmlDecl).(XML.Version)='1.0';
```

Even with generic XML, the order of creating parts of the XML message is important to avoid invalid XML being generated.

It's also important to create any new message headers such as the MQMD or MQRFH2 before creating body elements in the ESQL; otherwise, the message parser may simply treat them as additional body elements.

For more information on generic XML and ESQL, refer to the *WebSphere MQ Integrator ESQL Reference,* SC34-5923.

### 11.6.3 Using ESQL reference variables

One of the new ESQL features is *reference variables.* These variables can be used to make it simpler to navigate complex message trees. The use of these variables is not confined to working with the MRM or XML. We show how they can simplify the ESQL code by amending our example that outputs MRM XML messages.

Reference variables can be used as a short notation for fully qualified field names and they can also act as cursors or pointers into an array of element instances. This way you avoid a need to use array index variables and make your ESQL code easier to read and understand.

> **Attention:** The following note is given in the readme file that comes with WebSphere MQ Integrator 2.1.
>
> > Changes were made to the syntax of the CREATE, MOVE and SET statements primarily to avoid ambiguity of meaning. These changes were not fully reflected in *WebSphere MQ Integrator ESQL Reference,* SC34-5923.
>
> The readme file goes on to document the correct syntax.

Example 11-8 on page 290 is the complete ESQL code segment from our Compute node after being amended to use reference variables. Some points to note:

- ▶ Elements need to exist before they can be referred to, so use the CREATE or SET statement to make sure they exist (and do so in sequence if required).
- ▶ MOVE is used to increment the reference to the next element, but you cannot use MOVE unless the element exists, so CREATE any new one first.
- ▶ Avoid creating a new output element after processing the last input element by testing the LASTMOVE operation result.
- ▶ Use the user trace facility or the debugger to examine the MRM tree before and after the Compute node to make sure the results are as expected.

Use a new Compute node, add the DTD XML message set as output, click **Use as message body** and **Copy message header** and code below the generated ESQL.

*Example 11-8   Using reference variables*

```
DECLARE I INTEGER;
SET I = 1;
WHILE I < CARDINALITY(InputRoot.*[]) DO
    SET OutputRoot.*[I] = InputRoot.*[I];
    SET I=I+1;
END WHILE;
SET OutputRoot.Properties.MessageSet = 'D05T44S074001';
SET OutputRoot.Properties.MessageType = 'm_people';
-- Enter SQL below this line.  SQL above this line might be regenerated,
causing any modifications to be lost.
Set OutputRoot.Properties.MessageFormat = 'XML';
Set OutputRoot.Properties.MessageDomain = 'MRM';

DECLARE ptrin  REFERENCE to "InputBody"."person"[1];
CREATE FIELD "OutputRoot"."MRM"."person"[1] FROM ptrin;
DECLARE ptrout REFERENCE to "OutputRoot"."MRM"."person"[1];

WHILE LASTMOVE(ptrin) DO    /* while ptrin is within tree */
    SET ptrout."person_age"      = ptrin."person_age";
    SET ptrout."person_location" = 'Raleigh';
    SET ptrout."name"."first"    = ptrin."name"."first";
    SET ptrout."name"."last"     = ptrin."name"."last";
    SET ptrout."email"           = ptrin."email";
    MOVE ptrin  NEXTSIBLING;   /* move ptrin to next input person */
    IF LASTMOVE(ptrin) THEN   /* if move was still inside tree */
        CREATE NEXTSIBLING OF ptrout FROM ptrin; /* create next output person */
        MOVE ptrout NEXTSIBLING;  /* refer to next output person */
    END IF;
END WHILE;
```

This code is just meant as an example. If you really wanted to amend only one field you should copy the input message at a higher level and then amend it.

```
SET ptrout = ptrin;
SET ptrout."person_location" = 'Raleigh';
```

Copying the entire structure in one go also has the advantage of ensuring that the sequence of fields is the same in the output message as it is in the input message. As we have seen, it is essential to create fields in the correct sequence when using a compound type defined as an ordered set (or sequence).

However, if you were to use the ESQL statement SET "OutputRoot" = "InputRoot"; and then did *not* subsequently modify any of the message elements, the parser directly copies the input bit stream to the output bit stream without regenerating it, which means that any attributes in the output wire format layer do not take effect.

When you create or modify MQ headers, such as the MQMD, a message set definition for this (and other headers) is supplied with WebSphere MQ Integrator and can be added to your workspace, then used with the drag-and-drop feature of the Compute node.

It is possible for the Compute node to report an ESQL syntax error, when the statement is valid. For example, the following statement is flagged, but it is correct:

```
SET OutputRoot.MQRFH2.mcd.Set = OutputRoot.Properties.MessageSet;
```

# 12

# Developing and deploying custom nodes in Java

In this chapter we describe the process and requirements for developing and implementing custom-built Java plug-in nodes. We show some example programs for both standard plug-in nodes and input nodes based on the new Java support in WebSphere MQ Integrator.

The examples in this chapter were developed and compiled on Windows 2000 and tested on Windows 2000 and z/OS. If you remove all native references from your Java code, you should be able to deploy the same custom code on any platform that supports WebSphere MQ Integrator brokers and the same JDK level. It is assumed most custom nodes would be developed and unit tested in a Windows environment before deployment to z/OS for further testing and production operation.

## 12.1 What can you do with a Java plug-in?

With WebSphere MQ Integrator, there is new support for building custom plug-in nodes and parsers in Java or C. There is also new support for input nodes written in Java. This opens up the possibilities of dramatically expanding your message integration capability. By writing your own custom plug-in and input nodes, you can expand on existing functions or develop new nodes that are designed for very specific needs.

You may want to develop your own plug-in nodes so that a specific data element in an XML document would determine where a message should be routed. It is also possible that you would want to change this same data element to another value based on some rules.

With custom input nodes, it is possible to have a program read a file from a directory and bring it into the message flow. This eliminates the need for an MQSeries queue for input allowing your architecture to have more flexibility. Maybe you want the input node to listen to a specific port for a data stream. This is also possible. In the event that you would like to create a custom output node, simply utilize a custom-built Java plug-in node as the final step in the message flow and write the data to your preferred location, such as a database or a directory.

By using the information in this chapter, the *WebSphere MQ Integrator Programming Guide*, the javadoc that can be found in the JavaAPI directory of your WebSphere MQ Integrator installation (refer to <install_dir>\docs\JavaAPI\index.html) and some Java programming knowledge, you should be able to write your own custom plug-in and input nodes.

### 12.1.1 Plug-in nodes

In MQSeries Integrator 2.0.2 it was possible to build custom plug-in nodes using C, but now with WebSphere MQ Integrator 2.1 it is also possible to develop them in Java. These programs are compiled and packaged into a Java Archive File (JAR). These JAR files are loaded and cached by the broker on startup.

A Java plug-in node program can be written to have one input but an arbitrary amount of outputs. They do not have to have a node factory such as a custom node written in C.

The support for building custom input nodes is new for this release for both C and Java. We are going to describe the Java support here. Refer to the *WebSphere MQ Integrator Programming Guide* for more information about both possibilities.

The ability to write your own nodes in Java is achieved by extending interfaces and packages that are now shipped with the product. Specifically, jplugin.jar contains the important classes and can be found in the classes directory. If you would like to see the specific classes, unzip the JAR file in the directory from the <install_dir>\classes directory. You should find several new subdirectories creating the path /com/ibm/broker/plugin/. In the plug-in directory, you see several classes that should match the classes found in the Java API documentation found in:

<install_dir>\docs\JavaAPI      Windows NT/2000

<install_dir>/docs/JavaAPI      UNIX platforms including z/OS

There are two important interfaces that should be reviewed before attempting to write a new plug-in node. In the javadoc, you will see a listing for MbNodeInterface and MbInputNodeInterface. These interfaces are for standard Java plug-in nodes and Java input nodes respectively. The implementation and skeleton code is described in the JavaAPI javadoc for reference.

### 12.1.2 MbInputNodeInterface

The input node interface is designed to shield the programmer from the internal input operations of WebSphere MQ Integrator. Though most of the communication and specification has been encapsulated, you still need to follow several procedures, such as setting your new node to extend MbInputNode, creating the output terminal definitions (no need for input terminal), and assembling the new message using MbMessageAssembly. If an error does occur and you want WebSphere MQ Integrator to be aware of it for error handling, throw a message to MbException. All other processing logic can be built to suit your needs. Some examples of use may be to monitor a directory, FTP, HTTP, or telnet session. There are more examples in "Implementing an input node" on page 297.

### 12.1.3 MbNodeInterface

The node interface is the standard interface definition for all plug-in nodes other than input nodes. As with the MbInputNodeInterface, the developer has been shielded but must adhere to a general framework. The important aspects to note are that your plug-in node must extend MbNode. Unlike MbInputNode, you must define your input terminal at the same time you define your output terminals. MbMessageAssembly and MbException are used just as in the MbInputNodeInterface. All other processing logic can be built to suit your needs. You could use a plug-in node to process specific data formats such as XML, CSV or EDI using a robust rule set. Based on the content of the message you could route the message to one of multiple output terminals or even translate it into entirely new content garnished from multiple data sources. There are more examples in "Implementing a plug-in node" on page 313.

## 12.2 Getting started

This section outlines several steps to help you get your environment configured to quickly begin to develop and utilize custom plug-in and input nodes.

### 12.2.1 System requirements

Developing custom nodes can be accomplished on the same development workstation that manages a Control Center. Once a WebSphere MQ Integrator installation has taken place, verify the installation through the steps outlined in the "Getting Started" section of the respective installation guide for your operating system.

The only other software requirement is to have a Java Development Kit (JDK) installed and the path pointing to the correct bin directory. You can verify your JDK installation by opening a command prompt and typing `Java -version`. It is recommended that you use the most current IBM JDK (at the time of writing it is JDK 1.3.0).

You may choose to develop your programs with an IDE or GUI development environment such as VisualAge for Java, although a standard text editor will be sufficient for these examples.

### 12.2.2 Programming requirements

In order for your new programs to see the required classes during compilation, your classpath must also point to the new Mb*.classes found in the jplugin.jar. This can be done by setting your classpath to look at the directory:

<install_dir>\classes\jplugin.jar    Windows NT/2000

<install_dir>/classes/jplugin.jar    UNIX platforms including z/OS

### 12.2.3 Debugging and logging

When you run your own custom node, you can write events to the system log by using the static method MbService. There are some examples of this use in the code below.

Once you write a custom node, you can deploy it and restart the broker. There are some ways to view the activity that the node and broker are doing in real time. These instructions are for Windows NT/2000, but there are similar possibilities for UNIX and other operating systems.

On the services control window, set your broker to run with the local system account (assuming you are logged in as a user that is a member of the Administrators group) and select **Interact with Desktop**. When you restart the broker, you see two command windows open up. One of these windows displays standard output sent from your Java plug-in nodes when they execute. If you include such lines as:

```
System.out.println("This is my debug message")
```

you can see how your program is doing. This is only a temporary debugging feature for development. You should not rely on these messages for a production environment because the system-standard out settings will most likely be unusable and/or unpractical.

For a more permanent tracing and logging feature, you should instead have whatever messages that you need written to a log file. By using the attributes options in WebSphere MQ Integrator, you could set a tracing level such as "0, 1 or 2" and the path to where a file should be written. In this way, you should be able to write a custom node program one time in Java, but generate a logging file on many platforms if your dynamic path settings are correct.

The 1.4 version of Java (available in beta at the time of this writing) provides new Logging APIs. When this version becomes generally available, you can use these APIs to provide more robust logging capability, or continue to use your own code.

## 12.3 Implementing an input node

In this section we show how to develop a Java input node.

### 12.3.1 Working with the example provided with the product

This example program is simple, yet a very powerful tool. It lets you read a file from a system directory as the input to a message flow rather than from an MQSeries queue.

You can begin to write your input node based on the code found in this example and in Appendix B, "Source code for the Java extensions to WebSphere MQ Integrator" on page 333. The source files are available in the additional materials folder described in Appendix D, "Additional material" on page 355. For more assistance, refer to the *WebSphere MQ Integrator Programming Guide*.

## 12.3.2 Taking a look at the Java source

Code examples here are taken from a program that can read a file from a directory and receive data from a telnet data stream. We discuss the main flow of the controlling Java class. For the other supporting classes that you are going to need and for the full SocketNode.java code, refer to Appendix B.1.1, "SocketNode.java source code" on page 334. Whenever we use <class name> in this discussion, we mean SocketNode.

The main class for a input node should be declared as shown in Example 12-1.

*Example 12-1   Extending MbInputNode implementing MbInputNodeInterface*

```
public class <class name> extends MbInputNode implements MbInputNodeInterface
```

You also have to declare variables that correspond to attributes defined in the WebSphere MQ Integrator node installation and where the value can be set to the node in the message flow (Example 12-2).

*Example 12-2   Setting attribute variables*

```
String _filePath = "";
String _dataSource = "";
String _portNumber = "";
```

This is what tells a message flow what the names of the output terminals should be (on a standard plug-in node you also need to define an "in") (Example 12-3).

*Example 12-3   Creating Terminals example*

```
public SocketNode() throws MbException
{
  // create terminals here
  createOutputTerminal("out");
  createOutputTerminal("failure");
}
```

For every attribute that you define as conditional in the message flow, you have to use these statements (Example 12-4) to extract the values within WebSphere MQ Integrator. Simply stated, dataSource is the name of the attribute you declare in a message flow while _dataSource is the temporary variable that you use for internal processing in this program.

*Example 12-4   Get and set attributes example*

```
public String getDataSource()
{
  return _dataSource;
}

public void setDataSource(String dataSource)
{
  _dataSource = dataSource;
}
```

If you do want messages or errors sent to the system or event log file through WebSphere MQ Integrator, utilize the MbService as shown in Example 12-5.

*Example 12-5   MbService example*

```
private void logError(String traceText) throws MbException {
  MbService mbsLog = new MbService();
  mbsLog.logWarning(
    mbsLog.logWarning(
      this, methodName, "com.ibm.samples.SocketNodeMessages", messageID,
      traceText,new Object [] {});
}
```

The bulk of the input node program is reading data, building and passing the message. Example 12-6 shows how to call a build to the message.

*Example 12-6   MbMessageAssembly*

```
public int run(MbMessageAssembly assembly) throws MbException {
  byte [] generatedMessageBytes = null;
  if (_dataSource.equalsIgnoreCase("file")) {
    try {
      generatedMessageBytes = useFilePath();
    }
    catch {
      //some catch code here;
    }
}
```

Furthermore, you need to include some code (Example 12-7) to look for the file in a directory then read it. (The DirFilter is loaded as a separate class and can be found in Appendix B.1.4, "DirFilter.java source code" on page 339.)

*Example 12-7 Read in the file based on the file path*

```
private byte[] useFilePath() throws Exception {
  String [] inputFileList = sourceDirectory.list(new DirFilter());
  if (inputFileList.length >0) {
    File sourceFile = new File(
      _filePath + File.separator + inputFileList[0]);
    File newSourceFile = new File(
      _filePath + File.separator + inputFileList[0] + ".inuse");
    byte[] inputBytes = new byte[1024];
    InputStream in = new FileInputStream(newSourceFile);
    ByteArrayOutputStream byteStream = new ByteArrayOutputStream();
    int len;
    while ((len = in.read(inputBytes)) > 0) {
      byteStream.write(inputBytes,0,len);
    }
    in.close();
    newSourceFile.delete();
    return byteStream.toByteArray();
  }
}
```

This is the basic structure of the program that you can use to retrieve a file from a directory and pass it to WebSphere MQ Integrator as a message input rather than from a queue. It is important to note here that we did not show any error handling or exception catching scenarios in these snippets, but the full source code in Appendix B.1, "Java input node getting started example" on page 334 shows how to do this.

### 12.3.3 Packaging and loading the input node

Now that you have your Java classes written, you need to compile them using the correct package specifications and build a JAR file.

1. The first step is to ensure that you place your Java files in a directory structure that corresponds to the package structure that you specified in your programs. For this example, we used the following package path:

   `package com.ibm.samples;`

2. If you use the same package path, create a subdirectory structure below a self-created working directory such as javasource; for example:

   `<install_dir>\javasource\com\ibm\samples\`

Copy all of your Java source files to that samples directory.

3. You must ensure that in your classpath, there is a reference to the jplugin.jar. This file has the packages for the Mb*.class files that you are going to need for a successful compilation.

4. Now you are ready to compile your source files. Open a command window and make your working directory the current directory. This is the one that has the \com\ibm\samples\ below it, for example:

   `cd <install_dir>\javasource\`

5. Issue the command:

   `javac com\ibm\samples\*.java`

   If there are no errors, you should see the compiled *.class files in the same directory as the source.

   <install_dir>\javasource\com\ibm\samples\*.class

6. Now you need to create the JAR file. Change to your working directory with:

   `cd <install_dir>\javasource\`

7. Issue the following command in your working directory:

   `jar cvf SocketNode.jar com\ibm\samples\*.class`

   This command should create a SocketNode.jar file in your current directory. By issuing the command:

   `jar tvf SocketNode.jar`

   you should see output that lists all of the classes that were added. Ensure that all of the desired classes were added. In our case, the output should look as shown in Example 12-8.

*Example 12-8   jar tvf sample output*

```
com/ibm/samples/DirFilter.class
com/ibm/samples/SocketNode.class
com/ibm/samples/SocketNodeException.class
com/ibm/samples/SocketNodeMessages.class
some Meta File information
```

To test your new node and flow on Windows 2000, proceed with steps 8 through 10. If you are only going to test your new node and flow on z/OS, skip to steps 11 through 15.

8. Issue the command `mqsistop <broker_name>`.

9. All custom-built plug-in nodes should be placed as JAR files in the lilpath (loadable implementation libraries), which is defined during installation or customization. When installing WebSphere MQ Integrator on Windows 2000, the default directory is <install_dir>\jplugin\. Therefore it is necessary to copy

your newly created JAR file to this directory so that the broker will be able to access it.

> **Tip:** If you have a JAR file with the same name in the jplugin directory, attempt to delete the old one before copying in the new one. If you are not allowed to delete it, the broker or the Configuration Manager is still referencing it. If your Configuration Manager is on the same machine as the broker, you have to stop the Configuration Manager also.

10. You can copy the new JAR file by issuing the command:

    `copy SocketNode.jar <install_dir>\jplugin\SocketNode.jar`

11. Your z/OS broker will process Java packages from directories in the lilpath (loadable installation library) which is defined during installation or customization.

12. From a Windows 2000 command prompt window, FTP the Java JAR file from Windows to z/OS.

13. Log on to z/OS and copy the JAR file to the proper lil directory.

14. Exit FTP.

15. The broker must be stopped and started to refresh the lilpath.

16. Restart your broker with `mqsistart <broker_name>` or `S<broker_name>`.

17. You will need to restart your Configuration Manager if you had to stop it.

## 12.3.4 A simple message flow to test the input node

Now we are going to write a simple message flow to test our new input node.

1. Open the WebSphere MQ Integrator Control Center and proceed to create a new message flow. For this simple test case it is not necessary to create a message set. Expand the **Message Flows** node until you see IBMPrimitives. Right-click **IBMPrimitives** and select **Create Plugin Node**.

   You can use whatever Node Label you choose. It is best to make this something meaningful such as "InputNode". For the Node Identifier, you must use the value that is returned by the getNodeName function found in our program. For this example we used "ComIbmSampleInputNode".

> **Important:** For the first release of WebSphere MQ Integrator it is required that the Node Identifier end with the word "Node". However, there is also a known bug with this release where the word "Node" is added for you automatically. Therefore, for our entry we actually used "ComIbmSampleInput". Check the service pack level of WebSphere MQ Integrator you are working with to determine if you should do this or not.

2. Now we are going to add the terminals. Since this is an input node, defining an In Terminal has no effect. Therefore we choose the word "dummy" to hold the place value. The output terminals are, however, very important. Since this node only accomplishes input and not any level of filtering, we only need two output terminals, out and failure. Whatever values you use here must be the same as the value given to a createOutputTerminal function in your program. Figure 12-1 shows the Create a Plug-in Node window.

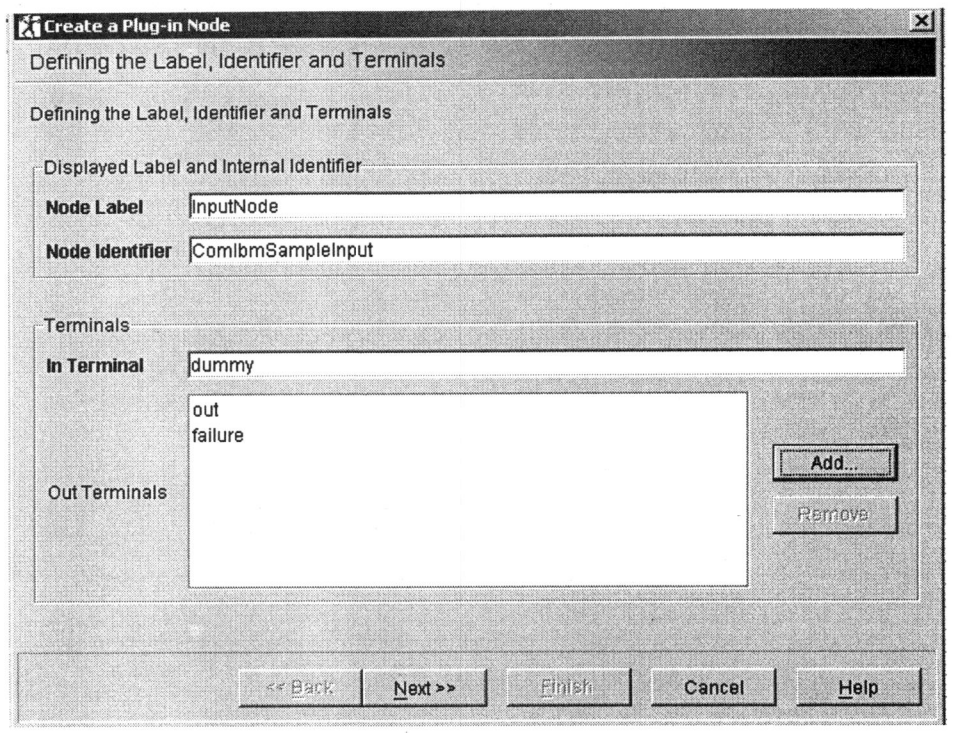

*Figure 12-1  Creating InputNode*

3. Click **Next** to specify the attributes. These attributes correspond to the fields that we specified in the various "set" methods in our Java program. For example, we declared (Example 12-9):

Chapter 12. Developing and deploying custom nodes in Java     **303**

*Example 12-9 Attribute extract from declare*

```
public void setDataSource(String dataSource)
{
  _dataSource = dataSource;
}
```

Where `dataSource` represents the attribute that we specify in this window. Click **InputNode** in the Hierarchy, then click **Create Attribute**. You must enter the attribute names exactly as you did in your program. They are case sensitive. For the first one we inserted `dataSource`. Repeat the procedure in this step until all of the attributes that you declared have been added. For this example we were able to accept the defaults for all of the other fields in this window. Go ahead and add the attribute `portNumber` (Figure 12-2).

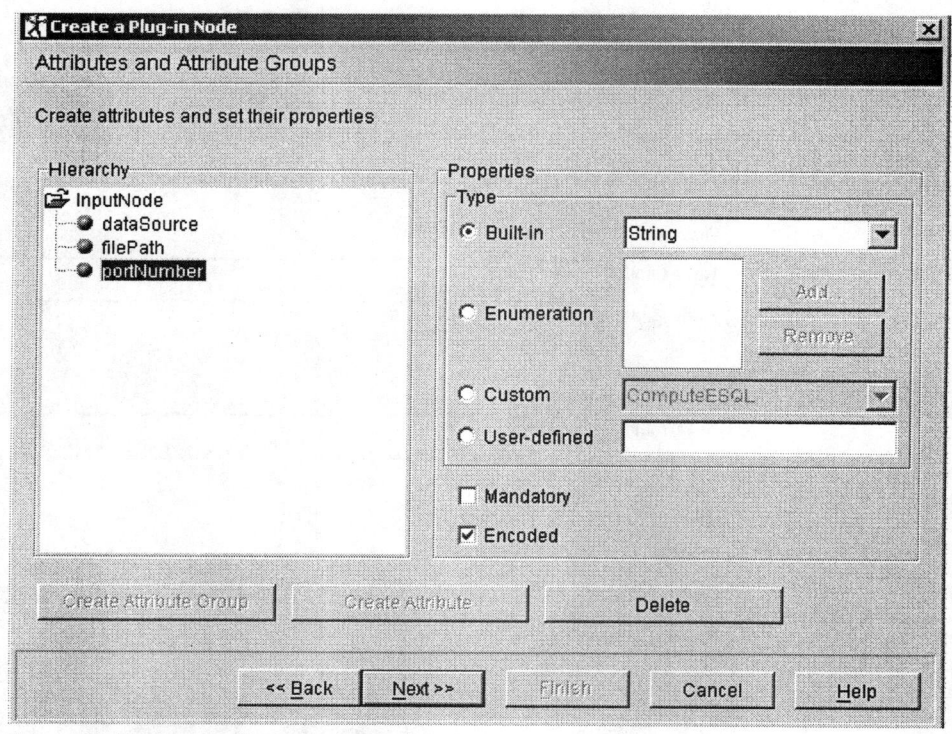

*Figure 12-2 Creating InputNode window 2*

4. Click **Next**. In the next window you can declare default values for the attributes that you just specified. We left these all empty so that there are no accidental parameter settings when you use this node. By clicking the **Description** tab, you can add a short and long description. It is

recommended that you do this here because once you click Finish, you cannot edit this parameter.

5. Click **Next**. In this window there are some other parameters that can be set. You can have WebSphere MQ Integrator create some templates for files, create a properties file (a file that contains startup/run-time parameters) or a Stub for a customizer. Refer to the *WebSphere MQ Integrator Programming Guide* for an explanation of these special features. Click **Finish** to create the node.

6. Now under IBMPrimitives you should see your new custom input node (Figure 12-3). The green box implies that this is a brand new node and is in its first checked-out state. You can right-click to check it in if you want.

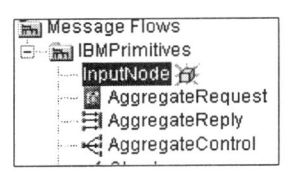

*Figure 12-3   New IBMPrimitive - InputNode*

7. You are now ready to create a test message flow. Right-click the **Message Flows** node and select **Create -> Message Flow**. Give it a test name like "InputNodeTestFlow".

8. Drag and drop your new InputNode into the pane to the right. Right-click the new node and select **Properties** (see Figure 12-4). In the first field, use the dataSource of file. In the filePath field, use something meaningful to you such as c:\temp\XML. This is where you are going to place test messages. If you want to add another description, do so now.

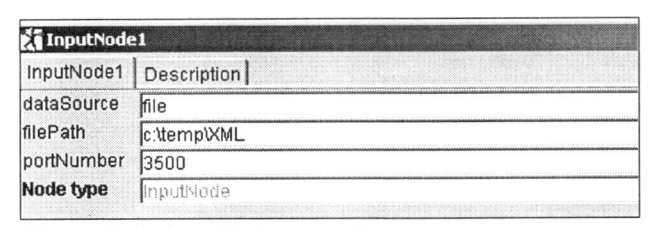

*Figure 12-4   InputNode properties*

9. Click **OK**. If you want, you can change the name of the InputNode1 to something else by right-clicking and selecting **Rename**.

10. Now drag and drop one Compute node from the IBMPrimitives to the message flow on the right. Since our message is coming from a directory and not from a MQSeries queue, we need to attach a header to the message. This is done by right-clicking the **Compute1** node and selecting **Properties**. Click

the **ESQL** tab without selecting either Copy message headers or Copy entire message. In the ESQL window, insert the code like the one shown in Example 12-10.

*Example 12-10   ESQL creating MQMD header*

```
SET OutputRoot.MQMD.MsgType=MQMT_DATAGRAM;
SET OutputRoot.XML=InputBody;
```

11. Ensure that there is no message that says `Syntax Error` and click **OK**. You can change the name of the node to "MakeMQMD".

12. Now we need to add three output terminals. Drag and drop three MQOutput nodes to the far right of the message flow. Rename each one of the output terminals to "Out", "MQMDFailure", and "Failure" respectively.

13. For the Out terminal (Figure 12-5), right-click and go to **Properties**. Click the **Basic** tab. You can leave the Queue Manager Name blank, because it defaults to whatever broker you deploy the flow to use. For the Queue Name, use OUT_Q.

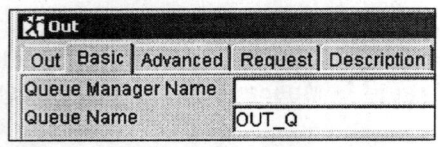

*Figure 12-5   Defining the Out Queue Basic tab*

Click the **Advanced** tab (Figure 12-6). In the Message Context field, select **Default**. If you do not want to add a description, click **OK**.

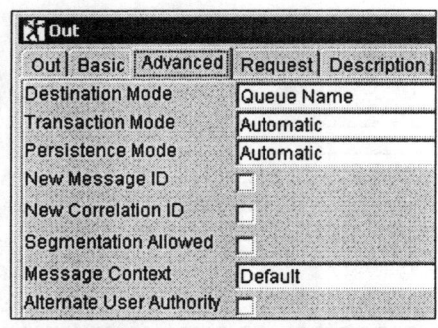

*Figure 12-6   Defining the Out queue Advanced tab*

14. Now set the Queue Names for the other output terminals. For MQMDFailure, choolse **MQMD_FAILURE_Q**. For Failure, choose **FAILURE_Q**. Make sure to remember to set the Message Context field to **Default** for each of them. Do

not worry that you have not created the queues yet; we are going to do it in another step.

15. Now that each of the output terminals have been defined, we need to connect the nodes together. Right-click **InputNode** and select **Connect -> Out**. Attach the Out connection to the MakeMQMD node. Connect the Failure connection to the Failure node (this is really just a dummy node; since there would be no MQMD attached, it would not be accessible).

16. For the MakeMQMD, attach the Out connection to the Out node and the Failure connection to the Failure node (see Figure 12-7).

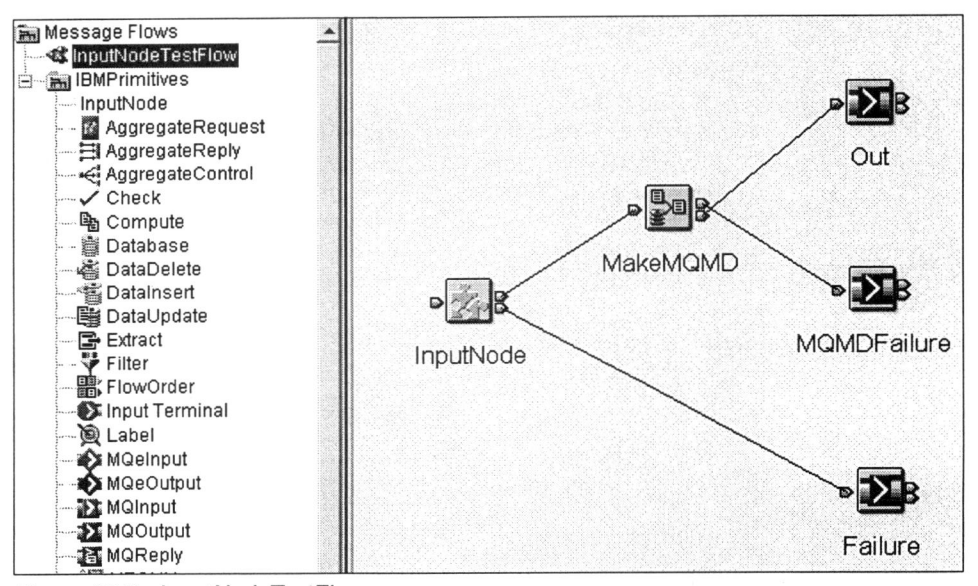

*Figure 12-7   InputNodeTestFlow*

17. Once you have set up your flow, click **File -> Check In -> All (Saved to Shared)**.

18. Before you deploy the flow, you need to create the queues on the respective broker's Queue Manager. Do this by selecting the **MQSeries Explorer** (Figure 12-8) and adding the queues with the exact names that we used above. If you used names different from our example, make sure that they are consistent with the message flow. You can make simple queue definitions and accept the defaults for this example.

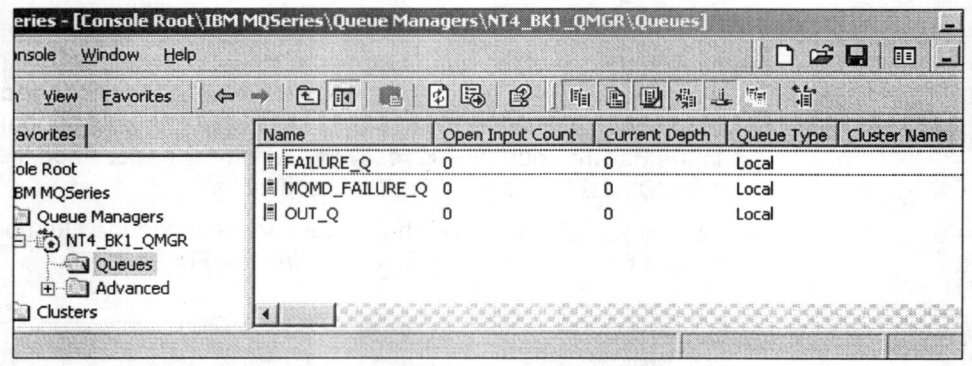

*Figure 12-8 Adding the correct queues to the Queue Manager*

19. Now that your have added the necessary queues, it is time to deploy your message flow to the broker. Return to the Control Center and select the **Assignments** tab (Figure 12-9). Check out the default execution group for your broker (if that is what you are using). Move the new message flow, InputNodeTestFlow, to the correct broker. Check in the default.

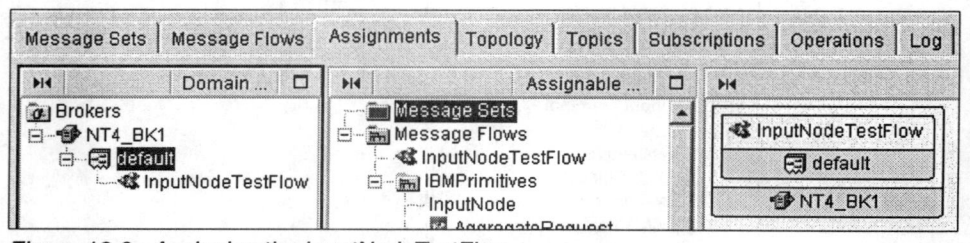

*Figure 12-9 Assigning the InputNodeTestFlow*

20. You may now deploy the changes to your broker by right-clicking the broker name in the left pane and selecting **Deploy -> Complete Assignments Configuration**.

21. Now by clicking the **Log** tab, and after waiting several seconds for the processes to finish, you should be able to click the **Refresh** button and see two messages returned to the display. If the deploy was successful, there should be two messages with blue "i" to the left. If the deploy was not successful, it is important to read all the error messages associated with deploying a flow with a custom-built node because the problem could be in several places. It can be a problem in your Java code or an error in a flow. Read these messages carefully to determine what went wrong.

## 12.3.5 How to test the input node

The version of the sample program that we used takes any file from a directory that we specify and places it into a WebSphere MQ Integrator message flow. For this first example, all that we did in the message flow test was to extract the file from the c:\temp\XML directory, add the MQMD header, and place the data of the file into a queue called "OUT_Q".

You might have noticed that when you deployed the message flow to the broker, some output appeared in one of the command windows that was started when you started the broker service. Look for that output now; it should look similar to Figure 12-10.

```
MtiImbParserFactory::MtiImbParserFactory
Searching for Incoming File...none found.
Searching for Incoming File...none found.
Searching for Incoming File...none found.
Searching for Incoming File...
```

*Figure 12-10   Sample Standard output messages*

To test your message, create a simple piece of XML data such as shown in Example 12-11, using a text editor such as Notepad:

*Example 12-11   Simple XML test file*

```
<data><action>add</action></data>
```

Ensure that there are no extraneous white spaces and save the file as TestMessage.xml, but do not save it into the c:\temp\XML directory. (You do not have to use a true XML file for this example, but the file must end with the .xml extension for it to be pulled from the directory. We are using a true XML file here so it can be reused because it will be required in a future example.)

22. Copy the message into the c:\temp\XML directory; you should immediately see it disappear from the directory. In the command window, you should see a message (Figure 12-11) that says `File Closed. Message created.`

```
File closed. Message created.
Searching for Incoming File...none found.
Searching for Incoming File...none found.
Searching for Incoming File...
```

*Figure 12-11   Sample standard output when file is created*

Chapter 12. Developing and deploying custom nodes in Java

23. Once you have tested your new node, you may want to stop the flow from the Control Center using the Operations tab (Example 12-12) and right-clicking the flow and stop. This will keep the messages from deploying to the window constantly or the process from taking up system resources while your are developing.

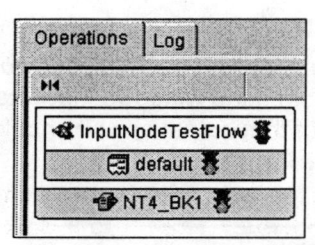

*Figure 12-12   InputNodeTestFlow stopped*

24. Finally, open the **MQSeries Explorer**. Double-click the **OUT_Q**. If your message was created, it should be in the list. To view the contents of your message, double-click the message then click the **Data** tab (Figure 12-13).

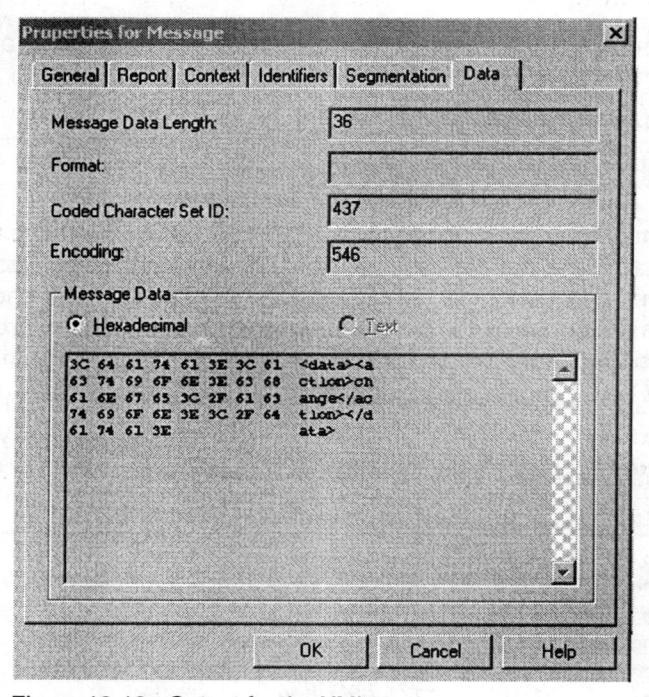

*Figure 12-13   Output for the XML test message*

25. That is all there is to it to test the input nodes directory reading ability. If you want to be able to change the location of the directory that is being read, you will have to change the filePath setting in the message flow and redeploy.

## 12.3.6 How to use the input node to read a telnet stream

Included with the sample program SocketNode.java, there is also the functionality to read data from a telnet stream and use it as an input to a WebSphere MQ Integrator message flow.

### Changes that need to be made

1. If you have not yet saved your workspace in your Control Center, do that now with a name like "InputNodeTestWorkspace.xml". Also this would be a good time to stop running your InputNodeTestFlow, if you have not done so according to the instructions above.

2. Make a copy of your current message flow by right-clicking the message flow and selecting **copy**. Then click the top-level message flow node and right-click and paste. The new copy will be given a default name. Change the name of the new message flow to" InputNodeTelnetTestFlow" or something that helps you remember the difference between the two flows (Figure 12-14).

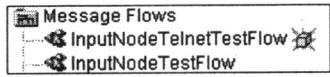

*Figure 12-14   New copy making InputNodeTelnetTestFlow*

3. Now open the new message flow (Figure 12-15) so that we can make some changes to the custom node definition. Right-click the input node and select **Properties**. For the dataSource, change it to say port. For the portNumber, you can use any valid port number that is not already being used by this machine. We are going to specify 3500, but the Java program will default to 3000 if you do not specify a specific port.

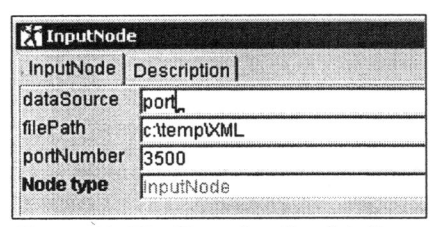

*Figure 12-15   Changing the dataSource*

4. Click **OK**. Check in All (Save to Shared). Check out the default for your broker and assign the new message flow to the broker. Check in the default. Deploy the Delta Assignments Configuration for the broker (Figure 12-16).

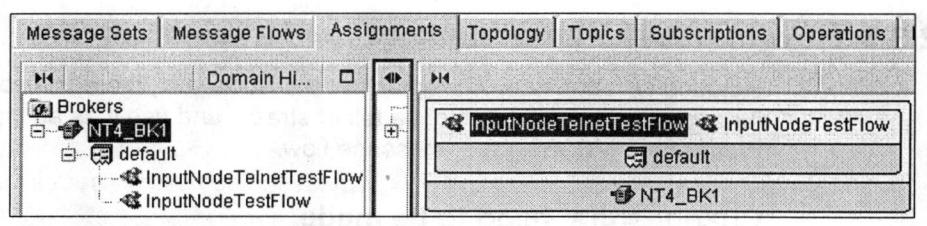

*Figure 12-16   Both Input nodes deployed*

5. Switch to the log view and wait for the confirmation messages to appear by clicking the **Refresh** button.
6. Once the new flow runs, in your standard output terminal (Figure 12-17) you should see messages stating that it is waiting for incoming data. This is because the Java program is monitoring the port constantly until it detects a new session being started.

```
Waiting for Incoming Data...
Waiting for Incoming Data...
Waiting for Incoming Data...
Waiting for Incoming Data...
Waiting for Incoming Data...
```

*Figure 12-17   Telnet session waiting for incoming data*

## Testing the telnet session input node

This test is based on having telnet access available and configured to the machine where the broker is residing. To configure telnet access, consult your network administrator. At the very minimum, they have to configure the telnet server to listen on the port that you specified.

1. Open a command window and run the telnet program by typing `telnet` and the IP address of where the broker is located. If the telnet server of the machine the broker is running on is listening to more than one port, you have to specify the same port that you defined in your node.
2. In your telnet session, you can begin typing XML directly into the session. This is a way of testing the socket functionality. You would not do this in production; rather this is a simple way of testing port listening capability. Instead, you would probably want to have XML come in through an HTTP session or a batch telnet stream. As you type your XML, be careful not to use the backspace or other nonsupported keys because on some telnet sessions,

this causes bytes to be placed in the stream. That will invalidate your XML. Make sure that you do not type extra spaces at the end of the string. Type something simple like the line shown in Figure 12-18).

```
<data><action>add</action></data>
```

*Figure 12-18 SImple XML line*

3. Now use the escape key-stroke for your telnet session. On Windows 2000 it is Ctrl+]. In your command window you should see messages confirming that a new message was created.
4. Check the OUT_Q to see if the XML data that you entered appears in the queue.

**Tip:** In this chapter we explained how to deploy a custom Java input node on a Windows 2000 broker installation. We did, however, conduct nearly these exact installation steps to deploy the same JAR file on Solaris and z/OS successfully without even recompiling the .java files.

## 12.4 Implementing a plug-in node

In "Implementing an input node" on page 297, we describe in detail the steps required to build a usable Java program, compile package and release it with a message flow. Since there is much overlap between an input node and a plug-in node, we are only going to discuss in this section the differences that you need to be aware of. It is highly recommended that you review 12.3, "Implementing an input node" on page 297 before completing this section. It is also recommended that you review the "Programming a plug-in node or parser" section in the *WebSphere MQ Integrator Programming Guide*.

### 12.4.1 Let us start

As with the input node example, this plug-in node example is a simple yet powerful tool that allows you to read the contents of an XML file and route the message based on the contents. The source code for the program is included with the full WebSphere MQ Integrator installation. It can be found in <install_dir>\examples\JavaPlugin\com\ibm\samples on a Windows 2000 installation. The file we are going to use is called SwitchNode.java, but in the same directory there is also a file called TransformNode.java. We are going to explain SwitchNode.java in detail, but TransformNode.java is also a useful program that shows you how to transform data from one value to another in an XML document based on content. After completing this section and reviewing the comments of TransformNode.java, you should have no trouble deploying this program.

The source code for both programs can be found in Appendix B.2, "Java plug-in node getting started example" on page 340 and also in the additional materials. You can learn how to access the Web materials from Appendix D, "Additional material" on page 355.

### 12.4.2 A look at another Java source

Start by opening the source file SwitchNode.java in your favorite text editor. Read the comments in the code to better understand what the program is used for. The program is going to parse an XML message looking for the first occurrence of the <action></action> tags. The message is then going to be routed to an output node with a name matching the value found there.

Notice that this program implements a different interface from the input node (Example 12-12).

*Example 12-12   Implementing MbNodeInterface*

```
public class SwitchNode extends MbNode implements MbNodeInterface
```

and that we also have to create an input terminal with:

```
createInputTerminal("in");
```

Otherwise, the structure of the program is very much like that of the input node. There are few value changes such as the string of getNodeName() as shown in Example 12-13.

*Example 12-13   getNodeName ComIbmSwitchNode*

```
public static String getNodeName()
{
  return "ComIbmSwitchNode";
}
```

Review the program to see if you can find other differences.

There are only two sections of code that provide the functionality that we require. We must parse the XML file and then determine where to route based on the value found. Parsing the file is accomplished through only two lines of code (Example 12-14) since MbElement is already provided for us.

*Example 12-14   Parsing the XML content*

```
MbElement rootElement = assembly.getMessage().getRootElement();
MbElement switchElement =
    rootElement.getLastChild().getFirstChild().getFirstChild();
```

Our example XML data is going to look like the following:

```
<data><action>change</action></data>
```

So the parser will be able to locate the appropriate tag. You can change the parsing order by altering the `getLastchild().getFirstChild()` statement.

Now that the parser has passed the value of the action field to the switchElement, we can evaluate its contents. First, we have to cast the switchElement to a string (Example 12-15).

*Example 12-15   Casting switchElement to a string*

```
String terminalName;
String elementValue = (String)switchElement.getValue();
```

Now that the value is housed in elementValue, we can evaluate it with simple if -> then -> else logic (Example 12-16).

*Example 12-16   Evaluating elementValue*

```
if(elementValue.equals("add"))
   terminalName = "add";
else if(elementValue.equals("change"))
   terminalName = "change";
else if(elementValue.equals("delete"))
   terminalName = "delete";
else if(elementValue.equals("hold"))
   terminalName = "hold";
else
   terminalName = "failure";
```

Notice that if the elementValue does not have a match, the message is routed to the failure output terminal.

The last step is to let WebSphere MQ Integrator know what terminal we want to send the message to. This is accomplished through defining the MbOutputTerminal value and propagating it as shown in Example 12-17.

*Example 12-17   Setting the MbOutputTerminal value and propagating*

```
MbOutputTerminal out = getOutputTerminal(terminalName);
out.propagate(assembly);
```

There are several features that you may want to add to a routing program, such as dynamic error handling or creating multiple input terminals. Review the API javadoc for some more ideas on how to use the other jplugin.jar features.

### 12.4.3 Packaging and loading the plug-in node

If you want to maintain a consistent development environment, copy the SwitchNode.java file to your new <install_dir>\javasource\com\ibm\samples directory. When you compile the source code, make sure that you specify the specific javasource name and not *.java. Otherwise you will recompile everything in this working directory. Also make sure that your classpath has been set to point to the jplugin.jar, as illustrated in the input node section.

For a quick review of the commands, follow these steps:

1. `cd <install_dir>\javasource\`
2. `javac com\ibm\samples\SwitchNode.java`
3. `jar cvf SwitchNode.jar com\ibm\samples\SwitchNode.class`
4. `mqsistop <broker_name>` (also `mqsistop ConfigMgr` if on the same machine)
5. `delete SwitchNode.jar <install_dir>\jplugin\SwitchNode.jar`
6. `copy SwitchNode.jar <install_dir>\jplugin\SwitchNode.jar`
7. FTP the Java JAR file from Windows to z/OS
8. Ensure the Java JAR file is in a directory in the lilpath
9. `mqsistart <broker_name>`

### 12.4.4 A simple message flow to test the plug-in node

As we did with the input node, we are going to define a new custom primitive using our JAR file as the source. Then we are going to expand on our current message flow (InputNodeMessageFlow) by creating new output terminals and adding the SwitchNode. The message flow then should be able to retrieve the message from a directory as before and route it to the appropriate queue based on the value found in the `<action>` tag.

If you did not choose to complete the InputNodeMessageFlow, you can simply create a new message flow using a standard MQ input node as input.

1. If your Control Center is not open, go to **Start -> Programs -> IBM WebSphere MQ Integrator 2.1 -> Control Center**.
1. Expand the **Message Flows** node until you see IBMPrimitives. Right-click **IBMPrimitives** and select **Create Plugin Node**.

2. You can use whatever Node Label you choose. It is best to make this label something meaningful, such as "SwitchNode". For the Node Identifier, you must use the value that is returned by the getNodeName function found in our program. For this example we used "ComIbmSwitchNode", but remember, you may have to leave off the trailing "Node" so that your actual input is "ComIbmSwitch".
3. You need an input terminal for this node so use "in".
4. You need several output terminals, called "add", "change", "delete", "hold", and "failure".

   Figure 12-19 shows the window you use to create a plug-in node.

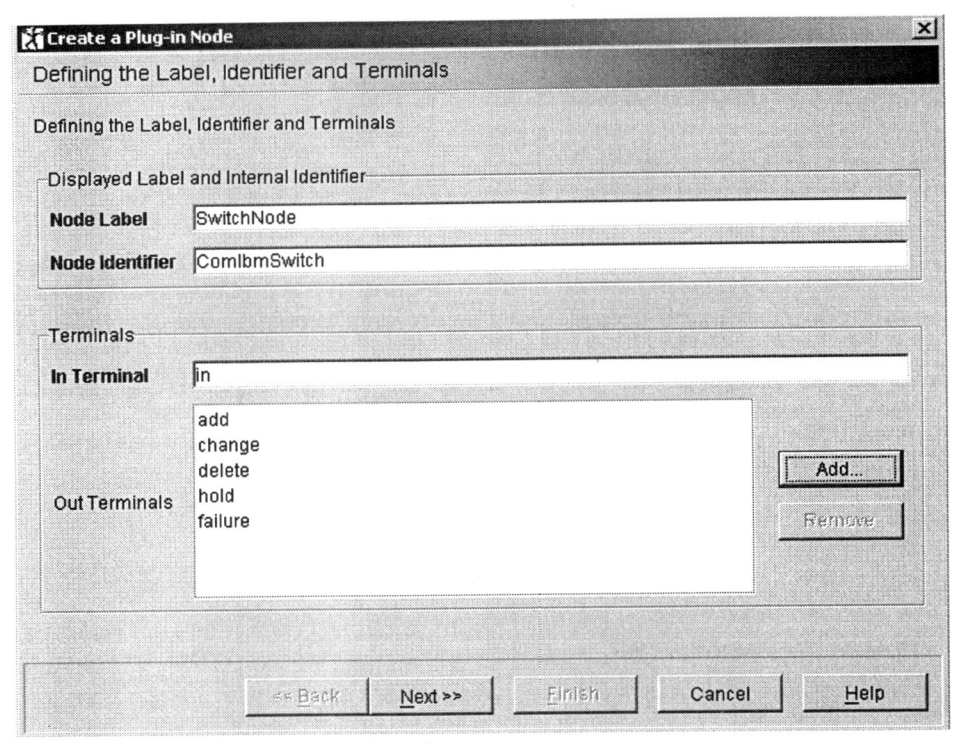

*Figure 12-19   Creating the plug-in node*

5. Click **Next**. There are no attributes that we need to define for this example.
6. Click **Next**. Add a description here.
7. Click **Next** and then right-click the **InputNodeTestFlow** and click **Check Out**.
8. Right-click the **Failure** node and click **Delete**.
9. Right-click the **Out** node and click **Delete**.

10. Drag-and-drop a new SwitchNode from the IBMPrimitives to the spot where the Out node had been.
11. Right-click the **SwitchNode1** and rename it to "SwitchNode", since it is the only one that we are going to use for this flow.
12. Drag-and-drop five MQOutput nodes from the IBMPrimitives to the far right-hand side of your message flow.
13. Rename each of the new output nodes to "Add", "Change", "Delete", "Hold", and "Failure".
14. Right-click the **Add** output terminal and click **Properties**.
15. Click the **Basic** tab and change the name of the Queue to "ADD_Q" (Figure 12-20).

*Figure 12-20  Defining the Add queue Basic tab*

16. Click the **Advanced** tab (Figure 12-21) and change the Message Context field to Default. If you do not want to change the description, click **OK**.

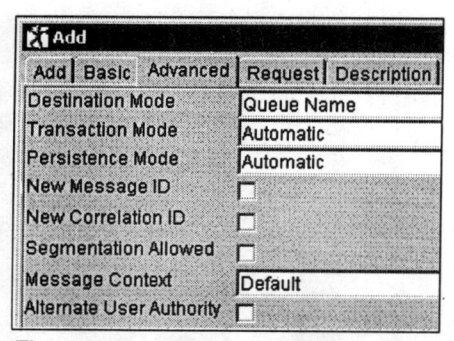

*Figure 12-21  Defining the Add queue Advanced tab*

17. For each of the terminals, name the queues "CHANGE_Q", "DELETE_Q", "HOLD_Q" and "FAILURE_Q" respectively. Make sure that you remember to change the Message Context field to Default for each.
18. Right-click the **MakeMQMD** node and select **Connect -> Out** and join then connection to the SwitchNode.
19. Right-click the **SwitchNode** and select **Connect -> Add** and join the connection to the Add terminal node.

20. Complete the last task for each of the output terminals.
21. When finished, your flow should look as shown in Figure 12-22.

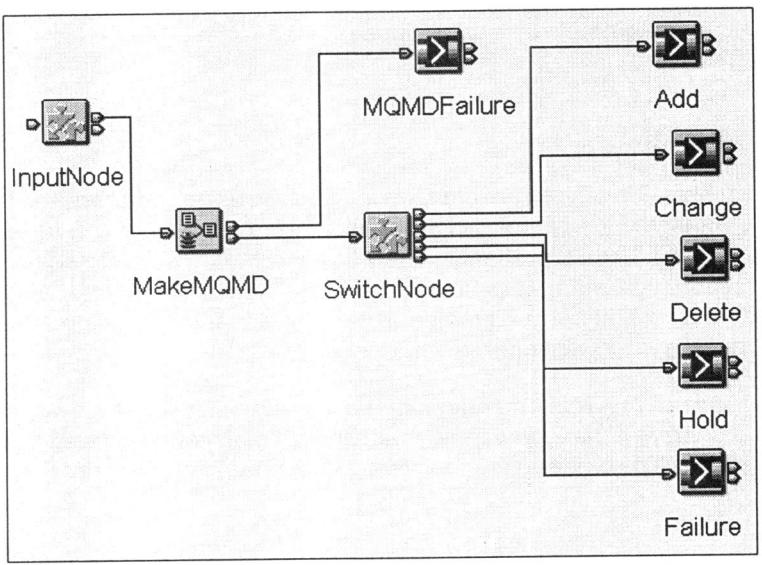

*Figure 12-22  InputNodeTestFlow with the SwitchNode added*

22. Click **File -> Check In -> All (Saved to Shared)**.
23. Go to **Start -> IBM MQSeries V5.2.1 -> MQSeries Explorer**.
24. For the Queue Manager that is deploying your test message, create the following queues: ADD_Q, CHANGE_Q, DELETE_Q, HOLD_Q, FAILURE_Q while accepting all of the default values for this test (Figure 12-23).

| Name | Open Input Count | Current Depth | Queue Type |
|---|---|---|---|
| ADD_Q | 0 | 0 | Local |
| CHANGE_Q | 0 | 1 | Local |
| DELETE_Q | 0 | 0 | Local |
| FAILURE_Q | 0 | 0 | Local |
| HOLD_Q | 0 | 0 | Local |

*Figure 12-23  Queue's required for SwitchNode test*

25. Return to the Control Center and redeploy your broker from the **Assignments** tab by right-clicking the broker with the existing message flow and clicking **Deploy -> Complete Assignments Configuration**.
26. Switch to the **Log** tab and refresh the window to ensure that the message flow deployed successfully.

Chapter 12. Developing and deploying custom nodes in Java  **319**

27. To test the message, simply copy and paste a version of the file TestMessage.xml that you created for the input node test into the c:\temp\XML directory. It should immediately be removed by the InputNode. By checking if your `<action>` tags contained the value `change`, you should see your complete message appear in the `CHANGE_Q`.

## 12.5 Summary

By now you should have a fairly good understanding of what it takes to create and deploy a custom-built Java node with WebSphere MQ Integrator. At this point you should probably review the programming guide again and the API javadoc to further emphasize the points the we made here. Also make sure to take a look at the Web materials for any last minute updates to these code examples or additional information.

There are several other custom features and classes that have been built into the **jplugin** API that you can take advantage of. Likewise there are limitless possibilities where you may want to consider implementing a custom java node.

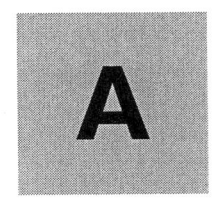

# Running a message flow trace

In this appendix, we detail how to run automated user traces using WebSphere MQ Integrator. These traces provide invaluable information when developing and modifying flows. The trace output describes what each node in a flow is doing, how variables have been interpreted and the contents of messages. This produces far more valuable information than the Control Center's graphic debugger.

Customers familiar with the distributed version of MQSeries Integrator will have become familiar with running and formatting traces to debug flows during development. This appendix discusses and provides samples of an automated version to run traces on Windows, z/OS and UNIX platforms.

All the command files and scripts are included in the additional materials referenced in Appendix D, "Additional material" on page 355.

For more information, refer to the *WebSphere MQ Integrator Problem Determination Guide,* GC34-5290.

## A.1 User traces for message flows

On all platforms, there are four commands that are required to run a user trace.

Once your flow is deployed, you must instruct the broker to start tracing. This is done with `mqsichangetrace` on the distributed platform and `changetrace` or `ct` on z/OS. Try and keep activity in the message flow you are tracing to a minimum to avoid creating unnecessary trace output. At this point you must test your flow.

Having been instructed to trace the flow, the broker creates log files. The broker could be tracing many flows, particularly in a development environment and may be producing many large log files. The next step is to extract the relevant data from all the log files being produced by the broker with the `mqsireadlog` command. This command creates XML trace files.

Next you can use the `mqsiformat` command to create a readable text trace file from the XML and finally you should instruct the broker to stop tracing with the `mqsichangetrace` or `ct` command again.

### A.1.1 Running the trace scripts

Running these four commands seems particularly arduous and it is therefore convenient to automate this process using command scripts as detailed in the next section. In each case start the script with the command below:

```
usertrace <Broker> <Execution Group> <Message Flow> [replace]
```

On z/OS and UNIX add .sh to the command.

## A.2 Tracing on Windows platforms

Example A-1 shows usertrace.cmd for Windows platforms. Place it in a directory in your path. After you execute the `mqsichangetrace` command, you will be prompted:

```
-- Now test your Messageflow
```

Test your flow and then click **Return** and the script will continue to process and pop up a Notepad window with the trace details. When viewing with Notepad, it is a good idea to maximize the window and set word wrap on.

Example: A-1   The usertrace command file

```
echo off
  rem ------------------------------------------------------------------------
  rem -- Program: Usertrace Utility "usertrace.cmd"
  Rem -- Version: 1.00
  rem -- Updated: 05/24/2000
  rem -- Purpose: start usertrace for a special messageflow (refresh the log)
  rem --          then wait (user can test the messageflow in another window)
```

```
  rem --            then dump the MQSI log to a file and use Notepad to view
  rem --            the results
  rem --            at last usertrace ist turned off again
  rem -- Required parameters are BrokerName, ExecutionGroup and MsgFlow -
  rem --            !!! THESE ARE CASE SENSITIVE !!!
  rem ---------------------------------------------------------------------

  echo ---------------------------------------------------------------------
  echo -- Usertrace Utility process started
  IF "%2" == "" goto BADPARAM
  IF "%3" == "" goto BADPARAM

:PROCESS
  echo -- Executing command: mqsichangetrace %1 -u -e %2 -f %3 -l debug -r
-c50000
  mqsichangetrace %1 -u -e %2 -f %3 -l debug -r -c50000
  echo -- Now test your Messageflow
  pause
  echo -- Executing command: mqsireadlog %1 -u -e %2 -o %3.tm$
  mqsireadlog %1 -u -e %2 -o %3.tm$
  rem ---------------------------------------------------------------------
  rem -- If the target file exists and REPLACE has not been specified then
  rem -- do not overwrite the file.  Report the error and end the process.
  rem ---------------------------------------------------------------------
  IF NOT EXIST %3.tm$ goto NOFILE
  IF NOT EXIST %3.txt goto OK
  IF "%4" == "REPLACE" goto REPLACEOK
  IF "%4" == "replace" goto REPLACEOK

:NOREPLACE
  echo -- ERROR !!!
  echo -- Output file %3.txt exists. (REPLACE option not specified)
  echo -- Specify replace option or delete the output file and try again.
  goto SYNTAX

:REPLACEOK
  del %3.txt
  echo -- Output file %3.txt deleted (REPLACE option specified)

:OK
  start mqsichangetrace %1 -u -e %2 -f %3 -l none -r
  echo -- Executing command: mqsiformatlog   -i %3.tm$ -o %3.txt
  mqsiformatlog   -i %3.tm$ -o %3.txt
  del %2.tm$
  rem ---------------------------------------------------------------------
  rem -- Make sure the output file exists before starting notepad
  rem ---------------------------------------------------------------------
  IF NOT EXIST %3.txt goto NOFILE
  echo -- Output stored in file %3.txt
```

Appendix A. Running a message flow trace

```
          echo -- Starting the Notepad editor to view the file
          echo -- Suggestion: Turn on word wrap in Notepad to easily view the output
          start notepad %3.txt
          goto FINISH

        :NOFILE
          echo -- ERROR !!!
          echo -- The process did not produce any output. Look for error messages
          echo -- from previous commands. Check parameters and try again.
          goto SYNTAX

        :BADPARAM
          echo -- Purpose: start usertrace for a special messageflow (refresh the log)
          echo --          then wait (user can test the messageflow in another window)
          echo --          then dump the MQSI log to a file and use Notepad to view the results
          echo --          at last usertrace ist turned off again
        :SYNTAX
          echo ---------------------------------------------------------------------------
          echo -- Syntax: usertrace [BrokerName] [Execution Group] [Message Flow] [replace]
          echo -- Remember, parameters are case sensitive!!!
          echo ---------------------------------------------------------------------------

        :FINISH
          echo -- Usertrace Utility process finished
          echo ---------------------------------------------------------------------------

        :END
```

## A.3 Tracing on z/OS and UNIX platforms

On z/OS, the broker needs to be modified to start tracing. The shell script shown in Example A-3 on page 325 echoes a message to instruct you to modify the broker, but there are freeware utilities that can be used to automate this step by directly issuing the MVS command from USS.

Having started the script and issued the MVS command you should test you flow and then press <ENTER> to continue the script. It will format the log and page the output to your window.

On AIX, Solaris and HP the **mqsichangetrace** command is used. The script uses the **uname** command to check which platform it is running on. In all other ways it should work the same.

On all platforms your user environment needs to be set up. Refer to the *WebSphere MQ Integrator for z/OS Customization and Administration Guide,* SC34-5919 or *WebSphere MQ Integrator Administration Guide,* SC34-5792 for details. For z/OS, we set up the environment as shown in Example A-2 on page 325.

*Example: A-2   Environment setting on z/OS*

```
export PATH=/usr/lpp/wmqi/bin:$PATH
export LIBPATH=/usr/lpp/wmqi/lib:$LIBPATH
export STEPLIB="DB7V7.SDSNLOAD"
export NLSPATH=/usr/lpp/wmqi/messages/En_US/%N:$NLSPATH
export MQSI_REGISTRY=/var/wmqi/MQV1BRK
export DSNAOINI=/var/wmqi/MQV1BRK/dsnaoini
```

*Example: A-3   usertrace shell command for z/OS*

```
#!/bin/sh
# ------------------------------------------------------------------------
# -- Program: Usertrace Utility "usertrace.sh" for z/OS
# -- Date 13/12/2001
# -- Version: 1.00
# -- Purpose: start usertrace for a special messageflow on z/OS
# --          then wait (user can test the messageflow in another window)
# --          then dump the MQSI log to a file and use pg to view
# --          the results and turns off trace
# -- Required parameters are BrokerName, ExecutionGroup and MsgFlow -
# --          !!! THESE ARE CASE SENSITIVE !!!
# ------------------------------------------------------------------------
# -- WMQI Environment variables must be setup with correctly for
# -- DSNAOINI, LIBPATH, PATH, STEPLIB
# ------------------------------------------------------------------------
# -- OECONSOLE #
# -- This is freeware which allows you to execute an MVS command from USS
# -- It can be used to automate the MVS commands in this script. It is
# -- available at:
# -- http://www-1.ibm.com/servers/eserver/zseries/zos/unix/toys/oeconsol.htm

TR1=trace.xml # xml trace file output
TR2=trace.txt # formatted trace output

###############
# Check Syntax #
###############

if [ "."$3 = "." ];then
   echo -- Purpose: starts usertrace for a messageflow resetting logs
   echo --          then wait for testing of messageflow in another session
```

```
         echo --              then dump the MQSI log to a file and use pg to view it.
         echo --              usertrace is then switched off and log reset.
         echo ----------------------------------------------------------------------
         echo -- Syntax: usertrace BrokerName ExecutionGroup MessageFlow
         echo -- remember, parameters are case sensitive!!!
         echo ----------------------------------------------------------------------
         exit -1
fi

##########################
# check file permissions #
##########################

for ITEM in $$.tmp $TR1 $TR2; do
   if [ ! -w $ITEM ];then
      touch $ITEM
      if [ $? -ne 0 ];then
         echo Error - Unable to write output files to current directory; exit -1
      fi
   fi
done


#############################
# Modify broker for tracing #
#############################

if [ `uname | grep -c 390` -eq 0 ]; then      # USS returns OS/390
   echo -- processing mqsichangetrace %1 -u -e %2 -f %3 -l debug -r -c50000
      mqsichangetrace %1 -u -e %2 -f %3 -l debug -r -c50000 > $$.tmp 2>&1
      if [ `grep -c BIP8071I $$.tmp` -eq 0 ];then
         echo mqsichangetrace command failed; exit -1
      fi

   else
   echo -- Please enter MVS console command:
   echo
   echo F $1,changetrace u=yes,e=\'$2\',f=\'$3\',r=yes,l=debug
   echo
   echo -- and wait for successfull command completion. You can then test
   echo -- your message flow and press ENTER when completed...
fi

read xxx         # Wait for message flow to be tested

###################
# Reading the log #
###################
```

```
echo -- processing mqsireadlog $1 -u -e$2 -f -o $TR1
mqsireadlog $1 -u -e$2 -f -o $TR1 > $$.tmp 2>&1
    if [ `grep -c BIP8071I $$.tmp` -eq 0 ];then
    echo mqsireadlog command failed; exit -1
    fi


#################
# formatting log #
#################

echo -- processing mqsiformatlog -i $TR1 -o $TR2
mqsiformatlog -i $TR1 -o $TR2 > $$.tmp 2>&1
    if [ `grep -c BIP8071I $$.tmp` -eq 0 ];then
    echo mqsiformatlog command failed; exit -1
    fi


##########################
# Modify broker trace off #
##########################

if [ `uname | grep -c 390` -eq 0 ]; then      # USS returns OS/390
   echo -- processing mqsichangetrace %1 -u -e %2 -l none
   mqsichangetrace %1 -u -e %2 -l none > $$.tmp 2>&1
       if [ `grep -c BIP8071I $$.tmp` -eq 0 ];then
       echo mqsichangetrace command failed - Please turn tracing off manually
       echo press ENTER to continue; read xxx
       fi

  else
  echo -- Please enter MVS console command:
  echo
  echo F $1,changetrace u=yes,e=\'$2\',l=none
  echo
  echo to switch tracing off...
  echo You can now press ENTER to view your trace
  read xxx
fi


##########
# Tidy Up #
##########
rm $$.tmp
pg $TR2
exit
0
```

## A.4 Trace nodes in message flows

When you use Trace nodes in your message flow, configure them to write the output as shown in Figure A-1. The data will appear in line (between information from its attached nodes) in your trace output which is easier to view, particularly when you have multiple trace nodes and complex errors.

To do this, configure the Destination field in the node properties to User Trace rather than File.

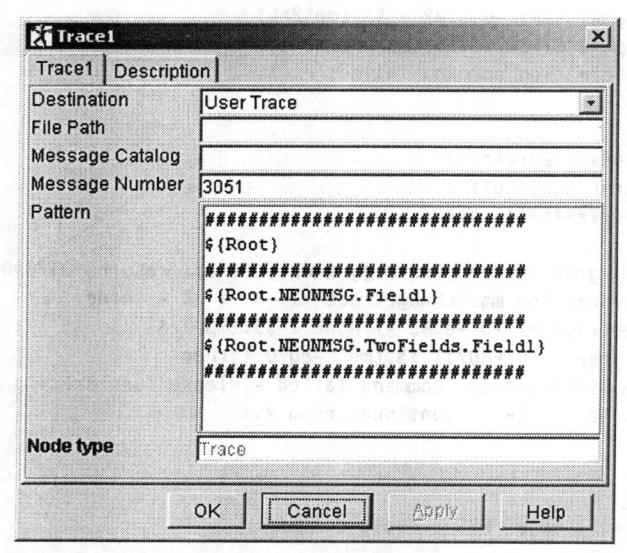

```
Trace1
Trace1 | Description
Destination      User Trace
File Path
Message Catalog
Message Number   3051
Pattern          ##############################
                 ${Root}
                 ##############################
                 ${Root.NEONMSG.Field1}
                 ##############################
                 ${Root.NEONMSG.TwoFields.Field1}
                 ##############################

Node type        Trace

        OK    Cancel    Apply    Help
```

*Figure A-1   Trace node properties configured to write to trace logs*

## A.5 Sample trace file output

Example A-4 shows some trace output with an error. This is a trace of the message flow in Figure 7-11 on page 139.

Between the ##### you can can see the output from the Trace node in the flow. Towards the end you can see the error:

`Reformat , TwoFields, 1004, Output format TwoFields not in database.`

This is an error from NEONMSG domain to say that it has no output format named TwoFields. This is in fact an input format.

*Example: A-4   Trace output*

Timestamps are formatted in local time, 300 minutes before GMT.

```
2001-11-29 11:15:36.547776        7     UserTrace    BIP2632I: Message being propagated to the
output terminal; node 'NEOFLOW1.NEON.IN'.
                                An input message received from MQSeries input queue in
node 'NEOFLOW1.NEON.IN' is being propagated to any nodes connected to the output terminal.
                                No user action required.
2001-11-29 11:15:36.548304        7     UserTrace    BIP6060I: Parser type 'Properties' created on
behalf of node 'NEOFLOW1.NEON.IN' to handle portion of incoming message of length 0 bytes
beginning at offset '0'.
                                The message broker has created a parser of type
'Properties' on behalf of node 'NEOFLOW1.NEON.IN' to handle the first part of an incoming
message. This parser has been given the portion of the message starting at offset '0' and '0'
bytes long.
                                No user action required.
2001-11-29 11:15:36.548576        7     UserTrace    BIP6061I: Parser type 'MQMD' created on
behalf of node 'NEOFLOW1.NEON.IN' to handle portion of incoming message of length '324' bytes
beginning at offset '0'. Parser type selected based on value 'MQHMD' from previous parser.
                                The message broker has created a parser of type 'MQMD'
on behalf of node 'NEOFLOW1.NEON.IN' to handle a subsequent part of an incoming message. This
parser has been given the portion of the message starting at offset '0' and '324' bytes long.
This parser type was selected as the best match given the value 'MQHMD' from the previous
parser.
                                No user action required.
2001-11-29 11:15:36.548832        7     UserTrace    BIP6061I: Parser type 'NEONMSG' created on
behalf of node 'NEOFLOW1.NEON.IN' to handle portion of incoming message of length '20' bytes
beginning at offset '324'. Parser type selected based on value 'NEONMSG' from previous parser.
                                The message broker has created a parser of type
'NEONMSG' on behalf of node 'NEOFLOW1.NEON.IN' to handle a subsequent part of an incoming
message. This parser has been given the portion of the message starting at offset '324' and
'20' bytes long. This parser type was selected as the best match given the value 'NEONMSG' from
the previous parser.
                                No user action required.
2001-11-29 11:15:36.549088        7     UserTrace    BIP2538I: Node 'NEOFLOW1.Trace1': Evaluating
expression 'ExceptionList' at (2, 3).
                                The expression being evaluated was 'ExceptionList'.
                                No user action required.
2001-11-29 11:15:36.549200        7     UserTrace    BIP2538I: Node 'NEOFLOW1.Trace1': Evaluating
expression 'Root' at (4, 3).
                                The expression being evaluated was 'Root'.
                                No user action required.
2001-11-29 11:15:45.701280        7     UserTrace    BIP4060I: Data
'#############START##################

######################################
(
                                (0x1000000)Properties = (
                                   (0x3000000)MessageSet      = ''
                                   (0x3000000)MessageType     = 'TwoFields'
                                   (0x3000000)MessageFormat   = ''
```

Appendix A. Running a message flow trace    329

```
                              (0x3000000)Encoding          = 785
                              (0x3000000)CodedCharSetId    = 500
                              (0x3000000)Transactional     = TRUE
                              (0x3000000)Persistence       = TRUE
                              (0x3000000)CreationTime      = GMTTIMESTAMP
'2001-11-29 15:54:00.588191'
                              (0x3000000)ExpirationTime    = -1
                              (0x3000000)Priority          = 0
                              (0x3000000)ReplyIdentifier   =
X'00000000000000000000000000000000000000000000000000'
                              (0x3000000)ReplyProtocol     = 'MQ'
                              (0x3000000)Topic             = NULL
                            )
                            (0x1000000)MQMD               = (
                              (0x3000000)SourceQueue       = 'NEON.IN'
                              (0x3000000)Transactional     = TRUE
                              (0x3000000)Encoding          = 785
                              (0x3000000)CodedCharSetId    = 500
                              (0x3000000)Format            = 'MQSTR   '
                              (0x3000000)Version           = 1
                              (0x3000000)Report            = 0
                              (0x3000000)MsgType           = 8
                              (0x3000000)Expiry            = -1
                              (0x3000000)Feedback          = 0
                              (0x3000000)Priority          = 0
                              (0x3000000)Persistence       = 1
                              (0x3000000)MsgId             =
X'c3e2d840d4d8e5f34040404040404040b6cf8823d08aa182'
                              (0x3000000)CorrelId          =
X'00000000000000000000000000000000000000000000000000'
                              (0x3000000)BackoutCount      = 0
                        (0x3000000)ReplyToQ      = 'NEON.IN                                                         '
                        (0x3000000)ReplyToQMgr   = 'MQV3                                                            '
                              (0x3000000)UserIdentifier    = 'MQRES4  '
                              (0x3000000)AccountingToken   =
X'06c1c3c3d5e37b0000000000000000000000000000000000000000000000000000'
                              (0x3000000)ApplIdentityData  = '                                '
                              (0x3000000)PutApplType       = 2
                        (0x3000000)PutApplName   = 'MQRES4A                                 '
                              (0x3000000)PutDate           = DATE '2001-11-29'
                              (0x3000000)PutTime           = GMTTIME '16:15:36.540'
                              (0x3000000)ApplOriginData    = '    '
                              (0x3000000)GroupId           =
X'00000000000000000000000000000000000000000000000000'
                              (0x3000000)MsgSeqNumber      = 1
```

```
                                    (0x3000000)Offset          = 0
                                    (0x3000000)MsgFlags        = 0
                                    (0x3000000)OriginalLength  = -1
                                    (0x3000000)Flags           = 0
                                )
                                (0x1000000)NEONMSG   = (
                                    (0x7000000)MessageType = 'TwoFields'
                                    (0x7000000)Format      = 'Content'
                                    (0x3000000)Field1      = 'helloworld'
                                    (0x3000000)Field2a     = 'dfggfdgg'
                                )
                            )
################END##################
```
' from trace node 'NEOFLOW1.Trace1'.
The trace node 'NEOFLOW1.Trace1' has output the specified trace data.
This is an information message provided by the message flow designer. The user response will be determined by the local environment.

2001-11-29 11:15:45.701824      7    UserTrace   BIP4067I: Message propagated to output terminal for trace node 'NEOFLOW1.Trace1'.
The trace node 'NEOFLOW1.Trace1' has received a message and is propagating it to any nodes connected to its output terminal.
No user action required.

2001-11-29 11:15:47.189120      7    Error       BIP2628E: Exception condition detected on input node 'NEOFLOW1.NEON.IN'.
The input node 'NEOFLOW1.NEON.IN' detected an error whilst processing a message. The message flow has been rolled-back and, if the message was being processed in a unit of work, it will remain on the input queue to be processed again. Following messages will indicate the cause of this exception.
Check the error messages which follow to determine why the exception was generated, and take action as described by those messages.

**2001-11-29 11:15:47.189200      7 ImbMqOutputNode::evaluate**
**2001-11-29 11:15:47.189216      7 Reformat , TwoFields, 1004, Output format TwoFields not in database**

2001-11-29 11:15:48.200208      7    UserTrace   BIP2631I: Backed out message being propagated to failure terminal; node 'NEOFLOW1.NEON.IN'.
Node 'NEOFLOW1.NEON.IN' has received a message which has previously been backed out because of a processing error in the message flow. The MQMD 'backoutCount' of the message exceeds (or equals) the 'backoutThreshold' defined for the MQSeries input queue. The message broker is propagating the message to the failure terminal of the node.
Examine the other messages and the message flow to determine why the message is being backed out. Correct this situation if possible. Perform any local error recovery processing required.

2001-11-29 11:15:48.200832      7    UserTrace   BIP2638I: MQPUT to queue 'NEON.ERROR' on queue manager '': MQCC=0, MQRC=0; node 'NEOFLOW1.NEON.ERROR'.
The node 'NEOFLOW1.NEON.ERROR' attempted to write a message to the specified queue 'NEON.ERROR' connected to queue manager ''. The MQCC was 0 and the MQRC was 0.

                                   No user action required.
2001-11-29 11:15:48.200928       7   UserTrace   BIP2622I: Message successfully output by
output node 'NEOFLOW1.NEON.ERROR' to queue 'NEON.ERROR' on queue manager ''.
                                   The MQSeries output node 'NEOFLOW1.NEON.ERROR'
successfully wrote an output message to the specified queue NEON.ERROR connected to queue
manager .
                                   No user action required.

Threads encountered in this
trace:

# Source code for the Java extensions to WebSphere MQ Integrator

This appendix contains all of the source code for the Java examples used throughout this redbook. Though they have been implemented and tested for usability, you should not use them in your production environment without conducting testing and quality assurance for yourself.

You can also find the source code in Web materials folder. The instructions for accessing the material can be found in Appendix D., "Additional material" on page 355.

# B.1 Java input node getting started example

In this section we provide the code for the Java input node example.

## B.1.1 SocketNode.java source code

```java
package com.ibm.samples;

import com.ibm.broker.plugin.*;
import java.io.*;
import java.net.*;
public class SocketNode extends MbInputNode implements MbInputNodeInterface {
   String _portNumber = "";
   String _filePath = "";
   String _dataSource = "";
   int FAILURE;

   ServerSocket server = null;

   public SocketNode () throws MbException {
     // create terminals here
     createOutputTerminal ("out");
     createOutputTerminal ("failure");
   }
   public String getDataSource () {
     return _dataSource;
   }
   public String getFilePath () {
     return _filePath;
   }
   public static String getNodeName () {
     return "ComIbmSampleInputNode";
   }
   public String getPortNumber () {
     return _portNumber;
   }
   private void logMessage ( String methodName, String messageID, String traceText) throws MbException{
     MbService mbsLog = new MbService ();
     if (messageID.endsWith ("W")) {
       mbsLog.logWarning (this, methodName, "com.ibm.samples.SocketNodeMessages", messageID, traceText,new Object [] {});
     }
     else{
       if (messageID.endsWith ("I")) {
          mbsLog.logInformation (this, methodName, "com.ibm.samples.SocketNodeMessages", messageID, traceText,new Object [] {});
       }
```

```java
      else {
          mbsLog.logError (this, methodName, "com.ibm.samples.SocketNodeMessages", messageID,
traceText,new Object [] {});
      }
    }
  }
  public int run (MbMessageAssembly assembly) throws MbException {

    byte [] generatedMessageBytes = null;

    // select correct routine
    if (_dataSource.equalsIgnoreCase ("port")) {
      try {
        generatedMessageBytes = usePortNumber ();
      }
      catch (InterruptedIOException e) {
        System.out.println ("Timed out");
        return TIMEOUT;
      }
      catch (SocketNodeException e) {
        return FAILURE;
      }
      catch (Exception e) {
        logMessage ("run", "4E", e.getMessage ());
        e.printStackTrace ();
        return FAILURE;
      }
    }
    else {
      if (_dataSource.equalsIgnoreCase ("file")) {
        try {
          generatedMessageBytes = useFilePath ();
        }
        catch (SocketNodeException e) {
          return FAILURE;
        }
        catch (Exception e) {
          logMessage ("run", "4E", e.getMessage ());
          e.printStackTrace ();
          return FAILURE;
        }
      }
      else {
        logMessage ("run", "0W", "");
        System.out.println ("Invalid datasource specified.");
        // use defaults and run port version.
        _portNumber = "3000";
        _dataSource = "port";
        try {
```

```
              generatedMessageBytes = usePortNumber ();
            }
            catch (InterruptedIOException e) {
              System.out.println ("Timed out");
              return TIMEOUT;
            }
            catch (SocketNodeException e) {
              return FAILURE;
            }
            catch (Exception e) {
              logMessage ("run", "4E", e.getMessage ());
              e.printStackTrace ();
              return FAILURE;
            }
          }
        }
        if (generatedMessageBytes == null){
          return TIMEOUT;
        }
        else {
          MbMessageAssembly outputAssembly = new MbMessageAssembly (assembly,createMessage
(generatedMessageBytes));
          MbOutputTerminal out = getOutputTerminal ("out");
          if(out != null) {
            out.propagate (outputAssembly);
          }
          return SUCCESS_CONTINUE;
        }
      }
      public void setDataSource (String dataSource) {
        _dataSource = dataSource;
      }
      public void setFilePath (String filePath) {
        _filePath = filePath;
      }
      public void setPortNumber (String portNumber) {
        _portNumber = portNumber;
      }
      private byte[] useFilePath () throws Exception {
        //check validity
        System.out.println ("Seaching for Incoming File...");

        File sourceDirectory = new File (_filePath);
        if (sourceDirectory == null) {
          logMessage ("useFilePath", "2E","Directory '" + _filePath + "'");
          throw new SocketNodeException ();
        }
        if (sourceDirectory.isDirectory () == false) {
          logMessage ("useFilePath", "5E", "Path '" + _filePath + "'");
```

```java
          System.out.println ("Source path is not a directory.");
          throw new SocketNodeException ();
        }
        // loop for 5 seconds or until a file is found
        long startTime = System.currentTimeMillis ();
        while ((System.currentTimeMillis () - startTime) < 5000) {
          String [] inputFileList = sourceDirectory.list (new DirFilter ());
          // only use first file
          if (inputFileList.length >0) {
            // open first file and rename to indicate use
            File sourceFile = new File (_filePath + File.separator + inputFileList[0]);
            if (sourceFile==null) {
              logMessage ("useFilePath", "3E", "File '" + _filePath + File.separator +
inputFileList[0] + "'");
              throw new SocketNodeException ();
            }
            File newSourceFile = new File (_filePath + File.separator + inputFileList[0] +
".inuse");
            if (sourceFile.renameTo (newSourceFile) == false) {
              logMessage ("useFilePath", "0E", "Source '" + _filePath + File.separator +
inputFileList[0] + "' Dest '"+ _filePath + File.separator + inputFileList[0] + ".inuse");
              throw new SocketNodeException ();
            }

            System.out.println ("\rFile found. Reading message ...");

            // copy file into byte array for propagation
            byte[] inputBytes = new byte[1024];
            InputStream in = new FileInputStream (newSourceFile);
            ByteArrayOutputStream byteStream = new ByteArrayOutputStream ();
            int len;
            while ((len = in.read (inputBytes)) > 0) {
              //append to input;
              byteStream.write (inputBytes,0,len);
            }
            in.close ();
            newSourceFile.delete ();
            System.out.println ("\rFile closed. Message created.            \n");
            return byteStream.toByteArray ();
          }
        }
        System.out.println ("none found.\n");
        return null;
      }
      private byte[] usePortNumber () throws Exception {
        System.out.println ("Waiting for Incoming Data...");
        // open server port if not already open
        if (server == null) {
          try {
```

```
          server = new ServerSocket (Integer.parseInt (_portNumber,10));
        }
        catch (Throwable t){
          logMessage ("usePortNumber", "1E", "Port '" + _portNumber + "'\r\nError:\r\n" +
t.getMessage ());
          throw new SocketNodeException ();
        }
      }
      server.setSoTimeout (10000);
      Socket sock = server.accept ();

      System.out.println ("\rConnection established. Reading message ...");

      byte[] inputBytes = new byte[1024];
      InputStream in = sock.getInputStream ();
      ByteArrayOutputStream byteStream = new ByteArrayOutputStream ();
      int len;
      while ((len = in.read (inputBytes)) > 0) {
        //append to input;
        byteStream.write (inputBytes,0,len);
      }
      in.close ();
      System.out.println ("\rConnection closed. Message created.      \n");
      return byteStream.toByteArray ();
  }
}
//EOF
```

## B.1.2  SocketNodeException.java source code

```
package com.ibm.samples;

public class SocketNodeException extends Exception {
  public SocketNodeException () {
    super();
  }
  public SocketNodeException (String s) {
    super(s);
  }
}
```

## B.1.3  SocketNodeMessages.java source code

```
package com.ibm.samples;

import java.util.*;

public class SocketNodeMessages extends ListResourceBundle {
```

```
/**
 * <p>static multi-dimensional array used as a catalog structure to store
 * messages containing a varying number of inserts, accessed via a msg
 * key</p>
 */
private static final Object[][] contents = {
  {"0E", "\r\nUnable to rename file.\r\n"},
  {"1E", "\r\nUnable to open port."},
  {"2E", "\r\nThe directory path specified is invalid.\r\nAborting read."},
  {"3E", "\r\nUnable to read from file.\r\n"},
  {"4E", "\r\nA general critial error occurred.\r\nThe stack trace is as follows:\r\n"},
  {"5E", "\r\nThe path specified is not a directory.\r\n"},
  {"0W", "\r\nThe data source specified is invalid.\r\nDefaulting to Socket mode, Port 3000.\r\n"},
  {"0I", "\r\n-Debug Checkpoint Data- \r\n"},
};
public java.lang.Object[][] getContents () {
  return contents;
}
}
```

## B.1.4  DirFilter.java source code

```
package com.ibm.samples;

public class DirFilter implements java.io.FilenameFilter {
  public DirFilter () {
    super();
  }
  public boolean accept (java.io.File dir, String name) {
    // accept if filename ends in .xml
    if (name.endsWith (".xml") == true) {
      return true;
    } else {
      return false;
    }
  }
}
```

## B.1.5  Compilation and packaging instructions

1. From a command window, add to your classpath:

    **set classpath=%path%;<install_dir>\classes\jplugin.jar**

    where <install_dir> is the drive and the directory where the WebSphere MQ Integrator installation is located, if the setting is not already in your classpath.

2. Write programs shown above in a text editor or copy them from the Web site.

3. Save programs to <install dir>\javasource\com\ibm\samples\. Ensure that you save the files with a .java extension and that a .txt or other extension is not attached.

4. From a command prompt, enter `cd <install dir>\javasource\`

5. Run the command `javac com\ibm\samples\*.java`

6. Create the JAR with `jar cvf SocketNode.jar com\ibm\samples\*.class`

7. Stop the broker with `mqsistop <broker_name>`

8. If the Configuration Manager is running on the same machine, issue the command `mqsistop ConfigMgr`

9. Delete old versions with `delete <install_dir>\jplugin\SocketNode.jar`

10. Copy the file with

    `copy SocketNode.jar <install_dir>\jplugin\SocketNode.jar`

11. For z/OS

    a. From a Windows 2000 command prompt window, FTP the Java JAR file from Windows to z/OS

    b. Log on to z/OS and copy the JAR file to the proper lil directory

    c. Exit FTP

    Your z/OS broker will process Java packages from directories in the lilpath that is defined during installation or customization.

12. Restart your broker and Configuration Manager services with the commands:

    `mqsistart <broker>`

    `mqsistart ConfigMgr`

## B.2 Java plug-in node getting started example

In this section we provide source code for the Java plug-in example.

### B.2.1 SwitchNode.java source code

```
/*
 * Licensed Materials - Property of IBM
 * 5648-C63
 * (C) Copyright IBM Corp. 1999, 2001
 */

package com.ibm.samples;
```

```java
import com.ibm.broker.plugin.*;

/**
 * Sample plugin node.
 * This node propagates the incoming message to one of several output terminals
 * depending on the content of the message.
 * A minimal test message for this node would be:
 * <data><action>change</action></data>
 */
public class SwitchNode extends MbNode implements MbNodeInterface {
  String _nodeTraceSetting;

  /**
   * Switch node constructor.
   * This is where input and output terminal are created.
   */
  public SwitchNode () throws MbException {
    createInputTerminal ("in");
    createOutputTerminal ("add");
    createOutputTerminal ("change");
    createOutputTerminal ("delete");
    createOutputTerminal ("hold");
    createOutputTerminal ("failure");
  }

  /**
   * This static method is called by the framework to identify this node.
   * If this method is not supplied, a default name will be generated
   * automatically based on the node's package/class name. In this case
   * it would be 'ComIbmSamplesSwitchNode'.
   */
  public static String getNodeName () {
    return "ComIbmSwitchNode";
  }

  /**
   * This evaluate message is called by the broker for each message passing
   * through the flow. The message assembly is passed in with the 'assembly'
   * parameter. It is possible for a node to have more than one input
   * terminal. The terminal that the message has come in on is represented
   * by the 'in' parameter.
   */
  public void evaluate (MbMessageAssembly assembly, MbInputTerminal in)
  throws MbException {
    // Navigate to the relevant syntax element in the XML message
    MbElement rootElement = assembly.getMessage ().getRootElement ();
    MbElement switchElement = rootElement.getLastChild ().getFirstChild ().getFirstChild ();

    // To aid debugging, text can be printed to stdout/stderr.
```

```java
      // On NT this can be viewed by selecting 'Allow sevice to interact with
      // desktop' on the NT Services properties dialog.
      // On Unix set the environment variable MQSI_RUN_ATTACHED=1 before
      // starting the broker.
      if(_nodeTraceSetting.equals ("debug")) {
        System.out.println ("Element = " + switchElement.getName ());
        System.out.println ("Value = " + switchElement.getValue ());
      }

      // Select the terminal indicated by the value of this element
      String terminalName;
      String elementValue = (String)switchElement.getValue ();
      if(elementValue.equals ("add"))
        terminalName = "add";
      else if(elementValue.equals ("change"))
        terminalName = "change";
      else if(elementValue.equals ("delete"))
        terminalName = "delete";
      else if(elementValue.equals ("hold"))
        terminalName = "hold";
      else
        terminalName = "failure";

      MbOutputTerminal out = getOutputTerminal (terminalName);

      // Now propagate the message assembly.
      // If the terminal is not attached, an exception will be thrown. The user
      // can choose to handle this exception, but it is not neccessary since
      // the framework will catch it and propagate the message to the failure
      // terminal, or if it not attached, rethrow the exception back upstream.
      out.propagate (assembly);
    }

    /* Attributes are defined for a node by supplying get/set methods.
     * The following two methods define an attribute 'nodeTraceSetting'.
     * The capitalisation follows the usual JavaBean property convention.
     */
    public String getNodeTraceSetting () {
      return _nodeTraceSetting;
    }

    public void setNodeTraceSetting (String nodeTraceSetting) {
      _nodeTraceSetting = nodeTraceSetting;
    }

}
```

## B.2.2 TransformNode source code

```java
/*
 * Licensed Materials - Property of IBM
 * 5648-C63
 * (C) Copyright IBM Corp. 1999, 2001
 */

package com.ibm.samples;

import com.ibm.broker.plugin.*;

/**
 * Sample plugin node.
 * This node alters the content of the incoming message before passing it to
 * its output terminal.
 * A minimal test message for this node would be:
 * <data><action>add</action></data>
 */
public class TransformNode extends MbNode implements MbNodeInterface {
  String _nodeTraceSetting;

  /**
   * Transform node constructor.
   * This is where input and output terminal are created.
   */
  public TransformNode () throws MbException {
    createInputTerminal ("in");
    createOutputTerminal ("out");
    createOutputTerminal ("failure");
  }

  /**
   * This static method is called by the framework to identify this node.
   * If this method is not supplied, a default name will be generated
   * automatically based on the node's package/class name. In this case
   * it would be 'ComIbmSamplesTranformNode'.
   */
  public static String getNodeName () {
    return "ComIbmTransformNode";
  }

  /**
   * This evaluate message is called by the broker for each message passing
   * through the flow. The message assembly is passed in with the 'assembly'
   * parameter. It is possible for a node to have more than one input
   * terminal. The terminal that the message has come in on is represented
   * by the 'in' parameter.
   */
```

```java
public void evaluate (MbMessageAssembly assembly, MbInputTerminal in)
throws MbException {
  // The incoming message assembly and its embedded messages are read-only.
  // New objects must be created using the copy constructors
  MbMessage newMsg = new MbMessage (assembly.getMessage ());
  MbMessageAssembly newAssembly = new MbMessageAssembly (assembly, newMsg);

  // Navigate to the relevant syntax element in the XML message
  MbElement rootElement = newAssembly.getMessage ().getRootElement ();
  MbElement switchElement = rootElement.getFirstElementByPath ("/XML/data/action");

  // To aid debugging, text can be printed to stdout/stderr.
  // On NT this can be viewed by selecting 'Allow sevice to interact with
  // desktop' on the NT Services properties dialog.
  // On Unix set the environment variable MQSI_RUN_ATTACHED=1 before
  // starting the broker.
  if(_nodeTraceSetting.equals ("debug")) {
    System.out.println ("Element = " + switchElement.getName ());
    System.out.println ("Value = " + switchElement.getValue ());
  }

  // Change the value of an existing element
  String elementValue = (String)switchElement.getValue ();
  if(elementValue.equals ("add"))
    switchElement.setValue ("change");
  else if(elementValue.equals ("change"))
    switchElement.setValue ("delete");
  else if(elementValue.equals ("delete"))
    switchElement.setValue ("hold");
  else
    switchElement.setValue ("failure");

  if(_nodeTraceSetting.equals ("debug")) {
    System.out.println ("New value = " + switchElement.getValue ());
  }

  // Add a new tag as a child of the switch tag
  MbElement tag = switchElement.createElementAsLastChild (MbElement.TYPE_NAME,
  "PreviousValue",
  elementValue);

  // Add an attribute to this new tag
  tag.createElementAsFirstChild (MbElement.TYPE_NAME_VALUE,
  "NewValue",
  switchElement.getValue ());

  MbOutputTerminal out = getOutputTerminal ("out");

  // Now propagate the message assembly.
```

```java
   // If the terminal is not attached, an exception will be thrown. The user
   // can choose to handle this exception, but it is not neccessary since
   // the framework will catch it and propagate the message to the failure
   // terminal, or if it not attached, rethrow the exception back upstream.
   out.propagate (newAssembly);
}

public String toString () {
   return getName ();
}

/* Attributes are defined for a node by supplying get/set methods.
 * The following two methods define an attribute 'nodeTraceSetting'.
 * The capitalisation follows the usual JavaBean property convention.
 */
public String getNodeTraceSetting () {
   return _nodeTraceSetting;
}

public void setNodeTraceSetting (String nodeTraceSetting) {
   _nodeTraceSetting = nodeTraceSetting;
}

}
```

## B.2.3  Compilation and packaging instructions

These two programs should not be contained in the same JAR file for obvious version issues, but the can be deployed at the same time. The instructions below follow this plan.

1. From a command window, add to your classpath:

   **set classpath=%path%;<install_dir>\classes\jplugin.jar**

   (where <install_dir> is the drive and the directory where the WebSphere MQ Integrator installation is located) if the setting is not already in your classpath.

2. Write programs shown above in a text editor or copy them from the Web materials.

3. Save programs to <install dir>\javasource\com\ibm\samples\. Ensure that you save the files with a .java extension and that a .txt or other extension is not attached to the end.

4. From your previous command window execute

   **cd <install dir>\javasource\**

5. Execute the command **javac com\ibm\samples\SwitchNode.java**

6. Create the JAR with

   `jar cvf SwitchNode.jar com\ibm\samples\SwitchNode.class`

7. Stop the broker with mqsistop <broker_name>
8. If the Configuration Manager is running on the same machine issue the command `mqsistop ConfigMgr`
9. Delete old versions with `delete <install_dir>\jplugin\SwitchNode.jar`
10. Copy the file with

    `copy SwitchNode.jar <install_dir>\jplugin\SwitchNode.jar`

11. Execute the command `javac com\ibm\samples\TransformNode.java`
12. Create the JAR with

    `jar cvf TransformNode.jar com\ibm\samples\TransformNode.class`

13. Delete old versions with `delete <install_dir>\jplugin\TransformNode.jar`
14. Copy with the file with

    `copy TransformNode.jar <install_dir>\jplugin\TransformNode.jar`

15. For z/OS

    From a Windows 2000 command prompt window, FTP the Java JAR file from Windows to z/OS

    Log on to z/OS and copy the JAR file to the proper lil directory

    Exit FTP

    Your z/OS broker will process Java packages from directories in the lilpath which is defined during installation or customization

16. Restart your broker and Configuration Manager services with the commands:

    `mqsistart <broker>`

    `mqsistart ConfigMgr`

# Using the Control Center Debugger

The Control Center provides facilities that help you to validate that a message flow is performing the desired actions under all conditions, and determine the cause of unexpected processing within a message flow. In this appendix we show an example of viewing a message flow with the debugger.

You find more detailed information on the debugger in the *WebSphere MQ Integrator Using the Control Center* manual, GC34-5602, and in the *WebSphere MQ Integrator Problem Determination Guide*, GC34-5920.

## C.1 Solving message flow problems with the debugger

Message flow problems can be analyzed with a user trace, using trace nodes and with the Control Center debugger. The debugger is an alternative window under the message flows view of the Control Center.

The debugger lets you define break points within a message flow. When a break point is encountered during message processing, control is returned to you, and you can then inspect and modify the message contents. This helps you to analyze and solve unexpected situations with the message flows, such as:

- Wrongly connected nodes, such as outputs connected to incorrect inputs

- Filter nodes with incorrect conditions
- Compute nodes with incorrect logic
- Database nodes making incorrect entries into their target databases
- Incorrect messages generated by applications, or having contents that the message flow does not expect
- Feedback loops that are never exited
- User-programmed plug-in nodes that contain errors, or are not reentrant

## C.2  Testing the message flow

In this example, a simple XML message is passed through a simple message flow. The message flow has one Compute node. The Compute node checks for one value in the message and changes another value based on the first value. The message and the ESQL from the Compute node are shown in Example C-1 and Example C-2.

*Example: C-1   XML message for debug testing*

```
MQMD

STRUCID                 MD
VERSION                 2
REPORT                  0
MSGTYPE                 1
EXPIRY                  -1
FEEDBACK                0
ENCODING                273
CODEDCHARSETID          437
FORMAT                  MQSTR
PRIORITY                0
PERSISTENCE             1
BACKOUTCOUNT            0
REPLYTOQ                MQREPLY
REPLYTOQMGR             M23BK59Z
USERIDENTIFIER          efletch
PUTAPPLTYPE             B

STARTDATA
<Message>
 <Version>2</Version>
 <CustomerName>
  <First>Ed</First>
  <Last>Fletcher</Last>
 </CustomerName>
 <Address>
```

```
      <Line1>Mail Point 135</Line1>
      <Line2>Hursley Park</Line2>
      <Town>Winchester</Town>
      <County>Hampshire</County>
      <Zip>SO21 2JN</Zip>
      <Country>UK</Country>
    </Address>
    <Complaint>
      <Type>Order</Type>
      <Reference>XYZ123ABC</Reference>
      <Text>
I placed an order on 15-11-99, well in time for Christmas and I still have not
had a delivery schedule sent to me. Please cancel the order and refund me NOW.
      </Text>
    </Complaint>
</Message>

ENDDATA
```

*Example: C-2   ESQL from Compute node*

```
SET OutputRoot = InputRoot;
SET OutputRoot.XML.Message.Admin.Dept =
CASE
  WHEN InputBody.Message.Complaint.Type = 'Order'
    THEN 'B01'
  WHEN InputBody.Message.Complaint.Type = 'Delivery'
    THEN 'C01'
  ELSE 'E01'
END
```

To debug a message flow, the flow should not be locked (checked out) and must be assigned to an execution group. Open the debugger by clicking the **Debugger** button (Figure C-1 on page 350) from the Message Flows view. Open the message flow to debug by selecting **Open Message Flow** on the Debug Action menu.

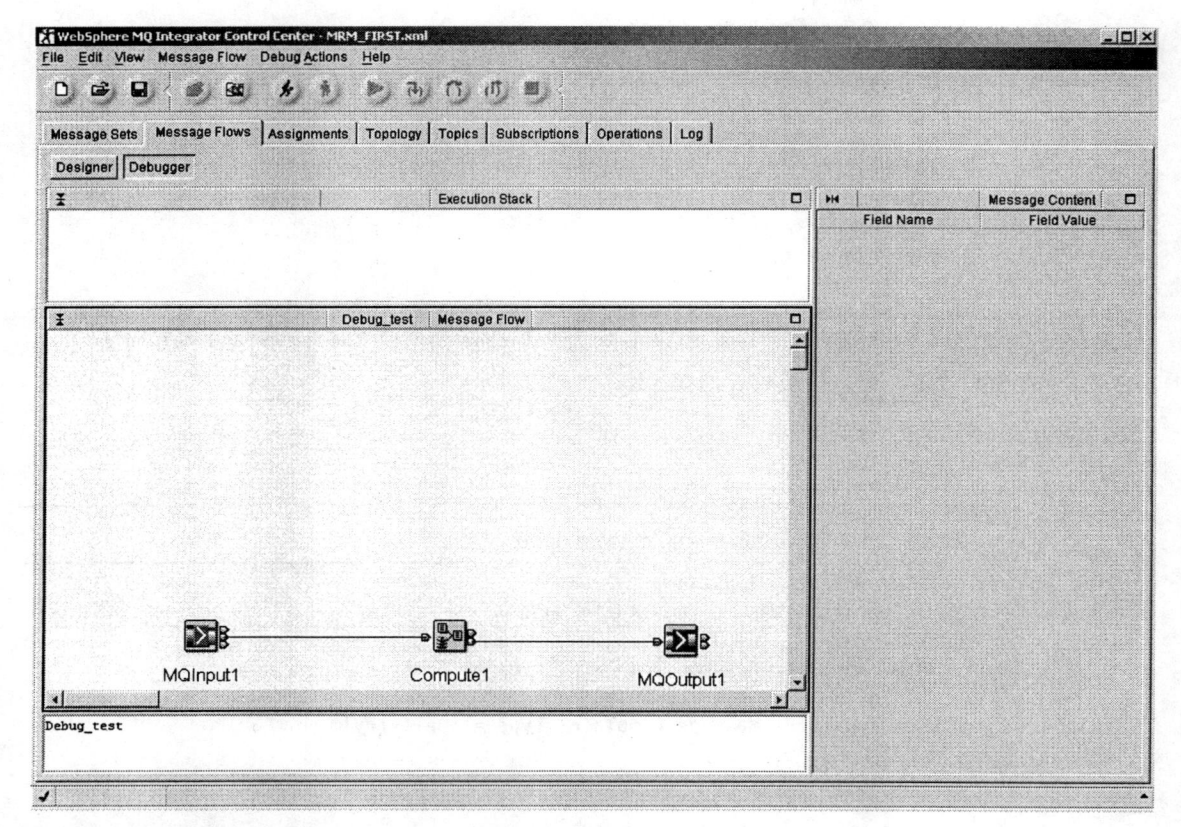

*Figure C-1   Simple message flow shown in the Message Flow pane of debugger*

You then need to decide where you want to look at your message as it is being processed through this flow. In this case, we are going to look at the message on the out terminal of the Compute node. We right click the Compute node and as shown in Figure C-2 on page 351, select **Break After**.

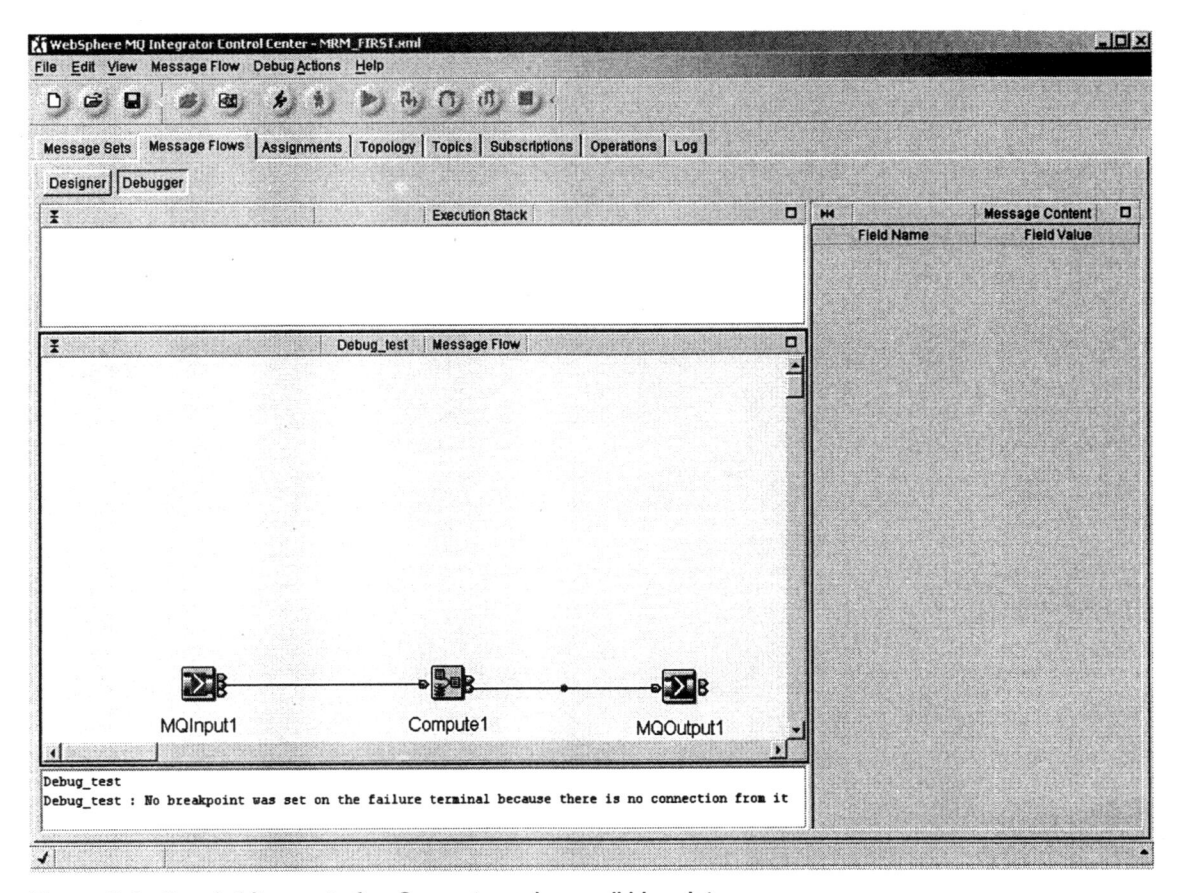

Figure C-2   Break After, set after Compute node, small blue dot

Because there was no failure terminal connected, a warning message was posted that can be ignored. You are now ready to process the XML message and take a look at the message immediately after the Compute node. The message text appears in the message content pane on the right, as shown in Figure C-3 on page 352 and Figure C-4 on page 353.

Appendix C. Using the Control Center Debugger   **351**

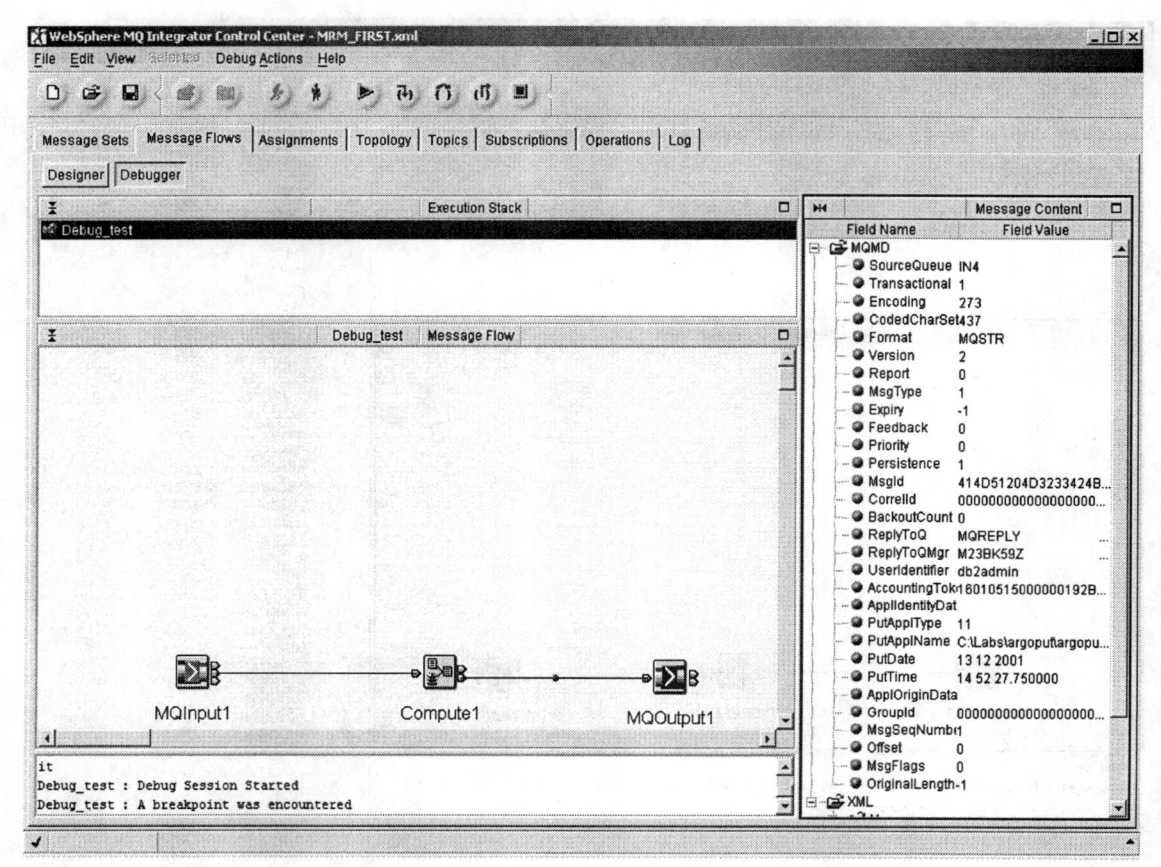

*Figure C-3   XML message content, header content*

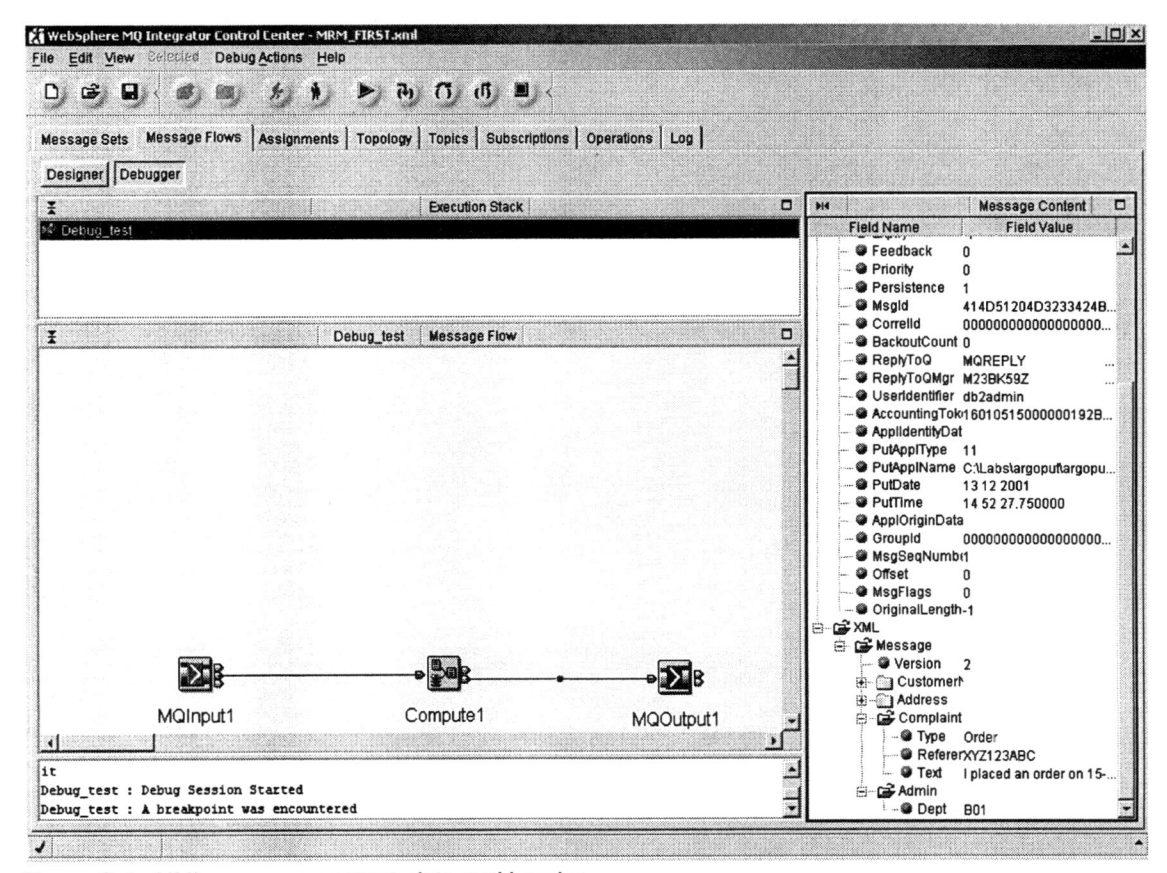

*Figure C-4   XML message content, data and header*

At this point, you can do a number of things to the message content. You can simply review it to see that the Compute node functioned properly. You can also change values by clicking the value to be changed and putting in a new value. You should be aware of the impact of your actions if you do make a change.

If a problem causes a message processing node to throw an exception, this exception is displayed in the message content pane.

There are a number of functions to control the progress of the message flow. These options (shown in Figure C-5 on page 354) are active only when a message flow is stopped at a breakpoint.

Appendix C. Using the Control Center Debugger   353

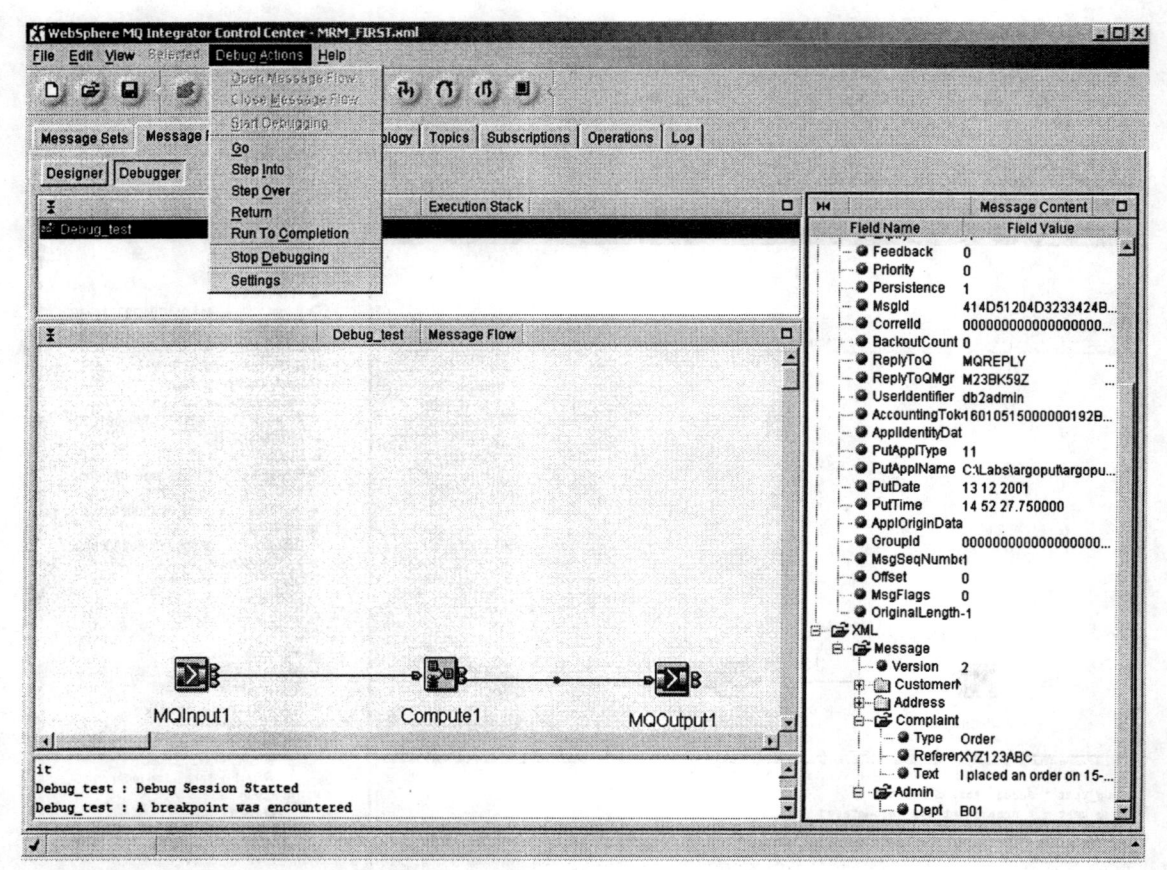

*Figure C-5   Message processing options*

These options are selected from the Debug Actions menu selection. The options are Go, Step into, Return, Step Over, and Run to Completion. Refer to *WebSphere MQ Integrator Using the Control Center* for more details.

You can stop the debugging by selecting **Stop Debugging** from the Debug Actions menu.

# Additional material

This redbook refers to additional material that can be downloaded from the Internet as described below.

## Locating the Web material

The Web material associated with this redbook is available in softcopy on the Internet from the IBM Redbooks Web server. Point your Web browser to:

    ftp://www.redbooks.ibm.com/redbooks/SG246528

Alternatively, you can go to the IBM Redbooks Web site at:

    **ibm.com**/redbooks

Select the **Additional materials** and open the directory that corresponds with the redbook form number, SG246528.

## Using the Web material

The additional Web material that accompanies this redbook is packaged in one file, called **SG246528.zip** and includes the following files:

| File name | Description |
| --- | --- |
| **Readme.txt** | References other files to book sections and instructs how to use them |
| **MsgFlow.exp.xml** | An export file of the message flow NEONFLOW1 used to verify the NEON support in WMQI |
| **nnsy.exp** | Two NEON formats used in NEONFLOW1 to verify the NEON support in WMQI |
| **DLM_TEST.mrp** | Export of delimited message set DLM_TEST |
| **TAGGED_TEST.mrp** | Export of tagged message set TAGGED_TEST |
| **CONTACTS.mrp** | Export of the DTD imported message set CONTACTS |
| **usertrace.cmd** | Windows command file that automates running a broker user trace |
| **usertrace.sh** | UNIX and z/OS USS shell script that automates running a broker user trace |
| java subdirectory | Contains the source and .jar files referenced in Chapter 12, "Developing and deploying custom nodes in Java" on page 293 |

## System requirements for downloading the Web material

The following system configuration is recommended:

**Operating System:** Windows NT or Windows 2000

**Tools:** WebSphere MQ Integrator V2.1 for Windows NT/2000, Java Development Kit 1.3

**Memory:** As required by the tools

## How to use the Web material

Create a subdirectory (folder) on your workstation, and unzip the contents of the Web material zip file into this folder. Then, follow the instructions in the readme file.

# Related publications

The publications listed in this section are considered particularly suitable for a more detailed discussion of the topics covered in this redbook.

## IBM Redbooks

For information on ordering these publications, see "How to get IBM Redbooks" on page 358.

- *Business Integration Solutions with MQSeries Integrator*, SG24-6154
- *MQSeries Publish/Subscribe Applications*, SG24-6282
- *Intra-Enterprise Business Process Management*, SG24-6173
- *Enterprise Java Beans for z/OS and OS/390 WebSphere Application Server V4.0*, SG24-6283
- *Enterprise Java Beans for z/OS and OS/390 CICS Transaction Server V2.1*, SG24-6284
- *CICS Transaction Server for OS/390: Version 1 Release 3 Implementation Guide*, SG24-5274

## Other resources

These publications are also relevant as further information sources:

- *WebSphere MQ Integrator Introduction and Planning*, GC34-5599
- *WebSphere MQ Integrator Using the Control Center*, GC34-5602
- *WebSphere MQ Integrator Programming Guide*, SC34-5603
- *WebSphere MQ Integrator Administration Guide*, SC34-5792
- *WebSphere MQ Integrator ESQL Reference*, SC34-5923
- *WebSphere MQ Integrator Problem Determination Guide*, GC34-5920
- *WebSphere MQ Integrator Working with Messages*, SC34-6039
- *WebSphere MQ Integrator Messages*, GC34-5601
- *WebSphere MQ Integrator for z/OS Customization and Administration Guide*, SC34-5919
- *WebSphere MQ Integrator for Windows NT Installation Guide*, GC34-5600

- *New Era of Networks Rules and Formatter Support for WebSphere MQ Integrator User's Guide*, SC34-6084
- *New Era of Networks Rules and Formatter Support for WebSphere MQ Integrator System Management Guide*, SC34-6083
- *MQSeries for OS/390 System Administration Guide*, SC34-5652
- *MQSeries for OS/390 System Setup Guide*, SC34-5651
- *z/OS UNIX System Services User's Guide*, SA22-7801
- *z/OS UNIX System Services Command Reference*, SA22-7802
- *z/OS UNIX System Services Planning*, GA22-7800
- *OS/390 UNIX System Services User's Guide*, SC28-1891
- *OS/390 UNIX System Services Command Reference*, SC28-1892
- *OS/390 UNIX System Services Planning*, SC28-1890
- *OS/390 MVS Setting up a Sysplex*, GC28-1779
- *OS/390 MVS Programming: Resource Recovery*, GC28-1739

## Referenced Web sites

These Web sites are also relevant as further information sources:

- WebSphere MQSeries SupportPac site

    http://www.software.ibm.com/ts/mqseries/txppacs

- O'REILLY XML site, DTD description

    http://www.xml.com/pub/a/98/10/guide2.html#DOCTYPEDEF

## How to get IBM Redbooks

You can order hardcopy Redbooks, as well as view, download, or search for Redbooks at the following Web site:

   **ibm.com**/redbooks

You can also download additional materials (code samples or diskette/CD-ROM images) from that site.

# IBM Redbooks collections

Redbooks are also available on CD-ROMs. Click the CD-ROMs button on the Redbooks Web site for information about all the CD-ROMs offered, as well as updates and formats.

# Special notices

References in this publication to IBM products, programs or services do not imply that IBM intends to make these available in all countries in which IBM operates. Any reference to an IBM product, program, or service is not intended to state or imply that only IBM's product, program, or service may be used. Any functionally equivalent program that does not infringe any of IBM's intellectual property rights may be used instead of the IBM product, program or service.

Information in this book was developed in conjunction with use of the equipment specified, and is limited in application to those specific hardware and software products and levels.

IBM may have patents or pending patent applications covering subject matter in this document. The furnishing of this document does not give you any license to these patents. You can send license inquiries, in writing, to the IBM Director of Licensing, IBM Corporation, North Castle Drive, Armonk, NY 10504-1785.

Licensees of this program who wish to have information about it for the purpose of enabling: (i) the exchange of information between independently created programs and other programs (including this one) and (ii) the mutual use of the information which has been exchanged, should contact IBM Corporation, Dept. 600A, Mail Drop 1329, Somers, NY 10589 USA.

Such information may be available, subject to appropriate terms and conditions, including in some cases, payment of a fee.

The information contained in this document has not been submitted to any formal IBM test and is distributed AS IS. The use of this information or the implementation of any of these techniques is a customer responsibility and depends on the customer's ability to evaluate and integrate them into the customer's operational environment. While each item may have been reviewed by IBM for accuracy in a specific situation, there is no guarantee that the same or similar results will be obtained elsewhere. Customers attempting to adapt these techniques to their own environments do so at their own risk.

Any pointers in this publication to external Web sites are provided for convenience only and do not in any manner serve as an endorsement of these Web sites.

© Copyright IBM Corp. 2002

The following terms are trademarks of other companies:

C-bus is a trademark of Corollary, Inc. in the United States and/or other countries.

Java and all Java-based trademarks and logos are trademarks or registered trademarks of Sun Microsystems, Inc. in the United States and/or other countries.

Microsoft, Windows, Windows NT, and the Windows logo are trademarks of Microsoft Corporation in the United States and/or other countries.

PC Direct is a trademark of Ziff Communications Company in the United States and/or other countries and is used by IBM Corporation under license.

ActionMedia, LANDesk, MMX, Pentium and ProShare are trademarks of Intel Corporation in the United States and/or other countries.

UNIX is a registered trademark in the United States and other countries licensed exclusively through The Open Group.

SET, SET Secure Electronic Transaction, and the SET Logo are trademarks owned by SET Secure Electronic Transaction LLC.

Other company, product, and service names may be trademarks or service marks of others

# Glossary

**Access Control List (ACL).** The list of principals that have explicit permission (to publish, to subscribe to, and to request persistent delivery of a publication message) against a topic in the topic tree. The ACLs define the implementation of topic-based security.

**AMI.** See **Application messaging interface**.

**API.** See **Application programming interface**.

**Application messaging interface.** The programming interface provided by MQSeries that defines a high level interface to message queuing services.

**Application programming interface.** An interface provided by a software product that enables programs to request services.

**BLOB.** Binary Large Object, a block of bytes of data (for example, the body of a message) that has no discernible meaning, but is treated as one solid entity that cannot be interpreted.

**Broker.** See **Message broker**.

**Check in.** The Control Center action that stores a new or updated resource in the configuration or message repository.

**Check out.** The Control Center action that extracts and locks a resource from the configuration or message repository for local modification by a user.

**Collective.** A totally connected set of brokers forming part of a multi-broker network for Publish/Subscribe applications.

**Configuration Manager.** A component of WebSphere MQ Integrator that acts as the interface between the configuration repository and an existing set of brokers.

**Configuration repository.** Persistent storage for broker configuration and topology definition.

**Control Center.** The graphical interface that provides facilities for defining, configuring, deploying, and monitoring resources of the WebSphere MQ Integrator network.

**Debugger.** A facility on the Message Flows view in the Control Center that enables message flows to be visually debugged.

**Deploy.** Make operational the configuration and topology of the broker domain.

**Distribution list.** A list of MQSeries queues to which a message can be put using a single statement.

**Document type definition.** The rules that specify the structure for a particular class of XML documents. The DTD defines the structure with elements, attributes, and notations, and it establishes constraints for how each element, attribute, and notation can be used within the particular class of documents.

**Domain.** See **Message domain**.

**DTD.** See **Document type definition**.

**Execution group.** A named grouping of message flows that have been assigned to a broker.

**Extended SQL.** A specialized set of SQL functions and statements based on regular SQL, extended with functions and statements unique to WebSphere MQ Integrator.

**Field reference.** A sequence of period-separated values that identify a specific field within a message tree. An example of a field reference might be *Address.Country.City.Street.HouseNumber*.

**Input node.** A message flow node that represents a source of messages for the message flow.

**Java Database Connectivity.** An application programming interface that has the same characteristics as ODBC but is specifically designed for use by Java database applications.

**Java Development Kit.** Software package used to write, compile, debug and run Java applets and applications.

**Java Message Service.** An application programming interface that provides Java language functions for handling messages.

**Java Runtime Environment.** A subset of the **Java Development Kit** that allows you to run Java applets and applications.

**JDK.** See **Java Development Kit**.

**JMS.** See **Java Message Service**.

**JRE.** See **Java Runtime Environment**.

**Message broker.** A set of execution processes hosting one or more message flows.

**Message domain.** The value that determines how the message is interpreted (parsed). The following domains are recognized:

- MRM, which identifies messages defined using the Control Center.
- NEONMSG and NEON, which identify messages created using the New Era of Networks user interfaces.
- XML, JMSMap, and JMSStream, which identify messages that are self-defining.
- BLOB, which identifies messages that are undefined.

**Message flow.** A directed graph that represents the set of activities performed on a message or event as it passes through a broker. A message flow consists of a set of message processing nodes and message processing connectors.

**Message processing node connector.** An entity that connects the output terminal of one message processing node to the input terminal of another.

**Message processing node.** A node in the message flow, representing a well defined processing stage. A message processing node can be one of several primitive types or it can represent a subflow.

**Message Queue Interface.** The programming interface provided by MQSeries Queue Managers that enables application program access to message queuing services.

**Message queuing.** A communication technique that uses asynchronous messages for communication between software components.

**Message Repository Manager (MRM).** A component of the Configuration Manager that handles message definition and control. A message defined to the MRM has a message domain set to MRM.

**Message repository.** A database holding message template definitions.

**Message set.** A grouping of related messages.

**MQRFH.** An architected message header that is used to provide metadata for the processing of a message. This header is supported by MQSeries Publish/Subscribe.

**MQRFH2.** An extended version of MQRFH being used by WMQI applications.

**ODBC.** See **Open Database Connectivity**.

**Open Database Connectivity.** A standard application programming interface for accessing data in both relational and non-relational database management systems. Using this API, database applications can access data stored in database management systems on a variety of computers even if each database management system uses a different data storage format and programming interface. ODBC is based on the call level interface (CLI) specification of the X/Open SQL Access Group.

**Output node.** A message processing node that represents a point at which messages flow out of the message flow.

**Plug-in.** An extension to the broker, written by a third-party developer, to provide a new message processing node or message parser in addition to those supplied with the product.

**Point-to-point.** Style of messaging application in which the sending application knows the destination of the message.

**Predefined message.** A message with a structure that is defined before the message is created or referenced.

**Publish/Subscribe.** Style of messaging application in which the providers of information (publishers) are decoupled from the consumers of that information (subscribers) through a broker.

**Publisher.** An application that makes information about a specific topic available to a broker in a Publish/Subscribe system.

**Queue Manager.** A subsystem that provides queuing services to applications. It provides an application programming interface so that applications can access messages on the queues that are owned and managed by the queue manager.

**Queue.** A WebSphere MQ object. Applications can put messages on, and get messages from, a queue. A queue is owned and managed by a queue manager. A local queue is a type of queue that can contain a list of messages waiting to be processed. Other types of queues cannot contain messages but are used to point to other queues.

**Self-defining message.** A message that defines its structure within its content. For example, a message coded in XML is self-defining.

**Subflow.** A sequence of message processing nodes that can be included within a message flow.

**Subscriber.** An application that requests information about a specific topic from a Publish/Subscribe broker.

**Terminal.** The point at which one node in a message flow is connected to another node.

**User Name Server.** The WMQI component that interfaces with operating system facilities to determine valid users and groups.

**Wire format.** A description of the physical representation of a message within the bit-stream.

**XML.** An eXtensible Markup Language, a standard for the representation of data.

# Abbreviations and acronyms

| | | | |
|---|---|---|---|
| AMI | Application Messaging Interface | IIOP | Internet InterORB Protocol |
| API | Application Programming Interface | IMS | Information Management System |
| ARM | Automatic Restart Management | ISPF | Interactive System Productivity Facility |
| BLOB | Binary Large Object | ISV | Independent Software Vendor |
| CAF | Client Access Facility | ITSO | International Technical Support Organization |
| CICS | Customer Information Control System | JAR | Java Archive |
| CIF | Customization Input File | JCL | Job Control Language |
| CWF | Custom Wire Format | JDBC | Java Database Connectivity |
| DB2 | Database 2 | JDK | Java Development Kit |
| DB2 UDB | DB2 Universal Database | JMS | Java Message Service |
| DLQ | Dead Letter Queue | JRE | Java Runtime Environment |
| DNS | Domain Name System | LAN | Local Area Network |
| DTD | Document Type Definition | LE | Language Environment |
| EAI | Enterprise Application Integration | MDAC | Microsoft Data Access Component |
| EDI | Electronic Data Interchange | MQ | Message Queuing |
| EJB | Enterprise Java Bean | MQI | Message Queuing Interface |
| ESM | External Security Manager | MQSI | MQSeries Integrator |
| ESQL | Extended Structured Query Language | MQWF | MQSeries Workflow |
| EXCI | External CICS Interface | MRM | Message Repository Manager |
| GID | Group Identifier | NEON | New Era of Networks |
| GUI | Graphical User Interface | NFS | Network File System |
| HFS | Hierarchical File System | ODBC | Open Database Connectivity |
| HTML | HyperText Markup Language | OS/390 | Operating System/390 |
| HTTP | HyperText Transport Protocol | OTMA | Open Transaction Manager Access |
| IBM | International Business Machines Corporation | PDS | Partitioned Data Set |
| IDE | Integrated Development Environment | PDSE | Partitioned Data Set Extended |

| | |
|---|---|
| **RACF** | Resource Access Control Facility |
| **RRS** | Resource Recovery Services |
| **SIT** | System Initialization Table |
| **SMP/E** | System Management Program/Extended |
| **SQL** | Structured Query Language |
| **SWIFT** | Society For Worldwide Interbank Financial Telecommunications |
| **TDWF** | Tagged/Delimited Wire Format |
| **TSO** | Time Sharing Option |
| **TSO/E** | Time Sharing Option/Extended |
| **TWF** | Tagged Wire Format |
| **UID** | User Identifier |
| **UNS** | User Name Server |
| **UOW** | Unit of Work |
| **UR** | Unit of Recovery |
| **URL** | Uniform Resource Locator |
| **VTAM** | Virtual Telecommunications Access Method |
| **WLM** | WorkLoad Management |
| **WMQI** | WebSphere MQ Integrator |
| **XCF** | Extended Connection Facility |
| **XML** | eXtensible Markup Language |

# Index

## Numerics
1414 MQSeries default port  86
4039 abend  74

## A
administration with console or OMVS commands  101
archive  34
Automatic Restart Management
    broker customization  217
    planning  217
    policy activation  219
    policy definition  218
    policy implementation  218
    subscription availability  228

## B
backout count  211
backout threshold  211, 213
BIPJRSTC job  103
BIPSLIB member  71, 79
BPXBATCH command  37
broker
    adding a User Name Server  104
    administration with console or OMVS commands  101
    backout procedure  210, 213
    definition  11
    deleting  103
    instance name  13
    listing execution groups  102
    mqsicreatebroker command  12
    mqsistop command  186
    release coexistence  187
    reloading NEON Rules and Formats  105
    resetting  103
    starting and stopping  102
    upgrading from V2.0  188
    upgrading from V2.0.1  187
    upgrading from V2.02  186
broker customization
    APF attributes of bipimain  65, 76
    broker directory  66
    creating the broker database  71
    creating the broker queues  72
    creating the STEPLIB member  71
    customizer's OMVS user ID  65
    defining the broker started task user ID  73
    deleting a broker  75
    editing the customization input file  68
    mqsicustomize command  71
    PDS creation  66
    Publish/Subscribe  225
    runtime environment  67
    verifying availability of threads  74
broker domain
    multiple User Name Server configuration  230
    single User Name Server configuration  229
broker network  221
broker startup
    bipbroker  107
    bipimain  107
    bipuns  107

## C
C language plug-in  294
collective  11, 223
comma separated variable message  238
comma separated variable message to XML conversion  254
commit coordination  46
component stopping and restarting  100
compound type  22, 251
Compute node  93, 96, 171, 255, 283
Configuration Manager
    deletion and recreation  184
    functionality  9
    mqsicreateconfigmgr command  11
Configuration Manager customization
    databases  83
    user ID  83
configuration repository  10, 104
console commands  37
Control Center
    adding brokers to topology  88, 199

© Copyright IBM Corp. 2002  **369**

Assignments tab   143, 258
checking in resources   16
checking out resources   16
connecting to the Configuration Manager   85
definition   15
Log tab   95
message flow creation   90, 93
message flow deployment   91
mrmimpexpmsgset command   17
online help   261
Operations tab   95
resource states   16
security exit   29
setup considerations   85
Topology tab   199
user roles   15
CSQBRSSI stub   48
CSQBRSTB stub   48
currentsqlid   126
Customization Input File   78
customization input file   68
Customization Verification Program   73

## D

daemon   33
Data Insert node   21
Data Update node   19
Database node
    transaction mode property   55
Database Source Name   99, 182
DB2 database heap size   84
DB2 LOCATION name   70, 99
db2trace utility   108
DDF location name   182
deployment option
    Complete   259
    Delta   259
DISPLAY THREAD command   47
Document Data Definition   26
Document Type Definition   235, 270
domain
    BLOB   5
    MRM   4
    NEONMSG   5, 118, 159
    XML   4
drag and drop   280
dubbing   33

## E

ESQL
    description   17
    new features   28
    PROPAGATE statement   286
    reference variables   289
execution group   11

## F

Filter node   21, 93, 171
fork   33

## I

input node
    deployment   303
    packaging   300
    reading a telnet stream   311
    testing   309
ISHELL command   35
IXCMIAPU utility   45

## J

Java Archive File   294
Java classes
    DirFilter   300
    MbInputNode   295
    MbNode   295
Java exceptions
    MbException   295
Java input node implementation   297
Java interfaces
    MbInputNodeInterface   295
    MbNodeInterface   295, 314
Java language plug-in   294
Java methods
    MbMessageAssembly   295
    MbService   296
Java Runtime Environment   30
javadoc   294
jplugin API   320

## L

loadable implementation libraries   13, 125, 301
logical partition (LPAR)   192

## M

message broker
   instance name  13
message domains  4
message flow
   coordinated transaction property  49
   database access  99
   debugger utility  107, 347
   definition  4
   deployment  200, 258
   fully broker-coordinated  51
   fully globally-coordinated  51
   functions  4
   migration from distributed to z/OS  181
   parallel execution by several brokers  205
   partially broker-coordinated  51
   Trace node  140
   Trace nodes  328
   tracing  321
   tracing on Windows  322
   tracing on z/OS and UNIX  324
   transactional behavior in Parallel Sysplex  213
   transactional coordination on z/OS  48, 183, 210
   transactionality  27, 49, 211
message identifier  245
message processing nodes  4
message repository  11, 185
Message Repository Manager
   components  22
   message model  22
   types  23
   wire formats  24
message sequence order and serialization  207
message set
   adding physical formats  242
   configuration for tagged data  261
   creation  239
   definition  22
   deployment  258
   DTD import  271
   identifier  241
message subflows  17, 21
message type  247
mount  33
mount point  33
MQI commands
   MQGET  17–18
   MQPUT  17
MQInput node
   Default tab  265
   transaction mode property  52
MQMD header  309
MQOutput node
   persistance mode property  54
   transaction mode property  54
MQReply node  96
MQSeries Client for Java  85
MQSeries commands
   DISPLAY THREAD  47
   RESOLVE INDOUBT  47
MQSeries messages
   CSQ3011  46
   CSQ3013  46
   CSQ3014  46
   CSQ3016  46
   CSQV435I  47
MQSeries Workflow  5

## N

NEON.ERROR node  142
NEON.OUT node  142
NEONMap node  170, 179
NEONRulesEvaluation node  151, 157
NEONTransform node  170, 179
NeonTransform node  141
New Era of Networks
   alternate formats  177
   broker customization  124
   building the Rules and Formats database  125
   Configuration Manager setup  129
   Consistency Checker  157
   current architecture within WMQI  118
   early product architecture  116
   ENVFILE file  124
   environment variables  130
   imbdfmignd.lil migration file  188
   importing formats  155
   importing Rules  156
   integration with MQSI and WMQI  117
   MQSIRuleng parameter file  119
   new feature overview  118
   NNFie and NNRie utilities  153
   NNFIE migration limitation  187
   NNGetmsg utility  121
   NNPutmsg utility  121
   NNSYMessageLog.nml file  150
   nnsyreg.dat configuration file  126

nnsyreg.dat file  128
-p import utility option  120, 155
problem determination for a broker  149
problem determination for NNSY GUI  150
problem determination for the Configuration Manager  150
propagate action  166
repeating formats  174
Rules and Formats database  124, 127
Rules Engine  152
setup verification  137
use of ESQL  171
using an MQRFH or MQRFH2 header  160
using MQRFH and MQRFH2 headers  157
USS environment variables  126
Visual Tester  136
workstation configuration  133

## O

OBROWSE command  37, 71
OCOPY command  37
ODBC source name  182
ODBC tracing  108
OEDIT command  37
OMVS command  35
OSHELL command  36

## P

Parallel Sysplex
    Coupling Facility  192
    definition  192
    message data shareability  193
    message high availability  198, 210
    message peer recovery  193
    message sharing  193
    Publish/Subscribe  224
    queue-sharing groups  193
    shared channels  195
    shared objects  193
    shared queues  194
Parsed Character Data  270
plug-in node  13, 18, 294
    deployment  316
    packaging  316
    parsing an XML file  314
    testing  316
Point to Point model  7
preserving configuration data  184

Publish/Subscribe
    basic model  7, 220
    broker networks  221
    Parallel Sysplex environment  224
    publisher  221
    subscriber  221
    subscription availability  228
    topic  221
    topic-based security  228

## Q

QMNAME keyword  47
Queue Manager
    definition as an XA Transaction Manager on Windows  49
queue sharing  45
queue sharing group
    definition  193
    shared objects  193
queue sharing groups
    message data shareability  193
    message persistance limitation  196
    message size limitation  195
    peer recovery  194

## R

RACF messages
    ICH4081E  110
Redbooks Web site  358
    Contact us  xiv
RESOLVE INDOUBT command  47
Resource Recovery Services
    ATRSCSS module  48
    CICS registration  44
    functionality  44
    ISPF panels  46
    MQSeries stubs  47
    MQSeries support  44, 46
    SRRBACK call  48
    SRRCMIT call  48
    supported Resource Managers  44
RFH2 format  244
rlogin command  62
ROOT  32
ROOT entry in BPXPRMxx  32

## S

security groups
    mqbrasgn 15
    mqbrdevt 15
    mqbrops 15
    mqbrtpic 15
shared objects
    channels 195
    queues 194
shared queue access
    exclusive mode 209
    shared mode 209
shell interface 34
SocketNode.java code 298
spawn 34
SQL code
    -803 216
    -911 215
SQL messages
    SQL1040N 111
SQL State
    51002 111
    57030 111
    58004 111
SupportPac
    IA72 - MQSeries Integrator V2 Aggregator Plug-In 30
    IC04 - MQSeries Integrator Business Scenarios 16
    ID05 - WebSphere MQ Integrator - Tagged/Delimited message examples 235
    ID06 - WebSphere MQ Integrator - MRM utilities 235
    ID11 - Writing New Era of Networks COBOL User Exits 121
    IH01 - WebSphere MQ Integrator Problem determination 106
    IH03 - MQSeries Integrator V2 Message display, test and performance utilities 236
    IP11 - WebSphere MQ Integrator for z/OS Performance report 191
SWIFT format
    example 25, 244
SYS1.PARMLIB members
    BPXPRMxx 32
    IEFSSNxx 45
System Affinity clause 72
System Affinity parameter 79

## T

tagged data formats 25, 235
tagged data message set 261
tagged message to XML conversion 261
tar UNIX command 34
TCP/IP Domain Name System 195
Trace node 140
transactionality 27
TSO commands
    BPXBATCH 37
    ISHELL 35
    OBROWSE 37, 71
    OCOPY 37
    OEDIT 37
    OMVS 35
    OSHELL 36

## U

UNIX System Services
    daemons 33
    environment variables 33
    file system 32
    MAXTHREADS parameter 75
    MAXTHREADTASKS parameter 75
    Path statements 35
    profile script 36
    services 32
    shared HFS 41
    shell interface 34
    users 35
User Name Server
    high availability 231
User Name Server customization
    creating the directory 77
    creating the PDS 76
    creating the queues 79
    creating the runtime environment 77
    creating the STEPLIB member 79
    defining the UNS started task used ID 79
    deleting the UNS 79
    editing the customization input file 77

## V

value constraints 24
VTAM Generic Resources 195

## W

Warehouse node   171
WebSphere Application Server for z/OS   44
WebSphere MQ Integrator
    applications   7
    architecture   8
    background   5
    thread availability   74
    utility jobs   105
    z/OS advantages   6
WebSphere MQ Integrator messages
    BIP2048E   110
    BIP2056I   143
    BIP2087E   188
    BIP2241E   188
    BIP2322E   111
    BIP4040I   143
    BIP4041E   188
    BIP8018E   100
    BIP8071I   102
    BIP8098I   113
    BIP8130I   102
    BIP8140E   101
    BIP914W   74, 80
    BIP9173I   68, 77

## X

XCF facility   41
XML messages
    amending DTD importer created names   276
    document type definition   270
    generic   26, 242
    mixing generic and MRM-defined   287
    MRM-defined   26, 242
    multiple entities   284
XML Model Building Process window   275